Japanese American Incarceration

POLITICS AND CULTURE IN MODERN AMERICA

Series Editors: Keisha N. Blain, Margot Canaday, Matthew
Lassiter, Stephen Pitti, Thomas J. Sugrue

Volumes in the series narrate and analyze political and social
change in the broadest dimensions from 1865 to the present,
including ideas about the ways people have sought and wielded
power in the public sphere and the language and institutions of
politics at all levels—local, national, and transnational. The
series is motivated by a desire to reverse the fragmentation of
modern U.S. history and to encourage synthetic perspectives
on social movements and the state, on gender, race, and labor,
and on intellectual history and popular culture.

Japanese American Incarceration

The Camps and Coerced Labor
During World War II

Stephanie Hinnershitz

PENN

UNIVERSITY OF PENNSYLVANIA PRESS

PHILADELPHIA

Published by
University of Pennsylvania Press
Philadelphia, Pennsylvania 19104-4112
www.upenn.edu/pennpress

Printed in the United States of America on acid-free paper
10   9   8   7   6   5   4   3   2   1

A catalogue record for this book is available from the
Library of Congress.
ISBN 978-0-8122-5336-8

CONTENTS

INTRODUCTION

In the summer of 1942, George Yamauchi worked nine hours a day, six days a week making camouflage netting for the United States Army. Yamauchi was one of twelve hundred workers at his factory who wove together long strips of nylon to make these crucial military supplies, using large wire fences to drape the massive nets as they grew with each woven row, arduous work in the sun. Rather than a large, sprawling plant like the ones where "Rosie the Riveters" or men who were not able to serve in the armed forces worked making munitions, plane parts, and other industrial products, this factory was located in the open, hot air of southern California's Santa Anita assembly center. As the sun set, Yamauchi's shadow cast over the netting, signaling that it was soon time to quit work for the day. He joined others in the mess hall for their evening supper, frequently hot dogs, baked beans, and a dessert of canned fruit or perhaps prunes, maybe a green salad.[1]

Yamauchi was a Nisei, an American-born citizen of Japanese descent, and a skilled weaver. For his daily work on the camouflage nets, he made fifty-three cents a day, or approximately sixteen dollars a month. With these wages, he bought clothing, snacks, and other sundries at the center canteen—for prices that seemed quite a bit more exorbitant than what he remembered as a free man in California. At the end of the day and after his evening meal, Yamauchi challenged some of the other incarcerees to a game of basketball or read the latest copy of the *Santa Anita Pacemaker*, the censored newspaper published by his fellow detainees at the center. But whatever he did to pass the time in the evening, every day ended the same way: Yamauchi removed his clothes, climbed into his cot with a straw mattress in his barracks, and drifted off to sleep, possibly thinking about the life he had before the Japanese attack on Pearl Harbor. Yamauchi, like other Nisei, Issei (first-generation Japanese migrants), and Kibei (Japanese American citizens educated in Japan), were detained in "assembly centers" along the West Coast during the late spring and early summer of 1942 as they awaited reassignment to one of ten "internment camps" from California to Arkansas. And, like the other imprisoned Japanese Americans, the administration at Santa Anita expected Yamauchi to work.[2]

Labor. Labor as a necessity for the American war economy. Labor as a means of preventing idleness and moral decay in the incarceration centers. Labor as a redemptive act necessary for the reclamation of American citizenship. Conceptions of and concerns about labor shaped the incarceration of approximately 115,000 to 120,000 Japanese Americans during World War II in ways great and small. The evidence for this is in plain sight, spread across documents in personal, state, and federal archives and in photos featured in museums and online exhibits.[3]

In observance of the seventy-fifth anniversary of Franklin Delano Roosevelt's decision to sign Executive Order 9066 in February 1942 designating areas along the West Coast as military zones, the FDR Presidential Library in Hyde Park, New York, displayed a special exhibit in 2017 titled "Images of Internment." The temporary exhibit featured photos by Dorothea Lange and Ansel Adams of wrongfully imprisoned Japanese Americans forcibly removed from their homes by the army. Many of the images depicted incarcerated Japanese Americans at work—young and old, first and second generation—farming, sewing, completing clerical tasks, manufacturing war materials, and constructing their own barracks.[4] Individual portraits of imprisoned Japanese Americans identify them by name first, occupation within the camps second.

The extraction of Japanese American labor looms just as large in the records of the War Relocation Authority (WRA), the Wartime Civil Control Administration (WCCA), and various divisions of the army in charge of planning and implementing EO 9066 and subsequent imprisonment of Japanese Americans. In memos, letters, and telephone conversations, the architects and administrators of incarceration expressed their fears that labor strikes in the camps would undermine order and that Japan would view the work performed by Japanese Americans as forced, using this to justify atrocities against American prisoners of war. Pulling these sources together reveals that the extraction of labor was a crucial component of the policy, planning, and implementation of the mass incarceration of Japanese Americans.

Although the photos of laboring Japanese Americans are no longer on the walls of the special exhibit hall at Hyde Park, gazing on them in collections

Figure 1. A member of the military police guards recently arrived Japanese Americans at the Manzanar prison camp. Photo by Albert Clem, April 1, 1942. Courtesy of the Bancroft Library.

held at the Library of Congress or the National Archives and Records Administration highlights the fact that labor was central to the experience of imprisoned Japanese Americans. Prisoners performed the same work on camouflage netting as Yamauchi did in the Poston and Manzanar prison camps during the summer and fall of 1942. In the spring of 1943, thousands of single men and families left the camps to work for private farmers in the Mountain States. These men and women were "freed" for work but were under threat of recall by the WRA either for violating myriad public proclamations limiting their activities or if their labor was required in the prison camps. Limitations on Japanese American freedom rendered their labor outside the camps as more of a work release program, and indeed the public often referred to these workers as "parolees" on "trial" leave.[5] Elsewhere, Japanese Americans built irrigation ditches meant to render tracts of the dry and dusty Arizona desert fit for Native American or GI Bill–eligible veteran settlement. Although Japanese Americans typically received between twelve and eighteen dollars a month and signed contracts with the WRA or private employers, labor disputes served as a catalyst for "riots" and strikes that revealed deep resentment over poor working conditions in and out of the prisons. Disillusionment and dissatisfaction over unpaid wages as well as exploitative and coercive conditions were central to the Japanese American experience of incarceration.

Japanese American Incarceration uncovers these experiences and argues that the incarceration of Japanese Americans created a massive system of prison labor that blurred the lines between free and forced work. This book is certainly not the first to note and discuss Japanese American laborers under EO 9066, but it is the first to categorize their experiences as coerced prison work. The decentralized nature of the WRA-run camps and the inefficiency of the agency provided some level of autonomy for each camp administrator to build different relationships with those imprisoned. Some prisoner-administrator relationships were antagonistic, such as those at the Tule Lake camp between director Raymond Best and Japanese Americans who refused to answer loyalty oaths. Others were less so with more room for self-government such as at the Poston camp in Arizona. Regardless of individual relationships between the administrators and the prisoners, Japanese Americans performed coerced labor in a variety of ways to benefit the prisons and the American war economy. This fact drew all camps and Japanese Americans together under one prison labor system. Military records, government documents, oral histories, and memoirs from Japanese Americans reveal that using Japanese American labor was an initial goal—not a convenient result—of the larger incarceration project. Administrators, the military, and private employers considered Japanese Americans a readily available labor force during the planning phases of incarceration through the dismantling of the prison camps.[6]

Executive Order 9066 and Imprisonment

Why have historians been hesitant to fully view the work performed by incarcerated Japanese Americans through the lens of prison labor? After all, scholars have rejected the various euphemisms used by the US government to describe and explain the incarceration project in 1942: "internment," "evacuee," "evacuation," "assembly center," and "relocation center." In 2010, the Japanese American Citizens League published the Power of Words resolution, which encouraged the wider public to use more accurate terms, including "imprisonment" or "incarceration" instead of internment (which as a legal concept applied specifically to foreign-born Japanese held in internment centers for "enemy aliens") considering that the majority of Japanese Americans forcibly removed (rather than evacuated) from their homes by the army and confined in detention centers (rather than assembly centers) were American citizens. From there, the army transported Japanese Americans to prison camps, not relocation camps or centers.[7] Even the Department of the Interior released a report on Japanese American incarceration in 1946 titled *Impounded People*, recognizing the detainment of Japanese Americans but using a term often designated for property rather than individuals.[8] Other scholars choose to use the then contemporary terms from the government to limit confusion and maintain historical accuracy, or reject the use of the Power of Words resolution's terminology, implying that it is overreaching or generalizing.[9]

The use of euphemisms to describe the imprisonment of Japanese Americans was not lost on contemporaries at the time. In his dissent on the 1944 Supreme Court case *Korematsu v. United States* pertaining to the constitutionality of Executive Order 9066, Justice Owen Roberts remarked that "an assembly center is a euphemism for prison" and that the exclusion orders were "but part of an overall plan for forceable detention."[10] More accurate words like "incarceration" and "detention" serve as a means to analyze and interrogate how and why Japanese Americans labored in the prisons after Executive Order 9066.

I use the resolution's suggested terms as they more accurately depict the wrongful detention of Japanese Americans but also echo the ways Japanese Americans themselves described their experiences with incarceration. Throughout this book, I use "prison camp" (or camp) because of the large-scale, government-funded projects Japanese Americans worked on while incarcerated. "Detention centers" (or simply centers) is the correct term for the temporary "assembly centers" Japanese Americans stayed in before going to the camps. I avoid the euphemisms used during the war to refocus on the elements of prison labor.

These terms also reflect changes in the narrative of the executive order and subsequent removal and imprisonment, opening opportunities for the exploration of incarceration as a history of prison labor. In 1981, following calls for redress within a growing Asian American movement for civil rights and equality, lawyers, scholars, activists, and survivors of incarceration served

as expert witnesses and provided heartbreaking testimony to congressional
hearings as part of the Commission on Wartime Relocation and Internment
of Civilians. The hearings resulted in an official report in 1982, *Personal Justice Denied*, and redress of $20,000 for every survivor (limited to American-
born and immigrants "residing legally" in the United States at the time; many
were no longer alive to receive their reparations) when President Ronald Rea-
gan signed the Civil Liberties Act of 1988.[11] The commission and its report
also offered a clear and concise explanation of the causes of incarceration and
specified which individual policy makers and government agencies should
shoulder the blame.

Following testimony and extensive legal and scholarly investigations, the
commission established that "race prejudice, war, and a failure of political
leadership" informed the incarceration of Japanese Americans.[12] These con-
clusions challenged the standard narrative that Roosevelt signed Executive
Order 9066 as a defense measure and for the protection of Japanese Americans from paranoid and vengeful residents on the West Coast—implicitly ac-
knowledging the racism and discrimination that affected so many Japanese
American communities economically, politically, and socially.[13]

The findings of the commission were inspired by, coincided with, and
shaped historiographical and scholarly interventions in the subject. More survivors opened up in interviews and oral histories about their experiences.
Historians and other scholars challenged the narrative of military necessity
on the basis of the longer history of anti-Asian sentiment on the West Coast.
As these activists and scholars discovered, and the hearings confirmed, many
government agencies and officials warned Roosevelt against signing the executive order given its potentially grave constitutional consequences. Assistant Attorney General James H. Rowe was an outspoken critic of the plan for
removal and incarceration, writing to FDR's secretary Grace Tully in early
February 1942, "It [Executive Order 9066] would probably require suspension of the writ of habeas corpus—and my estimate of the country's present
feeling is that we would have another Supreme Court fight on our hands."[14]
Attorney General Francis Biddle agreed with Rowe, and even Lieutenant
General John L. DeWitt, leader of the Western Defense Command of the
army, was initially wary of removing and incarcerating Japanese American
citizens and involving the military in civilian domestic matters, placing him
at odds with pro-incarceration members of the army such as Colonel Karl
Bendetsen (his assistant chief of staff). Despite opposition to the policy, the
government implemented first "voluntary relocation" of Japanese Americans

between March and May 1942 and later forced removal in May. Milton S. Eisenhower (former director of information for the Department of Agriculture and brother of Dwight Eisenhower) became director of the WRA despite his concern that long-term detainment would negatively affect Japanese Americans. (Dillon S. Myer assumed the position in the summer of 1942 when Eisenhower left for a position in the Office of War Information following his increasing disgust over incarceration).

Historians also identified incarceration not as an unfortunate yet isolated moment in American history but rather a culmination of long-standing anti-Japanese sentiment. Politicians and economic power players including farmers' and growers' associations capitalized on these feelings in California, Washington, and Oregon during heightened wartime hysteria and paranoia.[15] More recently, historians have also pushed the boundaries of incarceration physically beyond the United States and into the transnational realm, taking into consideration broader global patterns of wartime detention, the actions and experiences of foreign-born Issei in the prisons, and the removal and detainment of Japanese Canadians and Japanese Mexicans.[16]

For all of the reinterpretations of "internment" and with a view to incorporating analyses based on discussions of race, class, and gender, many of its links to imprisonment remain unexplored. Perhaps this is because of redress and the notion that this chapter of American history is closed, the former prisoners released and adequately compensated. Redress allowed the federal government and Americans to view incarceration from a safe distance, an anachronism or a misstep rather than part of a larger history of detainment. Embracing the connections between Japanese American incarceration and imprisonment forces scholars as well as the public to confront the insidiousness of the carceral state and how the rationales for incarceration of Japanese Americans "have morphed as they are applied to new target populations." The Japanese American prisons, as A. Naomi Paik reminds us, and the accompanying states of "rightlessness" for those held within "have hardly been eradicated from the country's arsenal of political strategies."[17]

Or perhaps it is because the prisons Japanese Americans were held in from California to Arkansas did not resemble exactly what we think a carceral system should look like. "Where were the uniforms?" a colleague once asked when I argued that incarceration was a more fitting term for "internment." They were referring to the standard-issue clothing associated with inmates in public and private prisons, a physical marker of difference. They continued by pointing to the fact that Japanese Americans were allowed to drive vehicles on prison property to complete tasks and therefore always had access to a means of escape, implying both that Japanese American prisoners were complicit in their own imprisonment and that even if they were not, conditions were not "that bad." Japanese Americans detained at the Topaz prison in Utah, for example, could enter and exit the camp through a hole in the fence. There were also instances of broken floodlights on guard towers at the Santa Anita detention center, implying that the lights remained broken because there was no concern for keeping Japanese Americans within the compound.[18]

All of these examples point to visual cues of imprisonment and physical restraint, no doubt a central part of the incarceration in limiting movement, but as interdisciplinary studies have shown, prisons and systems of incarceration operate in insidious and psychological ways. Not all restraints, or in the case of Japanese Americans, violations of basic Fourteenth Amendment freedoms including the rights to life, liberty, and property, were (or are) physical. If Japanese Americans had the means to escape, where would they go? Beyond barbed wire fences, searchlights, and guards, a system of surveillance and perceived and real danger cultivated by the government and prison administrators alike worked to limit the movement of Japanese Americans. The nineteenth-century detainment of Asian immigrants arriving at Angel Island as well as discriminatory immigration laws which limited movement by requiring papers to prove legal entry were part of the genealogy of the incarceration of Japanese Americans during World War II.[19]

Between March and May 1942, Japanese Americans living in the military zones along the West Coast had the option to voluntarily leave their homes and settle further east. Taking advantage of this mechanism ensured that property was accounted for, farm land leased and transferred to sympathetic friends, neighbors, or even employees, and jobs and residencies lined up elsewhere.[20] In total, approximately five thousand Japanese Americans left voluntarily before May 1942, many moving just outside of Military Area 1 and into Military Area 2, which were not initially part of the exclusion orders. Once exclusion applied to Military Area 2, however, the government forced Japanese Americans to move yet again in April and May. Others formed small farm cooperatives in Utah and Oregon or moved beyond West Coast states. In total, only 10 percent of the West Coast's Japanese American population relocated "voluntarily." The options for voluntarily leaving before forced removal—for uprooting families and searching for ways to protect property within a span of a few months—were out of reach logistically for most Japanese Americans.[21]

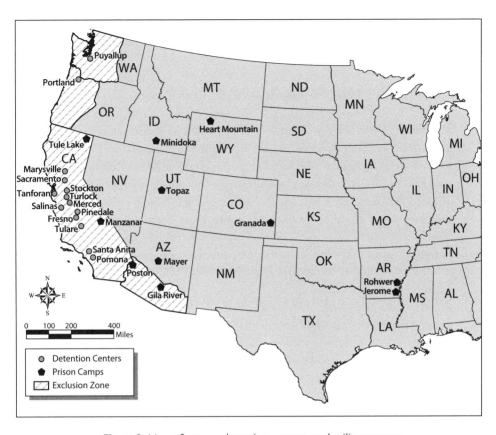

Figure 2. Map of camps, detention centers, and military zones.

Forced removal was hasty and in many ways disorganized, leaving little time for such life-changing and potentially economically damaging decisions. The WRA Evacuee Property Division and government depots operated as custodians for property, but many Japanese Americans were unable to trust the same government removing them from their homes with safeguarding their possessions. Also, the government had ordered bank accounts of Issei frozen since late 1941, making it more challenging for this generation and their families to voluntarily leave. As the government and military argued that time was of the essence, there were no opportunities for trials or loyalty hearings. As a result, many Japanese Americans lost their livelihoods because of EO 9066. Their Fourteenth Amendment rights to due process, equal protection under the law, and property ownership were, in essence, nullified.

Accepting imprisonment was in many ways the only option and the only way to ensure that families stayed together during uncertain times.[22]

Japanese Americans and Prison Labor

The limited options for avoiding forced removal and incarceration resulted in thousands of Japanese Americans laboring in the prison camps. The work performed by these men and women was essential for the functioning of the incarceration system. My use of the phrase "prison labor" to describe the work of incarcerated Japanese Americans is purposefully complex. Reaching for the simplest explanation, one could argue that if the government imprisoned (and wrongfully so) Japanese Americans and expected them to work to maintain the prisons, make profits for private employers who contracted with the prisons, and complete infrastructure projects adjacent to the prisons and chosen by prison administrators, then they engaged in prison labor. However, this is not a sufficient explanation in and of itself to apply such a loaded term to the experience of Japanese Americans during World War II. Why not simply refer to this as labor as others have done? Because EO 9066 created a specific, state-sanctioned form of exploitative work extracted from prisoners through coercion. Japanese American loyalty was suspect during the war, and the federal government used this suspicion to argue that Japanese Americans could prove their patriotism and dedication to the war effort by working on a variety of projects—many of which would benefit government agencies and private employers more than the prisoners.

Referring to Japanese American incarceration as simply "labor" also diminishes the unique aspects of the prison work system when compared to other wartime labor trends. With approximately sixteen million men and women serving in the war and other Americans moving to more lucrative military industries, various sectors of the economy suffered a decrease in available labor. Even war matériel plants could not keep up with demand placed on them by the War Department and various branches of the military. Agriculture fared far worse. While "Rosie the Riveters" sought wages in jobs that were typically reserved for their male counterparts, and men who were not qualified for service or granted exemptions found better-paying jobs in mining and manufacturing, large-scale farmers and corporations imported laborers from Mexico under the Bracero program beginning in 1942. Farmers also courted other migrant laborers across the nation to make up for their losses. Agricultural products were in high demand for war production as well. Working conditions in these industries varied, with some—such as what the braceros faced—more challenging and exploitative than others. Through propaganda and the promise of higher wages, the federal government called on Americans to do their part and use their labor to contribute to the war effort. Military leaders including General DeWitt also identified mobilizing the home front as crucial for victory and defense, tying the economy to the war effort. And the war effort in return was deeply intertwined with labor and demonstrations of patriotism. Racial tensions and gender discrimination within the very industries that recruited minorities and women, however, made patriotic labor challenging and, at times, dangerous.[23]

Connecting Japanese American labor to these trends adds more context and nuance, but denying the state-sanctioned, coerced nature of the labor that arose from incarceration obscures its unique challenges and experiences. Japanese Americans placed in prison camps with few opportunities to actively declare that they would *not* work or contribute to the war effort makes their wages of war different from those earned by other workers. How could administrators and the government harness Japanese American labor for a variety of projects without contradicting American principles and the antifascist ideals of the war? How could DeWitt—connected to incarceration through his post as commander of the Western Defense—prevent Japan from classifying the labor performed by Japanese Americans as "forced" and avoid potential retaliation on American prisoners of war in the Pacific? Japanese Americans—foreign and American born—were not prisoners of war, but army officials did not want to take any chances in appearing to violate international law, which forbade the forced and unpaid labor of captured enemies. These questions influenced many administrators and military leaders and illustrate a stark difference between the prison labor performed by Japanese Americans during the war and the labor of other workers.[24]

Beyond Japanese American incarceration, prison labor has a long history in the United States. Historians and scholars have cast a wide net in examining how and why labor (or peonage) became a core component of the American prison system from the colonial era through the late twentieth century.[25] As rudimentary approaches to prison reform in northern states during the mid-nineteenth century began, labor was seen as a rehabilitative and useful activity for convicts as opposed to simply a punitive measure. But even as (primarily religious) reformers worked to provide prisoners with the chance at redemption and salvation through their labor, in 1821 the New York or

"Auburn" system became a model for state penitentiaries. The Auburn model was representative of an "open market system" of imprisonment whereby convicts worked for private employers while the prisons profited from leasing or contracting the prisoners for outside work, shifting the focus of imprisonment from reform to profit for the state as well as private ventures.[26]

Imprisonment became part and parcel of an industrializing United States, setting the stage for later developments. After the Civil War, southern states turned to using African Americans imprisoned for violating the notorious Black Codes (laws that limited the basic rights of newly freed slaves and criminalized gun ownership, worshipping in "large groups" in churches, and "congregating" on streets after dark) for cheap or cost-free labor. The convict lease system became a hallmark of southern labor exploitation during the Jim Crow era as state prisons leased convicts—both men and women—to private employers for harvesting, planting, repairs, and other jobs (the lessee provided housing, clothing, and food for the inmates, although the definition of what was acceptable for these provisions varied across localities).[27] The panhandle of Florida as well as southern Georgia and southeastern Alabama hosted an intricate system of convict leasing that resembled an internal slave trade as private employers passed prisoners to one another as needed. Additionally, state officials put prisoners to work building roads and working on other infrastructure projects as part of the infamous chain gangs that changed the landscape not only of the South but of many states across the country.

As the nation rebuilt after the Civil War, imprisonment and labor worked hand in hand to assist a rapidly expanding economic system as well as westward settlement in a country dependent on exploitable labor for modernization. This system also assumed a racialized image as more minorities filled prisons.[28] Congress outlawed peonage in 1867 and the formal system of convict leasing eventually dissolved as the practice garnered negative publicity during the early twentieth century. Despite receiving enormous financial benefits, states began to abandon the system one by one. However, prison labor continued when Federal Prison Industries was established in 1934 to provide jobs and vocational training for those detained in federal prisons. Later, the agency became more closely tied to corporations as private prisons grew during the latter half of the twentieth century. While the 1930 Forced Labour Convention (held by the International Labour Organization) prohibited private employment of prison laborers, the United States and Canada did not participate in the accords as they still used prison labor in this capacity.[29]

With all of the variations, the hallmark of prison labor was the use of coercion or force to extract work and ensure compliance; even with wages, this was by no account a free or voluntary labor system.

Avoiding the image of forced labor was at the forefront of policy makers' minds when organizing and implementing Japanese American incarceration. According to the Geneva Convention of 1929 and previous agreements, Issei, or "enemy aliens," could not be forced to work; neither could prisoners of war, who would receive wages in scrip for their voluntary labor in line with their rank (as they did throughout the country).[30] Neither enemy aliens nor POWs could work on projects directly connected to war aims such as munitions manufacturing. Furthermore, the notion of imprisoning American citizens and forcing them to work was antithetical to both the war effort and American democracy.

To counter any claims of forced labor, the WCCA, WRA, and army took great pains to showcase the freedom Japanese Americans possessed when it came to their "choice" to work in the prisons. Repeatedly, the WRA maintained that no Japanese American was "forced" or "compelled" to work, and, in a technical sense, this was true. Japanese Americans signed contracts—the defining characteristic of free labor for administrators—and joined the Work Corps program for those held in the detention centers and later incarcerated in the prison camps. Yet, although they were paid a wage, Japanese Americans were required to labor until two weeks after the end of the war and were not allowed to quit a job without special permission from camp administrators. The same restrictions applied to those like Yamauchi who worked for the private contractors who set up factories in detainment centers and prisons, or prisoners working on agricultural leave for labor-strapped farmers and corporations outside the prisons. From the US government's perspective, every single worker had signed a contract and freely entered into an agreement exchanging labor for wages. Clearly, the army and WRA repeatedly argued, this was not forced labor.

But this emphasis on a contract as the foundation of free choice to work was belied by events. Some prison administrators repeatedly explained that if Japanese Americans wanted to eat, they would have to produce their own food, often in arid areas where significant land improvements were required prior to cultivation. The unforgiving physical environment of most prisons, as much as the WRA, compelled the prisoners to work.[31] Farmers who hired Japanese Americans and failed to provide adequate housing, withheld pay, or freely "traded" workers with limited federal oversight repeatedly violated contracts. Paychecks were frequently late or never received at all. The WCCA and WRA even initially sought to deduct subsistence charges for anyone not employed either within or outside the camps and centers in order to discourage "loafing." Administrators pressed Japanese Americans to enlist in the corps to prove their loyalty and disprove accusations of subversion, reminiscent of the "work or fight" order during World War I which required all able-bodied men to perform civilian tasks if they could not serve in the armed forces.[32] Japanese Americans held at the Topaz prison in Utah described themselves as forced laborers. As one noted, "We did not ask to come here. We were forced to leave our legitimate type of work for the Caucasians to take over and make money during the war."[33]

Free, Coerced, or Forced Labor?

Employing the term "prison labor" to describe the work completed by Japanese Americans in and out of the camps is also useful for considering the shifting conceptions of free labor during Japanese American incarceration. Although the WRA, WCCA, and the army strove to avoid the optics of forced labor, the work performed by imprisoned Japanese Americans challenged the distinctions among "free," "coerced," and "forced." Scholars and policy makers today frequently interchange terms describing circumscribed decision-making in labor scenarios. Concepts of "free" and "unfree" labor can be fluid in different time periods and contexts, with both labor systems existing at polar ends of the same continuum.[34]

In international law, a binary division of "free" and "forced" labor normalizes exploitative measures that happen daily yet do not fit the traditional image of "forced" labor (or slavery).[35] Convict lease labor in the South during the post-Reconstruction years where state and local governments and law enforcement arrested and imprisoned former slaves and then forced them to work for no pay is forced labor. Immigrants who came to the United States around the turn of the twentieth century and freely entered into labor contracts with employers yet found themselves in situations similar to indentured servitude muddy the distinction between "forced" and "free." "Coerced labor" born from socioeconomic conditions beyond the control of these workers is the more apt term to use in these situations.[36]

Turning again to international regulations, the United Nations' International Labour Organization explains that forced labor "refers to situations in

which persons are coerced to work through the use of violence or intimida-
tion, or by more subtle means such as accumulated debt, retention of identity
papers, or threats of denunciation to immigration authorities." Moreover,
such systems are characterized by limitations on freedom of movement and
the fact that "all work or service which is extracted from any person" is "under
the menace of penalty for which the said person has not offered himself voluntarily."[37] The Thirteenth Amendment of the United States Constitution
outlaws slavery and involuntary servitude (save for convicted criminals),
which has often led to more uncertainty on work arrangements for prisoners
and leaves wide open opportunities for the abuse and exploitation of laborers.[38] Others have argued that turning to human rights rather than
citizenship rights might more effectively cover the ways in which employers have historically coerced or forced workers to labor in ways that do not
cross the threshold into slavery.[39]

Taking these arguments into consideration, I frame this study around the
concept of prison labor, as it is useful in examining the multitude of ways in
which agencies, the military, private employers, and the imprisoned Japanese
Americans themselves sought to perform, discuss, implement and challenge
the work they performed. Forced and coerced labor were a part of this system. In the case of Japanese Americans, the concept of prison labor best reveals the dynamic continuum for defining how labor is coerced. The
imprisonment of Japanese Americans and their "social coercion," in which
prison administrators possessed "state-sanctioned power over workers'
well-being, families, and futures," describes the limited options for Japanese
Americans.[40] If a prisoner exercised his or her right not to work, they were
denied the opportunity to purchase medical supplies, clothing, and necessary dietary supplements for infants and the elderly in their immediate and
extended families. If they attempted to extract better working conditions
through individual complaints or collective action they risked the wrath of
the camp police or, worse, the Federal Bureau of Investigation for subversion
of the war effort. If found guilty, they faced transfer to a punitive camp for
"hard cases," away from their families.

Working within the camps was not without its complexities. Joining the
Work Corps also offered prisoners the opportunity to "prove" their loyalty
to the United States, assist with the war effort, purchase items, and develop
a sense of occupational achievement. Japanese American women, for example,
were able to work in a variety of positions for wages that provided them with
or increased their disposable income and loosened the ties of patriarchal

structures in their homes. Social scientists also disagree on whether or not incarceration had a positive or negative impact on the earning potential and career advancements of Japanese Americans. Some compare wages before and after World War II and argue that incarceration had a positive impact on earnings as a result of training opportunities in the camps and relocation to areas beyond the West Coast. Others suggest that once-prosperous farmers increased wage earnings after incarceration but lost property value and long-term assets over time. This variation in experience and outcome was the nature of this unique labor system.[41]

Given these realities, the government effectively created a new category of labor under incarceration, defined by exploitation of Japanese Americans for the benefit of both the state and private industry. The legal advisers to the WRA and the army argued that, while Japanese Americans were technically not convicts, the procedures governing convict labor and the ability to allow prisoners to leave on work release was a useful template for supervising and controlling the potentially subversive Japanese American population. Although Japanese Americans were eventually granted restricted freedom of movement beyond the prisons, this concession was for labor purposes only, and the army and federal, state, and local officials monitored their movement.[42]

Imprisoned but not convicts; supposedly not forced laborers yet with contracts that were casually violated and manipulated; allowed to leave for work but not free to travel. This was the carceral state at work, but a carceral state that intersected with the war effort. The government and private sector's exploitation of Japanese American labor was a product of this paradoxical wartime economy that valued labor as well as democratic principles of liberty and freedom during a global fight against fascism. Imprisoned Japanese Americans labored on public and private projects for the war effort while administrators attempted to balance between coercing Japanese Americans to work and maintaining the image of them as free workers. This was not a traditional form of prison labor; this was a system that arose specifically from a time of war.[43]

My focus on the prison labor aspect of incarceration is by no means designed to strip Japanese Americans of their agency. "Prison labor" adequately describes a larger system at play that circumscribed Japanese Americans' abilities to exercise free choice in their work conditions. This phrase does not mean that Japanese Americans did not want to support both their communities and the larger war effort. In oral histories and memoirs, Japanese

Americans have expressed pride in the work they completed while also detailing their feelings of disappointment and disillusionment with the nation that detained them during the war.[44] Japanese Americans (which I use to collectively denote Issei, Nisei, and Kibei) often used labor as a means to earn a living and maintain some sense of dignity or semblance of normality.

Though many of the examples in this book focus on manual work and its connections to meeting the most pressing labor demands in and beyond the camps, as well as strikes and protests, white-collar professions also fall under the complicated category of prison labor. Japanese American women often found career opportunities within the camps that were not afforded in their larger communities. Positions as clerical workers, newspaper writers and editors, nurses, and research assistants were available to those with the skills and training. As one Japanese American woman noted, knowing shorthand and how to type meant that she was "never out of a job" as she moved through the detention centers to the Jerome prison camp in Arkansas.[45] Competition with white women or a sense of familial responsibility and traditional gender roles and norms previously limited career choices for Japanese American women. In the camps—a manufactured world that upended traditional family structures—not only were those opportunities available, but the wages were a form of advancement as well. Though below the going rate beyond the prison camps, earning sixteen dollars a month as a professional worker was a chance at honing skills that could be useful after release from the camps. Other incarcerees also took pride in their work and found real contentment in their daily activities. Japanese Americans at Manzanar, for example, grew "victory gardens" or contributed their agricultural expertise to the cultivation of novel crops that fed the camps and contributed to the war effort.[46]

The above instances challenge cut-and-dried distinctions between free and forced labor. In the case of protests or strikes, labor activities served as a space where Japanese Americans could express broader dissatisfactions with their situation as prisoners and lack of rights as workers, among other grievances. Work—even when coerced—could itself become a catalyst for acts of defiance, as prisoners often used their labor as a tool in negotiations with camp administrators or to exercise agency over their surroundings and environment.[47]

Through withholding their labor during strikes at Manzanar, Tule Lake, and other camps, Japanese Americans also responded to a longer history of exploitation of Asian Americans. From the mid-1850s through the early twentieth century, Chinese miners and railroad workers in the West and farm laborers in the South after the Civil War, Sikh timber workers from India in the Pacific Northwest, and Filipino and Japanese migrant and agricultural workers were simultaneously valued for their cheap labor and reviled for their labor competition and contribution to a "yellow invasion" from Asia. In the case of Japanese, many West Coast growers' associations and politicians decried the productivity and skill of Japanese farmers during the early twentieth century and accused them of monopolizing agriculture through unethical practices.[48]

The contradictory desires for cheap labor and for limiting the influx of Asian immigrants resulted in a series of immigration policies with loopholes for employers. Congress modified the Chinese Exclusion Act of 1882 and the Immigration Act of 1890 to make exceptions for the entrance of Chinese traveling with Americans as servants, using immigration policy to create a body of domestic laborers who were easily exploited by middle- and upper-class employers.[49]

The federal government's use of Japanese Americans' labor during World War II and the assumption that their productivity was a valuable untapped resource were part of a longer legacy of viewing Asian Americans as easily exploited. The coercive nature of Japanese American prison labor in the camps was linked to the practice of coercive labor, unfair contracts, and poor working conditions created by railroad companies and southern planters in hiring Chinese "coolie" laborers in the nineteenth century.[50] Although wartime and defense measures presented the opportunity to use Japanese Americans' labor while imprisoned, the impetus for the treatment of Asian Americans as an expendable labor force was ingrained in the United States.

The emphasis of the WRA and the army that at no point were Japanese Americans forced to work colored publications, speeches, and memos arguing for the free nature of the labor despite the reality of coercion and exploitation. Much like scholars today argue that euphemisms such as internment conceal the carceral aspect of Executive Order 9066 (and indeed, the phrase "concentration camp" was often used by government officials when discussing incarceration), I argue that the justifications offered by the government to other agencies, the American people, and the Japanese American prisoners for requiring employment within the camps operate in a similar way, erasing the prison qualities of the coerced labor.

Administrators frequently used four rationales to explain the purpose and goals of incarceration to Japanese Americans, other government agencies, and the public. Common phrases and concepts detailed in the following paragraphs summarized these rationales and also serve as a framework for *Japanese American Incarceration.*

First, government officials and military leaders argued that Japanese American labor was essential for self-sufficiency, community building, and the promotion of a "pioneer spirit." In reality, explaining the need for these concepts in publications, memos, and to the incarcerated was a way to use Japanese American labor to complete infrastructure programs and ready land for use by other groups.

Second, administrators and members of the army stressed to each other and to Japanese Americans that their contributions to the war effort through their labor were essential for proving their loyalty and patriotism. Deploying the need for cooperation among civilians in the war effort was a successful motivating factor in many economic projects. WRA administrators used patriotism to encourage imprisoned Japanese Americans to sign up for private employment or for work in the camps directly making war matériel and subsidizing the costs of their own imprisonment.

Third, prison administrators explained that work was important for improving and sustaining morale among the incarcerated, particularly the American-born and -raised Nisei, whom administrators deemed vulnerable to despair and disillusionment. Concern for the well-being and industriousness of Nisei belied the fact that Japanese Americans were expected and coerced to work to maintain the prisons.

Finally, administrators insisted that work performed by Japanese Americans was free and voluntary as they signed contracts and received compensation for their work. In practice, contracts were often loosely enforced and created opportunities for exploitation. These justifications and explanations all factored into decisions—from where the prisons were located to their social and economic policies—made by the WCCA, the WRA, and the army following Executive Order 9066.

Approaching Japanese American incarceration during World War II as a labor history is an ambitious undertaking and one I have attempted to make more manageable by focusing on case studies that highlight specific elements of the prison labor system. At the camps and centers used in this study, approximately 40–60 percent of the Japanese Americans were employed. Numbers varied on the basis of age, health, and personal circumstances including child-rearing. WRA officials expected most prisoners to be put to work in agricultural projects. Self-sufficiency was a goal for the WRA for all the camps, and growing enough food to feed the prisoners (while surplus would be apportioned to the military) was considered an essential task. On the ground, most of the Japanese American employees worked in a variety of jobs—unskilled, skilled, and professional—that allowed the camps to function at an efficient pace and cost. Mess hall workers across the camps employed the largest number of employees as cooks, servers, dishwashers, and stockers; serving thousands of people at once in each block unit cafeteria (blocks were communities of barracks) required more personnel than the WRA initially expected. By 1943 most Japanese Americans were employed in a "community" position in some capacity or on furlough working in harvesting crops. Most Japanese Americans in the camps fell under the "skilled" designation and made sixteen dollars a month—when checks arrived on time and there were no discrepancies in pay. While the larger picture of the prison labor system provides opportunities for generalizations, key events and issues at specific camps and centers provide case studies for analyzing flash points.[51]

Each chapter focuses on a specific aspect of the labor system or a camp or detention center. *Japanese American Incarceration* begins after the government's decision to forcibly remove Japanese Americans from their homes and aligns with the arguments of scholars (as well as sources from the time) that the program was rooted in racism, paranoia, and political opportunism.[52] Chapter 1 details the central place labor assumed for the WCCA and the WRA in planning the locations and organization of wartime incarceration. Chapter 2 presents the rising challenges early in the spring and summer of 1942 in releasing Japanese Americans for private labor and confronting exploitation and violations of contracts that made "free" labor "coerced"—more akin to convict lease labor.

The third and fourth chapters focus on specific detention centers and prison camps: Santa Anita detention center, Manzanar prison camp in California, and the Poston prison colony in Arizona. Labor strikes at the Santa Anita center in June 1942 and later at Manzanar in the fall of 1942 highlight the experiences of Japanese Americans protesting their limited rights as laborers. In these cases, camouflage net workers at Santa Anita and "community" employees working on day-to-day maintenance at Manzanar often had little say in conditions and pay.

Chapter 3 also presents an example of the differences in labor expectations between the temporary detention centers and the later, more permanent prison camps. Community positions were necessary at the detention centers, but creating opportunities for Japanese Americans in producing war matériel was a more prominent goal for the army and WCCA. The army and the civilian administrators at the WCCA knew that their role was temporary; labor here existed for maintaining order amid a demographic thrust into an alien environment as well as for the production of necessary materials for the war effort.

At the camps, the WRA emphasized self-sufficiency and community positions to ensure the orderly operation of the camps with less oversight (and less money spent). Additionally, administrators at most camps were former New Deal liberals who held positions in the Works Progress Administration and other agencies designed to provide opportunities for out-of-work Americans. These administrators viewed self-sufficiency and employment of able-bodied Japanese Americans as goals that would promote productivity at the camps while also boosting morale. Unlike the army and the WCCA, the issue of forced labor and its impact on military strategy rarely crossed their minds, leading to problems between administrators and Japanese Americans who resented having limited workers' rights.

Each situation created a different set of problems that spoke to the coerced nature of the labor performed while imprisoned. At Santa Anita, workers at the camouflage netting company went on strike against poor working conditions and the notion that they were treated as "prison laborers," while at Manzanar—where Japanese American prisoners knew that they were there indefinitely—many protested a lack of say in their positions as well as back pay and disrespect from administrators.

Chapter 4 focuses exclusively on Poston for its unique position as a sociological experiment or "colony" established on the Colorado River Indian Tribes reservation. Poston was the largest prison camp (before Tule Lake became a segregation center) and employed Japanese Americans in a variety of positions. It also represented the challenge for both administrators and prisoners in determining the goals of the camps beyond self-sufficiency. Nonetheless, Poston also highlighted the problems of the prison labor system. The end of the incarceration project was in sight as repeated labor protests at Poston, combined with the strike at Tule Lake later in 1943, raised the ire of administrators and exposed the weaknesses of the WRA. Budget problems would eventually encourage Dillon S. Myer—then WRA director—to move to the "all-out relocation" program of eliminating positions at the camp to encourage Japanese American prisoners to leave Poston.

Chapter 5 picks up with all-out relocation and argues that "resettlement" was a parole system designed to place Japanese Americans in employment positions tied to war work. More specifically, WRA administrators made employment a condition for release from the camps. The resettlement process advocated for former prisoners to prove their loyalty and right to be released in a form of redemptive labor—though this process was not without its challenges.

This book primarily focuses on the design and implementation of Japanese American incarceration and the centrality of labor to both of these undertakings. It is not a comprehensive history of the topic nor does it examine the decision to remove and imprison Japanese Americans. I pay particular attention to the official government documents for what they reveal about the architecture of the incarceration labor system. It was almost a natural progression for the federal government, having already extensively violated the civil rights and liberties of Japanese Americans, to turn to conceiving of and exploiting the imprisoned Japanese Americans as a labor resource.

CHAPTER 1

The Economics of Incarceration and the Blueprint for Japanese American Labor

Just south of the Oregon border and nestled between the Modoc and Fremont National Forests is the small town of Tulelake, California. A sign welcoming visitors proclaims that it was "Built By Veterans," referencing the GIs who returned from World War II and purchased parcels of land auctioned off by the United States Reclamation Service (the Department of the Interior agency responsible for assisting with irrigation and water access primarily in the West). The Reclamation Service used the Civilian Conservation Corps (a public work relief program established in 1933) to construct irrigation systems and enlisted individual property owners and corporations to purchase land. The nearby town of Newell (population 305) was also a beneficiary of this infrastructure system. By the time veterans and their families formed the Newell Homestead Club in 1947 to build homes, a school, and a medical facility in preparation for auctions in 1951, Newell was a site of rapid growth. Deep wells, red cinder roads, surplus buildings, irrigation and sewer systems, electricity, a stop on the Southern Pacific Railroad, and the recently completed Highway 139 made the town an attractive place to settle.[1]

But Newell's history is more complicated than this idyllic picture of American frontier taming through persistence and grit. Rather than veterans, it was incarcerated Japanese Americans who completed most of the internal improvements and made significant progress on the Klamath Regional Irrigation Project. A historical marker serves as a pilgrimage site for those wishing to pay their respects to the thousands who lived—and worked—while imprisoned in the Tule Lake camp outside Newell, but the markers and local memory do not acknowledge the fact that Japanese Americans transformed the land for later settlement after the war. The US Army Corps of Engineers and the War Relocation Authority (WRA) explicitly chose Tulelake as a site for a prison camp so that the incarcerated Japanese Americans could cheaply and efficiently develop the region.

From the selection of sites to the control and operation of Japanese American incarceration, prison labor was key. On May 27, 1942, Japanese Americans arrived at Tule Lake from the Portland, Oregon and Puyallup, Washington detention centers to finish constructing housing facilities for the more permanent, WRA-administered prison camps. Apart from its location outside Military Zone 1 (designated by Lieutenant General John L. DeWitt for its defensive vulnerability following the Pearl Harbor attack), Tule Lake met the main requirement for hosting a prison camp: ample opportunities for work. The army (through the Wartime Civil Control Administration—its wartime branch and joint civilian agency established by DeWitt to oversee the removal and immediate detention of Japanese Americans) and the WRA assessed the suitability for a camp on the basis of a given area's need for agricultural, infrastructural, and/or manufacturing work. The selection process prized a site's potential for using the Japanese Americans' labor on rural improvement projects. The WCCA, WRA, and, later, private employers recognized economic opportunities in Japanese American removal and incarceration not long after the ink dried on Executive Order 9066. More importantly, members of the agencies in charge of designing and implementing incarceration decisively viewed labor exploitation as a benefit of this prison system *before* the first Japanese Americans left their homes in the spring of 1942.

The administrators' reasons for prioritizing labor in the blueprint for incarceration were varied, but all connected to the notion of creating a reservoir of readily available, cost-effective workers. Members of the WRA and WCCA claimed that work boosted the morale of Japanese Americans. Labor not only kept the prisoners busy and gave their lives meaning but also allowed them to use their skills in a productive way in nursing, teaching, weaving, or farming, among other occupations. Performing daily tasks for wages could help Japanese Americans temporarily accept their conditions and also build a community, with all prisoners working toward the common goal of creating a comfortable place to live. Japanese Americans could also prove their loyalty by accepting their situations and recognizing that detainment, though unfortunate, did not deny them their abilities to have as close to a "normal" life as possible. Compensation in the form of "cash advances" (a phrase used by the WCCA and WRA in the early planning stages of incarceration to differentiate the fruits of prison labor from civilian "wages") for the pur-chase of goods from camp canteens was a reward for Japanese Americans. This message of morale and loyalty is what WCCA and WRA officials as well as the directors of each detention center and prison camp delivered to the incarcerated. However, as found in internal memos, directives, letters, tele-phone conversations among representatives of various government agen-cies, and public statements, the administrators' motives for prizing labor had more to do with the economic and financial needs of different sectors of the wartime economy and the incarceration system than with Japanese American well-being.

The implementation of Executive Order 9066 was a massive undertaking, an extensive project that required the assistance of myriad federal agencies and bureaus to carry out each step in the process as well as a considerable amount of money. Early on, past-due bills from state and local agencies and private businesses that provided assistance with removal and incarceration piled up on the desks of federal and army officials. The estimated costs of con-structing and maintaining the prison camps—approximately $80 million for the first year alone—was staggering during a war. WRA administrators envisioned using Japanese American labor to create self-sufficient camps, which would reduce the cost of incarceration. Japanese Americans could also generate revenue that would then be passed on to the federal government by deducting some charges for subsistence from wages or selling agricultural products grown by Japanese American prisoners to the military. Finally, the military's drafting of Americans for service and industry's needs for work-ers to fill higher-paying jobs in manufacturing resulted in severe labor short-ages in agriculture, the production of ancillary wartime matériel (camouflage netting and cotton), and the completion of massive public works projects. These economic conditions created ready opportunities for both the federal government and private employers to consider the use of Japanese Ameri-can laborers to meet orders for wartime goods and food supplies.

The decision to use Japanese American labor was not an aftereffect of in-carceration but was at the very core of the system's goals from the start. Historians have long since dismissed the argument of military necessity for the forced removal and wrongful imprisonment of Japanese Americans, but administrators' decisions to implement incarceration reveal that they defined military necessity in a variety of ways, including the need for a steady supply of affordable labor to maintain productivity while America was at war.[2] The WRA's and WCCA's leaders' selection of Tulelake to host a prison camp because of its rural setting is only one part of the larger narrative of establishing and implementing incarceration. These agencies valued economic benefits as well as geographical location and prioritized exploiting Japanese Americans' labor. Their decisions set the stage for the government and the public to approach incarcerated Japanese Americans as convict laborers with curtailed civil and labor rights.

Locating the Detention Centers

Leaders of the Western Defense Command (the army command responsible for the defense of the western United States, primarily the Pacific Coast) initially supported "voluntary evacuation" of Japanese Americans from their homes to areas outside the military areas, hoping that the army could shift the responsibilities of removal onto Japanese Americans themselves. Lieutenant General DeWitt (commanding general of the Western Defense Command of the Fourth Army) envisioned that Japanese Americans would be able to relocate to the homes of friends and family members in the inland areas of California or farther east, failing to consider how connected Japanese Americans were to their communities and livelihoods on the West Coast. While some Japanese Americans were able to move to agricultural centers in the San Joaquin Valley of California and to privately owned Japanese American farms in Utah and beyond, DeWitt soon realized that voluntary relocation would be unsuccessful because Japanese Americans faced challenges in transferring property and finding residences among the unwelcoming attitudes of many communities farther east.[3]

A little less than a month after FDR signed Executive Order 9066, DeWitt issued General Order 35 on March 11, which established the Wartime Civil Control Administration (WCCA) to supervise and plan the army's forced removal of Japanese Americans from their homes to temporary detention centers. But the WCCA's responsibilities included more than the mass movement of people. Under DeWitt's order, the agency existed to "provide for the persons of Japanese ancestry from Military Area No. 1 and the California portion of Military Area No. 2 of the Pacific Coast with a minimum of social and economic dislocation, a minimum use of military personnel and maximum speed; and initially to employ appropriate means to encourage voluntary migration."[4] Efficiency in removal was the primary goal of the WCCA. On March 27, 1942, the period of voluntary resettlement officially came to an end, prompting the WCCA to begin its work. DeWitt placed Karl Bendetsen, a thirty-four-year-old recently minted colonel, in charge of the WCCA and the logistical planning of removal. However, Bendetsen and De-Witt were soon faced with another set of questions: where to hold the Japanese Americans for processing and how to care for over one hundred thousand people. The WRA would eventually take over the long-term planning and operations of incarceration and prison camps. In the meantime, the WCCA would be in charge of immediate detainment and all that this entailed. De-Witt soon realized that unless another agency stepped up to relieve pressure on the army for organizing detainment, the military would be saddled with an enormous task that went beyond its basic duties of establishing military areas and removing Japanese Americans. Where the army would place the Japanese Americans and what was to be done with them while they awaited the construction of the prison camps remained unaddressed by late February and early March 1942. Fortunately for DeWitt, a network of New Deal administrators was eager to help.[5]

Rex Nicholson, then assistant director for the western region of the Work Projects Administration (WPA), would prove to be of greatest assistance to the general. FDR established the WPA in 1935 (then the Works Progress Administration, before it was renamed in 1939) and tasked its administrators and supervisor, Harry Hopkins, with employing thousands of out-of-work Americans—skilled and unskilled alike—in public projects ranging from the construction of roads and dams to artistic projects for playwrights, painters, musicians, and other creative laborers. The WPA was not without its detractors, who claimed the agency was a waste of federal resources and run by inept opportunists, but its popularity varied by region depending on its impact on local economies. In the West, the WPA primarily oversaw public works projects that brought electricity, irrigation, and transportation routes to areas in need of development. Supported by the budget and administrative oversight of the Bureau of Land Reclamation, large-scale projects in California, Oregon, and Washington were antidotes for both high unemployment and economic underdevelopment. Nicholson made a name for himself in FDR's administration for his dedication and attention to detail in the management of WPA funds in the West, as well as his commitment to using work to instill pride in Americans who struggled during the Depression.[6]

On March 12, Bendetsen appointed Nicholson as chief of the Induction and Reception Division of the WCCA. Nicholson's new title made him largely responsible for overseeing the WPA's construction and maintenance of

temporary detention centers and work camps for Japanese Americans. The
WPA's involvement with stimulating wartime production appealed to DeWitt,
as did the agency's focus on labor as a promotion of both the war effort and
order and efficiency within the Japanese American incarceration system.
DeWitt suggested that the WPA would be the best agency to oversee the
centers, as "Japanese evacuees could be used to the fullest extent practica-
ble on jobs which they are capable of performing."[7] The army would remove
the Japanese; the WPA would construct the detainment centers and the
prison camps; and Nicholson would work with the WCCA to see that day-
to-day operations within the detention centers ran smoothly by utilizing Japanese American labor.

Before planning work projects for detained Japanese Americans, DeWitt
charged Nicholson and the WPA with deciding the "location, planning, constructing, and equipping of the Reception Centers."[8] Clayton E. Triggs, a
WPA administrator who became the project director of the Manzanar prison
camp, worked with Nicholson to identify detainment sites that were close to
the military zones. Proximity reduced the cost of transportation while miti-
gating the logistical nightmares inherent in removing such a large group of
Americans. Triggs and Nicholson initially suggested that areas with preex-
isting Civilian Conservation Corps (CCC) camps would be ideal locations
for the detention centers. Nicholson argued that shelters for the CCC's "tree
army" of young men were relatively easy to reequip for detaining Japanese
Americans, but Bendetsen and the WPA noted that they were not in good
working condition and lacked basic amenities (sewage and easy access to
water).

In response, Bendetsen dispatched two teams of army engineers to search
for sites that had the capacity to hold up to ten thousand people and could
be readily obtained with little disruption to local communities. Bendetsen
advised the teams to look for areas with "adaptable pre-existing facilities suitable for the establishment of shelter, power, light, and water within immediate availability, good connecting road and rail net, a short distance from
residences," and room for "some areas within the enclosure for recreation and
allied activities as the necessary confinement would otherwise . . . be completely demoralizing."[9] Bendetsen and WCCA administrators eventually approved public areas including the fairgrounds at Puyallup, Washington; the
Pacific International Livestock and Exposition Center in Portland, Oregon;
and the Santa Anita Park racetrack outside Los Angeles to host fifteen temporary detention centers and two permanent prison camps—Manzanar in

California and Poston in Arizona—despite the concerns of Puyallup and Santa Anita residents that the centers would interfere with the approaching racing and fair season.[10]

Constructing the detention centers before the arrival of thousands of Japanese Americans proved more challenging. Nicholson's and DeWitt's faith in the WPA's ability to complete its tasks in a timely fashion was short-lived. The WPA succeeded in recruiting hundreds of local, white, unionized workers to construct housing and basic structures for the detention centers by the April 21, 1942, deadline; however, the WPA still lacked adequate manpower and construction materials for the job. The task was too large to accomplish in such a short period of time. Disagreements about pay scales for both construction workers and federal employees as well as confusion relating to administrative responsibilities at each detention center slowed the process. General miscommunication between members of the WCCA and the WPA only made matters worse.

When forced removal began in May, Japanese Americans arrived at half-completed centers with insufficient housing and questionable living conditions. Nicholson tried to use press releases and reports from the Red Cross to assure other agencies and the public that the centers were comfortable places of temporary rest for the detainees, but Japanese Americans disagreed. Ted Nakashima's essay "Concentration Camp: US Style," published in the *New Republic* in June 1942, revealed the "mealtime queues [that] extend[ed] for blocks," with detainees standing in filth and mud while waiting for starchy meals devoid of nutrition at the Camp Harmony center near Seattle.[11] Nakashima described the crude bathroom facilities—wooden planks with six back-to-back cutouts placed over holes in the ground—that awaited Japanese Americans, who often suffered from severe gastrointestinal diseases that ravaged the centers. Visitors to Camp Harmony confirmed that detainees often went weeks without showers and suffered from a shortage of medicine and other medical supplies.

Bendetsen countered Nakashima's claims in a letter to the *New Republic* editor Bruce Bliven identifying a number of false statements. Bendetsen argued that the lack of fresh vegetables was simply "not true," quipping that "a good many American boys . . . quit their jobs to die on Bataan that Nakashima might be able to return to his 'little bathroom with the light coral walls, the open towel shelving and the pretty shower curtain' his family put up before they were evacuated." He challenged the *New Republic* editors to come and visit the centers for themselves. Bendetsen also laid guilt on Bliven for not

verifying Nakashima's claims and possibly jeopardizing the American prisoners of war in Japan if the Japanese found out about the camp conditions, a
common accusation Bendetsen levied against detractors and the media.[12]

Despite poor living conditions, Nicholson, Bendetsen, and others in the
WCCA did not view missing the deadline for completion of the camps as a
reason to petition for an extension to removal, and it was doubtful if this was
even a possibility considering the timeline set by DeWitt. Since postponing
their arrival was not an option, the WCCA turned to the detainees to complete center structures, encouraging Japanese Americans to make their
surroundings more welcoming by creating the appearance and feel of a
community.[13] In a memo to Bendetsen, Lieutenant Colonel Claude B. Washburne of the Fiscal Inspection Branch of the WCCA noted his dissatisfaction
with the state of the detention centers as well as his solutions to the problem.
"With evacuation only half completed," he began, "the problem of finding
something for the evacuees to do is already looming as a problem as indicated in field inspectors' reports and news items."[14]

Inspections confirmed the "inadequate installations" as well as the need
for the army engineers to "make extensive corrections and improvements."[15]
Living quarters were not partitioned before the arrival of the Japanese Americans, and multiple families were housed together in larger spaces at Santa
Anita, the Tanforan center near San Bruno, California, and others. There was
also no relief in sight to the shortages of materials needed to complete other
facilities at the detention centers. Washburne suggested that the utilities officers of the WCCA and Army Corps of Engineers turn to "utilizing evacuee
labor at the center as soon as possible" to complete construction and "occupy
the hands and minds of many evacuees who are becoming restless in center
areas with no place to go and nothing to do." Additionally, employing Japanese Americans would "promote the benefits of labor while working on a job
for the betterment of their own personal welfare and that of their friends and
relatives."[16] The WCCA issued a press release on March 30, 1942, explaining
that "the most important task after evacuees have been removed from military areas is to make it possible for them to perform work that contributes to
the maximum to the war production effort" utilizing their "wide range of useful skills and abilities," a task which required "a great deal of careful policy
making and planning."[17] Available white workers continued to build the
prison camps and detention centers while Japanese Americans arrived, but
the WCCA also tapped Japanese Americans to assist with construction.
Washburne's main concern was the need to complete the centers and occupy

the Japanese Americans with labor, which was a reward in and of itself; he paid no mind to the issue of compensation or wages.[18]

Beyond the logistical arguments for exploiting Japanese Americans, government officials were also aware of the tenuous social and political positions of Japanese Americans during and prior to the war. According to WRA policy, those Japanese Americans who were in the detention centers were "loyal." The army and Department of Justice technically placed any Japanese American suspected of subversion in an internment center for "enemy aliens." Among the "Guiding Principles" of the WRA was the belief that "it is possible to distinguish between the loyal and disloyal people of Japanese ancestry."[19] The WRA emphasized that Japanese Americans within the detention centers overseen by the WCCA "should not be confused with the program under which enemy aliens suspected of acts or intentions against the national security are interned."[20] Detention and incarceration were "concerned with a group composed mainly of American citizens and loyal individuals who have been removed from their homes . . . for their own bodily protection."[21] The WCCA and the WRA walked a fine line between upholding the loyalty of the incarcerated Japanese Americans to justify the cost of the program (the public would not readily support their tax dollars going toward providing food and shelter for disloyal Japanese Americans) and ensuring that Japanese Americans would prove their loyalty through contributions to the war effort.

Japanese Americans' citizenship was tied to their loyalty and vice versa, both of which were tenuous and scrutinized during the war. WCCA officials proclaimed that loyal Japanese Americans would accept their extraordinary conditions and perform work of any capacity to the best of their abilities. In 1942, Bendetsen explained in a memo to DeWitt that Japanese Americans should be recruited for labor on and off the detention sites, with WCCA and WRA officials "getting the evacuees to realize that this is a great opportunity for the evacuees to demonstrate their loyalty to the United States."[22] Similarly, a basic part of the oath sworn by Japanese Americans who signed up to be members of the Work Corps (a program which enlisted detainees for any job that might need filling as long as they were at least sixteen years old and willing to initially accept cash advances to use for goods at center canteens instead of wages) at the detention centers and prison camps was to "swear loyalty [to the United States] and perform faithfully all tasks assigned by the Corps authority."[23] Loyalty and work were intertwined for detained Japanese Americans, and this basic tenet at the heart of removal and incarceration made the "voluntary" nature of work more closely resemble coercion.

Imprisoned, with many of their rights suspended, Japanese Americans had few other options than to labor for the war effort, demonstrate self-sufficiency, and, in turn, prove their loyalty.

Labor as a Criteria for Prison Camp Sites

While the hasty construction of detention centers was underway, the WCCA, DeWitt, and the WRA turned their attention toward obtaining land for the construction of the more permanent "relocation centers" or prison camps. If the job of the WRA (with the initial construction financially backed by the War Department) was to "reestablish the evacuated people as a productive segment of the American population," then an "initial step" was the selection of the ten sites for the prison camps.[24]

In March 1942, WRA administrators met for a conference at the agency's regional headquarters in San Francisco, where they discussed basic principles of the WRA that placed a high priority on labor. WRA director Milton Eisenhower and his colleagues immediately recognized that "employment, or utilization of manpower, was a major part of the new agency's program." Eisenhower revealed to the others in attendance, which included state governors from the West and Bendetsen, his "Five-Point Plan" for incarceration. All points were grounded in using Japanese Americans for different projects including "services necessary for the operation and maintenance of the relocation communities"; "production of agricultural commodities needed for subsistence of the relocation centers" as well as for sale to or through the Office of Lend-Lease; "manufacture of various needed products or projects for the nation," including the army; and "useful public works." The plan also approved "private employment outside of the relocation projects." Eisenhower envisioned a "quasi-military" program like the Work Corps (modeled on the CCC) which would enlist Japanese Americans for work while also "binding" the incarcerees to WRA policy. The WRA would also run certain projects—such as camouflage netting—as "cooperative enterprises" that allowed for any profits made to be returned to Japanese Americans (though this would later become more complicated). FDR wrote the Work Corps into Executive Order 9102 when establishing the WRA, and Eisenhower later refined it during the March meeting. The WRA would eventually amend the Work Corps program multiple times before settling on a more standard application process for employment within and outside the camps.

Labor was a crucial component of the purpose of the WRA from its inception, which shaped decisions on locations for prison camps and detention centers.[25]

WRA administrators and the Army Corps of Engineers placed the potential for labor projects for Japanese Americans at the top of their list of specific requirements for a site to be considered for hosting a camp. A September 1942 report issued by the WRA described the selection process for the centers. "Since about 45 percent of the evacuees were engaged in agriculture before the war, the Authority naturally looked first of all for areas with good farming possibilities," paying special attention to soil, water supply, climate, and growing season.[26] Likewise, access to roads and other forms of transportation as well as electricity were important factors. Relatively remote locations that would not require displacement of current residents but could accommodate at least five thousand Japanese Americans were also favored. In order to satisfy these "rigid and sometimes conflicting requirements," the army and WRA turned to "wilderness" areas in the West just outside of the military areas—Wyoming, California, and Arizona, to name a few. First and foremost was the focus on "work opportunities for evacuees."[27]

In addition to agricultural labor that would promote self-sufficiency and tap into the Japanese Americans' skills in farming, WRA administrators also identified land improvements as suitable work projects for prisoners. WCCA officials agreed with the WRA. Peter R. Cooper, a supervisor at the Tanforan center, observed that "there are vast Federal Works Projects planned and awaiting only the labor to do them" and told DeWitt that "if the Army, WRA, Reclamation Service, and Federal Works Agency officials would get together they could work out a satisfactory solution to the question, 'What are we going to do with the Japanese?'"[28] The committees dispatched for choosing the sites "combed the country from the border of Military Area 1 to the Mississippi River" in order to "select the home communities for a large number of evacuees," making sure that they kept the number one requirement in mind: "The area must provide work opportunities throughout most of the year [in order] for the population to be relocated there."[29] "Public works" projects including "the development of land for irrigation, conservation of soil resources, food control operations, and range improvement" were desirable jobs for Japanese Americans as well as favorable factors in choosing sites.[30]

In a press release from April 13, 1942, Milton Eisenhower placed improvements of public land high on his list of qualifications for camp sites. "All reception centers must be located on public land so that improvements at public

expense become public, not private assets."[31] It was not a question of *if* Japanese American labor would be used on work projects to improve land, but
rather where, how, and to what extent. By early March 1942, Jennings B. Barge
(real estate representative from the Army Corps of Engineers) with E. J. Utz
and E. B. Whitaker (both from the WRA) conducted investigations of various sites (approximately three hundred) and compiled reports with the assistance of State Land Use Planning Committees (a branch of the WRA that
worked with state governments in identifying potential sites). They then for-
warded these reports back to Milton Eisenhower and Lieutenant Colonel
Crume of the Army Corps of Engineers, who passed them along to DeWitt
for final approval.

WCCA and WRA administrators tapped into existing WPA projects that
could be furthered with Japanese American labor during the war. From digging irrigation ditches, completing roads and dams, and felling trees, such
large-scale projects served as job opportunities for Americans during the Depression, and those who labored on them helped rural, underdeveloped areas grow and prosper. Electricity and access to water were required for land
cultivation as well as improvements for expanding urban areas, especially in
the West, the South, and the Southwest. Projects that were planned for Native American reservations since the early 1930s were also long overdue for
completion. Private industries, farmers, and landowners also became increasingly dependent on public works projects and the federal government's
support. Despite the United States waging a global, multi-theater war,
administrators in the WPA and Bureau of Land Reclamation argued that
completing and improving these internal improvements could not be put on
hold.[32] Fortunately for the bureau, the WRA and WCCA supported this idea,
as did other organizations. In Ketchikan, Alaska, the American Federation
of Labor–affiliated Central Labor Council, for example, passed a resolution
encouraging the government to consider using Japanese Americans to build
the Alaska highway connecting the contiguous United States to Alaska
through Canada for continued economic growth.[33]

The WRA and Army Corps of Engineers (who had previously helped
maintain some of the CCC camps during the Depression) worked together
with the Bureau of Land Reclamation in acquiring prison camp sites. Selecting areas in need of internal improvements was a logical decision from a variety of angles for the agencies involved. The Bureau of Land Reclamation
already oversaw the internal improvement sites that were on federal land and
could be easily obtained. These areas were also far from larger populations,

limiting the potential for widespread panic or hysteria among those who would be less than welcoming to Japanese Americans. Many of the land reclamation sites also hosted CCC camps with some existing access to needed resources like water pumps. While using Executive Order 9066 as a means to continue to "settle" the West and protect government investments, the emphasis in reports and memos on the desire to have enough works projects to keep Japanese Americans busy indicates that all agencies recognized that exploitation of imprisoned labor was crucial for this process.[34]

Some possible sites, such as the proposed Cambridge relocation center in the Republican River valley in Nebraska, failed to live up to potential after consideration despite ample job opportunities for imprisoned Japanese Americans. The Fort Riley army installation base (used for infantry training since the Civil War) in Nebraska was a possibility, as acquiring the land would be easy. The initial report from the camp selection committee also listed some of the positive qualities of the area, including twelve thousand acres of readily available land, seven thousand of which could "feasibly be irrigated" by Japanese Americans. Considerable need for additional labor on the farms throughout the Republican River valley also offered the promise of jobs for Japanese Americans. Between the possibility for land improvement through irrigation and the need for agricultural labor on private farms in the region, Cambridge was a prime choice. Eisenhower, however, wrote to Bendetsen in June 1942 advising him to think carefully about approving the site as "the demand for farm labor was scattered throughout a larger area" (making it difficult to supervise the Japanese American laborers), and opportunities for manufacturing employment were limited. Even the prospect of putting Japanese Americans to work on irrigation systems would be challenging as "the balance of the area is subject to flooding or too irregular to be irrigated." Eisenhower was concerned about wasting labor on an irrigation system that might prove useless in the long run, and a resulting dearth of work for Japanese Americans, making Cambridge inefficient, unproductive, and costly.[35] Other areas the WRA considered for prison camps were Harper County, Oklahoma; Wallace County, Kansas; and Reeves County, Texas; but administrators eventually deemed them inefficient for lack of large-scale work projects.

Other proposed sites offered more in terms of manageable agricultural and infrastructure projects and the chance for permanent land improvement. For example, the prison camp selection committee ranked Tulelake highly for its agricultural prospects as well as the necessity of land improvements.

The US Bureau of the Interior already managed the Tule Lake division of the larger Klamath Irrigation Project, designed to make the inland region of northern California—a dried-up lake bed—easier to farm and settle. Despite being owned by the Bureau of the Interior, much of the land was leased to small farmers who primarily grew barley, which created a stable living but was not in high demand during the war. Acquiring the land would be challenging considering the leasing system, but "because of a potential labor shortage, it [was] believed that most of the lease-holders would be willing to relinquish their leases for modest considerations, probably little more than the value of the improvements which they had installed."[36]

The only catch was that the bureau depended on the revenue from the leases to continue the Klamath Irrigation Project, meaning that "if these lands were appropriated by the Government for colonization by the Japanese, it would probably be necessary to reimburse the Bureau."[37] But this was a small price to pay for cheap access to a prison camp site. The WRA proposed to complement the existing 2,500 acres of irrigated and cultivated land with the use of Japanese American labor to "level the additional acreage and construct necessary irrigation and drainage facilities with the object of having 6,700 acres in production by 1943."[38] In addition to continued, non-WPA work on the irrigation project, Tulelake was "well-suited for intensive farming by Japanese labor," and "by encouraging the cultivation of crops with high labor-requirements, many of these people can be gainfully employed here."[39] Rather than the efficiently grown barley, which required fewer farmers to plant, harvest, and process, the WRA would employ Japanese Americans to work the black loam soil and produce potatoes, berries, alfalfa, peas, carrots, and other "hardy variety of vegetables" for cash advances to purchase items at prison camp stores.[40]

Similarly, E. R. Fryer, the western regional director of the WRA, praised a proposed site in Jerome County, Idaho, for its ability to accommodate ten thousand Japanese Americans, "who will help to bring this Idaho desert area into full production for the 'Food for Freedom' effort."[41] In his further recommendation of Minidoka in Idaho, Fryer alluded to the WRA's "policy of using the relocation camps to bring new territories into use and develop natural wealth . . . in this area," as well as its "hope to be able to develop some industrial activity" despite it being a primarily agricultural community.[42]

The camp selection committee also heralded the proposed sites for the Jerome and Rohwer prison camps in Arkansas based on the availability of labor opportunities. Located in the Mississippi Delta region of the state and with an economy largely based on timber and cotton, Jerome and Rohwer—separated by approximately thirty miles—were on land owned or leased by the Farm Security Administration (FSA) to farming cooperatives or individual farmers. The FSA originally established its cooperatives during the Depression in an attempt to assist landowners, as well as the sharecroppers who worked for them, in increasing crop revenue and stability. The idea was to encourage group farming as a way to provide a means of landownership, which was otherwise unobtainable, as well as to promote conservation and modernized farming practices. However, by the spring of 1942 agricultural output faced larger challenges including stalled infrastructure programs and a severe labor shortage.[43] Agricultural opportunities, work projects, and relatively easy access to land already controlled by a government agency (save for two larger cooperatives, Kelso Farms and Alluvial Farms, which leased land from the FSA but which the WRA was sure it could offer reasonable compensation for) made Arkansas a prime location for prison camps.

The selection committee reported to Eisenhower and DeWitt that "the proposed area is in the heart of a large amount of undeveloped land," and "as fast as land is cleared and drained, it will be used for subsistence farming and for crops which are in greatest demand for the war effort."[44] Anticipated demand from private farm owners for assistance in harvesting cotton in the late summer and early fall also appealed to the planners. Additionally, Rohwer and Jerome were not without potential for public works projects, as the "amount of labor that could profitably be used on public work in Southeast Arkansas [was] already tremendous."[45]

The Delta was in drastic need of new drainage canals for irrigation and flood control (caused by a large amount of yearly rainfall) as well as forest clearing, which would be vital to the continued economic development of the region. In promoting Arkansas as an ideal host for prison camps, the committee played up the solution of the drainage problem as one of "great interest to the Reconstruction Finance Corporation and other investors and drainage district bonds" as well as locals who could recover revenue from land that was devalued by malfunctioning drainage systems. Local farmers in the Delta would also benefit from the program as they could not individually afford to fix drainage systems. Using Japanese American prisoners to improve drainage would not only diversify crops to include alfalfa, wheat, and fruits and vegetables in addition to cotton, but "the land, if placed in a state of cultivation, would be highly desirable for use in resettling families released from war industries during post-war adjustment."[46] At the time, white and black sharecropping and tenant-farming families who benefited from FSA programs occupied the land, but the WRA was relieved that only "minimal" dislocation would occur if it was acquired for the construction of two prison camps.

The proposed Colorado River prison camp (or Poston, as it was commonly referred to) in Yuma County, Arizona, was an especially complex yet profitable site. The land the WRA identified for the camp was located on a portion of the Colorado River Indian Reservation that was overseen by the Office of Indian Affairs, the WRA, and the Department of the Interior. At the time, no Native Americans lived on that sector of the reservation. A lack of facilities (particularly a school and medical pavilion) and stalled construction of an irrigation system left the land uninhabitable. According to the WRA, these circumstances made it an excellent choice for hosting imprisoned Japanese Americans. Prisoners could complete an irrigation system that would link water from the Head Gate Rock Dam (six miles away) to the reservation—allowing crop cultivation for self-sufficiency—as well as construct adobe brick schools. The WRA estimated Poston could accommodate twenty thousand Japanese Americans who could cultivate forty-one thousand acres of land and "develop a green, irrigated valley for their own use during wartime and for post-war use by the Indian tribes."[47]

Once the WRA and the Army Corps of Engineers identified appropriate sites for the prison camps, convincing state governors that hosting Japanese Americans would be in their best economic interests was the next step in the process. Technically, even if some of the land was owned or leased privately or a governor protested (as some did), the army could still overrule any objections. Building relationships and trust with state governors simply made the job easier for the government as well as the army, which would be required to send troops to serve as guards for imprisoned Japanese Americans.

Some officials, such as Republican governor Ralph Carr of Colorado, were, in fact, cooperative. Carr agreed to assist his government in any way possible and spotted an opportunity to contract labor in the beet fields that made many Colorado farms profitable after they sold their produce to the military for sugar production.[48] Some, like Utah governor Herbert Maw, were cautiously accepting, seeing economic promise in an agreement to host a prison camp, but Maw was also concerned about how his constituents would view the "enemy" living within their state's borders. Suspicions over how much responsibility would be placed on Utah to financially and logistically provide for the maintenance of the prison camps also concerned the governor. Maw was particularly vocal in his stipulations for hosting Japanese Americans. In April 1942, he sent Bendetsen a detailed list of conditions for full cooperation with the WCCA and WRA, including "that the Federal Government should either assume full responsibility for handling the Jap problem or give full authority to the states, with the funds to do the job," "evacuees should not only be self-supporting but should contribute to defense productions," and "evacuees are to be used immediately for agricultural work, if production is not to suffer."[49]

Others were not as cooperative. Despite the WRA's insistence on Arkansas as a site for the prison camps as well as the selection committee's assurances that the inhabitants of the state were supportive, the prickly response from Governor Homer Adkins revealed a different reality. The committee initially reported that "the local people will cooperate in every way with the War Department and the WRA"; in fact, they "were anxious to cooperate in any Government program connected with National Defense" as well as with any projects that would help with the economic development of their state—so long as Japanese Americans would not be permitted to remain in their state permanently, as "they would think it unwise to inject a third race into the negro and white racial problem existing now."[50] These statements were all based on a slim volume of data collected by the committee and displayed in an appendix accompanying its report.

One person they did not contact was Governor Adkins, who protested against the presence of any "Japs" in Arkansas. Adkins frequently wrote to DeWitt and urged him to reconsider using the Delta to resettle "enemies of my country in my state—for no matter how long or for what reason."[51] Adkins was wary of hosting Japanese Americans for fears of subversion, but also because he worried they might become wards of the people of Arkansas, a prospect which his economically struggling state could not afford and did not want.[52]

Adkins proved difficult to cajole, and eventually DeWitt resorted to issuing demands. Writing to Adkins in June 1942, "I desire to inform you," the general began, "that under the provisions of Executive Order 9066, it has been found necessary to establish a relocation center for 10,000 Japanese evacuees . . . in your state."[53] DeWitt promised Adkins that "the project will be completely under federal supervision and control" and that "the housing will be constructed by the War Department and military police guard under control of the War Department will be provided," so as not to place a financial burden on the state of Arkansas. Bendetsen also assured Adkins that Japanese

Figure 3. Construction begins at the Manzanar prison camp. Photo by Albert Clem, April 2, 1942. Courtesy of the Bancroft Library.

American labor would be used (at no cost to Arkansas) to complete work projects of economic benefit to his state. Adkins later declared, during a meeting in Oregon in 1942, that "we've got 20,000 of your Pacific Coast Japs in my state and they ain't going to stay there after the war, I'll tell you that right now." But ultimately he had little choice but to open his state to prison camps. Offering military guards as well as opportunities for extracting economic benefits from Japanese Americans were methods of persuading governors to cooperate with removal and imprisonment. Incarceration frequently became an extension of New Deal politics and work projects.

The Central Role of Labor

Early on, WCCA and WRA administrators turned to Japanese American labor as a means of controlling the operating costs of the temporary detention centers and permanent camps. Any large-scale federal project does not come cheap, and the incarceration of Japanese Americans was no exception once planning was underway. The multilayered administration of the program required an increase in the flow of money to the agencies assisting with removal and detention. The FSA required an increase in staff to organize and oversee the transfer of Japanese American–owned and leased land to custodians who volunteered to manage the property and crops while the owners were imprisoned. On March 14, 1942 (the day Roosevelt issued Executive Order 9102 establishing the WRA), DeWitt wrote to the chief of staff of the War Department explaining that in order for the army to "orderly accomplish the mission assigned [to it]," it was imperative "that someone at the federal level make available more funds for the FSA to make loans available to those willing to work the land left behind by Japanese Americans" in order to avoid the loss of crops planted by Japanese Americans prior to their removal.[54] Likewise, the Department of Alien Property Custodians required significant increases in the number of employees required to perform such a large operation. The creation and staffing of the WRA also required funds as a multiunit agency charged with the often unwieldy task of ensuring efficiency in the creation and administration of the program. From the army to the civilian agencies, bureaucracy at the federal level expanded and required extra resources for implementation and maintenance of a complex new federal incarceration and resettlement program—a tall order during wartime.

At the forefront of all officials' minds were the overall costs of incarceration more generally: the construction, maintenance, and administration of this bureaucratic behemoth. In March 1942, the Army Corps of Engineers estimated that initial construction of the prison camps would cost approximately $33,148,560—and this was simply for construction. This amount did not encompass costs for the administration, maintenance, food, and wages and salaries paid to the personnel from various agencies who would have skilled jobs at the detention centers and, later, the prison camps.[55] In July 1942, Rex Nicholson revealed to Lieutenant Colonel I. K. Evans that an additional $1,707,560 would be required for operating the detention centers just in August and September (removal and detainment in the spring and early summer of 1942 cost roughly the same, including travel, shelter, utilities, and the payment of personnel).[56] The confirmed and estimated costs for the continued operation of incarceration as an overall program were staggering and, when combined with the already accrued costs associated with removal, transportation, and detention as well as other administrative duties, created financial anxiety among government officials who were placed in charge of the program. By November 1942 alone, incarceration had cost the government $88,679,716.[57]

When Evans expressed concern over the mounting costs of incarceration, Nicholson ensured him that "we plan to use Japanese labor in the assembly and reception centers to staff the kitchens, warehouses, clerical requirements, fire department, hospitals, education and recreation and to do any and all work in connection with the maintenance and operation of the camp," and promised that "Japanese labor will be used to the fullest extent . . . in the centers in the future."[58] In a special report distributed to governors and state legislators (or "sponsors") who might be interested in hosting a prison camp, WRA secretary-manager F. O. Hagie described the creation of the Work Corps, a program designed to "mobilize the energies, skills, and abilities of employable evacuees to undertake programs of constructive work on Relocation Centers" and to "assign individuals to work for which they are most fitted by training experience . . . and provide additional training to adapt old skills to new jobs and to develop new techniques."[59] The first job for enlistees would be the construction of schools so that children could continue their education, and the completion of any housing or infrastructure projects on the grounds of the camp, valuing self-sustaining agricultural production thereafter.

The Work Corps was a voluntary endeavor in which any incarceree over the age of sixteen could enlist to work in either skilled (teachers, tailors, draftsmen, stenographers, and doctors) and unskilled positions (drivers, woodcutters, janitors, seamstresses, and general "laborers," to name a few) required for maintaining and operating the centers. Later, enlistment in the Work Corps would also include positions in manufacturing jobs and agricultural labor inside and outside the camps. The members of the corps agreed to continue to perform duties in any capacity for the duration of the war plus two weeks following its end.[60] Enlistees would receive compensation for their work, initially identified as cash advances instead of wages to not raise ire or suspicion from the American public that Japanese Americans were receiving payment for doing little work. The advances would be made available to the workers only after administrators deducted the costs of incarceration from any profits made through the sale of agricultural products or savings in maintaining the prison camps and detention centers and/or value added to the land. In the report, Hagie admitted that at that time, "the precise method of keeping costs, making monthly cash advances to enlistees, and computing benefits earned by enlistees had not yet been exactly determined," but "in no event will the maximum monthly cash advances exceed the basic minimum wage of the American soldier—$21 a month."[61] This figure of twenty-one dollars was an important point for WRA director Milton Eisenhower as he feared public outrage if Japanese Americans received more, despite his acknowledgement that, "actually, of course, each private soldier costs the Federal Government about $150 a month" with all resources considered including pay.[62]

Eisenhower's initial solution was to "charge all evacuees for board, room, medical services, and so on and then to pay a cash wage sufficiently high to liquidate this debt and to leave a small amount for incidentals." Based on prevailing wages and estimating the costs for each family or individual, Eisenhower estimated that wages would range from forty dollars a month to ninety-five dollars—an amount that he figured would lead to the "public crucify[ing] us." Eventually, Eisenhower and Bendetsen settled on not charging for basic necessities (this would change once Japanese Americans could be employed in private labor) and instead paying wages that ranged from twelve dollars to nineteen dollars (plus a $3.75 clothing allowance) per month for the most qualified, with coupon books for incidentals.[63]

Testimony from a variety of West Coast residents, politicians, business owners, and public agency representatives during the Tolan Committee hearings in February and March 1942 reflected similar ideas on using Japanese American labor to offset the cost of their imprisonment. The House Select Committee Investigating National Defense was established in 1940, headed by John Tolan, a New Deal Democrat from Oakland, California. Initially, the committee was created to investigate the movement of Dust Bowl refugees to the West, as reflected in its original title: the Select Committee to Investigate the Interstate Migration of Destitute Citizens. Following America's entrance into the war in 1941, Congress renamed the committee to reflect its role in analyzing the movement of Americans for defense work. The Tolan Committee turned its attention toward the growing discussions of the removal of enemy aliens and American citizens of German, Italian, and Japanese descent by February 1942, and traveled to San Francisco, Portland, Seattle, and Los Angeles following Executive Order 9066 to hear testimony on the decision for removal. The official report of the committee was not released until May 1942 and had no direct bearing on the organization and structure of removal and incarceration, but many who testified before the committee influenced the process.

Many of the suggestions reflected those of the WRA and WCCA at the time, especially toward the use of Japanese Americans as a source of labor.

In San Francisco, J. Murray Thompson, chief of the Economic Section of the Western Division of the New Deal Agricultural Adjustment Administration (AAA), testified that the Department of Agriculture supported "permitting these people to hire out as agricultural wage earners . . . and earning the going wage," but also argued that "it could be possible to use a part of that wage for their keep and care, thereby decreasing the expense to the Government."[64] Samuel Goldblatt, secretary-treasurer of the California State Industrial Union Council (an affiliate of the Congress of Industrial Organizations), also testified in San Francisco before the committee and stressed the importance of ensuring that "no concentration camps or forced labor should be imposed" on Japanese Americans during removal (which he ultimately supported). But the army and federal government should ensure that "Japanese can perform useful work for the Nation" and that they are "given the fullest opportunity to demonstrate their loyalty to this nation in the performance of useful work."[65]

Goldblatt's testimony, as well as that of a key member of the AAA, revealed the complicated nature of using Japanese Americans' labor during their removal and detainment. No official or architect of incarceration desired to be seen as forcing Japanese Americans to work during a time when US war propaganda repeatedly emphasized the barbarities of German and Japanese forced labor operations. Emphasizing that Japanese Americans should prove their loyalty through work was itself exploitation, ultimately designed to reduce operating costs and economically assist the government. Goldblatt himself was a proponent of "accord[ing] Japanese Americans full civil liberties, the right of movement outside of restricted areas, and the right to work."[66] But Japanese Americans were imprisoned and would face restrictions on their right of movement and their rights to negotiate terms of a contract and to choose their occupations. Their choices were limited to the work the government identified as crucial to the war effort and to maintaining the detention centers and prison camps.

While officials internally discussed the importance of using Japanese American labor to reduce maintenance costs, the WRA stressed the importance of "self-sufficiency" to incarcerees in order to create a sense of order and make life in the prison camps seem as "normal" as possible. "Initially," the WRA explained, "the government will provide the minimum essentials of living—shelter, medical care, and mess and sanitary facilities," but the incarcerees were expected to "work together . . . for self-support."[67] But rather than a cost-cutting measure, the WRA proposed that self-sufficiency in the centers was a way to provide "each project a setting in which normal activities of life can go on as nearly as possible like those of an ordinary American community." This statement was promptly followed by a listing of all the ways in which Japanese Americans were prisoners (restrictions on movement, guarded by military police, assignment of duties) rather than "normal Americans."[68]

Later in 1942, WRA director Dillon Myer (who succeeded Eisenhower in the position) echoed these thoughts in a meeting with a group of journalists covering the WRA's policy. He stated that his agency's job was "to help [Japanese Americans] forget that there was an evacuation" through self-sufficiency, community building, and self-governance.[69] Leaders of the WRA recognized early on that removal and incarceration were difficult processes particularly that arose from "cutting off the normal business, social, and economic relationships of the evacuees."[70] If the WRA identified the economic and business problems as the most pressing, then emphasizing employment and "self-sufficiency" were the best solutions.

The promotion of self-sufficiency reinforced the general messages that the federal government delivered to the American people. As America's involvement in the war deepened and more goods were shipped overseas to American soldiers and their allies, food consumption became a point of concern for the government. Many of the canned and processed goods produced in factories were shipped internationally because of their shelf life. Limits on the use of rubber and steel (useful for war matériel) increased transportation costs and limited the availability of fresh produce. Food in a variety of forms became scarcer while the demand remained the same, prompting the Office of Price Administration to introduce food rationing on March 1, 1942. Rationing books ensured that products such as canned goods, beef, sugar, and cooking oil would be evenly distributed across American markets; when a household ran out of ration stamps for beef, they would receive no more until they obtained a new book. Fresh produce, however, was not placed on the rationing system, reviving the notion of the "victory garden," first introduced by Herbert Hoover and the US Food Administration during World War I.[71]

In addition to buying bonds, encouraging American families to plant their own victory gardens was a way to support the war effort. WRA administrators applied the use of rationing and victory gardens to Japanese Americans in the prison camps, encouraging agricultural and "environmental patriotism."[72] Administrators did not want to delay the process of self-sufficiency and stressed in March 1942 that "it is highly important that agricultural production be started on each relocation center as rapidly as possible."[73] In order to accomplish this, "all enlistees with agricultural experiences and all others with experience adaptable to agricultural work will be employed immediately in preparing land for cultivation, constructing irrigation canals, and planting, cultivating, harvesting, and processing of crops," in hopes that all "relocated communities would become self-sufficient in food production within the turn of a season."[74]

The WRA also informed Japanese Americans upon their arrival at the detention centers that food cultivation would help them to "embrace the pioneer spirit" of the prison camps. In addition to helping to feed those in the prison camps, Japanese Americans could also use their agricultural skills to conserve rations that could be shipped overseas and prove their loyalty to their country and the war effort. Newspapers as well as government officials often referred to the relocation centers as "colonies" or "pioneer camps," phrases that held heavy meaning, as most government euphemisms do. Japanese immigrants often referred to themselves as "colonists" after traveling east into the wild terrain of the American West, building up the land, and moving as far south as Florida to help the soil thrive.[75] Referring to the centers as colonies and the Japanese as pioneers, an idea reflected in a 1942 propaganda film *Japanese Relocation* by the WRA and featuring Milton Eisenhower, made the concept of forced removal and imprisonment more palatable for the public.

The pioneer message also called on Japanese Americans to participate in a fully American enterprise: settling the land and working as a community to help the wartime economy and transform the landscape of the nation. The US government would indeed use Japanese Americans as colonists to subjugate the land or continue an oppressive system of centuries-long subjugation in the case of Native American reservations in Colorado. Also, the allusion to the camps as colonies referenced a term that had been applied to Japanese immigrants since their first arrival to signal their "clannish" behavior and isolation. The effect was twofold in that these terms allowed the Japanese to remain "othered" while also functioning as useful tools of colonization and economic development.

The WRA ensured that all Japanese Americans—regardless of physical capabilities or age—would be put to work for the betterment of the community. In its first quarterly report, the WRA noted that "the task of planning work projects at the relocation centers was complicated to some extend by the peculiar age distribution of the American Japanese people."[76] Because the early wave of immigration from Japan to the United States consisted of mainly single men and married workers who later sent for their wives, there was a tendency for Japanese parents to have children "relatively late in life." Combined with the "virtual non-existence of Japanese immigration since 1924," the age distribution created a "marked sparseness of individuals in the supposedly most productive years of middle life." To address this issue, the WRA placed "special emphasis on jobs requiring limited skills and tasks on which the older evacuees could perform without undue physical hardships." Such activities would come to include sewing, light kitchen work, and housekeeping duties as well as secretarial work for those who were more skilled. Every Japanese American could contribute to efficiently operating the camp and their own imprisonment. Administrators looking to increase production and self-sufficiency rarely considered issues of safety and well-being in any depth during the planning stages of incarceration.

A Manufacturing Crisis in the Making

Japanese American participation in wartime manufacturing became a key component of incarceration and an assumed by-product of forcibly removing and imprisoning American citizens without due process. Employing incarcerated Japanese Americans as well as convicts in other penitentiaries was also an answer to a growing labor shortage in the United States as a result of the war. After Pearl Harbor, millions of men enlisted or were drafted into the armed forces. Many others who remained on the home front for medical or other purposes were pulled into lucrative employment in wartime manufacturing. Women followed suit and joined their remaining male compatriots in working on the front lines of war material production. Propaganda posters urging Americans to join the war effort through employment, and the relatively high pay, drew many employees away from undesirable and poorly compensated jobs in agriculture and less lucrative positions in the production of nylon and camouflage netting. Americans from all walks of life would eventually answer the call to serve in domestic employment, but estimated labor shortages weighed on government officials from the Bureau of Labor all the way up to FDR and his cabinet members.[77]

The United States was not prepared to meet the labor demands of war in early 1942. At a President's Council meeting on February 6, 1942, Attorney General Francis Biddle recorded in his notes that "[Secretary of Labor] Frances

Perkins thinks that we will have a serious labor shortage in the fall of 1942."
Perkins suggested that by "working more women into industry . . . taking the
self-employed into more direct industrial work [and] eliminating certain
physical requirements, using old people, etc., etc.," the problem might be mit-
igated but would remain "most acute."[78]

In early April 1942, FDR received a letter from the War Production Board
(WPB) that further emphasized the squeeze on production capabilities. Board
director Donald Nelson delivered the news that production goals for munitions and other wartime goods were not met. In December 1941, shortly after
Pearl Harbor, Nelson met with FDR and other federal and military advisors
to devise a war production plan. At the time, the president and his advisors
agreed that "it was within our economic potential to produce completed munitions, war facilities, and military construction to the value of $40 billion
in calendar year 1942 and $60 billion in 1943." Initially, the WPB had faith
that specific objectives set for the production of airplanes, tanks, anti-aircraft
and anti-tank guns, and merchant shipping necessities were accomplishable
within the established production programs and available plants and labor
supplies. But by the winter of 1942, and following an escalation of demands
for wartime goods, the feasibility of the WPB's goals was grim. The new requests from the army, navy, and Maritime Commission for $62 billion in war-
time goods in 1942 and another $110 billion in 1943 placed far too much
stress on Nelson and the WPB's capabilities. "I have examined the production possibilities," he explained, "and must report, that in my judgment, it
will not be possible to provide all of the items set forth in your list of objectives (including domestic and military products) and at the same time produce everything else now called for under the programs of the Army, the
Navy, the Maritime Commission, and Defense Aid." Nelson described an
"impasse" in his organization's ability to plan for production and feared
that he would "fall short of providing for a complete mobilization of our
resources."[79]

Propaganda, wage increases and protections, and other mobilization programs assisted in alleviating the labor shortage to a degree, but the federal
government also turned to tapping into prison labor as a solution with some
legal maneuvering. Depression-era regulations on the use of prison labor created a flurry of legislation that prohibited the sale of prison-made goods
across state lines. Francis Biddle's release of Circular 3591 in 1941 also prohibited (technically) private employers' use of leased convicts—a system that
had proliferated across the country following the end of the Civil War—in

order to limit competition in the public market with cheaply made goods.[80] Congress did, however, create loopholes that allowed the federal government to take advantage of the ready supply of exploitable prison labor. In 1934, FDR used his executive powers to establish the Federal Prison Industries, a corporation owned by the federal government that used prison labor to produce goods that were then sold back to the government and distributed nationwide. FDR and his administrators grappled with the shortage of labor in meeting production goals in early 1942 and turned to prisoners as a source of cheap and steady labor.

Questions on the legality of private industries that received government contracts employing the incarcerated created some confusion about the extent to which the federal government ventured into prison labor. In February 1942, FDR requested that D. W. Turner (a former governor of Iowa who then served as the consultant on materials under the War Production Board's Bureau of Governmental Requirement) to investigate the utility of prison labor in "supporting the productive power of our armed forces" as well as the Lend Lease program.[81] Turner enlisted WPB director Nelson to carry out the investigation, and in May 1942, Nelson reported that there "was available in [state prisons and other correctional institutions] the labor of approximately 100,000 inmates not fully employed as well as millions of dollars' worth of industrial equipment which is idle a great deal of time."[82] Nelson and Turner then directed their attention toward maneuvering around any legal restrictions under New Deal legislation and regulations on the use of prison labor for private military contracts. FDR tasked Nelson and Turner with forming an Institutional Supplies Committee under the WPB that would work with the Department of Labor and Department of Justice to ensure that legal procedures were followed while using prison labor—if such use was, indeed, legal.

Fortunately for FDR and the WPB, Nelson consulted with Biddle on the possibility of prison labor in wartime production, and the attorney general confirmed that there was "nothing in federal law which prevents the departments and agencies of the Federal Government from purchasing goods produced in federal and state prisons." Biddle suggested that the only possible existing restrictions on the use of prison labor in this capacity would be found under the Walsh-Healey Act (1936) that guaranteed fair wages and forty-hour work weeks to employees working on government contracts that exceeded $10,000. Although the Walsh-Healey Act forbade the employment of convicts in such contracts, FDR enlisted Secretary of Labor Frances Perkins to work with Congress in issuing an exception (ultimately granted in April 1942) for the use of convict labor with lower wages and longer hours.[83] By the summer of 1942, approximately 4,500 prisoners at state penitentiaries manufactured war material, and the WPB estimated that by the spring of 1943, prisoners were to produce wartime goods worth $18 million, not only assisting with the war effort but also demonstrating an "enthusiasm and patriotic spirit which equals the most patriotic group on the outside."[84]

However, even with the use of prison labor, shortages in manpower remained in the spring of 1942, a reality that also shaped the decisions and goals of incarceration. The WCCA suggested in a March 1942 memo that "a variety of work projects should be established [in the centers and camps] to absorb further employment of both men and women"; in particular, "the production of underclothes, fatigues, bags, and other sewing projects would not only meet the needs of the evacuees, but for other purposes as well . . . and could do great many kinds of work for the armed services." According to another official, the creation of more work projects would not only supply labor and materials for the armed forces but also limit the "number of able-bodied nonworkers" in the center.[85]

The army's control of the detention centers through the WCCA reflected the goal of using Japanese American labor for meeting production goals and maintaining order. Following suit, the WRA explained in a report from May 1942 that in addition to using Japanese American labor for running the prison camps, prisoners could also be used in the production of wartime manufacturing, either on-site or—potentially—through furloughs granted to those looking to work outside the designated military areas. Japanese Americans could be put to use in the "manufacturing of goods requiring a great deal of skilled hand labor, including . . . those needed in the national production program, including wood products, clothing, ceramics, netting, and woven and knitted materials."[86]

Working in wartime production would serve as a way for Japanese Americans to assist with the war effort and prove their loyalty at a moment when the government and fellow Americans questioned their commitment to the war cause. Japanese Americans "had many skills and abilities that [were] immediately needed in national production effort," and "as swiftly as possible, they must be given an opportunity to make use of those for the welfare of the nation and their new communities."[87] Using the specific skills of confined Japanese Americans for the war effort was exploitation at its most basic level. The WCCA and the WRA would invite private contractors into the assembly centers and later the prison camps to set up mobile "factories" for the production of a variety of wartime materials as early as May and June 1942.

To be sure, at no point during early discussions did administrators in the WRA and the WCCA equate Japanese American incarcerees with penitentiary laborers. What was evident was an almost automatic assumption that Japanese Americans, once detained, were available to be used to offset labor shortages in wartime production. Officials discussed the use of Japanese Americans as a labor safety valve in the same vein as prison labor: an exploitable resource that might be out of bounds in most cases for producing goods for private contractors and the government, but exceptions were to be made in times of war. Japanese Americans would be used *in conjunction* with prison laborers in penitentiaries to assist with the war effort. More importantly, as would occur later in the incarceration process and as already indicated by reports, assisting with wartime production would be a way for inmates at penitentiaries and the incarcerated Japanese Americans to earn the respect of the American public and their government through their labor and compliance.

Farm Labor Shortages and the Irony of EO 9066

Labor shortages of all varieties were pressing issues at the time, but most stressful was the gap between the number of agricultural workers available and the number of agricultural workers needed for harvesting and planting key crops by the spring and summer of 1942. Farmers across the country lacked access to agricultural workers who abandoned their former bosses for wartime work, but for those on the West Coast, EO 9066 presented an ironic conundrum. White planters in California and Washington previously benefited from a legacy of anti-alien land laws passed by state legislatures during the early 1900s. Japanese immigrants were restricted from owning land under such restrictive legislation but found a profitable loophole by placing property and farms in the names of their American-born children. Japanese American farmers did well for themselves by specializing in more intensive crops such as asparagus, lettuce, and strawberries, a practice known as truck farming. By 1940, 45 percent of Japanese Americans on the West Coast were engaged in farming (which spurred the growth of wholesalers and grocers), and Japanese Americans contributed around 9 percent of the nation's agricultural production. Compared with the value of the average crop acre (thirty-eight dollars), Japanese American–owned acres were valued at $280 each.[88] Under these circumstances, farmers should have welcomed EO 9066 as a means of stamping out competition in certain crops, and certainly white farmers were some of the most ardent supporters of removal in its early phases.

Farmers engaged in large-scale agricultural faced a different scenario. The impending removal of thousands of Japanese Americans who either worked for them, dealt in business with them, or sold produce wholesale threatened the annual profits of white planters. Removal actually exacerbated a labor shortage on the West Coast. The impact of EO 9066 on farm labor created complex and varied reactions among those who viewed removal as a boon and those who pleaded for exception to the policy so that they could retain Japanese American labor. Others argued that using Japanese Americans for farm labor once they were removed could bolster agricultural production elsewhere in the United States by exploiting their labor as a way to prove their loyalty.

Many private landowners and state representatives along the West Coast immediately wrote to Bendetsen, DeWitt, or FDR begging for an exemption under EO 9066 so they could continue to employ Japanese Americans. Japanese Americans were successful truck farmers and individual entrepreneurs, but many also worked in fields for wages or supplemental income. They were a crucial component of the West Coast economy, which was threatened by their removal.[89] "I am an orchard farmer in Clayton Valley, Contra Coast County," Willard F. Williamson wrote to Bendetsen in March 1942, "specializing in walnuts, pears, nectarines, grapes and tomatoes primarily and for years we have depended upon Japanese labor to cultivate the ground . . . and harvest our crops." While these perishable crops were not in high demand from the military or the "Food for Freedom" program, Williamson argued that the Japanese Americans in his area rendered a valuable service and suggested that "the recent order should be so far relaxed as to permit the retention in their present employment of these Japanese."[90]

Williamson was certainly not alone in his concerns. A letter to the editor from a shipping firm in San Diego lamented that "all the hardships won't be borne by those Japanese who are loyal to the country of their adoption . . . about the fifth columnist Japanese there is no occasion for commiseration—they are the cause of all the grief and the disruption of California's truck-garden industry, which means hardships for all of us in that fresh vegetables will be getting scarcer and scarcer and higher in price."[91] Farmers in Western

Washington were divided over the prospects of a planned removal of 120,000 Japanese Americans from their region. Some wanted officials "to take their time" with removal in order to have labor on hand to help with crops, while others wanted Japanese Americans gone as soon as possible to free up economic opportunities.[92]

Farmers in other states spotted an opportunity to import Japanese American laborers rather than sending them to prison camps. From the Mountain States to the Midwest, governors or state representatives flooded the administration with letters requesting exemption from removal or assistance from the government in meeting labor shortages. E. R. Bittin, secretary of the Building Trades Council union located in Great Falls, Montana, wrote to DeWitt and conveyed his organization's "objection to bringing of Japanese labor into the state as there are plenty of unemployed men here" and "the small minority [of farmers who do] only want cheap labor at the community's expense."[93] Others pressed for access to Japanese American labor. Ranchers from Nevada and Utah wrote to DeWitt asking for the right to use Japanese Americans for tasks on their properties.[94] Governor of Illinois Dwight H. Green wrote directly to FDR in 1942 to inform him of a resolution passed by representatives from the state farm bureau, state grange, state agricultural colleges, the USDA War Board, and the US Employment Service in Chicago during a meeting, which argued that "military, industrial, and agricultural groups should formulate a program that will make available man power to agriculture" to produce necessary food. It concluded: "The nation must mobilize to utilize its manpower to the best advantage."[95]

In April 1942, Colonel M. F. Haas, from the army's Civil Affairs Division, attended a conference hosted by farmers in the Sacramento Delta and San Joaquin Valley to hear grievances on the impact of Executive Order 9066 on their economic well-being. Neil MacLane, a successful farmer from the region, argued that the irrigation system of the Delta, which was essential to farming, "was different from any other in the state," a fact that made Japanese Americans and their specialized skills of cultivation vital for crops, such as celery, onions, and lettuce, that were the economic backbone of local farmers, even if they were not deemed military necessities. "The Japs know every mole hole in [the land]," MacLane exclaimed. "We can replace Mexicans, Filipinos at any time, but the Japs—they cannot be replaced." One of MacLane's fellow farmers, J. Zuckerman, agreed: "I couldn't today go out and irrigate a field and set the water like the Japanese." Representing the farmers in the area, Lawrence Hewes, the regional director of the FSA, suggested that the army establish a reception center on nearby King Island, which was only accessible via one bridge connecting it to the mainland and could be easily guarded to allow Japanese Americans to leave the center for employment and return at night. The conversations at the conference and the insistence of the local farmers on the prized skills of Japanese Americans were in sharp contrast to the outpouring of hatred and racism directed toward Japanese Americans in the early twentieth century. Japanese Americans, once economic threats who held a monopoly on farmland, were now a valuable component of the local economy that could not be extricated without serious disruptions.

Haas disagreed with the proposition that agricultural labor should supersede military necessity for removal. "I want you to know that we feel your problem and we are giving it every consideration we possibly can," Haas commiserated with those in attendance. "But there is another side to the picture: Those areas contain Japanese which are extremely dangerous to certain military projects or military installations which are of military importance." He pleaded with the farmers to understand that "those Japs will have to go and go first and we have been pounding to get those Japs out because it is of utmost danger at the present time." For Haas and the army, using Japanese American labor within the prison camps was one thing, but allowing them to remain in the military areas indefinitely was out of the question—initially.[96]

Predictions of devastating shortages in agricultural labor moved to the top of the list of concerns for various federal and state agencies as the war progressed through the spring of 1942. The Federal Reserve Bank of San Francisco warned of the unknown, yet concerning impact of Japanese American removal on the West Coast and the nation's economic strength. Federal Reserve representatives noted in their monthly review that the removal of Japanese Americans would "naturally create certain problems of economic adjustment," not only in farming but also in the services they provided to smaller communities.[97] Other farmers and business owners wrote to FDR, Bendetsen, and DeWitt with pleas for assistance, claiming that they had exhausted a variety of both standard and unique solutions to their labor shortages including recruiting women, children, and college students to enlist for harvesting work. Not only were some of these groups unfit for the job, but there were simply not enough workers able and/or willing to do the job.

Not all farmers along the West Coast expressed the same concerns about the removal of Japanese American farmers. D. M. Rutherford, a farmer who wrote a letter to the editor to the *Pacific Rural Press* in February 1942, asked if the West Coast actually needed Japanese American farmers. Rutherford referred to "a story circulating in the East that California is utterly, completely, and abjectly dependent upon the produce of the Jap farmers," a rumor "no doubt predicated by a certain amount of regional jealousy." He explained that Japanese Americans had already quit farming because of their uncertain fate. This was a fair statement, as many refrained from tilling their soil to prepare for future crops.[98] Furthermore, Rutherford emphasized that the crops Japanese Americans were known for growing—radishes, lettuce, cucumbers— were not in high demand from either the army or the public. "Japanese are garden farmers, not commercial farmers," and they had a reputation among white farmers for violating the Tomato Zone Prorate, which required farmers to allow inspections of the size of the fruit at markets.[99] For Rutherford, the Japanese Americans were a "thorn in the side" of the white farmer, and he relished their removal.

Regardless of the protests, many saw the value in using Japanese Americans for labor. A February editorial from the *Grand Junction Sentinel* in Colorado called for support of the employment of Japanese Americans in agricultural labor for another reason: punishment. "Did you hear about that chap from New Jersey who is now a prisoner in Japan over the radio the other day? He was broadcasting a statement to his family and at the close of it he said, 'I am all right. I am working in the rice fields.'" In retaliation, the editor, Charles Swain, suggested, "Why not put the Japanese who are here to work? I don't care whether it is in the sugar beet fields or what, but put them to work." It occurred to Swain that "if our boys are working in the fields over there, it won't hurt their boys to work in the fields over here."[100] "Their boys" referred to Nisei, who should be punished for their inherent ethnic and racial betrayal with POW field work, as opposed to US prisoners of war who were captured as combatants in Japan. As with other sectors of the wartime economy, agriculture was unprepared for the demands thrust on it after 1941. Fortunately for many farmers, members of the WCCA as well as the WRA identified agriculture as a vital area where imprisoned Japanese Americans could assist.

The planning phases of incarceration were often marked more by a concern for meeting labor shortages for the war effort than concerns for security or self-defense. Incarceration *was* a matter of military necessity for both the military and civilian agencies placed in charge of removing and detaining Japanese Americans. The definition and interpretation of "military necessity" in this case was simply reframed to mean war production rather than a more traditional sense of isolating Japanese Americans for fear of another attack on the United States.

Initially, using Japanese American labor was a straightforward solution for limiting costs, promoting morale within the camps, and completing long-standing infrastructure programs. For the administrators in the military, the WCCA, and the WRA, there was nothing exploitative about making labor a crucial component of incarceration. After all, what able-bodied American would want to remain idle during a time of national emergency, or would not work to pass the time and maintain his or her dignity? These questions drove much of the planning of incarceration from the forced removal to the construction of prison camps at Tule Lake, or the "land that veterans made."

As Japanese Americans moved into the detention centers during the spring of 1942, the calls for labor from private planters, governors, and politicians grew more urgent, and the government realized how necessary certain crops were to the war effort. Even before Japanese Americans arrived at Santa Anita, Tanforan, or Manzanar, the WCCA and WRA already struggled with creating an efficient way of allowing Japanese Americans to leave the centers and work for private employers. What was envisioned as an answer to two problems—providing Japanese Americans with work and assisting with the war effort—soon turned into a logistical conundrum for the military and the government. Questions of wages, supervision, and, most importantly, what constituted "free" and "coerced" labor came to shape the exploitation of Japanese America.

CHAPTER 2

"What Good Was My Contract?"

From Free to Convict Laborers

By April 1942, Colonel Karl Bendetsen had reached his breaking point. He had been subjected to a flood of requests from independent farmers and businesses to manipulate the implementation of Executive Order 9066 to suit their economic needs. "The Army is not the Department of Agriculture," Bendetsen dictated to Floyd Oles, a prominent wholesale buyer and shipper of Japanese American–grown produce in Western Washington. Oles had hounded Bendetsen for information on the removal process and requested that the army increase the speed of transferring Japanese American–owned land to lessees to prevent a loss of crops during the 1942 harvesting season. Bendetsen explained to Oles (for the fourth time that spring) that the Department of Agriculture, under the guidance of Secretary Claude Wickard and with the assistance of the Farm Security Administration (FSA), was the agency in charge of doling out loans for individuals or corporations to assume the responsibility of operating Japanese American land. Oles was not pleased with the FSA's current record of accomplishment and was concerned that such inefficiency would jeopardize his partners' profits come summer. Oles requested earlier in April that the army take over the loan process, but Bendetsen reminded Oles that he "did not intend to look at a single loan application as [he doesn't] know a cucumber from an ant hill," and encouraged him to take up his concerns with the Department of Agriculture. "I realize that the evacuation of Japanese from the farms in the King-Pierce County area upsets the economic order," Bendetsen cajoled Oles. "I realize that shippers are much disturbed because of the necessity for making new arrangements for dealing with the growers because the old growers are being evacuated. I know what this means to you and others, I regret it, but it is because of military necessity." As for Oles's concerns about agricultural production in his region, Bendetsen remarked acridly, "So far as the Army is concerned we may have to get along with fewer heads of lettuce, tomatoes and strawberries. If we have to we will."[1] Following his exchange with Oles, Bendetsen delivered an address before the Commonwealth Club of San Francisco in May 1942 and took the opportunity to explain once more that the army was not directly involved with either agricultural production or the employment of Japanese Americans; that was the realm of the War Relocation Authority (WRA).[2] With the harvest season approaching, farmers and agricultural corporations increasingly turned toward powerful growers' associations with state lobbying power to pressure the army and the federal government for access to Japanese American prison labor. Using Japanese Americans for private agricultural work was a long-term goal for the WRA, but Bendetsen and the WCCA did not expect to be approached for the release of Japanese Americans so soon.

Try as he may, Bendetsen's insistence on maintaining the army's distance from questions of labor and profits would soon be of little importance. The WCCA and WRA became increasingly responsible for overseeing the employment of imprisoned Japanese Americans in agricultural labor for private businesses. Government concerns about labor shortages on farms increased during the spring of 1942 as the army removed Japanese Americans from their homes and detained them while the need for agricultural goods increased from both the military and consumers. Not all farmers who wrote to the administration requesting assistance were engaged in farming crops that were military necessities. Many, like Oles, were more concerned with profits and their bottom lines, yet they attempted to play up their respective crop's importance for the military cause. However, other crops were still required for military production and shipments under obligations of the Lend-Lease Act of 1941, and a shrinking pool of labor made it more difficult for farmers to meet these demands.

The Department of Agriculture encouraged Americans to take up small-scale agricultural output in addition to rationing food as part of the war effort. The Food for Freedom program—developed in late 1942—went beyond victory gardens and urged Americans to think more concretely in terms of the problems that American farmers faced in meeting wartime demands. Defending America's abundant way of life defined by a cornucopia of healthy and delicious food was also crucial.[3] In a pamphlet distributed to Americans that summarized the proposed agricultural program, Secretary of Agriculture Claude Wickard compared farmers to soldiers, explaining that "there's no other group, with the exception of our military boys, who are being asked to do more" in order to feed the military, keep Americans well-fed, and also ship "boatload after boatload after boatload" of food to allies in Europe.[4] Cultivation of the "Will to Do" among Americans in terms of appreciating farmers and lending a hand, be it through donations of machinery or volunteering labor, was the goal of the Food for Freedom program.[5] The government did not exclude Japanese Americans from its expectations of agricultural patriotism.[6]

Once Japanese Americans arrived at the detention centers, the push for their limited release for employment on private farms increased, and the pleas of governors of western states became more desperate. From beets in Idaho, Utah, Montana, and western Oregon to cotton in Arizona, governors who were once hesitant or outright resistant to imprisoning Japanese Americans within their states now looked to exploit their labor in key crops. Even Governor Culbert Olson of California wrote to General John L. DeWitt and requested that Japanese Americans be allowed to leave the detention centers and travel throughout his state to harvest crops. Both employers and WRA administrators viewed Japanese Americans as units of production to be moved and allocated as needed. In the process, Japanese Americans were dehumanized by those who sought their labor. Racism and economic opportunism may have driven the initial support for removal and incarceration of Japanese Americans, but profits and labor still held sway when, ironically, removal contributed to a farm labor shortage.[7]

These requests left DeWitt, Bendetsen, Milton Eisenhower (then director of the WRA), and other officials and administrators with larger questions. If forced removal and imprisonment were deemed military necessities, could Japanese Americans be released for work—especially considering that some of the farmers requesting assistance were located in proximity to the vulnerable military areas? How would the public view the army's acquiescence to the labor demands of private employers? How much could Japanese Americans receive in payment, and how would contracts be established and regulated? What were the rights of Japanese American prisoners when it came to labor, and what is the boundary between voluntary and coerced labor when dealing with a group of incarcerated citizens? In other words, how do you maintain exploitation in private employment without it appearing as (in the words of officials) "forced labor"? Japanese Americans maintaining camps and working on public works projects was one thing; releasing them for work in a private system that could resemble convict leasing was another.

While farmers assumed that Japanese Americans were free for exploitation—as many white employers had done for decades with regard to Asian Americans—the labor shortage in agriculture presented new problems for the architects and administrators of Japanese American incarceration. Similar to other marginalized groups, including African Americans, Latinos, and Native Americans, who were subjected to low-paying jobs as a result of false choices in an exploitative labor system, Japanese Americans were forced to work under wartime imprisonment for the government or risk being labeled as disloyal or suspect.[8] The Bracero program (or the Mexican Farm Labor Agreement) is perhaps the most well known and documented example of an exploitative agricultural labor program dependent on Mexican migrants, but imprisoned Japanese Americans presented a more complicated form of wartime labor. They entered a geographic and economic space inhabited by capitalists and a rotation of cheap labor among largely poor whites, Mexicans, and Black migrants from the Caribbean, but their legal status was unique.[9] Between the spring and fall of 1942, Japanese Americans would be released to work on private farms under specific and often restrictive conditions, a scenario that highlighted the forced nature of their employment and turned incarceration into a full-blown prison labor system. While the WRA and WCCA agents ensured that Japanese Americans could volunteer their services to the private growers, the nature of the system and its implementation once Japanese Americans left the detention centers and prison camps more closely resembled coerced labor. Japanese American laborers, however, pushed back against this system of coercion and insisted on their rights as laborers.

Public and Political Pressure for Access to Japanese American Labor

From California to Oregon, Colorado, Utah, and as far away as Montana and South Dakota, sugar beets made many a man and corporation financially comfortable and employed thousands of tenant and migratory farmers in the production of what amounted to crystalized gold. Early German settlers mastered and brought to the West the process of turning beets into sugar during the mid-nineteenth century. Tariffs on the importation of sugar from Hawaii and Cuba during the late nineteenth century resulted in the entire sugar beet industry—from planting to refining—falling into the hands of a few powerful companies. The California-based Holly Sugar Corporation (organized through consolidation with the Sheridan Sugar Company in 1916) and American Beet Sugar Company, the Crystal Sugar Company in Montana, the Utah-Idaho Sugar Company, and the Oregon-based Amalgamated Sugar Company were among the most prominent examples.[10] While water manipulation is perhaps the most well-known example of wealth accumulation, speculation, and questionable business practices in the West, these sugar companies (described by a California economist at the time as "Rockefeller companies") formed a virtual monopoly on the industry mainly as a result of the labor- and property-intensive nature of the crop.

Beets required massive tracts of land and an even larger amount of cheap "stoop" labor. The growing season was divided into four phases, with slight alterations depending on the region: the winter planting, the early spring "blocking" (creating space around a beet sprout with a handheld hoe to encourage growth), the early summer "thinning" or weeding the tangled tops of the plants to leave the strongest beet sprouts, and the late summer or early fall harvest ("pulling and topping"). Few of the steps in the labor-intensive production process could be mechanized, least of all the thinning, which in California alone required approximately 280,000 man-days of labor on 140,000 acres of fields.[11] Harvesting called for nearly the same amount of time and effort. Beets were also highly perishable and not easily transported. Processing centers were located close to the fields and were owned and operated by the same sugar corporations that controlled the planting and harvesting—recreating the type of vertical integration that characterized American steel production in the early twentieth century. By the 1920s, it was nearly impossible for any outsiders to enter into sugar beet growing because the sugar companies owned most of the land and controlled a large portion of the migratory labor that the industry depended on—mostly performed by Chinese, Japanese, and Mexicans in California and white workers farther east. Employers used racial antagonisms to weaken solidarity and requests for workers' rights among the multiracial crews. Despite multiple attempts at strikes in California during the mid to late 1930s, beet workers made little headway in their demands for higher wages and contract negotiations (unlike the more skilled laborers in the processing plants, who successfully unionized in the 1930s).[12]

Come World War II, with many men enlisted overseas or fleeing to other forms of employment, sugar growers faced severe labor shortages. Even with those who chose to stay and work in the Montana and Dakota beet fields because of family or medical responsibilities, corporate managers scrambled for the workforce to sustain their profits. The military (responding to wartime restrictions on imported sugar from the Philippines) also placed heavy demands on the corporations for sugar that was used in the production of industrial alcohol as well as synthetic war materials like rubber.[13] Struggling to meet these orders, the sugar corporations blamed the federal government for failing to thoroughly investigate the labor shortage or provide subsidies.

Generally, sugar beet corporations had hoped to rely on Mexican migrant laborers—or *betabaleros*—who came to the Pacific Northwest, Intermountain States, and Great Plains to work the fields.[14] By August 1942, the United States and Mexico would enter into an agreement and create the Bracero program to allow thousands of Mexican migrant workers into the country to labor in beets and other crops, but the war initially made such importation of labor and negotiations between the two nations over wages difficult. Both Bendetsen and Colonel Ralph Tate (assistant secretary of war) also discussed possible complications with new foreigners arriving—even if they were not enemy aliens.[15] Uncertainties relating to how many and how soon Mexican laborers could move across the border in time for the various phases of beet production led corporations and farmers to seek a substitute labor source. Descriptions of the sugar beet industry during World War II typically emphasize the relations among the largely Mexican migrant workers, small farmers, and large corporations; however, a fourth entity—the WRA and the federal government—became a fixture of the industry as well.[16]

Scores of petitions, letters, and resolutions from beet growers' associations and corporations continued to flood the WRA's offices and Bendetsen's increasingly cluttered desk at his office in San Francisco. While Governor Samuel Ford of Montana wrote to DeWitt in April 1942 expressing his discontent with rumors he heard of Japanese Americans being relocated to his state to work in agriculture, his constituents voiced different opinions.[17] S. J. Boyer of the Utah State Farm Bureau Federation wrote to Bendetsen and declared that he and others in Utah "don't love the Japanese, but we intend to use them," while beet growers in Idaho protested the planting of new crops until they knew for certain that they would receive Japanese American laborers.[18] Similarly, Governor Harlan J. Bushfield of South Dakota requested 675 Japanese American workers to come and work the two thousand acres of sugar beet fields in his state, a move which an editorial in the *Sioux Falls Argus Leader* supported: "It is perhaps unnecessary to state that we would prefer to not have the Japanese . . . but this is war . . . the Japanese are to be placed somewhere and it is certainly advisable to employ them in productive work rather than permit them to remain idle."[19]

In early March, the Malta (Montana) Commercial Club and the Phillips County Agricultural Planning Committee sent a copy of a resolution the two groups passed during a recent meeting in the Milk River Valley requesting help from the government. "Whereas the federal government is urging an all-out agricultural production effort to maintain the nation's food supply and create surpluses for the use of our allies," the petitioners argued, "large numbers of these prospective evacuees are skilled in agriculture" and could be used in Montana.[20] Because both organizations believed that "it [would] be of greater national advantage to put these evacuees to useful employment in raising vitally needed food crops rather than maintain them in idleness as public charges," they "formally requested the Federal Government to assign at suitable points in the Milk River Valley a sufficient number of foreign born nationals or their American-born descendants who are trained in agricultural pursuits to constitute a labor reservoir for use at going rate of pay in planting, tending and harvesting of food crops."[21] The organizations promised that Japanese Americans would be guarded, kept safe, and paid prevailing wages (approximately $9.34 per acre for blocking, $3.00 per acre for hoeing, and $13.94 per hour for topping), and they advised Bendetsen that their proposal "be presented to the proper authorities and pushed for action as speedily as possible."[22]

The petitions sent by the beet growers and their various representatives and partners in the industry revealed a pattern of how private employers related to the imprisoned Japanese Americans and the government. Above all, the "requests" and "urgings" of corporations and associations read more like demands or at the very least assumptions of the government's role in securing labor for them. Eisenhower, Bendetsen, and DeWitt were hesitant to use Japanese Americans as private laborers so early in the removal process, as their initial goals were eviction and detention. Corporations and farmers viewed the relationship between imprisoned Japanese Americans and exploitable labor as organic. Not only were Japanese Americans racially othered, but now they were incarcerated, and farmers viewed Japanese Americans' agricultural skills as going to waste as they languished in the detention centers. Japanese Americans became an easily exploitable "labor reservoir" (to use the phrase that corporations often used themselves).

Private employers assumed that if Japanese Americans were not working, then they remained idle and became a hindrance to the war effort as well as a drain on American taxpayers. The federal government created an imprisoned work force that would go to waste if not employed outside the detention centers; in placing demands on the military and government for access to exploited Japanese Americans, private employers treated the government as a labor broker. The basic idea that the government and private employers shared a mutual goal in ensuring the continued operation and survival of the market and capitalism during war fueled the search among private growers for exploitable labor. The government played a large role in ensuring the continued effectiveness of the economy during the New Deal (particularly with the protective tariffs of the Sugar Act of 1937), and considering this fact—coupled with America's long history of the government's involvement with promoting and protecting capitalism—it would be no surprise that a similar expectation existed during World War II.[23] Private employers also worked hard to convince the government that their crops were military necessities and crucial to the war effort to prove that their motives were driven as much by America's victory as private profits.

Corporations and beet growers' associations emphasized time and again in their resolutions that the use of imprisoned Japanese Americans for labor would help them to meet the responsibilities that were foisted on them by the military and the federal government. And they assumed that it would be the government's job to assist them in doing so. While some private farmers revealed fundamental beliefs about the otherness of Japanese Americans as well as the use of labor as a form of punishment—such as a member of the Southeastern Montana Counties Association who explained during an association meeting that he would "just love to see these same Japs working in the Montana sugar beet fields to aid our boys in whipping other Japs across the sea"—most couched their demands in a mix of support for the war effort and concern for the morale of imprisoned Japanese Americans.[24]

Bendetsen, DeWitt, and Eisenhower fended off the requests from private farmers, the beet corporations, and their representatives and associations as long as possible, but the pressure for access to Japanese American labor mounted throughout the late winter and early spring of 1942. Employers became agitated as the season progressed with no word on whether or not Japanese Americans would be available for work. State governors grew weary of being criticized by their constituents and representatives of the sugar corporations for their lack of initiative in securing Japanese American laborers.[25]

By late April 1942, the momentum shifted for the sugar beet growers as discussions of allowing Japanese Americans to be used for private employers gained traction among government officials. Thomas Holland, chief of the WRA's Employment Division, recounted later in a 1943 memo to newly minted WRA director Dillon Myer (who would take over when Eisenhower resigned in late July to take a position in the Office of War Production—in large part because of disagreements with others over the trajectory of incarceration) that "when the break came in the sugar beet labor situation, it came quickly . . . and the sugar beet companies were instrumental in bringing the state and local officials around to an acceptance of the evacuees as temporary laborers in the sugar beet fields."[26] Confirming Holland's account, on May 1 Eisenhower received a telegram from H. E. Dodd, an administrator with the Agricultural Adjustment Administration (AAA), who informed the director of how dire the situation was in sugar beet production. Dodd also bemoaned the pressure he received from the beet growers and their associations. "Labor situation in sugar beet areas becoming more acute each day," Dodd warned.[27] "I have information that either state civil authorities or sugar beet processors would be willing to resume responsibility for housing and guards." Dodd did his best to deny requests, but "pressure [was] getting severe" over at the AAA.[28]

In early April 1942, members of growers' associations from Idaho, Montana, and the Dakotas met with representatives from the AAA as well as the Department of Labor and further pressed for assistance addressing labor shortages in their regions.[29] Governors grew more demanding in their requests while facing the wrath of the growers' associations and corporations for supposedly not fighting hard enough for the importation of Japanese American labor (even if most of the residents of their states opposed their arrival—the corporations won in this case). In response, Eisenhower went over Dodd's head and right to Secretary of Agriculture Claude Wickard to express his consternation with being pressured by corporations, citizens, and various civilian agencies. The frustrated director described the miscalculations in assuming that Japanese Americans were an ideal solution to labor shortages. "I find it is a tendency to look upon the evacuated Japanese as a much larger potential agricultural force then they actually are," Eisenhower surmised.[30] True, they were readily available, and any help was worthwhile, but the demographics of the removed Japanese American population did not reveal a robust work force. Approximately forty thousand men and women were over the age of fifteen and therefore cleared for labor; however, "a large portion of the people of working age will be occupied in the management of their community business life (doctors, nurses, school teachers, cooks, waiters, etc.) and in the raising of foodstuffs for subsistence and sale," thereby reducing the "total number of potentially available for private employment."[31] Using Japanese Americans for private labor was embedded in the WRA's early plans, but for Eisenhower, "the prevailing idea was that almost all the evacuees would remain in the centers during the war."

On April 5, Eisenhower revealed his growing anxiety over the labor situation in a letter to a fellow administrator. "New pressures are developing," he lamented. "In the sugar beet crop areas of the west, the demands for stoop labor are rolling in. Politically, these demands are going to be hard to withstand, but if we break down the orderly program and begin to rush Japanese families here and there simply to meet demands for labor, we are once again going to raise fears in the West." Eisenhower stood by his desire to see the best possible outcome for Japanese Americans following the war and stated that he would not acquiesce to any demands unless "the Japanese are fully protected." He wryly noted that "many of the same people who wished to have the Japanese evacuated in the first place are now asking that Japanese labor be kept available for various types of work."[32]

On April 7, 1942, Eisenhower met with ten western state governors as well as representatives from the WRA, the Department of Justice, and the army (including Bendetsen) in Salt Lake City, Utah, to address the requests for labor in the beet fields. The governors presented often contradictory viewpoints to Eisenhower. Many, like Governor Clark of Idaho, reluctantly agreed to host Japanese Americans but wanted a guarantee from the army that "when the war is over, they will return to the place from where they came."[33] Similar to Arkansas governor Homer Adkins, Governor Nels H. Smith of Wyoming also wanted Japanese Americans banished from his state after the war and insisted that the army provide supervision and guards for the prisoners, a demand that Bendetsen immediately rejected on grounds of logistics. Eisenhower balked at the demands for preventing Japanese Americans from resettling in the western states because it smacked of "predetermination" as well as (ironically) the violation of "the democratic process of the people to decide for themselves."[34]

While Eisenhower and Bendetsen grew weary of fielding what they considered absurd and high-maintenance requests from the governors, George Aiken, executive secretary to Oregon governor Charles Arthur Sprague, proposed the "Oregon Plan" for Japanese American removal. Aiken's solution for evicting approximately four thousand Japanese Americans from Oregon rested on their resettlement among the fields of eastern Oregon, where thousands of acres of sugar beets were at risk of rotting. Aiken had supported removing Japanese Americans and employing them in agriculture since January 1942, but his most recent plan was more readily adapted to save the state's beet crops. Rather than moving Japanese Americans to a detention center, Aiken suggested that they take up residence in a former CCC camp in the eastern portion of the state and be released as needed in neighboring beet fields. Farmers and corporations in eastern Oregon supported the plan when word got out, as did Governor Herbert Maw of Utah, who saw potential for agricultural help in his own state. Maw backed Aiken's plan so that "every possible effort [could] be made to meet these needs" of farmers and corporations, and to continue work on soil conservation during the off-season.[35] Aiken followed up with Bendetsen after the meeting and further promoted his plan by suggesting that Japanese Americans could be used for railroad construction on the Great Northern and Southern Pacific lines as well as on the Klamath Irrigation Project—work that CCC crews began before the war.[36]

But neither Bendetsen nor Eisenhower fully agreed with Aiken. First, the process of removal was in its earliest stages, and attempting to introduce private employment into the mix would be a logistical nightmare. Eisenhower, who was perpetually afraid that anti-Japanese violence would ensue if Japanese Americans were placed in areas that lacked security, lingered on the challenges of safeguarding the incarcerees. Leaving Japanese American prisoners largely in the hands of private employers tempted fate. "It is clear that this government cannot under any circumstance afford a single untoward incident in connection with evacuation," Eisenhower chastised members of the Montana-Dakotas Beet Growers' Association when they pressured him for direct access to Japanese Americans for private employment. In advocating for secure confinement, Eisenhower also attempted to appeal to the potential fears of residents that any Japanese American outside the prison camps might be a security risk. "The safety of the United States, of communities, and of evacuees must be considered more than anything else," Eisenhower explained. He promised that "if safety can be assured either through the use of military police on fairly large projects or through the State, you will not find anyone in the Federal Government discouraging private employment for evacuees."[37]

Bendetsen and DeWitt also questioned the feasibility of Aiken's plan. During the early stages of removal, there were no guarantees that Japanese

Americans would be paid prevailing wages by private employers or have their basic needs met without some sort of oversight by a civilian federal agency. DeWitt worried that private employers could recruit Japanese Americans to drive down the wages offered to the local employees who remained on the home front. In a letter to Lieutenant Colonel I. K. Evans (director of the Temporary Settlement Operations Branch of the WCCA), Bendetsen relayed DeWitt's views on unnecessary labor competition between Japanese Americans and whites in the construction of the detention centers and remarked that the general was "extremely anxious that it be thoroughly understood that Japanese labor will not be used in competition with union and other labor." DeWitt advised his staff to emphasize the same point in other requests for agricultural work.[38] As Bendetsen explained numerous times to private growers and state politicians, removal was under the purview of the army, and the army was not in the business of overseeing private employment. Of course, from a security perspective, Bendetsen was also concerned that moving Japanese Americans from one portion of a West Coast state in Military Zone 1 to another region of the same state would invalidate the entire process of removal and detainment. Why bother with removal at all if Japanese Americans would be released for private employment nearby? Nevertheless, Bendetsen assured Aiken that despite all his objections to removing Japanese Americans for the purpose of employing them in private projects, he and Eisenhower would consider the plan carefully.[39]

By early May 1942, when "voluntary relocation" became involuntary removal and Japanese Americans were filing into the detention centers, pressure for their release for sugar beet labor was felt at all levels of local and federal government. Small growers and larger corporations harassed Governor Charles Arthur Sprague to push harder to allow Japanese Americans into their state. On May 9, Sprague wrote to Bendetsen practically begging for the release of Japanese Americans "to save Oregon's beet crops" for both domestic and foreign use in the war effort.[40] With Eisenhower's abandonment, by this point, of Aiken's initial Oregon Plan, it seemed unlikely that the government would budge on using Japanese Americans for private labor. Once again, Bendetsen insisted that no farmer or corporation should even consider tapping into Japanese American labor until work and safety guarantees were made. Frustrated, Sprague went well over the heads of the leaders of the Western Defense Command and wrote to President Roosevelt himself in a last-ditch effort to secure relief. In his letter, Sprague adjusted Aiken's Oregon Plan to apply only to Malheur County in eastern Oregon (where a majority of the sugar beet crops existed) and to request Japanese American laborers only after they had been removed and placed in detention centers.[41] It was not completely out of line for Sprague to contact FDR directly and assume that he would lend a friendly ear. Regulating sugar prices and working to establish tariffs to protect domestic sugar growers were early goals of New Deal administrators, and corporations found a friend in the Roosevelt administration by appealing to the importance of farming for job creation and growth.[42]

Sprague's appeal worked. In early May, FDR spoke with the Department of Agriculture and strongly encouraged the agency to work with the WRA in promoting the use of Japanese Americans for labor in the sugar beet fields.[43]

Roosevelt's support of the use of Japanese Americans for private labor not only clashed with the views of Eisenhower, Bendetsen, and DeWitt but also presented the WCCA and the army with a series of challenges. First was the question of whether Japanese Americans who were supposedly subversive could be released for work. Or, more directly, should Japanese Americans—as prisoners and security risks—be allowed to engage in private employment at all? Did private labor demands overrule the supposed necessity of removal and imprisonment? Larger questions and the logistics of Japanese American labor remained.

The Conundrum of Free Labor

Both Eisenhower and DeWitt remained unsure about the legality of letting Japanese Americans leave the detention centers to work for private employers. In response, they called on WRA attorney Maurice Walk—who had advocated for a form of furlough or work release early in the developmental phase of incarceration—to further investigate the matter.[44] Walk argued in a memo submitted to DeWitt and Eisenhower that "before we can decide policy or devise administrative procedure, it is of paramount importance to form a clear and distinct conception of the legal status of evacuees after they leave their place of detention."[45] He raised an important point in his legal analysis of the situation: What was the legal status of detained Japanese Americans who could receive work furloughs? Not one WRA or WCCA administrator had defined the legal rights of the removed Japanese Americans, leaving little guidance on how to view those who would potentially be released for private employment. Walk's concerns for the status of furloughed Japanese Americans rested on their freedom of movement beyond the detention center and their right to refuse work or seek other employment. Legally, once the army decided to release Japanese Americans for work, did that mean they were no longer prisoners?

Walk suggested that releasing Japanese Americans to a private employer could create legal challenges that neither DeWitt nor Eisenhower wanted. When a Japanese American "left a zone or encampment which has been declared a military area in the physical control of the military authority . . . he will find himself in an area where there has been no military necessity to justify such a detention" as there was in eastern Oregon.[46] Walk wondered, "If being a citizen of the United States, how, then, can he be controlled by military authority and how can he be constrained to return to the place of enforced assembly?"[47] If Japanese Americans were detained by the army under Executive Order 9066 (which applied only to designated military areas) then did leaving for work limit the ability of the army to dictate right of movement? Did releasing Japanese Americans from detention sites for contracted work automatically restore some of their rights or at least give the impression that it did?

Walk also openly addressed the contradiction between using Japanese Americans for work in the prison camps and detention centers and using them for private employment. Specifically, he was troubled by the undefined boundary between voluntary and involuntary labor in this case. In order to ensure that a Japanese American who left for private employment agreed to return to their camp when the job was done, DeWitt had decided that the prisoner and the WRA should enter into an agreement. A Japanese American would sign a contract guaranteeing that when the job was complete, they would return to the prison camp. But Walk balked at this suggestion and demanded that it "be dismissed out of hand," explaining that "such an agreement is not specifically enforceable . . . and more importantly, it impliedly waives the continued authority of the military power of the detainee and places his obligation to return on a consensual basis."[48] According to provisions of Executive Order 9066, there was nothing consensual about Japanese Americans' relationship with the army once they were forcibly removed and placed in the detention centers and prison camps. In response, Walk toyed with the idea of using the Work Corps as an intermediary for private employers, but "you can't very well enlist people in a work corps at enlistment wages and then make them available for work in private employment at prevailing wages." Such a scenario would complicate the pay scale currently offered in the detention centers and perhaps encourage Japanese Americans to demand higher wages for the work they performed in the centers and camps.[49]

Walk also compared the Work Corps in the centers to private employment in thinking through the appropriate way to regulate the release of Japanese Americans for farm work. He advised that "the acceptance of private
employment is to be a purely voluntary matter, whereas enlistees in the work
corps, subject as they are to corps discipline, will do what they are told." His
statement clarified what the legal arm of the WRA believed to be the basic
element of labor performed behind barbed wire. Japanese Americans could
not be told what to do by private employers in the same way as they could by
military personnel in the detention centers and prison camps, for "to make
enlisted personnel available for private enterprise would expose the whole
venture to the imputation of involuntary servitude."[50]

Walk's hesitancy for any work performed by Japanese Americans to be
seen as forced or involuntary preoccupied the minds of all administrators in
the WRA and the WCCA. Bendetsen, DeWitt, and other leaders of the WCCA
went to great lengths to avoid referring to Japanese Americans as prisoners.
Captain Hugh Fullerton was sure to emphasize in a telegram to Bendetsen
that "there are no 'military installations' under the jurisdiction of the WCCA,"
and "while assembly centers were constructed by the Army and are under
the jurisdiction of the Army . . . they are not 'military installations' consistent with our past stand that evacuees are not 'prisoners of war' or 'internees' but merely temporary residents evacuated from a military area."[51] German
prisoners of war worked in agriculture in Nebraska, North Carolina, and
other regions where labor shortages were severe. They typically engaged in
amicable relationships with the community, received the going rate of pay
for officers in their respective military branches, and were, by most accounts,
housed and fed well. They could be put to work so long as it did not contribute to the war effort (per the 1929 Geneva Convention). Japanese Americans,
both citizens and Japanese nationals, were not prisoners of war nor were they
prisoners—according to the government.[52] DeWitt wished to avoid classifying Japanese Americans in a way that likened their situation to incarceration in order to mitigate any potential retaliation from Japanese who held
American POWs.

Also, the WRA's mission of emphasizing that "internment" was not imprisonment hinged on the understanding of the American public and the
allies that Japanese Americans were still citizens detained for their own safety.
Any notion of forced labor might raise concerns among Americans and
civil rights organizations. DeWitt was also cognizant of the role that civilians played in supporting the war effort in the Western Defense Command.

Societal mobilization for the war effort made the army particularly concerned with how the public would view some of its actions and strategies,
specifically those that had a direct impact on the home front.[53] Civilian support
for the army's plans was crucial. Forcing Japanese Americans to engage in
private labor was simply undemocratic and unconstitutional (whereas their
work in the detention centers and prison camps—no matter how question-
ably voluntary—was for their "self-sufficiency" and morale). As the growing
and harvesting season of 1942 marched along, the WRA and WCCA would
become more concerned with maintaining the perception of voluntary agricultural labor as demands increased.

But for Walk, DeWitt, and Bendetsen, the immediate concern was whether
or not acquiescing to the demands of corporations and private employers
would jeopardize military authority and control over the Japanese American prisoners. Private employment could not be seen as a step toward freedom and a reclamation of rights; military power must be maintained if
DeWitt would concede to basically violate the tenets of Executive Order 9066
and allow Japanese Americans to venture beyond the detainment centers and
prison camps. So, what to do about the increasing pressure to comply with
the demands of private employers while maintaining order among Japanese
Americans, who might be inclined to think that their private employment
undermined their "unfree" status and the authority of the army?

In response, Walk invoked "the only practical alternative approach to the
problem": the doctrine of constructive custody.[54] Constructive custody is a
legal premise which states that even if an individual is not under physical control by a legal authority, their freedom is still curtailed by said authority. The
clearest example of someone held under constructive custody would be a parolee: they may not be directly detained by a prison, but their freedom is
contingent on complying with and obeying the authority of law enforcement
officials. Walk concluded, "The Japanese . . . once . . . taken into detention or
custody by the military authority, remains under the control, actual or constructive, of that authority for the duration of the war," per the powers granted
to the military and the WRA by Executive Order 9066, and Executive Order
9102, which established the WRA.[55] "There is no inconvenience or difficulty,
legal or doctrinal, with that proposition; on the contrary, our legal system is
replete with examples of constructive custody, with instances, that is to say,
where a constituted authority has the right and power to reassert its physical control and to impose loose restraints upon the subject who has been
conditionally allowed his freedom from it." Walk listed "the custody of the

runaway child, the guardian over the runaway ward, and the master over the runaway apprentice" as "obvious examples of constructive custody" in this sense.[56]

Walk applied constructive custody and how it related to prisoners to Japanese Americans. Walk compared a Japanese American to "a prisoner enlarged on probation under a suspended execution of his sentence remains in the custody of the court throughout the unexpired period of his sentence." Japanese Americans' labor was bound by no specific domestic statute and was not within the realm of the Geneva Convention that allowed the use of prisoners of war in employment so long that it was not tied to the war effort, "but the military, in the instant case, has ample power to issue regulations . . . under . . . Presidential proclamations, governing the departure from declared military zones, and these regulations have the force of law."[57] More specifically, Walk compared Japanese Americans in the detention centers to "convicts [who are] often farmed out for agricultural labor and the more reliable of them—trusties as they are called—are often allowed considerable privileges outside of the physical control of the prison guards." "Would anybody suggest, although the prison authority had lost actual custody in the sense of physical control as a matter of fact, that its constructive custody had been impaired in the sense of its legal power to regain physical control by summary seizure?" Walk asked rhetorically. He reiterated that "the doctrine of constructive custody is the best available legal notion for the novel status of a citizen who, though not imprisoned, is under continuing legal disability, for the duration of the war, upon his freedom of locomotion and who is subject in that respect to the regulation of the military power."[58]

The position of Japanese Americans in the detention centers, behind barbed wire fences and under constant military guard, was thus equated in status, if not in name, with that of prisoners. By extension, they could be released for private employment (drawing on the example of convict laborers of the past) because they would still be under the constructive custody (detainment) of the army. Walk's application of constructive custody to Japanese Americans set the standard for all questions pertaining to the employment of the prisoners moving forward. He was able to pin down a legal status for the Japanese Americans that balanced what the army and the WRA wanted: a labor source that was technically not imprisoned yet also not free. This category simultaneously recognized that Japanese Americans were not convicts in name, but they could be controlled for labor using a similar legal concept. The agencies tested the line between "evacuee" or "detainee" and prisoner when they discussed the right of mobility and the right to contract freely with employers. War, racism, and labor shortages led to the creation of a new exploitable source of labor. With Walk signing off on the legal requisites for releasing Japanese Americans, DeWitt, Bendetsen, and Eisenhower turned to hashing out the logistics of providing labor to private employers.[59]

Planning for Private Labor

On May 11, 1942, Colonels Evans, George Moffitt, and William Boekel, along with E. R. Fryer (Pacific Coast regional director for the WRA), met with representatives of the Amalgamated Sugar Company of Oregon (one of the most ardent and insistent supporters of Japanese American labor in the sugar beet fields) to discuss the lingering questions surrounding the release of Japanese Americans for private labor. While all were in attendance at the meeting in order to ask questions and share ideas, it was primarily the WCCA and the WRA agents who posed the inquiries. The Amalgamated representatives were barraged with questions about the type of bedding provided ("straw tick or more standard mattresses?"), accessibility to showers and toilets, and how many blankets would be available. Ability for "recreation on days off," access to workmen's compensation and liability insurance, and protection from "direct action from the lawless elements among the Caucasians" were all topics opened for discussion by the WCCA and WRA men. The concerns of the WRA and the WCCA about the ability of the employers to provide basic necessities rested again on how much upkeep and care both organizations would be responsible for if they acquiesced to the demands of the private corporations and growers. The WCCA did not wish to have any extended oversight responsibilities for the detainees, just as the WRA hoped that it would not accrue extra costs in providing Japanese Americans with the basic needs that the corporations either could not or did not want to provide.[60]

Amalgamated was dedicated to meeting the demands of the war effort as well as turning a profit, and these interests were reflected in their guarantees to the agencies. First, everyone in the room agreed that the WRA would ultimately be responsible for the safety and care of Japanese Americans once they left the detention centers by fall of 1942. Second, the Amalgamated representatives agreed that Japanese Americans would be employed directly by them. The WRA would not function as a "middleman" or a subsidiary in supplying the corporation with workers, as this might appear to be a scheme akin to indentured servitude or involuntary labor. Japanese Americans would also be "allocated for work on individual farms and the wages for the evacuees are to be deducted from the proceeds of the crop before settlement with the growers." Amalgamated agreed to cover workmen's compensation, liability insurance, and social security deductions from the checks of the Japanese Americans—admirable steps in ensuring that the employees were laborers rather than convict workers or indentured servants (an agreement that would become more complex in practice).[61]

The list of requirements for a private employer to receive Japanese American workers was lengthy. First, the United States Employment Service would serve as the labor broker between the Japanese Americans and the private employers. Employers could only recruit members of the voluntary Work Corps for outside agricultural labor. Families would be allowed to accompany anyone who joined the Work Corps and volunteered for agricultural employment, but in order for an employer to recruit an entire family or even a single worker they were required to ensure that living facilities met the basic standards established by the Employment Service. Finally, any corporation or private grower underwent an investigation whereby a representative of the Employment Service would physically examine the living facilities and give a grade of "satisfactory" or "unsatisfactory." "Adequate housing and sanitary facilities" were required, as was access to medical care. Mess halls where employees could eat meals or kitchens where workers could cook as well as pit latrines were also minimum requirements. Any employer who wished to use Japanese American labor would need to request a specific number of employees and then demonstrate that they could adequately care for them.[62]

The WRA also expected corporations and private farmers to pay Japanese Americans prevailing wages. This was key to ensuring that the public did not come to see Japanese Americans as being forced to labor by private employers. Fair wages were also a mechanism to assure Americans that local workers were not deprived of jobs as a result of "greedy" employers seeking to exploit the prisoners. Any application for labor submitted by a corporation would require a statement of approval from the Employment Service that "local labor or labor within a shorter distance [from the centers to the fields] cannot be secured at wages or working conditions equivalent to the WRA."[63]

At the core of this newly fashioned labor system was the contract between the two parties, which technically set it apart from forced or convict-lease labor. The WRA operated under the idea that labor is free and voluntary so long as there is a contract and an agreed-on set of working conditions between the employer and the employee. In this case, the conditions were established by the WRA on behalf of the employee, but the fact that any employment agreement required the signature of a voluntary member of the Work Corps was important. "The required labor standards, the type of work to be performed, and the place of duration of employment shall be explained to each worker in the language he understands and each worker shall be given a written contract of employment." The WRA instructed workers that private employment was technically a contracted "furlough" from their normal Work Corps duties in the detention centers and prison camps. The employer "shall make every effort to provide fulltime employment during the contract period," and if "for any reason the employer cannot furnish full-time employment, at least two-thirds of fulltime wages for the duration of the contract must be paid." Furloughs consisted of one-month increments and could be extended on a month-to-month basis as needed. If an employee's services were no longer needed in the fields, they were to report back to the camp (if they were living on premises at the fields during their furlough) or they could enter into a new contract—going through the same procedure as stated above—with another employer. A Japanese American, could not, unlike convict lease laborers, be transferred from one employer to another without notice or consent per the rules of the Employment Service and the WRA. With such safeguards in place, there would be no way for the public to confuse a legally employed Japanese American (under the doctrine of constructive custody) with a forced laborer or a prison laborer. After all, the contract was the hallmark of a free system of work.[64]

But there were regulations that would remind government officials as well as Japanese Americans that they were not, in fact, "free" laborers. First and foremost, a governor who allowed Japanese Americans to enter his state for private employment would have to sign an agreement that declared that "law and order would be maintained" by local enforcement. The ever-present surveillance of the Japanese Americans who decided to take up private employment was a constant reminder that they were not free laborers, as their movement was restricted or guarded. Laborers were also "not permitted to leave camp without being accompanied by a deputy except when going to beet fields and in that event, they will be accompanied by the farmer who will be responsible for their protection, or deputized representative of the Amalgamated Sugar Company." Furthermore, the US Employment Service required that "records . . . be maintained so that at any time of the day we may be able to furnish information as to where the evacuees are engaged in work."[65]

DeWitt also issued general instructions regarding the movement of Japanese Americans who were employed in agricultural labor outside Military Areas 1 and 2. Using Walk's constructive custody doctrine, DeWitt proclaimed that evacuees were "under the jurisdiction of the War Relocation Authority at all times and are subject to recall to an assembly or relocation center at any time the Director of the Authority deems it necessary."[66] Personal safety or community conditions could prompt a recall, but more often the WRA would issue recalls if a laborer's work was required in the detention centers (further qualifying the definition of "voluntary" or "free" labor). The Employment Service equipped all Japanese Americans with travel permits that they were to carry with them at all times as they were free (under DeWitt's directives) to move about within whichever county they were domiciled for work. Although the WRA did not place any general restrictions or curfews on Japanese Americans for their movement within a county, "such regulation, if any, has been left entirely in the hands of the local authorities who have guaranteed your protection." Not only was it impracticable for the army to supply guards and military police for the Japanese Americans who worked beyond the centers and camps (as Bendetsen repeatedly stressed) but, as an WRA publication explained in late 1942, "it is hardly necessary to point out that the use of heavy guards and other obvious restrictions which convey the impression that the evacuees are war prisoners are extremely unfortunate from a public relations point of view."[67] Any member of the Work Corps who accepted outside employment could not return to the detention center or prison camp without the permission of the Employment Service or the WRA. Perhaps the type of labor system created by the WRA for private employers was voluntary, but it was certainly far from "free."

Required wage deductions that Japanese Americans handed over to the WRA also demonstrated the limits on their freedom. While all government agencies theoretically supported the payment of prevailing wages, larger questions remained as to the appropriate deductions for upkeep and maintenance of the detention centers and prison camps. With employers paying for the transportation and board of the workers, the WRA would be less responsible for meeting the basic needs of the Japanese Americans who left camp. But what of family members who remained? Once members of the Work Corps could be recruited for private employment and receive prevailing wages, prison laborers would be required to pay to offset the costs of the

imprisonment of his or her family. The WRA hired bonded officers to ensure that payment from the Japanese Americans was received for the upkeep
of their families. "If the evacuee is financially able to do so, he will pay to the
bonded finance officer $20, $40, or $60 (depending on the number of depen-
dents involved) each month and such funds will be deposited in the Trea-
sury of the United States as miscellaneous receipts."[68] If a prisoner who had
signed up for work and then for whatever reason was forced to leave the job
early and not receive his or her full pay, "he will pay such part of the charge
that he can and the balance will be entered as debit in the evacuee's account."[69]
If a prisoner chose not to enlist in the Work Corps performing duties in the
detention center upon their return, "and therefore does not aid in the community in which he lives," he would be unable to pay the charges and he and
his family would be moved to another center "in the name of public interest."[70] The mere fact that Japanese Americans could go into debt to the federal government while pursuing private employment (before a more
generalized wage scale was developed by the WRA later in the summer and
early fall) spoke to the questionable nature of the labor scheme developed in
response to growers' and corporations' needs.

Corporations could not and would not seek to "conscript" Japanese American prisoners into working for them, and the agreement to pay prevailing
wages was also seen as a crucial protection against forced labor or convict
leasing. But that was where the voluntary nature of the employment ended.
Typically, only one sugar corporation would be contracted to recruit labor
from any given center, limiting the choices that Japanese American prisoners had in their employment—they could either remain in the camp and earn
less money while receiving cash advancements, or they could work for the
corporation (through a private farmer) for more money, while having their
wages garnished to pay for their family members still in detention. The definition of voluntary labor among the corporations and the WCCA and WRA
officials consisted of being free to enter into an employment contract or refusing—a definition that excluded many of the rights and bargaining powers that were granted to workers under the New Deal.[71]

After outlining the plans for release, on May 19 Governor Sprague submitted his plans for the recruitment of Japanese Americans to work in beet
fields near Nyssa, Oregon, to E. R. Fryer, the regional director for the WRA.
In order to secure the release of Japanese Americans held at the Portland detention center, Sprague, along with the district attorney, sheriff, and judge of
Malheur County and the Amalgamated Sugar Company, guaranteed that

they "had met fully all of the requirements and conditions governing the release of Japanese evacuees for work in the beet fields," including certification from the US Employment Service that housing and health facilities at Nyssa were adequate, that the Japanese Americans would be paid prevailing wages, and that "the evacuees are being voluntarily recruited." In attesting to their meeting of these requirements, Sprague and the others hoped that the WRA would approve of the release of two hundred Japanese American evacuees from Portland by May 22 to work for the Amalgamated Sugar Company.[72] As soon as word got out that Japanese Americans were available for work in Oregon, representatives from Idaho, including the governor and county attorney of Madison County (where Japanese American labor was most needed), also wrote to Bendetsen and Eisenhower vowing that with the assistance of the employer—Utah-Idaho Sugar Company—Japanese American labor would only be used when no other options were readily available. There were also agreements that "evacuee Japanese recruited from Japanese Reception Centers are to be brought to the Farm Labor Camp in Madison at the expense of the Utah-Idaho Company through arrangements with the Farm Security Administration" (which technically held oversight over the camp), that only voluntary labor would be used, and that state and local law enforcement would provide protection of the Japanese Americans from departure to arrival.[73]

With the WRA in support of granting furloughs to Japanese Americans for private labor, it was up to the WCCA and the army to make exceptions to Civilian Order No. 1, which called for the detainment of Japanese Americans who lived within Military Areas 1 and 2. The sugar beet fields of Oregon were largely within the protected military areas, making it impossible for any recruitment to occur without the intervention of the Western Defense Command. Also, feeling pressure from President Roosevelt, DeWitt made a decision that would later produce a number of headaches for the army in dealing with labor issues and civilians. He removed the restrictions under the initial civilian order to acquiesce to the demands of private industry. DeWitt feared (correctly) that such a move would usher in a flood of requests for private labor in and outside the military areas. Nevertheless, he issued Civilian Order No. 2 on May 20, 1942, which allowed for the recruitment of four hundred Japanese Americans by the US Employment Service from the Portland detention center for work in Malheur County. This order only applied to Japanese Americans in Oregon, but it was the beginning of both an exploitative agricultural work system and a variation on the military necessity of incarceration that rested on agricultural production rather than security.[74] In many cases, labor demands overrode purported issues of national defense.

The Farm Security Administration shouldered the responsibility for providing shelter and basic necessities for the soon-to-be labor camp in Nyssa. Initially, the WRA was under the impression that an abandoned CCC camp could accommodate the prison workers, but the facilities had fallen into disrepair during the onset of the war. With the CCC facilities no longer able to pass inspection for housing workers, the FSA agreed to construct a camp made of numerous canvas tents with heating elements to house and shelter approximately 350 Japanese Americans following DeWitt's new orders (DeWitt would later issue more civilian orders through May 27 that would allow for the release of 1,500 Japanese Americans from the Puyallup, Pinedale, and Sacramento detention centers and another four hundred from Marysville, California).[75] William T. Geurts, the migratory labor camp chief of the FSA, quickly got to work inspecting other CCC camps in Oregon and Idaho for their suitability in hosting Japanese Americans.[76] While the FSA hurried to complete construction of the tent city, the Amalgamated Sugar Company worked through the Employment Service to recruit from the Portland detention center as early as May 22. With the promise of prevailing wages ($9.50 per acre for thinning, $2.50 acre for the first hoeing and $1.50 for the second, and $0.50 an hour for harvesting), a hot meal, comfortable housing, and an ability to move beyond the camps, the Employment Service had little reason to doubt that they could sign up at least two hundred Japanese Americans and possibly their families for work in the sugar beet fields.

Recruiting Japanese Americans for Beet Field Labor

Japanese Americans detained at the Portland center were less enthusiastic about beet labor than corporations had hoped. Despite the Employment Service's repeated guarantees of "[the] highest wages, good climate and best living conditions," when representatives came to recruit at the Portland center, the *San Francisco Examiner* reported that the "voluntary migration" of Japanese Americans to Nyssa only consisted of twenty volunteer workers.[77] News of the failure of the Employment Service to recruit Japanese American for work traveled along the West Coast press and beyond. In a *Portland Journal* article titled "To Beet or Not to Beet; That Is Question Stumping Japs," the author despairingly reported that only twenty Japanese American workers and their families would be sent to Nyssa, and the "possibility that no [more] Japanese will go from here to Eastern Oregon sugar beet fields developed today."[78] Twenty Japanese Americans were a far cry from the two hundred who were originally promised by the WRA and the WCCA in press releases.[79] Newspapers later contrasted the seemingly enthusiastic response of prisoners from state penitentiaries and county jails in California for volunteering for sugar beet labor in exchange for parole—nearly 90 percent—with the "unpatriotic/work-shy" Japanese Americans. The *Los Angeles Times* compared this number to the dismal 44 percent of Japanese Americans that would eventually sign up for work, creating for readers a contrast between the eager and hardworking criminals and the "stubborn and disloyal" Japanese Americans in the headline "Prisoners Favor Farm Labor Plan; Japanese Do Not."[80] Others questioned Japanese Americans' loyalty when even criminals and convicts were willing to prove their worth through their labor for the war effort.

WRA and WCCA administrators scrambled to understand why so few Japanese Americans detained at an international livestock exposition center in Portland with an uncertain future would shun volunteer work in beet fields. Unsurprisingly, Japanese Americans were puzzled by corporations recruiting them for work when they had just recently been forced out of their homes and into the detention centers in the name of military necessity. Hito Okada, the National Secretary of the Japanese American Citizens League (JACL), who voluntarily relocated to Salt Lake City in the spring of 1942, confirmed these fears in a letter to Governor Sprague. Okada jumped on an opportunity to prevent any potential denunciations of Japanese Americans as a result of their less-than-stellar turnout for recruitment. "Realizing the misunderstanding that may come from the small number of evacuees that have volunteered to go to Oregon to assist in thinning work," Okada offered explanations for "some of the reactions of the evacuees on this subject matter."[81] The Employment Service as well as the WRA had come to count on the JACL for raising support for the farm labor program, making Okada's letter an important insight into the problem. Okada confirmed the *Idaho Daily Statesman*'s suggestion that fear prompted the hesitancy to enlist. "I believe it is too much to expect the evacuees to jump at the opportunity of working in the sugar beet fields, when you consider that the very area from which the request comes now, only a few weeks ago made the statement to your office that they would take vigilante action if the Japanese were allowed to go into Malheur County."[82]

Okada also provided damning evidence of the two-faced nature of Idaho governor Chase Clark in his drive to bring Japanese Americans to his state. He contrasted Clark's guarantee of the "finest treatment" for workers who came to the beet fields with the governor's earlier remarks that "the Japanese people act like rats and that the solution to the Japanese problem in Idaho and the nation would be to send them all back to Japan and then sink the island."[83]

Japanese Americans were also hesitant to embrace beet field work because of general confusion about the working conditions. Okada noted that the Japanese American prisoners declined to volunteer because they were in many cases unfamiliar with the type of stoop labor they were expected to perform. "Most of the [Japanese American] farmers from Oregon are operators," Okada informed Sprague, "so there are not many people that we could classify as itinerant laborers."[84] Many of the five hundred Japanese American men who would eventually sign up for beet labor in Idaho by June 1942 were originally "white collar" workers or former landowners rather than migrant field laborers.[85] Corporations and farmers would come to praise the laborers for saving Idaho's $16 million beet crop, but many initially noted that the volunteers (including young Japanese American men who had studied at colleges or universities before they were detained) knew little about farm labor.[86] A manager of a bank in Ontario, Oregon (near Nyssa) even complained to Governor Sprague about the inexperienced workers after he "learned that quite a number of these Japs are not experienced farmers, having come in here from the Seattle District where they operated as merchants and shop owners."[87] He noted that "when they are put in our fields to harvest our sugar beets, they are no better than the average white office worker."[88]

Beliefs that Japanese Americans performed field work better than a white middle-class worker spoke to the racial stereotypes of Japanese Americans as easily exploited "stoop" laborers. Not only did the administrators believe that the prisoners would embrace the opportunity to work the beet fields to earn money and prove their loyalty, but they also incorrectly assumed that there were no distinctions between generations, the regions of the West Coast where Japanese Americans originated before arriving at the detention centers, or class background (all characteristics that would create tensions later in the prison camps). As Okada noted, perhaps the recruiters would have had more luck by initially turning to the detention centers in California, where Japanese Americans from the central and southern regions of the state were more accustomed to agricultural labor.[89] Also, recruiters and federal agents overlooked the generational differences in occupations between the Issei, Nisei, and Kibei (those born in America but educated in Japan before returning to the United States). Many Issei were more familiar with physical farm labor as a result of their inability to own property in many West Coast states, whereas a large number of the Nisei and Kibei were either students or employed in white-collar jobs prior to removal. Variations between what constituted a "farmer" were also unclear to administrators. Landowners often grew smaller crops to sell at local markets or to wholesale distributors and hired workers to perform the physical labor for them, whereas others worked the land themselves with the assistance of their family. But the WCCA and WRA officials either ignored or were unaware of these distinctions and targeted all Japanese Americans for the beet fields. They assumed that there was an innate and inherent predilection for this labor and an acceptance of exploitative agricultural work.[90]

Lieutenant Colonel Frank E. Meek (a supervisor with the WCCA) also observed during an inspection of the Nyssa camp that Japanese Americans suspected that they would be forced to work without pay and against their will. After speaking with a number of Japanese Americans who did make the journey to Nyssa (some with their families), Meek discovered that distrust and confusion—mainly regarding the Employment Service's description of the work to be performed and living conditions—discouraged the prisoners from enlisting in the Work Corps and traveling to the beet fields. "[A] matter that apparently caused confusion and uncertainty was the apparent misunderstanding in the instructions given to them [Japanese Americans] as to what liberty or lack of liberty they would have when they arrived at their destination," Meek explained.[91] Local law officials placed Japanese Americans under curfew and restricted their movement save for two days a week when they granted workers permission to enter the town of Nyssa for leisure (so long as they had copies of their documents certifying that they were employees and not escapees from the detention centers or camps). But no one adequately explained this.[92]

The enlistment papers that volunteers signed when joining the Work Corps also added confusion. Form WRA-1 outlined conditions "provided for their [Japanese Americans] transfer from one Center to another from time to time, as determined by the [WRA]" for employment purposes if a laborer finished one job early or was needed for work at the center.[93] The directive caused anxiety among the prisoners, prompting them to interpret the clause regulating transfers as a means to separate them from their families as punishment or as a requirement for their service. Japanese Americans were so suspicious of the form that the Employment Service abandoned the requirement, but it "apparently caused a feeling of uncertainty and unrest" that lingered.[94] Overall, Meek opined that "there was no real unwillingness of Japanese to volunteer for this work, but that they became skeptical because of apparent high pressure methods used at the out-set and the many confusing instructions and statements made to them."[95] Such high-pressure methods of recruitment on behalf of the Employment Service included framing participation in the Works Corps as voluntary yet suggesting that refusing to participate could result in prisoners paying extra in maintenance fees; that volunteering for beet work could forestall involuntary transfers to other centers for work; and that enlistment in the corps would ensure that once released from the camps, Japanese Americans would be viewed more favorably by white Americans for their participation in the war effort.[96] It is unclear how common such tactics were, but the evidence that they existed suggests at best a complicated labor system and at worst, a deceptive recruiting practice.

In coercing Japanese Americans to sign up for voluntary labor, some Employment Service agents exploited the fears of Japanese Americans that the labor the federal agencies expected them to perform was indeed involuntary and more akin to indentured servitude. One detainee even likened the pressure he felt to sign up for the Work Corps and his ultimate lack of choice in the matter to slavery.[97] While a drastic comparison, the sense of a lack of control over their own labor speaks to the prison work system the WCCA and WRA promoted in the beet fields.

Despite the initial setbacks, corporate supervisors, beet farmers' association members, and individual farmers were so pleased with the use of Japanese American prisoners at Nyssa that others pressured the WCCA for the creation of prison camps in their own states. By hosting a camp, corporations could more easily facilitate the transfer of Japanese Americans from the prison to the fields and also reduce the costs of transportation (which the companies were ultimately responsible for). In other words, a Japanese American camp would cut costs and increase profits at the expense of the American federal government (which could in turn deduct money from the payment of the Japanese American employees for the care and upkeep of their families who remained behind). Both Bendetsen and DeWitt, however, were not impressed with the arguments in favor of establishing a camp in Montana, for example. Not only were they concerned about the potential pressure from other states if they acquiesced, but they also rejected such proposals based on sheer logistics—discussing Japanese Americans in correspondence more as units of production than individuals.

During a phone call on July 7, 1942, Bendetsen informed DeWitt that Senator Charles Murray of Montana used his connections with the powerful Military Affairs Committee in Congress to pressure the WCCA to establish a camp for approximately nine thousand Japanese Americans at Fort Peck, Montana, near the sugar beet region of the state.[98]

"The thing about it is," DeWitt explained, "it seems to me it is a matter for the War Relocation Authority . . . let them handle this thing. I think we don't enter into it all. And we simply don't have any more Japs to give them. We turned [that] down once already because we just ran out of Japs."[99]

"I think that's the answer, sir. That we have reached our capacity and then some with a——of 9,000," Bendetsen responded.[100]

Bendetsen and DeWitt ultimately decided to tell Murray that they could not support the establishment of a camp in Montana due to "military necessity."[101] "Of course, that is not the case and we, of course, can't permit that to go by, because actually—it wouldn't be any more dangerous to have a camp there than it would to have one at Poston, Arizona," DeWitt admitted, knowing that "military necessity" and "security" were satisfactory excuses to have on hand to justify actions that simply defied logistics in the operation of removal and incarceration.[102] Despite the labor demands, there were simply not enough Japanese Americans—"units of production"—left to justify moving nine thousand to Montana. Military leaders and federal agency representatives dehumanized and reduced Japanese Americans to tools for labor meant to meet demands.

Japanese American Experiences in Private Agricultural Work

Eventually corporations, farmers, the Employment Service, and the WRA declared the farm furlough program a success, in large part because of the number of Japanese Americans who later volunteered to work in the beet fields. By the end of June 1942, an estimated fifteen hundred Japanese Americans thinned beets in Idaho, Montana, and eastern Oregon. Many of those employed in the summer would stay on well after the thinning phase to help with the fall harvest, and others would enlist in the Work Corps between August

Figure 4. Japanese American man working on a beet farm near Shelley, Idaho.
Photo by Russell Lee, July 1942. Courtesy of the Library of Congress.

and November, most from the Poston and Manzanar centers. Governor
Herbert Maw of Utah declared Japanese Americans vital to his state's economic success and ability to meet the demands faced by farmers and corporations for beet production, while farmers from as far away as Nebraska would
seek to recruit Japanese Americans for work during the beet off-season. By
1944, thirty-three thousand Japanese Americans signed contracts to work for
farmers, most in the beet fields.[103]

Why did fifteen hundred prisoners decide to join the Works Corps and
travel to the beet fields? The reasons varied, and Japanese Americans published

opinion pieces and notifications of recruitment opportunities in center and later camp newspapers that offer some explanations.[104] But there are challenges to utilizing these sources. The WRA's censorship of camp newspapers and prohibition of most Japanese-language material as well as "subversive" content was central to maintaining order in the centers and camps, with degrees of varying success. Also, camp reporters who worked on the papers were technically government employees and were paid the monthly wage of twelve or sixteen dollars, making the authors and contributors particularly susceptible to self-censorship.[105] However, placing the papers, like any source, within the context of labor history creates a vast and rich collection of primary documents. Opinion pieces and articles provide examples of the image Japanese Americans wanted to project (if not their reality) as well as the importance of work for their acceptance as minorities labeled disloyal during the war. If the camp papers are heavily self-censored with overly patriotic messages from Japanese American editors and other prisoners, then this censorship—especially in terms of labor—speaks to how important proving loyalty through work was in the camps and how significant labor was more generally.

Following the initial arrival of embarrassingly few Japanese Americans to Nyssa, the US Employment Service encouraged those who decided to work in the fields to send good reports back to others in the detention centers.[106] Ben Mitsuda left the Santa Anita center in late summer 1942 to work on the beet harvest, and the *Santa Anita Pacemaker* published his "first impressions" of working in the fields in September. "The country here is great and we have become attached to it already," Mitsuda declared, reflecting on his and his fellow workers' impressions of their new home in Glasgow, Montana.[107] He arrived in Glasgow with thirty-four other employees, and they immediately noted that "the farmers greatly appreciate our help and show it with consideration."[108] Mitsuda concluded his report with descriptions of friendly townsfolk and a pleasant boss who let him and the others go into his private garden and gather potatoes and tomatoes for delicious meals.[109] Earlier in May, after the Employment Service began to recruit from the Portland detention center, editors from the *Portland Evacuazette* noted that more volunteers signed up for beet labor "instigated by encouraging letters and phone calls from friends and relatives already at the beet fields," calling for a "contingent of pioneers" headed for eastern Oregon and later elsewhere. Here, the editors of the *Evacuazette* adopted the language of the administrators in describing the workers who chose to leave as embracing a pioneer spirit.[110]

In other ways, articles and editorials published in the camp newspapers drew on the possibility of performing beet labor as a means of contributing to the war effort. Overtly patriotic and positive messages of the inherently good and loyal nature of work were themes throughout many of the pieces. A front-page article titled "Work Corps to Aid U.S." from the May 21, 1942, edition of the *Manzanar Free Press* declared the patriotic and dutiful nature of volunteering for work in the beet fields. Editors of the *Free Press* described the Work Corps as "an opportunity to make tangible contributions to the American war effort" and suggested that enlistment in the corps and the obligation of taking a loyalty oath confirmed "patriotism and loyalty to the United States."[111] An editorial in the *Pacemaker* from June titled "Victory Volunteers Are Loyal" not only celebrated the two hundred detainees who left Santa Anita to work in the beet fields of Idaho but also commended the "volunteers for victory" who "gave lie to those who would impugn, on a wholesale basis, the loyalty of the great mass of Japanese Americans."[112] The author ensured readers that through volunteer service in the beet fields, "loyal American Japanese will not tolerate, will not forgive any injury done to America."[113] The center newspapers' cheery support of victory gardens, agriculture, and beet labor reads as a facade for a heavily censored publication. The fact that editors and authors tied loyalty to private farm labor, however, was a testament to the survival tactics and strategizing of Japanese Americans while detained.

Once settled in their new jobs, Japanese Americans often provided written accounts of their experiences that revealed a complex picture of the system they labored under. Following an increase in the number of Japanese Americans leaving to go to Idaho, Montana, Colorado, Utah, eastern Oregon, and Nebraska in the summer and fall of 1942, WRA administrators encouraged Japanese Americans to send letters detailing their experiences back to the camps. Leaders of the employment divisions in the camps often received scores of letters from Japanese Americans out in the fields. Other laborers also wrote to Employment Services representatives, a habit that pleased the agency as it could use the letters to entice other volunteers to sign up or initiate investigations of poor conditions if deemed necessary. Such correspondence appears in the personal papers of prison camp administrators and among the collections of official government-employed sociologists and social scientists deployed to study the experiences of the imprisoned (particularly in the Poston, Arizona, camp). If the camp newspapers were heavily censored and perhaps do not offer a true description of work in the fields, the letters from Japanese Americans to WRA agents are surprisingly detailed

and raw. Authors expressed emotions ranging from joy in the newfound freedom in the fields relative to the detention centers and camps to disgust at the
unexpected exploitation and indentured-servitude conditions encountered
while hundreds of miles away from friends and family.

Letters from Japanese Americans working in the harvest from late August through October abound, and many initially detailed favorable experiences. Jack Nakagawa left the Poston, Arizona, prison camp in late August
to travel via rail with a group of Japanese American men recruited from Manzanar and Heart Mountain, Wyoming, to work in the beet fields of a private
farmer in Scotts Bluff, Nebraska. Nakagawa took a moment from his harvesting work in mid-October to pen a letter to Hugh Evans (his employment
division chief at Poston) while he still had a "fairly clear picture" of his situation in Scotts Bluff, having arrived ten days earlier. While most of his fellow workers were "quite happy to be in a community such as Scotts Bluff,"
where the desperate need for labor among the farmers and townsfolk overrode any prejudice when they ventured into town for a "hamburger, steak and
beer . . . which allowed even the most bitter ones to forget the trials of evacuation days," Nakagawa noted that "the overall attitude of the evacuee
labor[ers] is somewhat mixed."[114] Some came because of "economic necessity,
others to see what Nebraska looked like, some to see the prospects of obtaining permanent employment outside of the camp [when they would be re-
leased], and the rest to 'get away for a while' and to have a taste of beer once
again."[115] Because a "good portion" of those who traveled to Nebraska to get
away and swig beer with their buddies had never held a farm job before, they
"knew not what the demands farm labor imposed on them—sore backs, ach-
ing muscles, early to bed and early to rise, no Sundays or holidays, etc." Nakagawa noted that those who came to Nebraska on a lark were the ones to
complain the loudest about the physical hardships of their labor, but those
(such as himself) who joined the Work Corps to earn money "are not finding things so bad."[116] Nakagawa reasoned that because many of the young
men who signed up to work were college kids desperate to get out of the
camps, their experiences would be negative.

Others echoed Nakagawa's sentiments and views on agricultural labor.
Perhaps the most comforting and surprising aspect of arriving to work in the
fields was the generally pleasant attitude of the community. One employee
who came to work for Henry Frank, a potato farmer in Gering, Nebraska,
offered enthusiastic remarks on the local folk. "The public at large treat us
all very nice," he explained, and noted that he and the others "go anywhere

at anytime and no one gives a damn," a clear violation of the civil orders.[117] "The people that wait on us at the stores are very friendly and helpful," and he even noted that "many are sympathetic and some even surprised and shocked to learn that we had been evacuated to places that resemble concentration camps."[118] The desperation among farmers and the corporations for workers appeared to defuse many negative encounters between the locals and the Japanese American laborers.

Japanese American Work Corps members also reported reasonably comfortable living conditions, considering the circumstances, as well as decent pay and good bosses. William Fujito left the Portland detention center in the spring of 1942 to go to the Nyssa camp and remained in the Work Corps to take up harvesting beets on a private farm owned by Alan Conforth in Weiser, Idaho. On October 10, he wrote to William Bonack, the US Employment Service representative for Nyssa, and described the good housing conditions he and the others were able to enjoy. "The houses are fair and have a nice warm stove and everybody in our group has no complaints." Fujito did describe fairly cold and damp weather in the fall, but this was "beyond Mr. Conforth's help."[119] Conforth also paid his employees fifty cents an hour for harvesting (some received fifty-five cents for doing extra work) for a typical ten-hour workday. Fair pay, understanding bosses (many of whom were German Americans—either first- or second-generation farmers), and suitable housing (if not ideal climates) summed up the experiences of these and other letter writers to Employment Service representatives or camp administrators, friends, and family members. One employee answered the question of what he liked about his experience as a furlough worker in the Work Corps with a simple statement: "I just like the feeling of being free!"[120]

But not all accounts of life in the fields were glowing. Japanese Americans wrote letters that revealed disturbing conditions and the exploitative nature of the employment system that challenged its characterization as "free." One fact throughout all of the letters—positive and negative—remains: variations in region, the crops worked, and individual bosses and farmers should be accounted for when assessing the Work Corps and private agricultural employment. Groups of men who labored together on the same farm often expressed similar praise for their boss as well as living and working conditions. In other cases, camp administrators and the Employment Service received clusters of letters from men who worked in other places and spoke of the demoralizing and horrid conditions they encountered.

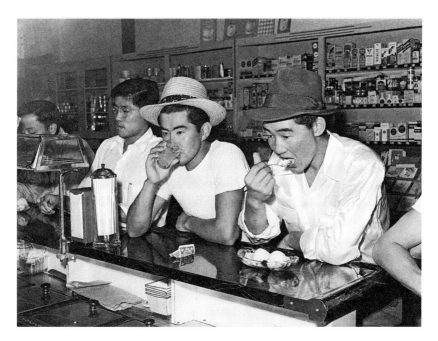

Figure 5. Japanese American beet laborers from the Nyssa Farm Security Administration camp visiting a drugstore downtown during a break. Photo by Russell Lee, July 1942. The FSA used images like this of Japanese Americans enjoying some leisure time to encourage others to sign up for labor leave clearances. Courtesy of the Library of Congress.

Many of the complaints from the laborers went beyond the gripes about backaches and boring food that Nakagawa had mentioned. The basic regulations for housing and food that were required of any farmer or corporation in order to acquire and maintain a labor force from the centers and camps were blatantly disregarded in these cases. "Our living conditions are terrible," an employee working in Baylor, Nebraska, wrote to Hugh Evans of Poston on October 15, 1942.[121] Whereas the farmer was required to provide ample heating, bathroom facilities, and enough cots or mattresses for every employee, five employees were crowded into a "shack" of twelve by fourteen feet infested with mice and flies and with "one rickety cot" to take turns sharing.[122] Another violation of the agreement between the farmer and the Employment Service was the lack of proper bathroom facilities; the employees had access to an old outhouse, but it was "filled to the brim" and they were forced to dig another hole and place a piece of cut-out cardboard over it so that they could sit down when needed. There were also no bathing facilities.[123] Another worker on the same farm confirmed the conditions in his own letter. He understood that the living conditions would not be "comfy," but he was surprised to discover that "Poston shacks seem like the Ritz compared to this Poston Jr.," as he referred to the work camp at the farm.[124]

On July 16, 1942, Lieutenant Colonel Frank Meek stopped by the Turlock detention center in California to make an inspection and received information from another administrator on the poor working conditions of forty-five Japanese Americans who had left in June to go work for the Crystal Sugar Company in Montana. The workers were in different groups and stationed at different farms. Two groups reported favorably, while the others "complained bitterly as to living and working conditions."[125] The workers stated that they had to walk two miles just to get access to drinking water, and although they received thirty-five dollars a week in wages, their boss required them to pay forty-two dollars a month in board—a violation of the agreement between private employers and the WRA that housing was to be provided for free by the employer. The workers signed their letter, "Four Suckers" and Meek prompted an investigation by the Employment Service into the matter. The workers were eventually passed off to another farm also associated with the Crystal Company, but there were no punishments meted to the employer who violated the agreement.

In addition to housing, workers often complained of the miserable situations they found themselves in when it came to food. Under the contracts between the employers and the WRA and Employment Service, cooking utensils and appliances were to be provided for employees to cook meals, or their employers should prepare meals for them in communal dining spaces. But this could create a tricky situation as the laborers often arrived with little to no money and were forced to wait until their first paycheck to purchase groceries from local stores if there was no mess hall. Employees reported incidents of extortion and exploitation from their employers, who would refuse to let them go into town to buy groceries and would charge them on a "credit" system to purchase food and necessary items on-site. Employers would often drastically inflate the price of goods. A boss in Montana provided milk for his employees but forced them to pay one dollar a day, adding the totals up and deducting it from their pay at the end of the week or month.[126] Another employee on a farm in Oregon reported that his employer also charged one dollar and a half per day for food.[127] One dollar per day for meals (approximately seventeen dollars today) was not astronomical, but the employer in these situations took advantage of Japanese American workers who had no means for food except to rely on a credit system that resembled that of a sharecropper or company store. In Colorado, there were reports that Japanese Americans working in the beet fields earned four or five dollars a day and were "in the red" because of borrowing food on credit from their employer or grocers.[128] Another employee who worked in carrot fields in Nevada in the summer before moving on to the beet fields in Idaho reported that his employer required eighty-five cents a week for board—again, perhaps not a large amount but still a violation of government contract agreements that clearly stated that in exchange for access to Japanese American laborers, employers were not allowed to collect money for accommodations.[129]

Perhaps most troubling for Japanese Americans who went to work for private farmers was the realization that the contracts that dictated the rules and regulations for the labor system were often loosely enforced. With so many private farmers working for corporations spread throughout the West, Great Plains, and Intermountain States, it was difficult for the Employment Service to consistently inspect farms to ensure appropriate working conditions. As a result, violations in pay, the type of assigned job, and the length of the contracts were common complaints in letters from Japanese Americans.

Jack Nakagawa wrote to a camp administrator at Poston to explain his ordeal upon arrival in Clearfield, Utah, in early September 1942, before eventually settling in a more favorable work environment in Nebraska. "The first day we arrived here, the farmer that we were supposed to work for, never even showed up for us," so one of the other Japanese American men traveling for work invited Nakagawa and his crew to come with him so that they might find work. Unfortunately, the farmer wasn't interested in hiring Nakagawa or any of his group; he took one look at them and drove them back to town. They were "fired before they even started." A "white guy" who happened to be at the train station when Nakagawa and the others arrived offered them work in his tomato cannery. Not knowing what else to do, Nakagawa and his crew accepted the offer and rode with the man in his truck to the cannery, where they were immediately put to work that night since the owner had no place for the crew to sleep. After the men worked from 8 P.M. to 5 A.M. the following morning (after a grueling fifteen-hour train ride), the cannery owner found a "shack" to house Nakagawa and his eight coworkers. They had no beds and no access to bathrooms. They worked without food for the next day (Nakagawa said he had to eat tomatoes before they went into the cans) and were informed by the foreman that they were going to be making sixty cents an hour working in the cannery. While this pay was not dismal, the men had no idea who their boss was, where they were, or what to do. The camp administrators at Poston informed the Employment Service of this unauthorized transfer, but it is unclear what happened to either the crew or the employment situation.[130]

The men at the cannery technically worked with no contract or formal agreement and were easily passed off from one private employer to the next, a trend that characterized the experiences of other laborers. Despite the emphasis of both the WRA and the Employment Service on the need for authorized transfers of employees between employers, Japanese Americans were frequently traded with no oversight. One group of laborers from Poston arrived too early in Layton, Utah, for the beet harvest in early September, so they were passed along by the farmer initially responsible for them to another who needed help picking string beans in his fields. The Japanese American laborers arrived believing they would make fifty cents an hour harvesting beets but were put to work harvesting beans for one and a half cents per pound instead. Before the beet season arrived, these men grew so frustrated with not only the low pay and their lack of say in where they worked but also the irregular hours due to weather that they quit reporting to work and tried to pool their resources to purchase transportation back to Poston.[131]

John Katano from Poston was also disturbed when he arrived in Bayard, Montana, at 6 A.M. having agreed to work for a farmer named Sam Milchas (a lessee of the Great Western Sugar Company) but was met instead by a Mr. Ginn (the manager at Bayard). Ginn informed Katano and his crew that they would actually be working on the farm of a Mr. Thompson and that he would soon be there to pick them up. Mr. Thompson never showed and the men grew cold and hungry while waiting for their mystery employer. Katano noted that there was another group of Japanese American men from California who also wondered where their employer was. Fortunately for Katano, the crew was able to find his address and go to his farm, where Thompson met them. Katano wrote to Evans at Poston seeking assistance, because he and the others were not willing to work for Thompson without a contract. Thompson respected their wishes but also did little to provide them with food in the meantime. Katano took it upon himself to contact Ginn at Great Western Sugar again, and the manager ensured him that "changes in contracts were being made regularly" and that he and the crew had nothing to worry about. This all did not sit well with Katano and "seemed highly irregular."

"What good was my contract?" Katano asked. "I signed in good faith and the sanctity of the contract and all those things came to mind."[132]

Another member of Katano's crew, Johnnie Fukushima, expressed similar dissatisfaction with the way the WRA and the Employment Service ran the labor system and added some more details to Katano's account. At the train station, when Milchas did not show up, Ginn informed the crew that Milchas no longer required their services because "he already had his labor wants filled" with another crew from Poston that had arrived two days earlier. Fukushima was dissatisfied with this explanation and began to worry. Ginn eventually informed them that "it was the policy of the sugar company to take laborers from relocation centers and move them about after their arrival at destination to suit the sugar company's most urgent needs" and "that after all, we were all working for the same company," which Fukushima thought "was poor management and unfair to the worker."[133] The volunteers were allowed to choose the individual farmer they were contracting with while still at the centers and camps based on factors including living accommodations and proximity to the nearest town. When the sugar company shifted employees without their permission, however, the terms of the contract the employee initially agreed to were different from what they encountered.

Fukushima's and the others' indignity over the violation of their contracts highlighted a particularly pernicious, yet subtle hallmark of the employment agreement. Though each employee did sign a contract stating that they would work for an individual farmer for specific conditions and wages, the reality was that they were contracting not with an individual farmer but with the sugar company the farmer worked for. The Employment Service acted as a broker between the WRA and the sugar companies, recruiting laborers for the needs of private industry as part of their duties under the Manpower Commission of the Department of Labor. Although employers were expected to notify the Employment Service when a transfer occurred, there was no rush to do so, and the sugar companies were correct in assuming that since they were the employer, they could make decisions based on their needs—all of which fell under Walk's interpretation of constructive custody.

With little oversight of the various employers, pay fluctuations and irregular wages were common for Japanese Americans employed in agriculture. For those not accustomed to farm work, the impact of weather on wages was particularly frustrating, as many complained of the effect of "too much H_2O" during the rainy falls to be able to do any work outside, cutting into their expected wages.[134] While the inability to make agreed-on wages due to climate

patterns was beyond the employers' control, they would sometimes set unobtainable goals for compensation in the contract which went unnoticed by
laborers without planting or harvesting experience.

Mitsukane Kaneko wrote to Vernon Kennedy, chief of the Employment
Division at Poston, to explain how difficult he and his crew were finding their
work harvesting beets. The employer agreed to compensation per acre so long
as by the end of the harvest, everyone was able to harvest fourteen tons of
beets per acre. Kaneko remarked that "several boys who signed up . . . are actually turning out only two to four tons per acre," with the average being
well under fourteen tons.[135] "These boys are working from 6 A.M. when the
sun comes up to 6 P.M. when it gets dark and only making from 2–4 dollars
a day," Kaneko decried, with some making less than ten dollars for a week.[136]
When contracts were complete and the workers returned to their camps they
discovered that their wages for the same job paid by different employers varied significantly: some received only twenty cents an acre for harvesting beets
while others received upward of eighty cents or more.[137] Regulating wages
for men who were forced to pay for any dependents who remained in the
centers while they were in the fields was relatively easy for the Employment
Service and the WRA. Irregularity in wages for those without dependents,
however, often went unnoticed and uninspected by the Employment Service while they were burdened with other tasks related to wartime labor
needs.

The Army and the Problems of Agricultural Labor

Despite the problems Japanese Americans faced with their work in the beet
fields, other farmers and corporations clamored for access to their
labor—much to the annoyance of Bendetsen and DeWitt. Governor Culbert
Olson of California proved to be a thorn in the side of WCCA administrators because of his persistent requests for labor, which more often than not
resembled demands. Faced with a severe labor shortage in the summer of
1942, Olson requested that Japanese Americans be permitted to return to the
farming areas within Military Areas 1 and 2 to assist with the planting and
harvesting of crops come late summer and early fall.[138] After repeated rebuffs
from Bendetsen, who cited military necessity as well as a lack of troops available for guarding the prisoners in the work zones, Olson issued a statement
to California newspapers that accused DeWitt of "turning down his [Olson's]

suggestion that Japanese be allowed to work in California orchards and fields outside of the strategic military areas."[139]

DeWitt was not amused. "They [farmers in California] are applying it to the fruit crop, the pickle crop. I just got a message from Olson this morning again demanding to give furloughs to troops to pick crops. I won't do it," the general vented to Assistant Secretary of War John McCloy during a telephone call in early September.[140] When the yellow slips summarizing the daily headlines on incarceration came across DeWitt's desk on July 6, 1942, the commanding general was incensed and quickly dialed Bendetsen. "So, you see instead of saying I had refused to stop the evacuation, he put it the other way," DeWitt explained to Bendetsen while also suggesting that Olson was only pushing so hard because he needed political support from his constituents.[141] DeWitt's subordinate agreed and issued an official statement to Olson closing the case for good, but the damage was done. Bendetsen continued to receive requests for Japanese American labor from private farmers within and outside the military areas, including one who demanded that a "Jap labor draft" be instituted by the army to be able to supply workers against their will.[142]

Maintaining the optics of completely voluntary and free labor was at the forefront of DeWitt's and Bendetsen's minds when confronted with a labor shortage for harvesting long-staple cotton in southwestern Arizona. Stronger and more durable yet also more difficult to cultivate and harvest in the dusty soil of the southwest, long-staple, or pima, cotton was in high demand for many war products, including canvas cloth, but there was a severe shortage of labor in Arizona to harvest the prized plant. Ranchers who grew pima traditionally relied on migrant Mexican workers who crossed the border every late summer and early fall in search of temporary agricultural employment. However, diplomatic disagreements between Mexico and the United States—similar to those faced by beet growers—created a shortage in the number of Mexicans arriving in time for the rapidly approaching cotton harvest.[143] Having exhausted other options, including recruiting high school students and college men for the work, ranchers pressured their governor, Sidney Osborn, to request assistance from the government in the form of Japanese American labor. Osborn, still riding the high of securing a victory during the gubernatorial election of 1940 and hoping to secure another term, happily obliged and turned to DeWitt for help.[144]

DeWitt, however, was unconvinced of the necessity of releasing Japanese Americans for work in the cotton fields. First, unlike the Intermountain and

Great Plains regions, where Japanese Americans worked in the beet fields, southwestern Arizona (where the pima ranches were located) was well within the boundaries of both Military Areas 1 and 2. When Assistant Secretary of War John J. McCloy called DeWitt in early September following up on Osborn's requests, the general expressed his hesitation in allowing the release of Japanese Americans in Arizona. "I'd like to think about it a little while because it's putting them in an area we have just gotten them out of," DeWitt responded, referencing earlier concerns about the undermining of removal and incarceration as a military necessity among the public.[145] DeWitt was also unconvinced that pima cotton was an absolute military necessity since there was such an emphasis on sugar and other crops for supplying food to allies, troops, and other Japanese American prison camps.

Most importantly, DeWitt stressed the necessity of maintaining the appearance of voluntary and free Japanese American labor. Reports from the provost marshal general as well as German POWs themselves in agriculture confirmed that their conditions were acceptable under the Geneva Convention, but DeWitt feared that the Japanese government could respond negatively if even the American-born of Japanese descent were forcibly made to work. If Japanese Americans were to be released to work in the cotton fields, then military guards would be necessary to ensure order and control as the region was within the most vulnerable military areas. "If we put troops to guard them," DeWitt explained to McCloy, "then it will look like forced labor and we'll just have all sorts of difficulties," not limited to a potential public relations nightmare and retaliation from the Japanese if they found out that Japanese Americans were being forced to work while imprisoned. "I have insisted in every one of these labor questions that there be no tendency at all to apply forced labor methods," DeWitt reminded McCloy. And should he consider releasing Japanese Americans for this purpose, he would insist on prevailing wages and that recruitment be "purely voluntary."[146]

Unfortunately for DeWitt, his objections were unconvincing for War Department officials who believed that Japanese Americans should be released for work in Arizona. Secretary of War Henry Stimson caught wind of DeWitt's denial of the necessity of pima cotton to the war effort and wrote to DeWitt directly on September 12. "Long staple cotton is essential to the production of gliders, parachutes, balloons and certain other vital implements of war," Stimson informed, backed by data collected from surveys conducted by the War Manpower Commission describing the severe shortage of labor that threatened this vital crop. Although Stimson recognized and understood

DeWitt's hesitations based on free labor and the maintenance of the military necessity of EO 9066, he added, "The War Department, however, finds that the harvesting of long staple cotton at this time is an urgent military necessity and I inquire whether it may be feasible for you to make satisfactory arrangements whereby volunteer Japanese evacuee labor can be made available for the harvesting of this vital crop."[147] Seeing that he ultimately had little say in the matter, DeWitt conceded to the demands of the War Department. He may have been the commander of the Western Defense Command, but other agencies and officials consistently questioned DeWitt's designs for security and preparedness, particularly with regard to Japanese American incarceration.

On September 15, 1942, DeWitt issued General Order 17, allowing Japanese Americans from the Gila River camp in southwestern Arizona to leave and work for private ranchers in Pima County. With the military maneuvers for allowing such an act established, Bendetsen worked with the WRA to ensure that the army would have as little to do with this employment system as possible and also to ensure that Japanese Americans were afforded the same rights and regulations as those who left to work in the beet fields. The US Employment Service would once again serve as broker between the WRA and the private ranchers. The main difference between the setup with cotton and the system established for beet labor was the extent to which the WRA was involved in the care of the Japanese Americans employed. Rather than the ranchers being held solely responsible for the Japanese Americans, the WRA would assume some responsibility. Because Pima County was located in military zones, Japanese Americans who volunteered to work in cotton harvesting would be relocated to tent camps closer to the fields and would be recruited from there rather than directly from the Gila River camp. Also, while Governor Osborn agreed to enlist local law enforcement to ensure that those Japanese Americans who did go to work for private ranchers were protected, Bendetsen was forced to use troops associated with the Southern Frontier Command to guard the area around the delimited zones in Military Areas 1 and 2 where Japanese Americans would work—a responsibility that Bendetsen detested.[148]

Recruiting Japanese Americans for work in the cotton fields proved to be a disaster. DeWitt, Osborn, and the Employment Service initially estimated that between five thousand and seven thousand Japanese Americans would volunteer, particularly after DeWitt issued another civilian order (number 22) that extended the delimited areas to Maricopa, Pinal, and Yuma Counties. However, the hot weather, and the odd distribution of wages earned by Japanese

Americans into a community trust fund from which payments for each worker would be disbursed after the WRA deducted allotments for food and housing (in essence forcing Japanese Americans to cover the costs of their own incarceration), were not enticing. Despite the challenges, approximately 283 Japanese Americans engaged in a short-lived "noble experiment" of working for private cotton ranchers under the guard of troops from the Southern Frontier Command. In a few months, however, it became evident that the costs to the army to quarter troops in the region for overseeing the Japanese American employees far outweighed the economic benefits to the war cause and the private ranchers. On November 6, 1942, DeWitt issued a memo to the chief of staff of the army citing "the negligible response of the Japanese evacuees, for whatever reasons" to the cotton project as well as the requirement of "18 officers and 657 enlisted men of this command to control the areas wherein evacuees are employed" as justifications for formally ending the cotton program, as the "loss of combat training" for the men was too high of a cost.[149]

Following the failed cotton-harvesting program, some openly blamed the Japanese Americans for failing to answer the call of duty when needed to supply private employers with labor. Earl Maharg, executive secretary of the Arizona State Farm Bureau Federation, claimed that "failure to obtain sufficient volunteers from the Relocation Center at Parker and Gila River is an attempt at sabotage on the part of the Japanese and that this action is obstructing the war effort." Maharg followed up with a comment to the *Los Angeles Times* expressing his frustration with the lack of interest of the Japanese American prisoners, saying that they were sabotaging the war effort and "obstructing the winning of the war." DeWitt was not pleased and issued a memo to the Civil Affairs Division of the WRA, responsible for public relations, asking it to watch this situation carefully and see that there "was no pressure being brought to bear on the Japanese in these Relocation Centers to force them to work." "Publicity of this kind is dangerous," DeWitt explained, "and indicates a leaning toward forced labor. While I do not want to recognize this statement publicly, I do want the situation carefully watched to see that recruiting efforts in the camps for Japanese cotton pickers in Arizona do not take on a pressure tinge."[150] Maintaining the optics of voluntary and free labor was a crucial goal for the army and the WRA while the United States waged a war against fascism and tyranny. But ensuring readily available labor at an affordable price for private employers was also part of the war effort and military necessity of incarceration, creating exploitative conditions for many who signed up for pay or other reasons. As Maharg's comment demonstrates, Japanese Americans were aware that their loyalty was tied to their labor—an idea that the Employment Service as well as the WRA reminded them of constantly while the agencies placed them in employment situations that were far from free.

By the fall of 1942, the agricultural furlough program for Japanese Americans was a staple of Work Corps employment options. As Japanese Americans were once again moved from the detention centers to their more permanent prison camps, private agricultural employment continued to provide some money and some freedom. For farmers and corporations, Japanese American labor often became a crucial component of their operations and helped them to meet the demands placed upon them by the government and the army.

All was not well, however, and the furlough program showed signs of distress as more Japanese Americans became dissatisfied and downright angry about the exploitative nature of their employment. Farmers in Colorado who hired Japanese Americans to help with the beet harvest were appalled when the prisoners began to demand "better living accommodations than Mexican [laborers] would be satisfied with," including "shower baths and other conveniences."[151] They also refused to work in fields "which were very muddy or had a low yield, apparently feeling that they were in a position of choice as to where and under what conditions they wanted to work."[152] Other incarcerees challenged the notion that they had little say in whom they contracted their services with and flouted the Employment Service and military policy by picking up and leaving in search of another employer (a move which ultimately ended in their return to the camp they came from) or demanding more pay and a shorter workday in the fields.[153] Once the Jerome and Rohwer camps in Arkansas were opened in October and November 1942 (respectively), local farmers turned to imprisoned Japanese Americans for help in completing small-scale irrigation systems on their Delta farms or helping with crop diversification there. Japanese Americans who voluntarily signed up for these jobs expressed similar annoyances with their positions and engaged in similar demands for better pay, working conditions, and freedoms, prompting locals to even suggest to the WRA that "the Government ought to permit the exploitation of the evacuees at low wages, since they were war prisoners and a burden to the taxpayers."[154] The outright calls for exploitation, the conflations of Japanese prisoners of war with American-born citizens of Japanese descent, and the haphazard and risky attempts of the Japanese American prisoners to engage in negotiations over their contracts reveal the complications of the WRA's employment system. Approaching Japanese Americans as units of production beholden to the notion of constructive custody also belied the rhetoric of the WRA that laborers were free and productive "pioneer" farmers in the detainment centers and prison camps.

The problems for the WRA and its management of Japanese Americans (which increasingly fell under scrutiny as rumors of "coddling" the prisoners circulated following Dillon Myers's assumption of the position of director of the WRA after Eisenhower's departure in June 1942) did not end in the fields. In January 1943, the *New York Times* picked up a story of chaos among the prisoners at Jerome who had "turned the camp into a nest of sabotage and unrest" while engaging in slowdowns and walkouts. Like other camps, those at Jerome were expected to join the Work Corps and engage in farming, construction, maintenance, and other general day-to-day tasks in addition to constructing irrigation ditches and clearing trees for land development. While greatly exaggerated in the news descriptions from New York to Milwaukee, Japanese American lumber workers at Jerome did indeed engage in multiple strikes and protests against the often dangerous working conditions and corresponding low pay. One prisoner, Haruji Ego, had died when a trailer carrying woodcutters overturned, prompting others working on the project to call for a strike unless camp director Paul A. Taylor—notorious for his callousness toward workers—resigned.[155]

The labor protests and strikes at Jerome were far from isolated incidents as the removal and imprisonment of Japanese Americans continued after 1942. Repeatedly, in the detention centers or the prison camps, WRA administrators were faced with challenges by Japanese Americans who refused to tacitly accept their new positions as prison laborers with few rights and unable to negotiate their own employment terms. Tensions grew between WRA leaders, who viewed the Work Corps as voluntary and reasonable work to bolster morale and provide aid for the war effort, and the Japanese Americans themselves, who argued that the work they were often coerced to perform violated their civil and labor rights. As a result, both parties edged toward showdowns at the various camps over a "free" system of labor that was often anything but free.

CHAPTER 3

═══════

"Worse Than Prisoners"

Labor Resistance in the Detention Centers and Prison Camps

By August 1943, the Tule Lake prison camp near the California-Oregon border was a site of labor unrest. A sit-down strike among Japanese American prisoners working in the agricultural department of the camp resulted in an estimated loss of a "million and a half dollars' worth or more of crops," including potatoes, onions, cabbage, carrots, broccoli, "and all that sort of stuff that could be used by the Army," Colonel Verne Austin (commander of the 752nd Military Police Battalion at Tule Lake) noted during a phone conversation with his colleague Colonel Moffitt.[1] Both men were part of the military attachment assigned to Tule Lake once the WRA declared the camp to be a "segregation" center earlier in July. A segregation designation meant that thousands of "disloyal" Japanese Americans from other prison camps who responded incorrectly to a questionnaire designed to gauge loyalty to the United States and willingness to serve in the armed forces were detained in Tule Lake. Some responded in ways that made their loyalty appear questionable on purpose as a means of protest; others (particularly Issei) answered incorrectly as a result of confusion. Many refused to answer the questionnaire at all. Shortly thereafter, the WRA identified Tule Lake (which held the largest number of "disloyal" Japanese Americans based on their survey responses) as a maximum-security camp. What the WRA, Tule Lake director Raymond Best (who developed a reputation for inhumanity and harshness toward the Japanese Americans at Tule Lake), and the army overlooked, however, was the fact that the 3,500 new Japanese American arrivals to Tule

Lake included known labor organizers and leaders. Or, as Austin referred to them, "the bad boys from Topaz and Manzanar" who had been "agitating in the camp" since their arrival, trying to "get control" of the prison.[2] The "bad boys," who were experienced with protesting working conditions, arrived at a time when other prisoners at Tule Lake were also demanding their rights as laborers. Tensions flared at Tule Lake between prisoners and administrators throughout the summer. Later, a sit-down strike (termed a "riot" by the press and the WRA) became part of a system-wide wave of labor protests that had been growing since 1942.

Living and working conditions in the prison camps were inseparable; when Japanese Americans cried out against the abnormal carceral space they inhabited, they protested both. Resistance was difficult but not impossible.[3] Japanese American expressions of dissatisfaction with their labor conditions and acts of resistance to the violations of their civil rights ranged from the mundane to the tragic. At the Fresno detention center in California, Japanese American editors of the *Grapevine* scolded thieves who had stolen both materials from the mess hall and "government equipment" needed to finish maintenance and construction jobs. A report also noted that at Fresno, "several people have lost their minds. One was shot trying to escape . . . through the barbed wire."[4] Other Japanese Americans refused to report for work assignments. There were also those who lashed out, as in the case of a Japanese American man from Tule Lake who had a pass to travel into town as a part of his construction duties. When faced with a local who asked if he was Japanese and why he was outside the camp, he exclaimed "You're damn right I am!' and asked "What are you going to do about it?" right before he punched the local and "knocked out his false teeth."[5] Still others, such as one Japanese American member of the timber clearance crew at the Jerome prison camp, committed suicide.[6]

Japanese Americans also orchestrated large-scale protests, such as the strike on Tuesday, June 16, 1942, at the Santa Anita detention center (a former racetrack) in Arcadia, California, where they awaited transfer to a prison camp. Approximately 1,500 Issei, Nisei, and Kibei out of 18,719 detainees worked as weavers and boxers for sixteen dollars and eight dollars a month (respectively) at an on-site camouflage net factory operated by a private contractor. A delay in pay, unsanitary work conditions, and a general sense of exploitation among those employed in camouflage netting came to a head when 1,200 net workers walked off the job. The director of the Santa Anita center, Russell Amory (a former Work Projects Administration leader), was flabbergasted. No one forced the Japanese American detainees to work. The administration paid for their labor per the directives of the Work Projects Authority (the agency initially placed in charge of employment at the centers) and provided them with thirty-minute breaks during the workday. Yet, for reasons unknown to Amory, these Japanese American industrial workers joined 847,000 American workers who went on strike nationwide in 1942.[7]

These incarceree laborers, viewing themselves as wrongfully imprisoned American citizens, demanded their rights to a safe work environment, adequate pay, and more control over hours and working conditions. Their insistence on workers' rights and resistance to their imprisonment clashed with the belief of WRA and WCCA officials that Japanese Americans were free laborers with good pay and good jobs. Japanese Americans temporarily held at Santa Anita lacked a WCCA-sanctioned form of self-governance, though they did organize informal evacuee councils to handle day-to-day business and some interaction with the predominantly white administrators. The evacuee councils differed from the more detailed and organized governing system (which consisted of labor groups designed to report to and negotiate with administrators) implemented by the WRA in the prison camps. For the army, self-governance was unnecessary for a temporary stay in the detention centers when order and control were the primary concerns. Japanese Americans who went on strike at Santa Anita did so with no clear path to approach the administration without a formally recognized and representative body, unlike the incarcerees at the permanent prison camps. Nonetheless, the administration at Santa Anita faced the challenges of managing and controlling a prison workforce when confronted by the camouflage net workers.[8]

The events at Santa Anita were indicative of the tense labor relationships that became commonplace by the end of 1942. WCCA and later WRA officials saw themselves as managing voluntary workers while the Japanese American employees resisted their new identities as prison laborers. These conflicting perspectives challenged the prison labor system in wartime incarceration. Shortly after the camouflage net workers walked off the job at Santa Anita, strikes in the mess halls soon followed, indicating that maintaining order in the detention centers and within the larger system of wartime incarceration would prove challenging. The incident at Santa Anita was a prison labor strike, despite the WCCA's descriptions of work stoppage as a "riot" or period of vague "unrest." Japanese Americans informed the state that they would contest violations of civil and labor rights through their resistance in all of its manifest forms.

The camouflage net strikers at Santa Anita proved that labor would serve as a catalyst for protests in the prison camps, including the Manzanar "riot" of 1942. WCCA officials, military leaders, and later WRA administrators debated who was responsible for quelling labor disturbances and what was to be done with Japanese Americans who went on strike or otherwise interfered with wartime production. Strikes and protests at Santa Anita, Manzanar, and other camps prompted administrators to examine the root causes of labor disputes (believing that they were caused by psychological trauma or inherent racial characteristics and traits) and develop plans to prevent future disturbances.

The explanations administrators and military officials offered for understanding the Santa Anita protest and later strikes at Manzanar rested on the simple theory that supposed disloyal saboteurs used strikes to undermine the war effort. Such theories, however, clashed with the arguments of Japanese Americans in their demands for workers' rights and recognition of their loyalty. The camp administrators' definition of free labor was a far cry from that of Japanese Americans who fought for their rights to negotiation and to enumerate grievances.

From Prison to Factory

Thousands of Japanese Americans from the Los Angeles area arrived at the Santa Anita detention center in the nearby city of Arcadia, to the northeast of the City of Angels, in the spring of 1942. On first glimpse, however, the former racetrack where Los Angelenos wagered on horses little resembled a habitable place for people. Japanese Americans debarked from the trains that took them in some cases only minutes from their homes and waited in line to receive their identification numbers and their belongings before finding their way to their assigned barracks. Refurbished horse stalls (where many reported that they could still see horsehair in the paint on the wooden walls) with cots served as crude lodgings prior to the completion of barracks. "Streets" named after great racehorses like Man O' War and Seabiscuit divided Santa Anita into smaller neighborhoods. Dining was a communal experience in large mess halls, as was using the bathroom—detainees were forced to share spartan outdoor latrines before proper sewage systems were installed. One incarcerated woman recalled "fences and searchlights" on her first night at Santa Anita, noting that her family of four shared a small room with four cots and nothing else. She slept by the window and was constantly woken up throughout the night by the searchlight from the guard tower sweeping throughout the detention center.[9] Santa Anita was so hastily transformed into a detainment center that sewage and trash from the mess halls and latrines created a horrible stench that detainees remembered for years.[10] Even Thomas Holland, head of the Employment Division of the WRA, and Dillon Myer, soon to be director of the WRA, were "horrified" by the conditions they encountered on an inspection tour of several of the detention centers and suggested that the "evacuees should be removed as soon as possible [to prison camps] because these centers were not normal places to live and were not good from any standpoint."[11] Santa Anita's conditions were similar to those of the other fourteen detention centers (two of which—Manzanar and Poston—would become permanent prison camps) and characterized a sprawling, temporary detention system designed to accommodate forcibly removed Japanese Americans.

Descriptions of the prison-like conditions that Japanese Americans lived under in Santa Anita also filtered out to the public through the media. Methodist missionary Charles Iglehart visited the detention center in early June 1942 and recorded his views of Santa Anita and incarceration more generally in an article published in the *Nation*. Iglehart was skeptical that forced removal was required for the protection of Japanese Americans, and he could not "escape the conclusion that even as a war measure evacuation was unnecessary."[12] Upon his visit to Santa Anita, Iglehart's suspicions were confirmed by the "citizens behind barbed wires" that he encountered at the converted racetrack and fairgrounds. Iglehart described the sparse conditions and restrictions on prisoner movement and argued that "pressure should be brought to bear upon the federal government to discontinue the assembly centers as a way of dealing with the problem of [Japanese American] removal."[13]

In addition to the spartan features of confinement, the American Civil Liberties Union (ACLU) objected to the "prison rules" which detainees lived under at Santa Anita. An August 1942 article published in the ACLU's *Union News* periodical argued that "virtual prison conditions have been established in the Japanese American assembly centers operated by the Army's Wartime Civilian Control Administration."[14] Japanese Americans were "not only detained for unlimited time without trial or hearing in concentration camps guarded by soldiers, but conditions have gradually been imposed in the Centers that make a mockery of the liberties guaranteed under the Bill of

Rights."[15] The article cited "Hitleresque" controls over gatherings among detainees at Santa Anita, including regulations requiring requests for meetings to be submitted in writing to the camp directors and that "one or more Caucasian American citizens representing the management must be present at all meetings to act as observers," as well as restrictions on printed material and censorship of camp newspapers.[16]

The bleak conditions at Santa Anita led to mounting boredom and depression among detainees, with many taking advantage of temporary labor "opportunities" to help the days go by. Initially, "work" meant the tasks required for the day-to-day functions of the center. The WCCA expected the centers to be as self-sufficient as possible, with incarcerees completing every chore from teaching to trash removal as overseen by both Japanese American and white supervisors. Laborers at Santa Anita and the other detention centers who wanted to work enrolled in the Work Corps, a complicated labor arrangement based on "cash advances" in amounts of twelve, sixteen, and nineteen dollars a month (based on skill) that WCCA administrators dispersed after tallying the total expenses for the centers at the end of the year and subtracting savings from duties performed by the workers. Members of the Work Corps also would have the opportunity to work in agriculture. After the needs of the center were met, surplus products were sold to the military and the public. If a profit resulted from these sales, the laborers received their advances. Initially, those who were eligible for joining the Work Corps but refused would be charged twenty dollars a month to cover basics provided by the WCCA, but Dillon Myer dropped this provision after assuming the position of director in mid-June. WCCA administers would take into consideration any previous employment and occupations of the detainees and line them up with similar jobs, though it was understood that the center directors could use them wherever they were needed—regardless of skill or experience. The WRA dissolved the Work Corps program as initially designed by December 1942, substituting straight wages for cash advances, but those at Santa Anita in the spring of 1942 operated under the original corps conditions.[17]

If a detainee did agree to work, the WCCA issued strict guidelines for ensuring maximum efficiency in daily operations. For example, intentionally or even unintentionally interfering with the smooth functioning of the centers meant that an employee was sabotaging the security of the center as well as the United States war effort. In general, "any stoppage of work by individuals or as a group," preventing or attempting to prevent another employee from working, "deliberately or willfully destroying or mutilating government

property," and/or not carrying out their job duties as specified by the "Caucasian supervisors" (although there would be Japanese American supervisors,
as well) was a violation of Public Law 503. This decree reinforced EO 9066
by making actions that disrupted camp life in any way criminal offenses pun-
ishable by up to a year in prison.[18]

Nevertheless, Japanese Americans often took advantage of labor opportunities in the centers. In a letter to the director of the Puyallup center in
Washington State, a group of Japanese Americans petitioned for "more labor
projects or working parties either within or without the center," "more stan-
dardized work schedules," and generally "more projects to choose from." The
prisoners desired "to do some more productive work for America . . . while
it is crying for more manpower." "There is nothing better to find comfort,
consolation, and relief in at this time than in work. To work productively
should not be our only desire, but, also, the nation's demand," the petitioners declared.[19] Work provided purpose for the incarcerated in this case and,
as they noted, also contributed to easing American labor demands during
the war. Many still held fast to their identities as patriotic American workers
with useful skills. By June, approximately 30 percent of Santa Anita's population were working (at its height, 12,919 Japanese Americans were detained
there), with most working in the mess hall and in other services to the center.

The WCCA soon realized that Japanese Americans' willingness to work
could be used to meet the need for low-cost war materials. The WCCA suggested in a March 1942 memo that "a variety of work projects should be established to absorb further employment of both men and women"; in
particular, "the production of underclothes, fatigues, bags, and other sewing
projects would not only meet the needs of the evacuees, but for other purposes as well." Through these projects, "[Japanese Americans] could do great
many kinds of work for the armed services." According to another official,
the creation of more work projects would not only supply labor and materials for the armed forces but also limit the "number of able-bodied nonworkers" in the center.[20]

In May 1942, the administrators of Santa Anita followed suggestions from
the army and the WCCA on using Japanese American labor and established
a camouflage net-making program under the guidance of the WCCA. Used
for a variety of purposes by all branches of the military, camouflage netting
was a crucial product, but one that was labor-intensive because the process
was not mechanized.[21] Skilled laborers were required to handcraft the nets
by weaving together large pieces of nylon while using fencing for support and

draping. Manufacturing centers had little incentive to hire workers to make the nets when there were more profitable government contracts to be found in the production of planes, guns, ships, and other military items.

Members of the Office of Production initially contemplated two options for the organization and control of net production in the centers. The first was a system operated under WCCA sponsorship, or a completely WCCA-driven program, with the agency having control and directly receiving pay from the military for distribution to the Japanese American laborers—taking into consideration the cost of maintenance of the centers.[22] The second option consisted of contracts with manufacturers resulting in the private employer, the center (the WCCA), and the incarcerees receiving wages, or a portion of the profits after selling the netting to the military—the center and the private manufacturers reaping the most benefits. Although laws had been in effect since the 1930s to ensure that cheap goods made by prisoners would not flood the market and create unfair competition, and despite Attorney General Francis Biddle's 1940 release of Circular 3591 (which prohibited convict leasing to private employers), the use of Japanese American laborers in wartime production was not deemed illegal nor was the use of inmates more generally.[23] Ultimately, the WCCA agreed to invite private contractors to establish "netting factories" in the centers employing Japanese Americans. The contractor prospered from the use of cheap labor and access to a ready consumer (the military), while the WCCA issued payment in the form of cash advances. These advances were used to purchase goods such as clothing and specialty foods from canteens, reducing the costs of the detention centers and subsistence costs for the incarcerees.[24]

And what benefits did Japanese Americans derive from this labor relationship? The WRA established a wage system because of its adherence to the WPA wage scale. When the administrators welcomed John Stahl, a private contractor from Los Angeles, into Santa Anita in May 1942, the WCCA set wages of sixteen dollars per month for the skilled weavers and twelve or eight dollars for other unskilled laborers (packers and cleaners for example).[25] The Army Corps of Engineers regulated the relationship between the contractor and the incarcerated employees and determined the appropriate profits, as the army was the customer. However, Japanese Americans technically worked directly for the contractor and not for the WCCA or the army (by the summer, camouflage net workers would work directly for the WRA at prison camps like Manzanar and Poston). The incarcerees received their pay from the contractor, but the WCCA (through the US Employment Service) distributed the monthly wages. White supervisors employed by the WCCA oversaw the production of netting in the centers and selected some Japanese Americans for positions as assistant managers with additional pay. Factory workers entered into sixty-day contracts (renewable based on performance and need), and those who could not perform their full duties (for any reason) would pay six dollars a month for room and board. State laws technically applied to laborers in terms of safety depending on where the centers were located (the enforcement of these laws was arbitrary and difficult to track), but employees who worked in netting were forced to waive their right to file for workers' compensation in the event of injury.[26]

In addition to establishing the basic parameters of operating a factory inside a detention center, administrators and army officials were preoccupied with questions of which incarcerees were eligible for war-related work. Santa Anita held both American citizens and foreign-born Japanese nationals, creating initial confusion as to whether or not Japanese "enemy aliens" could be employed in war work. The deputy provost marshal general Colonel Archer Lerch and Santa Anita director Russell Amory even questioned in a memo to Colonel Bendetsen if "Japanese internees *who are citizens* could be employed in making camo nets without their consent, and without pay."[27] Bendetsen did not respond to the request to force Japanese American citizens to work, but he did address other scenarios. Because camouflage netting was a war material, Bendetsen and his assistant, Colonel I. K. Evans, informed Amory that "it is not possible to use aliens on net production," and R. L. Nicholson (chief of the Reception Center Division under the WCCA) followed up by advising that "Japanese aliens may be assigned to perform work on the boxing of camo nets, but shall not under any circumstances be employed in any operation directly connected with the weaving of the nets themselves."[28] Bendetsen and Evans went further in advising Amory to simply abandon the idea of using aliens in any capacity on the net project and to "place these aliens in work [in daily maintenance on the camp] now being performed by American Japanese and in turn move these American Japanese to the net project."[29] In doing so, using only citizens in the production of netting would become a matter of "force put," meaning that the managers of Santa Anita could have complete authority over the incarcerated laborers and required "no further comment" from any other agency beside the Army Corps of Engineers or the WCCA. Using Japanese American citizens as prison labor was more convenient than employing enemy aliens, as Japanese American imprisonment was part of EO 9066 and required less oversight and protection of rights. The Geneva Convention protected Japanese nationals but not American citizens. In the end, the WRA agreed to employ nationals as well, but only in the boxing of nets at eight dollars a month.

With the basic questions answered as to who could labor and under what circumstances, Santa Anita became an experiment in employing imprisoned Japanese Americans in net manufacturing. If all went well, the WCCA and WRA planned to install similar operations at the Manzanar prison camp and the Tanforan and Sacramento detention centers. Shipments of nylon and other materials required in net production arrived at Santa Anita after May 15, 1942, and the overall production line included laborers unpacking the raw materials, others garnishing and weaving, and Japanese nationals repacking the nets for shipment to eastern depots.[30] Nets that were thirty-six by forty-four feet in size were in high demand in the military, with a projected requirement of 33,500 nets in total for the remainder of 1942. The planning branch of the WCCA, however, was far more optimistic. They estimated that by using Japanese American prison labor, the detention centers could produce closer to 225,000 nets, with each weaver producing approximately one thousand feet of netting in a day. Typically, approximately two hours were required for the construction of smaller nets and twenty-five hours for the construction of each larger net. Even then, WCCA officials believed "that the above time estimate will be decreased considerably by [utilizing] Japanese labor."[31]

By early June 1942, the net project was well underway. When the Personnel Division announced the need for at least 650 laborers on May 27, workers immediately signed up for the job. By the first week, over a thousand detainees (including both men and women, American citizens and Japanese nationals) enlisted for the work and the project was "operating at full capacity." Nicholson, chief of the Reception and Induction Division of the WCCA, noted in an early report that "the overall response on the project has been gratifying" but also warned that "the success of the project will require full cooperation of the entire center population."[32]

The Santa Anita Strike

Santa Anita administrators soon discovered how difficult it was to maintain full support for the project among the prisoners. For most of early June, operations at the net factory "hummed along merrily" with few complaints from either the laborers or their managers, but this quiet obscured growing

Figure 6. A group of Japanese Americans working at the camouflage net factory at the Santa Anita detention center. Photo by the US Army Signal Corps, 1942. Courtesy of the Library of Congress.

unrest among the Japanese American workers.[33] When more than 1,200 workers went on strike at the net factory, the action caught the administrators off guard. But for the Japanese American laborers, the strike was a long time coming.

At 1 P.M. on Tuesday, June 16, 1942, workers initiated the strike. American-born Shuji Fujii (who was employed in the boxing division of the net factory) along with fellow American citizen Jotaro "George" Ban, Hawaiian-born Nisei Koji Ariyoshi, and Japanese national Shuji Matsui (all known for their more radical tendencies—particularly pushing for a Japanese-language newspaper at Santa Anita) organized the laborers—both foreign and American-born as well as incarcerees from Hawaii—in a peaceful walkout of the factory.[34] Considering that Fujii and the rest of the employees appeared to be relatively tolerant of their positions (although another contributor, Hawaii-born Ernest Wakayama, had proposed that the Spanish consulate investigate the poor conditions at Santa Anita), John Fitzpatrick, manager of the camouflage net project, was taken aback by the protest. Immediately after the workers walked off, Fitzpatrick phoned F. H. Arrowood, chief inspector of the Interior Police at Santa Anita, to inform him of the situation. Fitzpatrick had little information to offer except that the only reason Fujii (who became a de facto leader of the striking laborers) provided for the strike was that "they [Japanese Americans] did not like the sauerkraut which was served for the noontime meal."[35] Arrowood then compiled a report that he passed along to Major Ray Ashworth (chief of the Interior Security Branch of the WCCA) later that day, explaining that initially only a handful of workers followed Fujii, but later over a thousand also walked off the job and either returned to their living quarters or sat in the nearby racetrack grandstand, where they discussed their next steps. Arrowood noted that the demonstration was peaceful and orderly with no physical violence or damage done to any equipment or netting. In fact, by June 18, 75 percent of the workers who had walked off the job were reported to be back at work and making up for lost time in meeting their production goals.[36] Internal police and FBI agents arrested and interrogated Shuji Fujii and his American and foreign-born associates and placed their names on a list for transfer to a more secure facility.[37]

News coverage of the strike reflected the unalarming reports provided by director Russell Amory to journalists. On June 18, the *Madera Times* reported that "eight hundred Japanese who stopped work on an assembly center project, reportedly over the serving of sauerkraut for dinner, reportedly were back on the job today." The article supported the administration's claims that there was "no clear cut explanation of the sit down strike" among the Japanese Americans and that the unrest "might have begun by agitators at the center." Other newspapers referred to the strike as the work of "troublemakers" such as Fujii and others. Although unreported at the time, long-standing conflicts between Nisei Kay Sugihara, who recruited Japanese Americans to work in netting, and Fujii, who blamed Sugihara for the poor working conditions of the employees, also played a role in the lead-up to the strike. However, the standard narrative of the strike was established: subversives like Fujii capitalized on misgivings about mess hall food and created a chaotic and ultimately unsuccessful attempt at a riot to undermine the war effort (ironic as Fujii was a noted Communist and dedicated to the American war effort because of his political affiliation).[38]

While the initial cause of the strike was attributed to displeasure over lunch, further investigation by the FBI and center police revealed more sweeping demands among the laborers. At 9:30 A.M. on June 17, Amory met with representatives of the workers to discuss the strike and later attended a meeting with Fitzpatrick and Arrowood where they analyzed the protest and "all concurred on one thing—that Shuji Fujii was the instigator and leader of the strikes."[39] Fujii did not protest this accusation and admitted to distributing a petition among Japanese Americans to demand the right to publish a Japanese-language newspaper. A member of the Japanese American auxiliary police unit (a group established by the WCCA to promote greater self-policing and trust among the incarcerated, and staffed by a majority of English-speaking Nisei) discovered the petition. The auxiliary police also discovered a pamphlet in multiple barracks encouraging protest among the Japanese Americans employed in net making. The police argued that Fujii and his collaborators were the ones responsible for the pamphlet. The FBI obtained the original document and used it to build a case against Fujii for federal offenses of subversion and sabotage.

The fact that it was Fujii, an American citizen, who was identified as the man behind the circulated pamphlet prompted the center administrators to argue that this was the work of a disloyal prisoner rather than a protest by a loyal citizen. A close reading of it, however, suggests that this was more than an instigation by a subversive individual; it was an American's protest against labor injustice and civil rights violations. The pamphlet, addressed to "Nisei Camouflage Workers," listed grievances of the workers as well as some demands. The author identified Nisei net workers as "loyal for America" but then questioned why they remained loyal considering that they were asked to "sacrifice themselves in . . . service" while in the centers at the expense of their health, a necessity for a "nation's future" as well as "survival." Loyalty to their country was something to be proud of, but not when they risked their well-being to make camouflage nets under the hazardous conditions further outlined in the pamphlet. "Well, do you understand what you are doing now? You are working in the poisonous factory without medical or hygienic protection."[40] Indeed, employees in the net factory did not have proper face protection and inhaled fibers and dust particles that sent some to the infirmary with persistent coughing that produced mucus and blood. Crude masks fashioned from discarded bandages were eventually made available for those workers who requested them, but they offered inadequate protection. Later, weavers at other centers and camps without gloves often complained of blisters and sores on their hands.[41] The contractors evaded responsibility for the medical risks at the factory.

Beyond health issues, the pamphlet also compared the detained Japanese Americans working in the net factory to imprisoned criminals. "Formerly, camouflage work has been done by prisoners of state penitentiaries. <u>BUT</u> they quit. You know why? Yes! Because it is unhygienic work for even prisoners." Although inmates at San Quentin State Penitentiary in California were put to work making anti-submarine nets beginning in 1942, there is no indication that they were ever used in camouflage net making or that they protested the work. Regardless, this did not stop the author from further comparing Japanese Americans at Santa Anita to "common" prisoners. "Well, where do you stand? Is the value of our life [sic] as Japanese American citizens cheaper than state prisoners?" The author drew a sharp distinction between the "cheapness" of Japanese Americans and the higher valuation of state prisoners. A rumor that camouflage net work had been rejected by San Quentin and pushed onto the detainees by the WCCA was enough to spark comparisons between the treatment of Japanese American citizens and criminals. They were performing labor that was not only beneath them but practically forced upon them. "Where is DEMOCRACY? There is no democracy for [the] Japanese race, even if we are born in this country—first we are in camp, now we are worse than prisoners." The author linked the unhealthy labor performed by Japanese Americans in the net factory to a slippery slope of exploitation. Initially, they had been detained for security purposes, but now—being coerced to labor for the military, the government, and a private contractor—they were "worse" than prisoners as they had committed no crime yet their loyalty was questioned.[42]

Yamato Ichihashi, a Stanford University professor detained at Santa Anita, maintained detailed accounts of his time at the center in diaries and letters and identified the causes of the strike, many which corroborated those in the pamphlet. Writing to a friend immediately after the strike, Ichihashi explained that "the newspapers made a joke of it, saying that the workers objected to sauerkraut served at lunch . . . this is a lie." Ichihashi emphasized the coercion that accompanied recruitment for work in netting. "First, the workers are supposed to [be] volunteers, but [were] 'drafted' by the application of high pressures," he explained. He then listed the "immediate causes" of the strike, including the small portions served at lunch, the "hot, dusty, and poisonous" conditions at the net factory, and the fact that laborers had "not received a penny" for their netting work and others employed on different projects had gone almost two months without their pay.[43]

Despite the ideological objections to working in the net factory, the author of the pamphlet did not wish to see the factory removed. Rather, he or she listed "demands" that the Japanese Americans should make to the administration if they desired more profits and an end to the strike. At the top of the list were a four-hour workday and "regular Army pay, $41 a month," (the amount paid to a regular enlisted soldier after adjustments by Congress in 1942) followed by "special medical protection for this type of work" and "medically-approved masks." If the demands were not met, the workers knew what to do: "S-T-R-I-K-E." The Japanese Americans—like Fujii—employed in the camouflage netting factory withheld their labor during a temporary walkout to demonstrate the power they held to disrupt production, but they chose to return to work in order to prove their loyalty to the United States. The net workers (many of whom were Nisei who held the higher-paying weaving positions) protested labor injustice during the walkout while also showcasing their dedication to the war cause when they decided to resume their jobs. They created a dilemma for the center administrators, who sought to maintain order and productivity without appearing to further punish imprisoned Japanese American citizens or force them to labor.

The complaints and demands listed in the pamphlet were also echoed among the Japanese Americans who met with members of the administration (including Amory) in the immediate days after the strike. On June 19, the *Santa Anita Pacemaker* (the WCCA-supported and censored paper published by detainees) reported on the meeting between Amory and the strikers. Amory addressed workers from in front of the grandstand on the racetrack and dismissed many of the concerns from the protest, particularly that Japanese American prisoners were being taken advantage of by both the center administration and the private contractors. "This project is part of the war effort," Amory reminded them, "the American Army needs these nets quickly." Therefore, "in time of war, in a combat area, anyone found agitating is subject to fine and imprisonment . . . any agitation from now on will not be tolerated." Amory chalked up the strike to the "rumor-mongering of subversives" who were looking to undermine the war effort and maintained that it was actually "a very small portion of workers who wanted to go on strike." Most importantly, Amory stressed that despite what some might think, "there is absolutely no exploitation of Japanese labor by private interests."[44] Amory conceded that forming employment committees could potentially help in opening up lines of communication between management and the workers, but ultimately he (and others in the administration) viewed the strike as less of a labor protest and more the work of disloyal agitators and subversives who capitalized on the frustration of the incarcerated. This interpretation ran counter to the demands of the Japanese Americans for workers' rights. Although the strike ended, the discrepancies between how the administration and the prisoners interpreted the walkout shaped the legal response for punishing the leaders of the protest, both foreign and American-born.

Treason or Strike? Punishments for Labor Leaders at Santa Anita

While the strike was quickly resolved, WCCA administrators and FBI officials believed that punishments for the suspected leaders of the walkout should be meted out as quickly as possible. United States commissioner David B. Head arraigned five Santa Anita "troublemakers" on June 25, including those directly associated with the strike and others described by the FBI as subversive for holding secret meetings in Japanese.[45] Considering the recent labor unrest, any action that was in violation of center rules would be scrutinized going forward. Fujii and Ban (the supposed leaders of the strike) were charged with "conspiring to circulate a petition in the center demanding publication of a Japanese language newspaper," and they were held at the Tuna Canyon detention center in Tujunga, California, while they awaited their July hearing. But the larger issue for the WCCA and the military was the strike itself.

Because administrators at Santa Anita largely refused to acknowledge the reasons for the strike provided by the incarcerees, arguments that the walk-out was a product of disloyalty and subversion pervaded discussions of punishment. Initially, Bendetsen suggested to General DeWitt that the strike violated certain state laws in California relating to defense and security during the war. Attempting to prosecute the leaders of the strike under state codes appeared to be the easiest way to deliver punishments and send a message to other incarcerees, but Lieutenant William Boekel, Bendetsen's assistant, was not convinced. Though Boekel was unable to speak directly to attorney general of California Earl Warren, he did speak with Warren's assistant, chief deputy Robert W. Harrison, who explained that "in his offhand opinion . . . there is no offense against the State of California, and no offense against any citizen of the State of California." Instead, "the offense, if any, is one against the sovereignty of the Federal Government, namely, a violation of the custodial authority of the Army."[46] Harrison recommended that Bendetsen contact both Warren and the US attorney general "requesting the opinion on the facts of this case in order that the groundwork may be laid for prompt action in other or similar cases."[47]

DeWitt wrote to Warren in late June arguing that the Japanese American citizens should be punished harshly for violating a number of laws and statutes designed to protect the United States during times of war. Despite the large number of workers involved, DeWitt viewed the "so-called sit-down strike" not as a collective action taken by all of the workers to demand better conditions and pay but rather an act of sabotage "induced by certain leaders . . . for the purpose of interfering with, or at least cutting downtime total production of camouflage nets for the use of the Army."[48] From this perspective, the strike went above and beyond violating the prohibition on such activities in the centers; the walkout was an act of subversion that deserved to be addressed by both federal officials and courts rather than simply by the administration at Santa Anita.

Bendetsen and Boekel continued to pursue legal action against the strikers, fortified by DeWitt's belief that "these and similar questions would undoubtedly arise in the future" if more incidents occurred.[49] United States attorney general William Fleet Palmer initially told Boekel that based on investigative reports into the strike from the FBI and other sources, "the conclusion remains that there is not now enough evidence of the violation of a federal statute to warrant indictment of the citizen-Japanese now in custody, much less to prosecute them."[50] However, Palmer and his staff proceeded to investigate whether or not "any new federal statutes" that were created specifically for war contained authority for indictment and prosecution under the facts of this case.

Palmer's findings were not promising. In a memo to Boekel, Palmer outlined in detail the shortcomings in attempting to prosecute the Japanese American strike leaders under a variety of existing statutes and laws. No evidence existed in the case to try the strikers under the Espionage Act, nor did prosecution under the Sabotage Act hold up, as "this act contemplates positive action on the part of the accused—that is, he must destroy or injure war materials or war utilities . . . or make defective war material or war utilities."[51] The strikers refused to make the nets but did not destroy them. Bendetsen had suggested that codes prohibiting work stoppages at armories or arsenals also be applied to the case of the strikers, but Palmer instructed that the centers were not armories or arsenals and, regardless, there were no other reported cases of prosecutions under such codes. The only option Palmer identified for prosecution was calling up conspiracy charges, but he doubted their applicability considering the "tenuous evidence" and the fact that the Japanese American citizens would be difficult to prosecute under these charges (unlike Japanese nationals).[52] Boekel was losing hope of appeasing DeWitt, scrawling "We appear to be on thin ice in this matter" at the top of the memo from Palmer before forwarding it along to Bendetsen.[53]

Nevertheless, in a Los Angeles federal court on July 1, 1942, Palmer charged Ban and Fujii with conspiracy and attempts to "defraud the United States" through their refusal to contribute to the war effort. Ultimately, even if conspiracy charges did not stick (and Palmer doubted they would), Ban and Fujii violated Section 503 of the Public Statutes by leading an illegal strike. Despite the dubious charges, on July 2 the grand jury issued true bills against the Japanese Americans. Palmer was surprised, while Boekel was hopeful that the army would be relieved of this "headache" and the federal government would set a precedent for others who considered similar actions.[54]

Much to Bendetsen's and Boekel's dismay, there were no indictments handed down to Ban, Fujii, or the others. There was no evidence the workers went on strike in order to directly undermine the war effort. Furthermore, the fact that the strike was resolved in a timely fashion, with most workers returning to their jobs by that following Monday, also weighed against prosecution. The striker leaders may have been troublemakers, but conspirators they were not. Although strikes did violate public codes issued to support Executive Order 9066's power, the defendants did not receive fines but were punished just as harshly. They were sent to higher-security detention centers in Fort Missoula, Montana, and Santa Fe, New Mexico, and later the Tule Lake segregation center in California (although Fujii would later find work with the Office of War Information as a consultant in using the Japanese-language press to build support for the war effort).[55]

The desires of high-ranking military and government officials to seek punishment for the strikers speaks to the anxiety the incarcerated laborers created. More so than the administrators at Santa Anita (who considered the strike an annoying yet easily controlled display by a few troublemakers), Bendetsen, Boekel, and DeWitt identified the strike as a direct challenge to maintaining order and control in the centers. In their eyes, the strike was a deliberate act of defiance against the United States despite the fact that the incarcerees justified their actions in the familiar language of a peacetime labor dispute. Japanese Americans employed in the net factory demanded their rights as workers and challenged their positions as convict laborers, whereas the administrators, in their repeated identification of the strikers and their leaders as saboteurs, refused to view them as anything other than dangerous prisoners of the state. While administrators and military officials emphasized the importance of Japanese American labor for morale, the war effort, and the basic functions of incarceration, their responses to the Santa Anita strike reminded the imprisoned workers that their status as free laborers was tenuous. The WCCA expected Japanese Americans to display their patriotism through their labor, while the military expected strict order and control at the detention centers. The strike exposed the tensions between Japanese Americans who attempted to maintain their dignity, demonstrate their loyalty, and protect their workers' rights and the administration.

Later in October, incarcerees who volunteered to assist with the movement of people and goods to the WRA prison camps also used their crucial role as leverage to contest their working conditions. Beginning in September, the quartermaster called on Japanese Americans at Santa Anita to assist with gathering and shipping construction materials to Heart Mountain, Jerome, Rohwer, and Topaz prison camps in addition to their current jobs at the center. The extra duties required the workers to be on site and ready to work at 4:30 A.M. for the move and then return to their normal responsibilities as outlined in the Work Corps contract. The WCCA work manual also limited the number of hours that a detainee could work to forty-four hours per week, with no opportunities for overtime pay. This was the WCCA's attempt to ensure that there would be "no forced labor" in assembly centers nor anything that remotely resembled it.[56] The workers who volunteered for the additional shifts, however, far exceeded their forty-four hours per week. Many prisoners believed that (despite the WCCA prohibitions) they would receive additional pay or an increase in wages because the administrators surely understood what they were requesting of the workers. When the workers were informed that they would not receive extra wages, they "walked off the job," frustrating administrators but leaving them without a remedy, considering the WCCA prohibition on overtime.

Center manager Gene Wilbur (who eventually replaced Amory) complained that out of 7,677 detained at Santa Anita "there were able-bodied Japanese among the population [who could help with the movement, but did not], but again, 'forced labor' has not been the policy in operation of the center."[57] The administrators, as much as they would have liked to in this case, could not force men to work on voluntary projects, and the Japanese Americans detained at Santa Anita were well aware of this. The detainees used the prohibition of forced labor to slow down operations and protest against working conditions. As another incarceree stated during a later meeting on labor with camp administrators, "Unless he is getting some satisfaction as to working conditions and mutual cooperation, you cannot just go and tell any individual what to do and order them to do it because he cannot be forced to work in here."[58]

Self-Government and Labor Disputes

Another site of camouflage net production, the Manzanar prison camp, would also come to see unrest and a labor dispute in 1942, but with a different ending. The Manzanar riot in December is traditionally viewed as an intergenerational conflict between Issei and Nisei, "loyal" and "disloyal" to the camp administration or at least questioning the motives and actions of the WRA. However, labor arrangements in the prison camp served as a catalyst for the widespread strike and protest. Combined with internal tensions over representative government positions among Japanese Americans in Manzanar, labor was a crucial component of the subsequent unrest.

While Santa Anita lacked a well-developed form of self-government, the Manzanar detention center (which later became a permanent prison camp) was a beneficiary of the WRA's belief in the importance of Japanese Americans achieving a sense of autonomy. Permanent self-government was not a

Figure 7. View of housing barracks at the Manzanar prison camp from the guard tower. Photo by Ansel Adams, 1943. Courtesy of the Library of Congress.

priority for the WCCA in its attempt to establish and maintain an orderly removal and temporary detainment. WRA administrators, however, argued that self-government was a means of promoting democracy among a group of people who had every reason to doubt their nation's dedication to such principles. Some, such as DeWitt, were less than enthusiastic about allowing Japanese Americans to have a say over aspects of prison life but did agree that in the long run it would ensure order via self-policing. Others, including Milton Eisenhower and Dillon Myer, argued that self-government promoted democratic principles within the camps and instilled or reinforced American ideals.[59]

Systems of self-government varied in the prison camps, but the emphasis on Nisei holding higher ranking and more positions than the Issei or Kibei remained a hallmark of the "liberal democratic management" of incarceration.[60] Each prison was organized into a block system with block units comprising various barracks. The lead WRA administrator (or "project director") appointed Japanese American block managers, or "paid resident director[s] to the Assistant Director," to help oversee day-to-day operations, including distributing goods such as soap, blankets, and other items; maintaining the block grounds; forming "block councils" to serve as a "channel of complaint" for represented residents; and collecting and distributing correspondence and publications, including Japanese American–produced newspapers and periodicals. Directors initially chose Issei and Kibei to serve as block managers in order to take advantage of their bilingualism and general authority among the Japanese American community. In many cases, block manager duties overlapped with camp bureaus and agencies staffed by white functionaries, thereby maintaining the image of self-sufficiency and self-government while undermining the power and authority of prisoners.[61]

In contrast to the block managers and the block councils, the community councils were all Nisei and represented the WRA's dedication to placing "pro-American" and "pro-Ally" citizens in relative positions of power to portray the prisons as orderly and patriotic. Administrators considered Nisei the most loyal and devoted to the American war cause. Milton Eisenhower first established the "temporary community councils" in May 1942 with the goal of creating a more permanent and engaged governmental body than the block managers. The temporary councils morphed into community councils designed to allow prisoners more say over legislation, enforcement, and legal actions (such as creating courts and judicial committees to try prisoners who violated community standards and committed petty crimes). To ensure full support of the WRA's goals, the administration restricted membership to the council to Nisei twenty-one and older. Many council members in camps such as Poston and Topaz were educated, middle-class Nisei who were members of the Japanese American Citizens League (JACL) and best represented the WRA's ideal leaders. Issei were initially barred from voting for community council members but were later enfranchised and also created their own informal committees and representative bodies.[62]

At Manzanar, the formation of self-government would contribute to labor unrest as well as conflicts between Japanese Americans and the administration. The block manager system had existed at Manzanar since its days as a detention center under the direction of the WCCA and was well entrenched by the time the WRA assumed operations in June 1942. While block manager positions were sometimes appointed by administrators in other prisons, at Manzanar a block could elect a leader (including Issei) once the population reached two hundred prisoners. When the WRA took control of the facilities, Manzanar was a massive settlement of ten thousand incarcerees, with most blocks electing their own leaders. This left the Issei, who were able to maintain the prewar political influence they had in their home communities before arriving at Manzanar, as the dominant faction within the camp population. The block managers successfully carried out their duties and maintained order. As a result, both the Issei and the camp administration saw no pressing need for a community council.[63]

Not all Nisei, however, were content with the Issei's domination of the block positions. While at the detention centers at Santa Anita and Stockton in California, many Nisei who later came to Manzanar had grown accustomed to a power shift after forced removal. Issei ran most of the traditional cultural associations that characterized so much of Japanese American life before 1942, but these associations disappeared or went underground during incarceration. This resulted in an intergenerational power vacuum in administrative and self-government positions within the prisons. Concerned with the continued stronghold of the Issei on positions of relative power, a group of Nisei at Manzanar scrambled to form a rival political body, claiming that "the Issei were only representing one point of view" and that "cases of discrimination and infringement of civil liberties had to be fought by a citizen group: i.e., Nisei."[64]

Nisei attempted to strike a balance between cooperation and resistance within the prison camps. They also recognized "that under existing social customs, only the elders in the community would be elected leaders," a challenge to how WRA-sanctioned leadership changes swept through the prisons. The Manzanar Nisei's cause was also assisted by Mike Masaoka and other leaders of the JACL when they lobbied in Washington, DC, to become the recognized political leaders in the prisons "as the only persons capable under law to vote and hold office." WRA director Dillon Myer was only too happy to endorse this proposition, considering that the WRA depended on support from the JACL.[65]

On July 14, 1942, Nisei at Manzanar gathered to form the Manzanar Citizens' Federation. The federation was an unofficial organization of Nisei designed to "act in accordance with the Constitution of the United States, and strive with the united efforts for the preservation of Real Democratic principles" as well as "to act in the capacity of intermediary in carrying out instructions of the authorities to avoid misunderstanding and complexity among the Issei, Nisei, and Kibei groups."[66] Organized by prominent members of Nisei communities in Los Angeles, including Henry Tsurutani (a Los Angeles attorney and former district chairman of a JACL chapter), the federation maintained open membership and named four objectives: "To improve conditions in camp; to educate citizens for leadership; to participate in the war effort; and to prepare a postwar program for all evacuees." Later, federation members openly proclaimed their patriotism by submitting a petition to FDR arguing for the use of Japanese Americans in military service.[67] Such a request alienated many in Manzanar—Issei and Nisei alike—who hesitated to offer their services so readily. The federation did not receive a warm welcome following its first meeting on July 28, 1942, with one prisoner proclaiming, "We do not need a Citizens' Federation or self-government. The government put us behind barbed wire, let it take care of us."

The Citizens' Federation struggled to gain traction until the fall of 1942, when Manzanar administrators formally recognized the group. On September 4, the WRA established Administrative Procedure 34, which stated that only citizens could hold elective offices in any center and set the standards for self-government in the prisons. As the federation was composed of Nisei and the block council dominated by Issei, Manzanar director Roy Nash appointed members of the federation as the *political* leaders of the prison, as opposed to the general leadership and maintenance overseen by the Issei block managers. According to Administrative Procedure 34, in order for community government to exist, a charter or constitution was required. Later in September, Nash appointed a charter committee to draft the governing document. Unsurprisingly, this committee was made up entirely of members of the federation. The committee's charter emphasized the political power that belonged to the Nisei in decision-making roles, as opposed to the block managers who supervised logistics like distributing goods and overseeing the day-to-day operations in the barracks. In order for the charter to be ratified, the WRA required that it be put to a vote by the prison per individual blocks. Arguments over the wording of the charter as well as outright opposition to the document by the block council left approval of the document in limbo. A self-governing document was not approved by the fall of 1942, leaving the Nisei in a recognized yet unofficial place of power in Manzanar.[68]

Tensions between Nisei and Issei over self-government and political power also influenced labor relations in Manzanar. Just as in the other detention centers and camps, incarcerees at Manzanar were responsible for maintenance tasks but were also given the opportunity to earn set monthly wages (twelve, sixteen, or nineteen dollars) for a variety of skilled and unskilled labor by joining the Manzanar Work Corps, though recruiters played on the Japanese Americans' need to prove their loyalty through work. The administration's invitation to the Southern California Glass Company to establish a camouflage net factory in the late spring of 1942 presented more job opportunities to those incarcerees qualified as skilled weavers. Many of the Nisei who held powerful political positions in the federation and worked closely with the administration were able to recruit other American citizens to work on the project, leading Issei to further speculate about the special privileges that Nisei received in the camps—first political and now economic.[69]

The Manzanar Riot: A Reconsideration

When Fred Tayama—a leader of the federation and prominent member of the JACL—returned to Manzanar after being released to travel to Salt Lake City as part of a joint conference between JACL leaders and the WRA leaders, he "returned a marked man."[70] The federation's close relationship with the camp administration fueled suspicions of Tayama's motives in attending the conference. Issei, Kibei, and frustrated Nisei accused Tayama and those affiliated with him of being FBI informants, or *inu* (dogs). These accusations mounted to a fever pitch by November. Attacks on suspected (and later confirmed) Nisei FBI informants or those who were simply too "cozy" with the administration (*eta* in Japanese) increased as did verbal abuse of Nisei who appeared to be too willing to go along with WRA and prison policy. Cooperation and acceptance of camp living and working conditions became synonymous with being *inu*. And this was the environment to which Tayama returned.

On Saturday night, December 5, six men sneaked into Tayama's room in Block 28 and brutally attacked him, beating his head and limbs to the point that he was rushed to the prison hospital. One of the prisoners nearby alerted the director and assistant project director, who called in the camp police to round up and question suspects. Officers arrested two Nisei men—Henry Ueno and another unnamed suspect—and held them in custody for questioning. Ueno was detained in the Independence jail, in the nearby town, while the other was detained in the Manzanar jail. Questioning continued throughout the night until director Ralph Merritt called off the interrogation at 5 A.M. Assuming that everything was under control, Merritt declined the police's offer to bring in a reports officer to begin a written account of the incident.[71]

By noon on December 6, however, Merritt discovered that he had misread the situation, as inmates employed in Mess Hall 22 called a mass meeting which grew to the point that attendees spilled outside just after lunch. At the meeting, Joe Kurihara expressed his dissatisfaction with the camp assistant director Ned Campbell and his decision to arrest and detain Ueno. Most of the crowd cheered and voiced their agreement while Kurihara continued to read aloud the names on an *inu* "death list" he had created (Tayama's name was at the top). The mass meeting was not in vain. Campbell recognized a Committee of Five from the group (a mix of Nisei critical of the administration, Kibei, and Issei) and named Kurihara the spokesperson. Merritt met with the committee, and both groups agreed that Ueno would be returned to Manzanar in exchange for the committee's pledge to forgo further demonstrations.

Guards returned Ueno to Manzanar by 3 P.M., but the crowd—now approximately two thousand strong—called for the committee to push for his immediate release. Later that evening, a smaller group ransacked the prison hospital in search of Tayama and others on the death list, while a group of five hundred made their way to the jail to free Ueno. Arthur L. Williams, the head of the internal security division at Manzanar, informed Merritt of the growing crowd. In response, Merritt called in the military police to stand guard and maintain order. Meanwhile, Japanese American members of internal security forces scattered, in fear for their lives, as soon as the crowd made its way over to the jail. At 8 P.M., when the crowd refused to disperse, the military police received orders to fire tear gas into the crowd. When one incarceree attempted to drive a car into the jail and others pelted the military police with rocks (according to an eyewitness), violence ensued. Two military police fired at the crowd, injuring nine and killing James Ito, a seventeen-year-old Nisei from Los Angeles. Protests continued throughout the evening until military police restored order by morning.[72]

The aftermath of the protest at Manzanar resulted in a reassignment of key incarcerees connected to the events. One group, including Ueno, was forcibly removed to a high-security prison in Moab, Utah, and later to another in Arizona before arriving at Tule Lake, which would become a prison for "disloyal" and "subversive" Japanese Americans. Many Nisei, including Tayama and other members of the federation, were removed for their safety and held at Cow Creek camp in California's Death Valley, a former CCC facility hastily refashioned by the WRA. No further disruptions of significance occurred at Manzanar, ushering in a period generally referred to by the administration as "the Peace at Manzanar."

Other camp administrators as well as the public refused to see the abatement of violence as a victory, however, and blamed ongoing generational and political conflict among the Japanese Americans as sparking the Manzanar "riot," as it came to be known.[73] In conversations among military officials, the cause for the riot was simple: "The military pro-Axis mob beat up on one of the people who was going along with as they put it the administration."[74] Looking for a way to steer clear of further involvement with the WRA and incarceration, Bendetsen and others stressed that the problems in the prisons were ideological and based on loyal versus disloyal factions, a social and political problem best left to the WRA to solve. As Bendetsen indicated in a memo, "If there is a breakdown inside the civil administration of any other Federal agency, the Army doesn't go in and correct it . . . the fact that we go in with MP's when there is a break-down—of civil authority—doesn't cure anything. We only have to pull out some time and the underlying causes haven't been cured."[75]

The WRA administration agreed with Bendetsen. In the final report on the Manzanar camp, Robert Brown (public information officer at Manzanar) and Ralph Merritt described the rift between "pro-Americanism" and "pro-Japanism" as a driving force in the riot. Interpreting the "incident" at Manzanar in this light reveals it to be a "microcosm" of World War II in which ideological in-battles between loyal and disloyal played out on a daily basis in the prisons.[76] In the decades following the end of incarceration, scholars disagreed with the official WRA assessment of the causes, citing an "ethnic perspective" that challenged the WRA and JACL interpretation as one of loyal versus disloyal. The loss of power among the Issei was exemplified by the imprisonment of an anti-administration incarceree (Ueno) and was better understood as a "revolt" (indicative of a long-term and growing problem) rather than an unorganized "riot" or a one-off "incident." In other words, the Manzanar revolt was "a logical culmination of developments originating with the administration's decision to bypass the community's natural Issei leadership to deal with its own artificially erected JACL hierarchy and to embark on a program of Americanization at the expense of Japanese ethnicity."[77] Other historians have worked within the same framework and emphasized the importance of the Issei's growing support for the Japanese cause in the war, stemming from dissatisfaction with prison conditions at Manzanar.[78]

In both interpretations, there is little discussion of the prison labor strike that followed the initial revolt at the jail to release Ueno. Although relying on WRA sources for information regarding uprisings in prisons is not without its challenges, a close reading of the reports from camp administrators reveals a strong labor dimension to the riots, which both stemmed from and reinforced existing tensions, disorganization, and miscommunication among the Issei, Nisei, and the administration. Even the final report on Manzanar— wedged between lengthy descriptions of camp life and the riot—admitted that "labels such as Pro-Americanism and Pro-Japanism . . . were more nearly handy labels to be pasted over old feuds rather than a representation of any real source of the struggle."[79] The protest by inmates against their working and living conditions at Manzanar was not a riot but a strike.

Harry Ueno was, as one incarceree recalled, "very popular" among prisoners at Manzanar, not least for his role as a labor leader. Ueno worked as a cook in Mess Hall 22, along with approximately 1,600 other incarcerees who were employed in mess operations. As in the detention centers, food service became one of the most important jobs for the camps. WRA administrators originally believed that food production and agriculture would be the jobs requiring the largest number of workers. Food cultivation proved to labor-intensive and necessary for feeding incarcerees at Manzanar as well as those in other camps. As early as June 1942, 125 recently arrived Japanese Americans worked in agriculture, but one-third of the 9,671 incarcerees worked in "operation services" for the camp. Unlike with agriculture, administrators vastly underestimated the number of employees required to cook and serve food as well as clean up after meals. By the winter of 1943, the WRA established training programs for junior cooks to learn the trade and paid most employees sixteen dollars a month. At the peak of its population in the fall of 1942—approximately 10,000 incarcerees—4,789 were employed, most in the mess halls. Food service employees held important roles in camp life and some, like Ueno, were not afraid to wield their influence.[80]

In late September 1942, Ueno organized other workers into a Kitchen Mess Hall Union. This group was not formally recognized by the administration but nonetheless met to discuss matters relating to the working and living conditions in the prison. At one of the early meetings of the union, Ueno raised concerns and accused project directors of stealing sugar from the mess halls to sell on the black market during wartime rationing. Merritt and Brown's final report identifies this accusation as "a story manufactured out of whole cloth" and dismissed the claim, but Ueno continued to build support for the union by addressing workers' concerns with hours and pay. He also worked closely with others at Manzanar who were dissatisfied or critical of the administration. And Ueno spoke for workers beyond the mess halls. For example, he decried some elements of the camouflage net factory at Manzanar. Net employees (many women, who made sixteen dollars a month) often incurred the annoyance of others at the camp because only Nisei were allowed to hold these skilled positions, and others argued that the pay was not commensurate with the skilled labor required for other essential jobs. However, Ueno saw things differently. "I did not have any opposition to the camouflage nets," he later explained. "The only thing I was against was the low wages. . . . the wages he [Southern Glass Company] offered were so low compared with wages outside . . . they tried to exploit the people in the camp."[81] Administrators identified Ueno as little more than a nuisance, but Merritt and Brown admitted in their report that workers at Manzanar, especially those in the mess halls, "were ripe for labor organization."[82]

Administrators' references to labor conditions as causes of the initial revolt are listed ad nauseam in the final report on the incident. Manzanar experienced a high turnover of administrators, particularly those who had antagonistic relationships with the incarcerees and failed to establish any real channels of communication. Incarcerees often witnessed unruly arguments among different administrators in the employment division over a lack of materials needed to complete construction and provide jobs for the incarcerees, followed by finger-pointing. As a result, Japanese Americans came to believe in "the ineffectiveness of the federal government" and questioned the administrators' ability to maintain control and order as well as care for the incarcerees in Manzanar. A hasty transition in control from the WCCA to the WRA in the summer of 1942 did not help matters. Roy Nash, the first project director, was focused more on maintaining good relations with the local townspeople than learning from the WCCA employees of the challenges of running Manzanar and implementing better living, working, and self-governing policies. Administrators removed all but six WCCA employees from their positions once the WRA assumed control, losing a sense of institutional stability. With little time to accommodate the rapidly expanding population once Manzanar became a permanent prison, chaotic planning and implementation of new policies—including self-government—ensued.[83]

More problematic were the wages (or lack thereof) for the incarcerees who voluntarily left their homes before forced removal in the spring of 1942 and worked to make Manzanar hospitable before the others arrived. Early on, when Japanese Americans were still held in the detention centers along the West Coast before coming to Manzanar, "the great need to keep busy, to be at work, to be producing things was a constant pressure on the evacuees," and "people were told early that they would be expected to work."[84] Eventually, all detainees would be given jobs that were in line with their skill sets, but first the prisons needed to be constructed. According to the final report, "the first Japanese to arrive at the Center received an impression that he would be paid Army wages . . . which probably stemmed from the fact that the Army was in charge of evacuation" and had already made clerical hires among Japanese Americans who were rumored to be receiving army pay (they were not).[85] A group of Catholic fathers from Maryknoll who came to the San Pedro detention center in California only made matters worse when they informed the detainees that if they volunteered to leave early and help prepare Manzanar for settlement, they would "probably" be paid army wages (forty-one dollars a month for a newly enlisted soldier). A manager at Manzanar who happened to be interviewed by a local paper also incorrectly spoke on behalf of the WRA and proclaimed that Japanese Americans who worked at Manzanar would be paid WPA wages, similar to those of the white employees at the prison. At the time, Japanese Americans were not barred from reading local and national news sources and were under the impression they would earn extra wages for prepping the camp.

"No decision came on wages for several months," creating more opportunities for exploitation and confusion among the detainees. "The management asked the evacuees to 'volunteer' their services to keep essential services going" at Manzanar while other prisoners arrived, promising unspecified additional wage compensation once everything was settled. As it turned out, after three months of construction, cleaning, farming, and other forms of maintenance, not a single Japanese American received compensation for their work. "Having been promised certain wages and then seeing the confusion and indecision on the part of the administration over the subject, and then failing to receive any wages for three months, is it any wonder that the first charges of 'broken promises' stemmed from this issue over wages?" Merritt and Brown asked.[86]

The first issues at Manzanar—well before supposed pro- and anti-American conflicts and intergenerational tensions and disputes arose—were grounded in money and wages. In fact, Merritt and Brown declared that the tension over wages was the "first national issue" that gained attention and concern at Manzanar—be it among the detainees over their lack of pay or Americans who were told in numerous outlandish media reports that Japanese Americans received up to ninety dollars a month.[87] While admitting that wage and labor disputes were at the heart of many of the issues in Manzanar, WRA administrators still emphasized the role of pro-Japanese saboteurs in riling up otherwise loyal and law-abiding Japanese Americans. "The broken promise charge," the report declared, "is an important turning point in the story of Manzanar as it was this weapon which was used by the anti-administration and the so-called pro-Japanese forces six months later to stir up the turbulence which resulted in the 'Incident' of December 6."[88] Wage disputes were pressing issues for Japanese Americans who unknowingly worked for free and challenged the notion of "volunteer" as the WRA defined it (agreeing to work for a job voluntarily and accept the fact that they would receive pay at a later, unspecified time). But it was the "pro-Japan" forces and "disloyal" and "troublesome" members of the Manzanar community who turned the labor grievances into an assault on the administration. The WRA administration argued that loyal prisoners did as they were told and worked to improve their community, while those who spoke out against the violations of their civil and labor rights did so only because they were looking to "stir up trouble" for more nefarious reasons.

Other work programs in and outside the Manzanar prison factored into the WRA's final report on the strike. Beyond wages, the announcement from WRA headquarters in Washington that the Kibei would not initially be qualified to leave the camps on furloughs for agricultural work also contributed to unrest. Many Kibei "felt that the order keeping them in the Center, even though they had legal American citizenship, was a great act of discrimination." In retaliation, the report noted that many Kibei, "led by anti-administration forces," renounced their American citizenship in public meetings and pledged their allegiance to Japan. The exact numbers of those who renounced their citizenship and actually carried through with the process were unclear, but for the administrators, this was the work of saboteurs rather than prisoners unhappy with unfair work restrictions.[89]

Following conflicts over the restrictions on the Kibei for leaving on furloughs, a number of "underground," "subversive" groups formed, including two calling themselves the Black Dragons and Blood Brothers. These organizations left their calling cards in kitchens and at the pit latrines, denouncing a variety of work programs in Manzanar. The groups issued "tirades" against the camouflage project, charging that this was a way for the government to exploit the loyalty of Japanese American citizens and foreign-born nationals who worked in the boxing department of the factories. Members posted notes and bulletins around Manzanar decrying the work furlough program: "The white man told us to get out of California; now they want to use us as economic serfs. Do not go on furlough." They also spoke out against incarceree-owned and operated cooperative stores that accepted cash advances for goods and items produced by Japanese Americans in the camps. Japanese Americans used their wages to purchase "luxury" items (extra clothing beyond the incarcerees' clothing allowance, or special medicine) that were not provided by the WRA and, in turn, contributed to a community fund. The WRA considered these co-ops economic enterprises that promoted business and morale, but the Black Dragons and Blood Brothers charged that the WRA required the co-ops to charge inflated prices and were part of an administrative plot to "impoverish" incarcerees."[90]

Camp administrators took a variety of steps to restore full order—with varying success. They reassigned those deemed responsible for the violence (suspected members of the above subversive groups included), as well as those who were vulnerable to retaliation from other prisoners, to other camps and centers. Captain Martyn L. Hall (commanding officer of the military police at Manzanar) established an increased military presence to dissuade further demonstrations. But even after the military and prison administrators initiated these measures, incarcerees still protested administrative decisions through work stoppages and strikes during the so-called Peace of Manzanar. In the aftermath of the uprising, "WRA and military authorities determined that essential center services, such as heat, water, light, food, garbage disposal, and supply deliveries, would be maintained during the emergency period following the violence." In order to continue to keep the prison functioning, small crews of trusted prisoners as well as WRA staff members performed daily tasks necessary for the maintenance of the prison. While WRA administrators reported that most of the crews that were necessary for maintenance reported for duties, the "plumbers and electricians failed to report to work" on December 12. Japanese Americans sought to maintain control over what was identified as their most valuable asset: their labor.[91]

While the stand-alone uprising of December 6 captures the attention of most of the scholarly literature on Manzanar, the prisoners' response in the form of constant labor strikes and protests at other camps is a crucial component of the labor history of incarceration. Withholding production to contest their status as exploited laborers was a feature of camp life. If more overt acts of defiance such as the uprisings at Manzanar and elsewhere were newsworthy, the day-to-day forms of labor protest were more characteristic of daily life in the camps.

On the heels of Santa Anita and Manzanar, more strikes would follow through 1944. In June 1943, nurses at the Heart Mountain prison hospital in

Wyoming walked off the job. In an analytical report on labor disputes at the camps, the WRA administrator noted that at Heart Mountain "no particular incident can be pointed to as directly precipitating the action" and that "the strike was poorly organized" with no clear leaders, and "many workers were vague on why they were on strike."[92] Nonetheless, using strikes as a means to voice displeasure with everything from working conditions to living conditions was common at Heart Mountain. Earlier, "evacuees had struck previously to attain the removal of a project steward, of a fire-protection and a police officer, and of an appointive employee in the Motor Pool." Imprisoned Japanese Americans had "frequently threatened to strike and had previously walked out several times."[93]

Later that year at the Topaz prison camp in central Utah, the garage repair crew "stopped work for eleven days and was followed by workers in units functionally unrelated to transportation services."[94] This particular strike concerned administrators because it appeared to have "great community approval" and threatened to continue to grow, undermining the day-to-day operations of the prison. The strike began when a military guard looking for smuggled liquor stopped a garage repair crew's truck. This was a well-established practice but was normally completed by an WRA administrator, not a member of the military. Incensed by what they assumed to be an increase in surveillance, the crew refused to stop and allow the vehicle to be searched, prompting the supervisor to order them to proceed with the inspection and "go to work or get off of the lot." The crew saw the threat by the supervisor (whom they had never gotten along with, charging him with discrimination and favoritism for certain workers) as a challenge, and they stopped working. They refused to return until they received a written apology for the supervisor's "manner" in which he dealt with his workers. Within a few hours, other employees at Topaz, including "200 agricultural workers along with carpenters, maintenance and operations men, plumbers, and the transport and supply crew went on a sympathy strike" and ceased operations in their respective occupations.[95] Particularly disturbing for the camp administrators was the prospect of the strike becoming center-wide and inhibiting the transfer of "disloyal" prisoners to Tule Lake. Although the supervisor never issued an apology, the strike ended when many of the employees returned to work within a day or two; they were worried about the loss of wages and cash advances for purchasing extra items. However, in reviewing the root causes of the strike by the garage repair crew, the WRA also identified threats of reduction in hours and pay as well as "anti-administration activities of a small group" contributing to the "mounting tensions" prior to the strike. There were prisoners who believed that "the government had caused the plight of the evacuees and should therefore be responsible for supplying their needs." "To this group," the section of the report on Topaz concluded, *work on the center was much the same as forced labor.*[96]

In January 1944, boilermen at the Minidoka prison in Idaho protested their working conditions, resulting in a "six-day suspension of janitorial and boilermen services, which involved an entire community" in the dead of winter. The report cited a reduction in the number of employees in maintaining the boiler and an attempt to merge the duties of the janitorial and boilermaker staff to accomplish more with fewer employees as the "igniting" factor in the strike.[97] When the administration called for men to work twenty-four-hour shifts to ensure that the boilers ran safely, the crew revolted and refused to report for duties. The administration then attempted to shift the responsibilities of tending the boilers to the general maintenance staff, who also protested the extra responsibilities and hours placed upon their already strained numbers. When the janitorial staff also refused to take on more work, the administration's hands were tied. The workers had a simple solution: hire more workers. The administration balked at this suggestion, prompting the prisoners to write to WRA director Dillon Myer demanding more employees. The strike only ceased when the administration was forced to enlist "volunteers" to perform maintenance and boiler work, which created such an uproar in the community that administrators ended the twenty-four-hour cycle and allowed for a slight increase in the number of maintenance staff. Administrators also "accepted as its own the responsibility for safeguarding government property" outside the janitor, maintenance, and boilermen's basic work hours.[98] In spite of the resolution of the dispute, the administration became increasingly concerned, as Bendetsen stated, that more of the imprisoned Japanese Americans would attempt to band together and "dictate, just like a union would, as to who shall work . . . and on what job."[99]

While manual laborers usually organized strikes in the centers and camps, this did not mean that all Japanese Americans resented the administration or their work. For many Japanese Americans, incarceration provided them with white-collar opportunities that might not have existed in their previous communities. Discriminatory employers and racist practices shut doors to careers for Japanese Americans along the West Coast. In the camps and centers, the need for all Japanese Americans to work in operational services meant that nursing, teaching, writing and editing for camp newspapers, and clerical work were options now available, especially for Nisei women. The camp wage for nurses or secretaries, for example, were not on par with those outside, but the opportunities existed.

Chiyoko Yano spent her incarcerated years at the Topaz prison camp in Utah and recalled a "very interesting job" working in Central Statistics. Topaz director Charles E. Ernst recruited Yano to assist with gathering statistics on the incarcerated at the camp and to create a census to send to the WRA headquarters in Washington, DC. Yano was a bookkeeper with North American Mercantile in San Francisco after leaving the University of California at Berkeley before completing her degree to help take care of her family when her father could no longer work. She worked alongside other Nisei men and women in Central Statistics; a Berkeley statistician, Fern French, supervised the project. She took a liking to Yano and arranged for Yano to leave Topaz for three months while getting additional data training in Washington, DC. Not only did the statistics job allow Yano to travel while incarcerated, but she also developed a good working relationship with Ernst. Yano described Ernst as "one of the very good project directors" and her work at Topaz as "very important." Other women who worked on the camouflage net projects at Santa Anita or Manzanar also found opportunities to earn their own wages while exercising independence from their patriarchal family structures. For incarcerees who did not participate in strikes or even see the need for them, life in the prison camps was a paradox of limited freedoms with opportunities for career development.[100]

The Tule Lake "Riot" and Labor Protests Throughout the Prison Camps

If the army and WRA wanted to discourage Japanese American labor resistance, the decision to make the Tule Lake camp a segregation center ran counter to their concerns. Administrators argued that segregating the "loyal" from the "disloyal" incarcerees would prevent "contamination" of the more cooperative Japanese Americans, but where to place the "bad apples"? There were those who were wary of such a program: How would forcing the "troublemakers" into one area possibly lead to anything but more control issues? One option for housing the dissenters was to use the true internment detention centers for "enemy aliens" such as those in Crystal City, Texas, and Santa Fe, New Mexico, or the "Citizen Isolation Centers" at Moab and Leupp, Arizona, designed to hold saboteurs or criminals.[101] However, these centers could not accommodate large numbers of prisoners.

In 1943, the WRA administered a loyalty questionnaire to all incarcerees to clear those seeking job relocations or recruitment into the army. The questionnaire was divisive, and many Japanese Americans viewed it as further insult to a population whose loyalty was already tested. Forty-two percent of Tule Lake incarcerees answered the questionnaire "incorrectly" (not proclaiming their denouncement of the Japanese emperor, or declining to serve in the military—further discussed in Chapter 5) or not at all.[102] Administrators argued that it would be easier to ship other "disloyal" incarcerees to Tule Lake than disperse the Tule Lake dissenters to other camps. The WRA (with pressure from the War Department, DeWitt, and members of Congress to address reports of misconduct and riots in the camps) converted Tule Lake into a maximum-security site. They installed a seven-foot-high barbed wire fence, delivered army tanks, and added guard towers around the prison grounds, including the farm areas where prisoners were expected to grow their own food as well as provisions for other camps. Many of those who answered the questionnaire as expected—confirming their loyalty—were moved to other prison camps to make room for the newly arriving dissenters, which resulted in Tule Lake's population ballooning from 15,276 to 18,789 during the summer of 1943—well beyond the prison's capacity despite the addition of extra barracks and facilities.[103]

Tule Lake's reclassification as a segregation center resulted in a volatile mix of prisoners. Among recently arrived Japanese Americans were Japanese nationals who longed to repatriate to their homeland, Issei and Nisei who were dissatisfied with their plight and resistant to the idea of Nisei serving in the military, and those who wished to renounce their American citizenship as a result of incarceration and anti-Japanese hysteria. Thousands of others were original inmates at Tule Lake and answered the questionnaire as expected, yet were neither "pro-Japan" nor anti-administration.[104] Intergenerational tensions that existed at other prisons took root at Tule Lake, and the myriad political and social beliefs at the new segregation center exacerbated the conditions.

Adding fuel to the existing fire was Raymond Best, the former administrator of the citizen isolation centers at Moab and Leupp. Myer appointed Best as director of Tule Lake in August (taking over for Harvey Coverly) on the basis of his experience as a level-headed and fair administrator. His previous stint as a disciplinarian at the higher-security centers more than likely influenced Myer's decision. Best was responsible for the final transformation of Tule Lake into a maximum-security prison, adding an entire battalion of army soldiers and placing restrictions on certain activities, particularly those that hinted at "pro-Japanism." Best developed a "no-nonsense" reputation when it came to dealing with the prisoners. He approached all the prisoners at Tule Lake as potentially dangerous and took a hard line when responding to the "demands" of the dissenters. And these "trouble-makers" held no qualms about speaking out on the conditions of the camps or "recruiting" other prisoners for "subversive activities," as WRA administrators explained.[105]

Japanese Americans soon tested Best on his leadership abilities. In July 1943, an anonymous source circulated a pamphlet around Tule Lake for "the benefit of the Manzanar people" who had recently arrived at the prison. "We hereby submit to you a brief outline, even though incomplete, of the true picture and facts of the pending confusion and present conditions at this center," the decree began. "Up to this time, ever since the present war, the definitive policy of the WRA was none other than to convert the so-called loyal elements as much as possible," which relied on using promises of money to "convert reluctant evacuees to so-called loyal ones." The anonymous authors of the pamphlet revealed their theory that when it came to making Tule Lake the prison which would house Japanese American dissenters, "they have selected a location, fitted for agriculture, for a segregation center. By mass production of war industry as their sole object, they had intended to slave the evacuees."[106]

Beginning in August 1943, dissatisfaction with working and living conditions manifested in multiple sit-down strikes and work stoppages. Prisoners proved that they were willing to once again use their labor as a weapon to push for demands, but they repeatedly ran into the equally strong will of Best to maintain order and control. However, a series of events would lead to a crescendo in November 1943 when a "riot" erupted in Tule Lake. On October 15, a group of workers employed in the agricultural department became the touchstone for subsequent protests when five were injured and one was killed during a truck accident as the employees rushed to complete their tasks in preparation for the fall harvest. The driver of the truck was underage and the other workers argued that the administration was to blame for the injuries and death because of their lax oversight of working conditions.

Relationships between the prisoners and administration only deteriorated further when agricultural employees responded to the administration's lack

of concern with a sit-down strike. As one laborer opined, "These farmers who
went over there to produce those vegetables, they worked for the government
for $15 a month and they [the prisoners] turned right around and bought the
items from the Government and ate them," referencing the idea that prisoners were required to purchase extra food items from canteens.[107] "From that,"
he continued, "you can clearly see that it is pure exploitation of labor on the
part of the U.S. Government."[108] The labor protest coincided with the harvest of crops the prisoners grew for themselves as well as other prison camps,
further annoying both Best and members of the army administration, who
became increasingly concerned about control at Tule Lake following its transformation to a segregation center. Best maintained that the strike was the
work of "disloyal" and subversive factions of recently arrived, pro-Japan prisoners from Manzanar and Topaz. Colonel Verne Austin echoed Best's theory and believed that "it would be the finest thing in the world" if the army
simply took the harvesting into its own hands and moved "the soldiers in [to]
harvest those God damned crops and haul them off and let those Japs go to
hell."[109] Best tried a similar tactic in informing the prisoners that "if they want
to eat, they're going to have to help in getting in the crops; if they don't want
them, why it just meant that they won't get that food."[110] Such a move was
unrealistic as Best was unable to let the workers starve. Moreover, the crops
were needed for a variety of purposes. Meanwhile, in response to the protest, Best brought prisoners from Poston and Topaz to harvest the crops, paying them one dollar per hour, which was more than the agricultural workers
at Tule Lake received, and housing them at an old CCC camp nearby, converted into an isolation center. Best's decision infuriated many of the Tule
Lake agricultural workers as well as sympathetic prisoners who continued
the strike.

   On October 26, 1943, representatives from the Tule Lake prisoners met
with Best to voice their concerns with the working conditions and safety of
the employees. They also demanded a public apology from Best for those who
were injured in the truck accident. George Kuratomi served as the leader and
spokesperson for the prison workers, and he charged Best and the other administrators with acting "very inhuman [sic]" in not formally acknowledg-
ing the death and injuries of the prisoners.[111] Best refused to engage with this
charge because, in his words, "Who is to be the judge" of whether or not he
was inhumane in his reaction to the deaths?[112] Best viewed the funeral of one
of the prisoners as a public protest, charging that on the day of the event some
"men were forced to go to that funeral" by pro-Japan or pro-Axis forces in

the prison.[113] When Kuratomi advised Best that the very least he could do was issue a public apology and asked that the administration take steps to "prevent further occurrence of such accidents," Best retorted, "You, or no one else, are going to tell me what to do."[114] Kuratomi had hoped that Best would "listen to reason" during the meeting and also agree that "termination [of the farm workers] would not be good."[115] Best, however, dug in, and the day after the meeting—according to Kuratomi, who later explained that the following statement was "not in the minutes of the October 26 meeting"—wrote while away in San Francisco that "all farm workers are terminated as of October 19."[116] After the meeting, Japanese Americans expressed "extreme distrust" of Best. Kuratomi and other representatives later took advantage of an opportunity to meet with Dillon Myer during a scheduled visit November 1. They requested that Myer force Best to resign from his position, but both Myer and Best reacted harshly to feeling cornered by the prisoners. Best subsequently denied further meetings with the prisoners.

The breaking point, however, occurred on November 4, when some prisoners witnessed trucks moving goods from the warehouse to the Tule Lake isolation center where Best housed the strikebreakers from other camps. Those who reported the movement suggested that Best was taking materials that were intended for the Tule Lake prisoners and giving them to the strikebreakers, making good on his promise to starve the prisoners in order to force them to return to work. When groups of confused, frightened, and angry agricultural laborers gathered in central areas in the prison, Best responded by contacting Austin and calling for troops to maintain order. The WRA internal security branch identified groups of suspected saboteurs and isolated and beat them into submission, while the army used tear gas, tanks, and weapons against those prisoners who even dared to attempt to return to their normal jobs. Many white WRA employees reacted strongly to the crowds as well as the increased presence of the army and cried for more protections from the potential danger the prisoners posed.[117]

In response, Tule Lake moved into a period of martial law under which the army gained control; issued curfews; seized Japanese-language materials, radios, and other items from the prisoners after raiding their barracks; and searched for members of Daihyo Sha Kai, the negotiating committee. Some of the leaders eventually turned themselves in to spare further invasions of privacy, resulting in their arrest and detainment for "crimes" that included being a "troublemaker" as well as being "too smart for [their] own good." Military units guarded the stockades, and detainees made a number of charges against the army, including being forced to work. Detainees eventually went on a hunger strike until Myer recognized their various grievances and charges, including "inhumane treatment," poor food and a lack of coal, "brutal beating[s]," and forced labor "at the point of a gun."[118] Military officials denied that those in the stockade had ever been "forced to work at the point of a gun," except perhaps when a guard may have used his rifle butt to "nudge" a detainee along, or "the fact that these people are to be accompanied by guards when they go out to get their coal, which they do so voluntarily."[119]

The incarcerees' withholding of their labor contributed to the WCCA and WRA's turn to the army for ending and discouraging strikes, in the form of martial law. Martial law was at an extreme end of a spectrum in suppressing strikes and labor protests, but the WCCA and army's initial responses to the strike at Santa Anita as an act of subversion was a forerunner to Tule Lake. Labor unions including the Congress of Industrial Organizations (CIO) and American Federation of Labor (AFL) had entered into a no-strike pact following the attack on Pearl Harbor, a move supported by FDR and the federal government to ensure high production levels for the war effort. Those who did not work, including incarcerated Japanese Americans, threatened America's defense. Both the CIO and AFL advocated for American workers to accept an "equality of sacrifice" stance: their agreement to avoid labor conflict and pull together in war material production was their own sacrifice as those who served put their lives on the line overseas.[120] Disillusioned and dissatisfied union members and employees, however, initiated wildcat strikes without union approval across the country as they feared that employers would take advantage of a no-strike pledge.

Japanese Americans in the detention centers and prison camps used wildcat strikes and labor organization for different purposes. While seeking better working conditions and pay, incarcerees also halted their duties to protest the administration's limits on their civil and labor rights. But the army, WCCA, and WRA viewed Japanese Americans as a *source* of labor (similar to units of production in the beet fields) rather than as *laborers*. What were Japanese Americans working for while in the centers and camps? Did they labor in operational services to improve the quality of their lives and communities—ensuring that food was cooked and served, facilities cleaned, and fellow incarcerees cared for when sick? Were they earning wages to purchase goods from community-owned co-ops? Or, as Japanese American protesters pointed out, were the government agencies merely taking advantage of them and using them to reduce the costs of the incarceration project? Plenty of Japanese Americans drew pride and meaning from the work. But for the administrators, what Japanese Americans received from the work—be it an increase in morale, pride that they were helping their nation, sharpened skills for when they were released, or "pocket" money for camp goods—was less important than what the camps, the administration, and the military received in the form of order, efficiency, reduced costs of operation, and war matériel. Through punishment, martial law, and unmet demands, those in charge of incarceration reminded Japanese Americans that while they desired workers who were as content as possible, those workers were not working for themselves. They labored for their country. They labored to improve the abnormal conditions in which they lived in the camps and centers. And they worked to prove their loyalty and their self-worth to Americans who doubted their contributions and their commitment to the war effort.

An "Unusual Employment Situation"

Administrators scrambled to understand why and how such widespread strikes occurred. The WRA recruited psychologists to analyze the mental health of Japanese Americans and assess its effects on their decisions to protest. On the basis of their observations, psychologists shifted away from examinations of the individual and more to the collective labor environment established under incarceration. Famed University of Chicago sociologist Robert E. Park conducted studies of the second generation of Japanese Americans and often focused on the "hyper racial sensitivity" of Nisei to both real and perceived racism, but the psychologists hired by the WRA delved deeper into the impact of incarceration on the community.[121]

A WRA Community Analysis Report that focused specifically on labor relations in the prison camps revealed that "both the underlying and immediate causes of labor trouble stem from the unusual structure of the center community and the relation of workers to it." Because the prisons "differ[ed] from normal communities outside, they [had] an unusual employment situation," with "evacuees . . . restricted in movement . . . lacking freedom of economic competition since all of their work is for the center and reimbursed by a small cash allotment—a weak bargaining point." The report also noted that "the difference in the economic and social status of the Japanese before and after evacuation affect[ed] labor relations—many who were self-employed on the West Coast in businesses or on farms find it hard to adjust to their role as employees." Japanese Americans sat down with interviewers and expressed opinions that reflected the above observations. "We did not ask to come here. We were forced to leave our legitimate type of work for the Caucasians to take over and make money on during the war, therefore if we choose not to work, the government still has the obligation to see to it that we are treated right," one noted. Another responded to the WRA's frequent requests that the incarcerees volunteer their labor for improvement projects on top of or instead of normal duties: "WRA is trying to get work for nothing in order to keep a good record for some of the administrators. The more we volunteer the more we will be expected to work for nothing, and it's little enough we get for what we do as it is."[122]

When supervisors insisted that Japanese Americans embrace better work habits to prove their loyalty, one incarceree exclaimed, "Don't give us the loyalty talk again! What the hell do you expect for $16 [a month]!" Even the author of the report admitted that this was a "paltry sum" for the job at hand. Authors of the analysis did not fully analyze race relations in the prison camps between the incarcerees and their white supervisors (noting that poor wages and working conditions made "workers less inclined to overlook real or fancied discrimination or dominating attitudes" in the prisons); they did describe the effects of mass incarceration and forced employment on the incarcerees.[123] Japanese Americans did not, as other administrators such as Amory argued, go on strike or stage a protest because they were subversive agitators but because they had legitimate concerns for their rights as laborers. Even Issei who lacked citizenship knew that basic workers' rights were important components of American employer-employee relationships, particularly under New Deal legislation. The reports themselves proved that the working conditions established by the WRA in the detention centers and the camps compounded the problems of forced removal and incarceration.

The events at Santa Anita, Manzanar, and other prisons in the fall of 1942 and through the winter and spring of 1943 revealed the growing protest movement among Japanese Americans. The standard explanations of the administrators approached the uprisings at Santa Anita, Manzanar, and Tule Lake as the result of a combination of rage over imprisonment, disloyalty, or intergenerational tensions. But the strikes were organized events with clear agendas. Japanese Americans fought for improvement in working conditions and more say in labor negotiations. Issei, Nisei, and Kibei all expressed dissatisfaction with their positions and their loss of power as a result of their imprisonment; more generally, they expressed their disapproval of being forced to perform certain tasks and duties for little or no pay. Japanese Americans forced the WRA and other agencies to reckon with the limitations of their plans for exploiting the labor of incarcerated Japanese Americans.

CHAPTER 4

A Prison by Any Other Name

Labor and the Poston "Colony"

In July 1942, John Collier, commissioner of the Office of Indian Affairs (OIA), stood before hundreds of Japanese Americans at the Parker (or Colorado River) Relocation Center in Arizona, readying himself to address the mass of prisoners. The Parker camp (or Poston as it became known) would become the largest of the prison camps for Japanese Americans with a population peaking at approximately seventeen thousand. Apart from holding the record for largest population (until Tule Lake surpassed it) and having joint WRA and OIA administration (until the WRA assumed sole control in 1943), Poston's other unique feature was its location. The federal government erected this camp on land belonging to the Colorado River Indian Reservation, home to the Diné, Chemehuevi, 'Aha Makhav, and Hopi and now operated by the Department of the Interior under the OIA—hence Collier's presence in the Poston mess hall on that summer evening.

Collier wiped the perspiration from his brow and turned to the increasingly anxious crowd before him. "I have to admit a feeling of rather acute humility in standing before you, and I feel rather tongue-tied," he explained. Collier acknowledged the "thousands and thousands of deep, bitter, individual injustices" the audience members experienced during removal and imprisonment, many of them arriving from detention centers in California or coming directly to Poston from their homes following the end of "voluntary relocation." Hot and tired from working and carving out a life among the dusty winds which were a perpetual nuisance in the remote area, Collier's audience sat patiently as he continued. "It came about that the organization of which I am chief was requested to administer this [Poston camp] . . . [and]

we agree to accept the responsibility upon a clear and written understanding that the administrative authority would be us—the Department of the Interior, Secretary [Harold] Ickes and me."[1]

Collier continued by outlining the loftier goals he had in mind for Poston. He explained that the job of the OIA was "to work with you [Japanese Americans] toward making this place a truly happy place where individuals and families will be giving themselves utterly to the community and winning a reward of inward power and inward joy greater than anything in the external world." He emphasized to his audience that their job while at the prison—beyond the self-sufficient duties required in the camps—was to build a successful colony, a "great social experiment" of self-government and shared work "that would be very inspiring and illuminating . . . , a flowering of mutuality, of teamwork, of cooperative thinking and cooperative work." By promoting self-government, labor, and economic self-sufficiency, Poston would become a successful colony and prove that even in challenging situations, American democracy could thrive. Americans would be able to learn everything from social organization to political structures and sound employee-employer relationships from the experiences of imprisoned Japanese Americans.[2]

Collier, however, had another agenda in creating a colony of Japanese Americans on a remote Native American reservation: the exploitation of prisoner labor for the completion of infrastructure programs. For decades, Collier and the OIA had scrambled to find the resources and manpower to complete desperately needed infrastructure projects on the Colorado River Indian Reservation, including digging irrigation canals, preparing land for intensive agriculture, and constructing adobe-brick schools.[3] Executive Order 9066 and the later establishment of the WRA created opportunities for the Department of the Interior and the OIA to gain the necessary and cheap labor to complete projects on the reservation. The WCCA and the federal government initially turned to the Department of the Interior (DOI) during the late winter and spring of 1942 for help in selecting prison sites that both could be easily obtained and benefit from exploited labor. Collier was eager to offer up the reservations, but Ickes and other officials in the DOI recommended their agency hold off from participating. Ickes was not sure he wanted the agency to be associated with the process of removing and detaining Japanese Americans.

By early March, however, Ickes included Collier in the planning process. WRA director Milton Eisenhower agreed to allow Collier to run the Poston prison with the assistance of the WRA, but when Dillon Myer assumed the

position after Eisenhower, he dashed Collier's dream of an unfettered sociological experiment. Myer embittered Collier by refusing to let the commissioner have complete control over Poston. He reined in Collier's lofty goals
and insisted that Poston be run like any other prison camp in the system.
Still, Collier worked to encourage a sense of pioneering spirit among the Japanese American prisoners. Poston was, according to Collier, an opportunity
for the OIA to "make history" with the "social experiment" established at
the camp when it officially opened and received its first 350 residents on
June 2, 1942.[4]

Collier's notion of self-government among Japanese Americans, for all of
its potential in preserving democracy, was also part of the incarceration process designed to ensure order and productivity. Social scientists including
Johns Hopkins–trained psychiatrist and former naval officer Dr. Alexander
Leighton and his team of assistants formed the Bureau of Sociological Research (sponsored by the OIA) and conducted extensive surveys and studies
of Poston. Leighton and his team also exploited Japanese American incarcerees for the sake of producing data sets on the "Japanese personality," eventually published as part of Leighton's account of incarceration, *The Governing
of Men*, in 1945. Leighton and another sociologist, Dorothy Swaine Thomas
(head of the Japanese American Evacuation and Resettlement Program,
which studied other prison camps beyond Poston), used paid Japanese American assistants from within the prisons to gather data and interview other
prisoners to examine larger issues of democracy, freedom, and labor. Poston's
unofficial status as a sociological experiment and its ties to the history of social science and racial relations are well documented. Leighton's observations of life at Poston (referenced extensively in this chapter) illustrate the
clash between administrative goals and the reality of Japanese American lives
at the work colony.[5]

Social experiment. Colony. Self-sufficient community. Collier, Ickes, and
the WRA's missions for Poston often conflicted with one another. They also
forced imprisoned Japanese Americans into roles as laborers, community
leaders, and colonized as well as colonizers clearing land on behalf of the DOI
and the reservation system. What was at the heart of the lofty visions for
Poston was the exploitation of Japanese Americans and their labor in craft-
ing a community for study by social scientists; clearing and improving land
for reservations; and easing the financial burden of the WRA. Because exploitation was crucial for success as defined by the agencies, Poston was—
above all else—a prison work colony consisting of white-collar and manual

laborers, a reality that did not escape many detained Japanese Americans. Rather than an anomaly, Poston's reliance on Japanese American labor was part and parcel of the larger prison work system under EO 9066. But the conflicting goals and interagency disputes over its governance, as well as challenges from Japanese Americans who questioned and rejected their duties, would eventually expose the insurmountable challenges of continuing such a project. Poston's status as a prison work colony would be the larger prison labor system's ultimate undoing.[6]

Self-Sufficient and Self-Supporting: The Abstract and Practical Underpinnings of Poston

It was no secret among the WRA, WCCA, and OIA administrators that Poston was to serve both as a colony for Japanese Americans during the war and as a means of improving the Colorado River Indian Reservation. Because the reservation was located on government land, the process for obtaining permission to build Poston was fairly straightforward; Secretary of War Henry Stimson, the OIA (representing the Department of the Interior), and the WRA were able to negotiate directly with one another. Unlike with other sites, including Jerome in Arkansas or Manzanar in California, there was little need for convincing on the part of any of the agencies to establish a camp on the reservation. With plenty of internal improvements to busy Japanese Americans, there was also little concern about the nonexistent opportunities for outside industrial or agricultural employment as it was almost guaranteed that the prisoners would be well-occupied for the duration of their stay.

The administrators' desire to use Japanese American labor for the completion of public works projects on the reservation was the result of a complex web of economic and social policies governing tribal lands. Collier fashioned himself as a friend and advocate to the United States' Indigenous peoples. A sociologist by training, he was interested in the effects of social institutions on culture and "personalities." His sociological research caught the eye of other organizations that spoke out against the long-held practice of "Americanizing" Native Americans through forms of cultural genocide, land use regulations (including the Dawes Act of 1877, which broke up tribal lands to encourage private ownership), and the ill-reputed "Indian boarding schools" for children. By 1933, Collier's dedication resulted in administrative

recognition. With Harold Ickes's blessing, FDR appointed Collier to the position of commissioner (or head) of the OIA.[7]

Once in a prominent position, Collier took the lead in establishing, outlining, and supporting what became known as the "Indian New Deal" as part
of FDR's sweeping economic, social, and political reforms. Collier abandoned
the program of assimilation and instead hired anthropologists and sociologists to study and document Native American life on reservations. Additionally, Collier was instrumental in ensuring the passage of the Indian
Reorganization Act (IRA) of 1934, which allowed for more self-governance
through the promotion of tribal council systems and abolished the land allotment program established under the Dawes Act. Collier also shepherded
the Johnson-O'Malley Act of 1934 through the legislative process, allowing
Congress to apportion federal dollars for the building of schools and medical facilities and the establishment of agricultural programs on reservations.
In conjunction with the Johnson-O'Malley Act, Collier took advantage of
both an increase in federal spending for Native Americans and FDR's devotion to creating jobs to form the Indian Division of the Civilian Conservation Corps. This division provided economic opportunities and eased
unemployment for Native Americans who worked on large-scale infrastructure programs on various reservations, particularly those in the southwest
in need of a stable water supply.[8]

Unfortunately for Collier, Congress slashed the OIA's budget by 1941 as
the nation prepared for war. Once-promising projects for land development
and irrigation that employed fifteen thousand Native Americans across the
West sat unattended by the end of the year. The long-standing ambitions of
the DOI to make land on tribal reservations arable and accessible to white
settlers as well as Native Americans were also challenged by the budget re-
prioritizations of the war economy. Dismayed by the sudden lack of cash flow
for his projects but still convinced of their potential, Collier and the DOI identified an opportunity for the continuation of their goals following FDR's
signing of EO 9066 and the WCCA and WRA's search for locations for prison
camps.[9]

The WRA emphasized the potential for land improvement in its justifications to the OIA for erecting a prison for Japanese Americans on a reservation. As part of the Indian New Deal, the Leavitt Act of 1932 amended the
process of determining to what extent tribes would be financially responsible for projects completed on reservation land, especially expansive and

expensive irrigation systems. Previously, the construction costs for DOI infrastructure projects on tribal land accrued to the tribes. This system placed the tribes in a position where it would be nearly impossible to pay back the debt of construction costs to the federal government and also inhibited their potential for self-sufficiency.[10] The Leavitt Act provided authorization for the DOI both to cancel long-standing charges for irrigation and other public works projects initiated before 1934 and to defer collection of charges for internal improvements until the tribes decided to sell the land (or in other words, indefinitely).

The Leavitt Act also created unique opportunities for both the WRA and the OIA. With the WRA's interest in reducing the overhead costs of incarceration and employing Japanese Americans for the war effort, and the OIA's desire to complete infrastructure improvements, framing any form of agricultural production as an internal improvement became common among both agencies. The WRA would receive access to labor to help with the war effort, and the OIA would receive access to Japanese Americans to construct infrastructure improvements at a low cost with little to no financial responsibility. The Leavitt Act freed the OIA of financial responsibilities, and the WRA was not a permanent organization, so whether or not it received compensation for the irrigation projects was of no immediate concern.[11]

When it came to the Gila River Indian Reservation (home of the Akimel O'odham and Pee-Posh peoples) and Colorado River Indian Reservation (home of the Diné, Chemehuevi, 'Aha Makhav, and Hopi peoples) in Arizona, multiple agencies benefited from manipulating agreements that were designed to assist Native American tribes. Under the Leavitt Act and general agreements among the OIA and other government agencies, both the approval of the tribes and just compensation were required for any alteration or use of reservation property. When initially approached by the OIA and the WRA for the use of the reservation for the incarceration of Japanese Americans, both the Gila River and Colorado River tribal councils were wary or outright opposed to such measures. The challenge for the OIA was to offer fair compensation for use of reservation land for imprisoning Japanese Americans in order to persuade the councils to look past the incarceration. Defining "fair compensation" required Collier and the DOI to draw on a long legacy of the OIA acting on behalf of Native Americans in determining their best interests. Despite Collier's dedication to the preservation of Native

American culture and sovereignty, he and others in his agency still believed that these goals could only be accomplished by embracing the plans of white administrators.

The OIA's offer to the Native American tribes emphasized infrastructure improvements in return for temporary access to land for incarceration. In April, the WRA, OIA, DOI, and secretary of war engaged in a flurry of memo writing and agreement signing to move toward the construction of the prisons on both the Gila River and the Colorado River Reservations. Before taking the final plan to the tribal councils, the WRA and Ickes hammered out their own agreement on the utilization of the land and the role of the WRA on the reservations. Both Ickes and Milton Eisenhower agreed that the DOI (through the OIA and Collier) would "determine the areas to be occupied and used by evacuees . . . and changes in program, policy or procedure will be made only with the approval of the WRA," and that the WRA would provide the same administrative staff (project director, assistants, a community analyst to sociologically study the camps, and so on) to the reservation prison camps as the others.[12] The WRA also agreed to establish a work corps for imprisoned Japanese Americans and to allow them to be transferred between Gila River and Poston as well as to other prison camps. Additionally, the WRA conceded to "advance to the Sec. Of the Interior for expenditure by the Office of Indian Affairs funds to cover the expenses of the work to be done by and under the direction of the Sec as provided in this memorandum, in accordance with a budget approved by the WRA."[13]

The crux of the agreement, however, was the WRA and DOI's justification of internal improvements to the tribal councils as fair compensation for access to their land. Both agencies agreed "the development and operation of the relocation project . . . so far as it involves the subjugation of the land and the development of irrigation facilities, will materially enhance the value of the land."[14] Moreover, benefits from this increased value would "accrue to the Indians as the owners of the land when the evacuees are removed after the end of the war."[15] Despite the emphasis on Japanese American self-sufficiency and morale espoused by administrators, they fully acknowledged that the work the Japanese Americans would perform would not be for their benefit but for the benefit of the government agencies in charge of reservation management. Eisenhower deemed the construction of irrigation systems and the subjugation of land for cultivation beneficial. Ickes agreed that "the value of such improvements left on the land will be fair and equitable compensation to the Indians for the use of their land."[16]

The Colorado River tribes agreed in April to allow the agencies to use their land for the duration of the incarceration project. "Agreed" is a problematic term, however, as there was unequal power at play among the different entities. As in many land dealings between federal agencies and tribes, coercion was at the root of agreements. In this case, promises of land improvements on reservations were held as bargaining chips. The Colorado River council voiced concerns over the use of their land for the containment of yet another minority group. According to OIA reports, tribal council members were also "extremely antagonistic toward the Japanese," though their ire was directed more "toward the Caucasians for permitting the Japanese to come on to the reservation."[17] In the end the tribal council agreed to the terms outlined by the OIA and the WRA, which included the use of Japanese Americans to install new irrigation systems and to help to clear and cultivate land for future use. On April 14, 1942, the Colorado Reservation tribes "consent[ed] to the use by the WRA and the Sec. Of the Interior of such areas within the reservation as may from time to time be designated by the Secretary for approximately 20,000 persons of Japanese nationality or descent," though true consent was an afterthought as the Army Corps of Engineers had already arrived on site to begin building the units before the agreement was signed.[18] The WRA also guaranteed that it would "remove at the expense of the United States . . . said internees . . . within a reasonable time after the termination of the war, and to assume full responsibility that this removal will in no way interfere with the rights and activities of the Indians."[19] The work performed by Japanese Americans on the reservation would be considered part of the OIA's contribution to the war effort.

Collier also had grand visions for the project beyond structural improvements. His goal of creating a colony for the study of Japanese Americans and their abilities to build communities and establish self-government while detained was not far removed from his work and support for the "Indian Personality Research Project." This large-scale, multiyear study was a joint venture between the OIA and the University of Chicago's Committee on Human Development (sponsored by the American Indian Institute).[20] The project's purpose was to "determine the degree to which the personality of the Indian child is able to develop fully, and the factors in the physical and social environment, including the influences of government programs."[21] Inspired by the "success" of the Indian Personality Project, Collier turned his eye to using a similar format to study the Japanese Americans imprisoned on the reservations. In addition to using Japanese Americans for structural improvements on Native land, Collier argued that a sociological study of how the prisoners reacted to their environments would be of great value to not only the OIA and the WRA but also any agency or institution looking to develop democratic and self-sufficient communities among its workers, residents, or other groups.

Collier was also quick to explain in reports to Ickes and the WRA that the proposed colony project at Poston would benefit Japanese Americans over the long term. He argued that after their stay at the Poston prison camp/ colony, Japanese Americans would return "to their normal place as members of the American community, not only as loyal citizens or resident aliens, but as better citizens, more realistically democratic in principle, in thought, and in effect."[22] Participating in community building would necessitate Japanese Americans honing their existing skills or developing new ones that would not only benefit the prison but improve their own chances of securing employment in the future. E. R. Fryer (a regional director for the WRA) echoed Collier's goals for Japanese Americans and emphasized the usefulness of labor in reshaping the land of the reservation and in community building. "The projects to be studied are designed to weld the evacuated Japanese into respected and self-respecting communities in a manner which is to assure a swift and efficient resettlement, full protection of American interests, and satisfactory use of Japanese abilities," Fryer explained in a report submitted to Milton Eisenhower justifying the purpose of the proposed research project at Poston.[23]

In order to accomplish the goals of the project, particularly "the develop[ment] of functional local democracies" among Native Americans and Japanese Americans, the promotion of self-governance in the prison was essential.[24] Eisenhower, who was only a hesitant supporter of long-term Japanese American incarceration as he feared the more permanent consequences on the psyche of the imprisoned, advocated for self-government in the form of temporary community councils composed of elected Nisei representatives from each block of residential barracks. Collier spotted an ally in Eisenhower. In April 1942, the commissioner spoke with the director on the necessity of not only self-government at Poston but the need to retain as many civil liberties and freedoms for the prisoners as possible if it were to become a truly revolutionary sociological experiment. Such freedoms and liberties included the ability to produce some reading material in Japanese, allowing council meetings to operate as freely and with as limited supervision from administrators as possible, and promoting a camp newspaper that was lightly censored in order to "concentrate . . . the richest possible stimulus in the direction of getting a vital democratic response [from the Japanese Americans]."[25] Collier was not necessarily as interested in ensuring that the prisoners' freedoms were respected as much as he was in creating as "pure" an environment as possible to measure the effects of incarceration on Japanese Americans and their commitment to democratic communities.

Collier also emphasized the importance of Japanese American self-governance. The WRA and OIA initially designed the structure of self-government at Poston to be similar to that of the other camps, but Collier's emphasis on self-governance also had an ulterior motive. The WRA and Collier agreed to provide more freedom in self-government for the incarcerees to also promote "cooperative living" or organization and discipline for the purpose of ensuring continued self-sufficiency, production, and labor. Above all—even beyond Collier's dream of using Poston as a social experiment—the WRA sought to ensure that "as quickly as possible, the community was to become economically self-sufficient," as "in time of war, with every dollar and all manpower in demand, it was important to convert the Center from an item of government expense into an asset." Because removal "had been a great shock to the Japanese," it was imperative "for their own welfare and future usefulness as members of the American nation" that they became "busy as quickly as possible in work that would provide independent livelihood, self-respect and an opportunity to make a record that the rest of the country could appreciate." In order to accomplish all of the outlined goals, "a program of self-government was envisaged that would develop gradually" to "emphasize the creation of a community that would provide security, stability and an opportunity to earn a living."[26] Self-governance maintained order and ensured that maximum productivity would allow the colony to be self-sufficient and cheaply maintained while also supporting the war effort and infrastructure projects.

Before Poston could become a self-sufficient colony, workers needed to complete the camp and prepare it for reception of its prisoners—which was more complicated than officials had perhaps expected. When Eisenhower arrived at Poston in April to take in the progress, he was appalled at what he discovered. There was no conceivable way Poston was fit to receive the first wave of "voluntarily" arriving Japanese Americans who would be leaving their homes within the next month. Earlier in March, Collier's assistant Walter Woehlke established a plan of action for whipping Poston into shape with the assistance of the War Department, which would be responsible for

Figure 8. Members of the Colorado River tribes at the Colorado River Indian
Reservation unload beds for Japanese Americans before their arrival at the Poston
prison camp. Photo by Fred Clark, April 1942. Courtesy of the Bancroft Library.

building the necessary structures. Woehlke sketched out the "three phases"
of the creation of the prison on the Colorado River Indian Reservation: "1)
The erection of barracks to house a minimum of 20,000 persons in six weeks.
Of necessity these quarters must be of flimsy construction, 2) Construction
of semi-permanent quarters, of utilities, public buildings and irrigation systems plus a certain amount of subjugation work, [and] 3) Operation of part
of the subjugated land for subsistence and for needs of Army."[27] The plans
were rough, but adequate in Woehlke's opinion to "plan for colonization of
the CRR before the first shovelful of dirt is moved by the Army engineers."[28]
Woehlke also called for the Japanese American "communities" or barracks
to consist of "strips of varying widths running from the north to the south
for use and occupancy by the different tribes" once the prisoners were gone.
Japanese Americans were to subjugate, irrigate, and cultivate the land around
these communities for food, with any surplus going to the army.

Eisenhower did not find even "flimsy" barracks for the housing of Japanese Americans let alone any of the resources that would be necessary for the prisoners to irrigate and subjugate the land. The lack of any discernable progress at Poston horrified the director. Looking around at the desolate landscape, Eisenhower wearily took in the scene: "The tar paper is blowing off of the roofs about as fast as it can be put on. The sand is blowing through wide cracks in the floor. The walls at the back of the stoves in the Mess Halls have not been insulated. The roads are of course in very bad shape. The water is bad, so much so that a chlorinator must be rushed over for installation."[29] "General Dewitt gave instructions on all of these points; correctives should have been underway weeks ago," an exasperated Eisenhower recounted.[30] Eisenhower was puzzled by went wrong at Poston (and, in fact, Leighton would issue a report the following year titled "What Went Wrong at Poston"), but the struggles of Poston to even get off the ground were similar to the problems faced in the establishment of the other camps.

Although Eisenhower was sorely disappointed with the lack of progress at the camp, by April the site was "a scene of great activity" where "speed was the keynote." The US Army Corps of Engineers supervised WRA-hired contractors, who hastily erected barracks to accommodate ten thousand Japanese Americans on arid land after clearing the few trees that provided shade within the complex. The newly constructed living quarters were organized by blocks, which consisted of fourteen barracks as well as a recreation hall, mess hall for meals, male and female pit latrines, and laundry facilities. While crude forms of these structures existed, hospital facilities, warehouses, water towers, wells, sewage disposal systems, and offices and housing quarters for the administrative personnel were still under construction. Poston would eventually consist of three separate camps or units (Poston I, II, and III)—jokingly referred to as "Dustin," "Roasten," and "Toasten" by the prisoners for their desert locale, all separated by approximately three miles—two of which were not yet completed in even the most rudimentary sense in April 1942. On completion, Poston would become one of the largest "cities" in Arizona as well as the most populated prison camp (approximately seventeen thousand at peak in September 1942) before Tule Lake became a segregation center in 1943.[31]

Leighton and other administrators would look back in amazement that Poston did not immediately collapse before it opened as "the constant threat that within a few days thousands of men, women, and children, including infants and invalids, would begin flowing into the center at the rate of 500 a day." Leighton credited the administrators for doing what needed to be done

Figure 9. Leftover materials from the construction of the housing barracks and other facilities at the Poston prison camp. Administrators expected Japanese Americans to use scraps to finish making their environment more "hospitable." Photo by Fred Clark, May 9, 1942. The original caption for this photo reads: "Poston, Arizona. Scrap lumber which will be put to many uses by evacuees of Japanese American ancestry upon their arrival." Courtesy of the National Archives and Records Administration.

to ensure that Poston opened on time and was ready to accommodate the thousands of prisoners soon to arrive. "That collapse did not occur was largely due to the mutual understanding of men in each of the organizations and their will to help," Leighton later noted, recognizing the administrators who "had the courage to assume responsibility for action in the emergency without knowing whether or not they would be backed up by the law, the Government or Congress."[32]

Building a "Modern Colonial Community": Life and Work at Poston

What Leighton overlooked was that it would be the unpaid labor of the prisoners themselves, or "pioneers" (as Collier would come to see them), that prevented the collapse of Poston in its earliest days. On May 8, 1942, the "physical shell of Poston began to fill with its human occupants," the first being the Japanese Americans who voluntarily arrived at the prison directly from their homes in Washington, Oregon, and parts of California (those from the detention centers in Santa Anita, Pinedale, and Salinas would arrive later) with the assistance of the WCCA and their army escorts. These volunteers—similar to those that arrived early at Manzanar—came with the goal of preparing the living quarters in exchange for a paycheck. They did not volunteer their labor for free but rather volunteered to arrive early and assist with preparing the camp, and to be paid for this work later. Eventually, Poston administrators figured out that they could use the eager volunteers to complete the camps, perform other administrative duties, and carry out maintenance tasks in preparation for the next arrivals. Within the first two weeks of May, 251 Japanese Americans arrived to work on construction crews, staff the hospitals, and serve as stenographers and receptionists. Leighton generalized descriptions of Japanese Americans and observed that they "proved to be diligent workers, were prepared for hardships, seemed cheerful, and were among those who had reacted to the evacuation situation by a determination to make the best of it."[33] Whether or not those who arrived early did so out of a genuine devotion to building a "modern colonial community" remains unknown; rather, arriving early may have meant more freedom in some areas (such as choosing occupations at the prison camp when the WRA administration phased out the Work Corps concept to a more traditional approach of responding to hiring ads by the fall of 1942) and more money (which in many cases would not materialize for months to come).

The volunteers were also put to work by the administration in the process of "intake" when the other prisoners arrived. Beginning the second week of May, "the new arrivals, coming in a steady stream, were poured into empty blocks one after another, as into a series of bottles" in order to be "processed" and assigned living quarters, provided supplies, and directed toward occupational opportunities at Poston. While the sun beat down on rubbish piles and row after row of black tar-papered barracks, the sound of hammers and the hum of motors in trucks, cars, bulldozers, tractors, pumps, and graders surrounded Japanese Americans who were ushered off the buses that transported them from the nearest train depot in Parker, Arizona. From there, the prisoners gathered their family members and bundles and were escorted by military police to the mess halls, where they were provided ice water, salt tablets (to help with dehydration), and wet towels. Administrative assistants—both

Japanese American and white—then guided the new arrivals into cramped offices with desks jammed next to one another and staffed with both white and Japanese American representatives in charge of intake. Cots lined the back wall so those who fainted from heat or exhaustion were able to lie down for a bit and stretch out—but there were too many weary travelers and not enough cots, forcing many to pass out on the floor. While the new arrivals tried to catch their breath and gain their bearings, interviewers sat at long tables and walked among the Japanese Americans waiting to be processed, suggesting that they consider joining the Work Corps. The idea was not fully explained except that it was a way to earn extra money and prevent idleness during their stay. Eager administrators continuously thrust application forms into the faces of the new arrivals while men and women, "still sweating while holding on to children and bundles," tried to process the options before them.[34]

Feeling flustered, overwhelmed, and tired enough to agree to just about anything to be free of the interviewers, many signed the form and enlisted in the Work Corps. The enlistees agreed to accept "whatever pay, unspecified at the present time, the War Relocation Authority determines" for jobs based on former occupations (when possible) and observe all rules and regulations. The Work Corps members also relinquished access to workmen's compensation and assumed all financial responsibility for the full value of any government property used while in the corps. The infraction of any regulations of the WRA rendered the enlistee liable for trial and suitable punishment. In the end, "a few read the form carefully and very few refused to sign."[35]

Japanese Americans who enlisted in the Work Corps had mixed reactions to the program's requirements. WRA administrators organized the corps around the principles that there would "be no scarcity in jobs" at the camps and that "jobs would be provided for everyone who wished to work under whatever conditions the Government would stipulate." Although the WRA abandoned this version of the Work Corps by fall, Japanese Americans at Poston came to view the whole setup as a "make-work situation," or that the job situation "was not a real one related to any economic necessities."[36] In other words, the Work Corps created busy work for the incarcerees. At first, many were eager to help set up their new communities, but soon, as one employee stated, confusion about wages and delays in their disbursement made "the whole thing stink." The employee didn't fault Poston's administrators for the mishaps but rather "the system—the system starting with a bang on a grand idea, without attention to details."[37] Another declared in an interview with a Poston researcher, "I'm not working yet. I don't feel like working. If they force me to I might have to."[38]

But there were also disagreements among the Japanese Americans and WRA administrators on "where the evacuee obligation to work began or ended." Some incarcerees spoke out against work and camp cooperatives because the WRA should be supplying what they need without labor—it was not the fault of the Japanese Americans that they were imprisoned. Some WRA administrators also believed that sixteen dollars a month was insufficient for the amount of work Japanese Americans performed; others grew frustrated with what they perceived as a lack of motivation among Japanese Americans and thought that perhaps sixteen dollars a month was *too much* for the bare minimum of work the WRA required from them. During a meeting, both Nisei and Issei leaders agreed that work to improve the camp was required for the benefit of all but were "wary of the vague, larger plans in terms of which the administration seemed to be talking" when describing pioneer projects and the construction of a colony.[39] However, there were also incarcerees who overlooked the issue of wages because they were "anxious to work for the people" or "were enjoying the feelings of responsibility, prestige, or authority" in the camps that came from working closely with white WRA supervisors, according to reports from anthropologist Edward H. Spicer, who also conducted studies at Poston.[40]

Regardless of early disagreements (which would resurface later at Poston), by 1943, approximately 50 percent of Poston's population (excluding children, the elderly, those physically incapable of work, and new mothers—approximately 25 percent) was employed in some capacity for the camp. Clerical work (particularly for Nisei women), farm work and food production, construction, and general operational services were the largest occupations at Poston. Professional and skilled opportunities were available at Poston; however, as Japanese American Evacuation and Resettlement Study assistant Tamie Tsuchiyama stated, "it is still more regrettable that those possessing intelligence and ability to do work of extended scope have had to find their efforts confined simply because the avenues to individual self-determination within the American society were so insurmountably barred."[41]

Life at Poston was organized around labor, meals, and—when necessary and appropriate—leisure, similar to the other camps. However, the burden of completing infrastructure projects for another colonized and subjugated people that rested on the shoulders of Japanese Americans made Poston unique. On July 16, 1942, Ira K. Evans (an administrator in the Employment

Division) addressed all of the unemployed residents (Issei and Nisei) of Poston I to plead for their participation in one of these many projects. Evans explained that he "knew how hot it is outside and how difficult it is to work on any project which requires working in the sun and dust," and admitted that the administration was not "here to dictate to you or compel you to work on any project against your will."[42] Instead, he appealed to the unemployed members of Poston to "improve their own city."[43] "Many, many working men" were required at the time for the subjugation and irrigation projects as well as the making of adobe bricks for constructing schools, yet still Evans insisted that this was only a call for volunteers who desired to "create a city [of] which they and the United States could be proud."[44] Little mention was made of the ultimate goal of Japanese American labor: improvement of the land for the betterment and savings of the OIA.

As a result of the woeful lack of preparation on behalf of the administrators and the focus on exploiting Japanese Americans rather than accommodating them, labor problems plagued Poston from the outset. From day one, the Japanese Americans who volunteered for the Work Corps were required to immediately form committees to handle trash, maintenance, and construction completion, making the goal of agricultural self-sufficiency and the promotion of "dignity" challenging. Block by block, the WRA established units to employ cooks, kitchen help, warehouse men, truck drivers, firemen, police, and "hundreds of other workers" (many of whom would have little to do in the first few weeks due to a lack of supplies).[45] In this sense, from its inception, Poston was always a prison labor camp rather than the free colony that Collier had envisioned.

Japanese Americans imprisoned at Poston were quick to note and react to the chaos and poor working conditions when they arrived. In the midst of scrambling to get Japanese Americans settled and ready to work, the administration took "little time to look after the adjustment and indoctrination of those evacuees who were past the initial stages of settlement in Poston," as more continued to arrive throughout the early summer.[46] Japanese Americans at Poston resented the administrators for failing to deliver on promises of banks, schools, playgrounds, special facilities for those with unique medical conditions or infants, a hospital, stores, and other facilities. Moreover, prisoners expressed to administrators, block managers, and supervisors that they were angry "at the nature of the Work Corps enlistment which seemed to require that [they] renounce all chance of reimbursement for losses, that they promise everything, and gain no definite assurance in return, not even as to wages."[47] They also "particularly resented that they had been asked to enlist during the first moments of arrival when they were too tired and exhausted to give proper thought."[48] Poor food, temperatures reaching over one hundred degrees in the shade, dust storms, and the inadequate living conditions merged with labor grievances.

Intergenerational conflicts also coincided with labor dissatisfaction during the early days at Poston. As at Manzanar, Poston administrators were quick to blame tensions between Issei and Nisei for the riots and strikes, emphasizing issues of loyalty and suspicion while downplaying the role of labor conditions in resistance to the administration. At Poston, there were simmering resentments between first- and second-generation Japanese Americans; however, it was the preference of the administration to have Nisei in positions of political and economic power that served as a catalyst for the strikes.

Nisei were many of the first arrivals at Poston. Leighton described these early volunteer laborers as doing an excellent job considering their circumstances, but in a new, prisonlike environment filled with uncertainty, "the abilities and motives of the volunteers were unknown to the majority of the people." Why did they rush to arrive and help set up their own prison? What were they expecting? Were they already "in good" with the administration? As Leighton noted, "The Isseis [sic] did not take well to having such young persons in high places and other Niseis [sic] felt that simply because the volunteers had not had personal responsibilities [at home] they had been able to rush in early and secure all the good positions." Hostility and suspicion flourished among those imprisoned at Poston in the early days, and many of the volunteers were accused of "siding with the Administration" instead of "with the people."[49] The fact that many of the volunteers were placed in charge of the intake duties only added to their fellow prisoners' distrust. The WRA followed the same procedure established at other prisons and in the detention centers to place more Nisei in positions of political power, but the administrators did little to stem the growing distrust of the Nisei volunteers among the prisoners or address the lack of pay for work performed by the earlier volunteers. "No plan was offered whereby the volunteers could be rewarded for their early services and then retired while jobs were thrown open on a basis of merit to old and newcomers alike," Leighton later noted.[50] "Instead, matters merely went on as they were," contributing to underlying social problems exacerbated by unclear and often unfair work policies.

Problems with pay also plagued Poston and did not go unnoticed by Japanese Americans. The first arrivals who enlisted in the Work Corps did not receive any wages until July 17—almost two months for some prisoners who had been working since May. In June, the WRA announced a pay scale of twelve dollars for manual labor, sixteen dollars for clerical work, and nineteen dollars a month for professional occupations, which immediately prompted protests in Poston. Hostility stemmed from workers' assumptions that they were to receive WPA (at least twenty-three dollars a month) or "army" wages for doing work of a similar nature and for the same agencies. Especially galling was the fact that the lower pay scale was not included on the form they signed (or were coerced to sign) when they enlisted in the corps.

Second, prisoners and camp authorities disagreed over which manual labor jobs were "skilled" and which white-collar occupations deserved higher wages. Those who worked outdoors in the sweltering heat slinging picks and axes resented their sixteen-dollar-a-month wages while those who worked in "easy jobs" in cooler offices received higher pay. Similarly, intergenerational conflicts bubbled to the surface once again after the announcement of the pay scale as older Issei who were skilled farmers and employed in the Agricultural Department received only twelve dollars, while younger Nisei fresh out of high school or still in college received the highest wages for desk jobs. Generally, there were protests against the rate of pay regardless of the job.[51]

The way the camp administration disbursed the funds also fostered anger and resentment among the prisoners. Even when paychecks were distributed in a timely fashion (which was not guaranteed), the process was disorderly and chaotic, resulting in "people standing in line all day" for their wages. In other instances the receipt of payment was "dragged out over a number of days."[52] Clerical errors and general disorganization in payment departments resulted in miscalculated wages, while poor card-keeping among white supervisors (who often showed little concern for such matters) often left little in way of a paper trail for prisoners to argue for their missing wages. One man employed in the fields who worked over two hundred recorded hours in the month of July received a check for nineteen cents. Even this obvious error took a month to correct. In the meantime, those who worked in manual labor were unable to replace their tattered clothing without their pay; the clothing allowances of $3.50 a month would not cover these costs. Poston was far from a well-organized colony in its early days.

Japanese Americans were also wary of the underlying motives for their labor at Poston, regardless of the utopian rhetoric of the camp administration. The decision to place a prison on a reservation raised suspicions among the incarcerated of the true goals of Poston. The very presence of supervisors and administrators from the OIA prompted complaints from Japanese Americans that the government wanted to "keep" them "all the rest of their lives on 'reservations like Indians.'"[53] Social scientists in the Bureau of Sociological Research at Poston frequently noted that the Japanese Americans believed that "Indians were forced to stay on reservations much like animals in a zoo and that the Indian Office was a sort of keeper."[54] When asked about his experiences with labor at the prison, one Japanese American exclaimed in an interview that he "would not be worked like an Indian," reflecting the suspicion that the WRA and the OIA simply wanted to lock Japanese Americans away on the reservation indefinitely and colonize them like they had the Native Americans.[55] Another prisoner, engaged in agricultural labor at Poston, decried his low pay as an "Indian wage . . . which may be good for them, but not for me."[56] Leighton observed that Japanese Americans regarded "Indians in a stereotyped manner as a lower race of people with whom it was an insult to compare the Japanese," a product of both a legacy of poor treatment of Native Americans and the complicated racial identities that surfaced in a colonized and carceral space.[57]

Japanese Americans' resentment of "work[ing] for the Indians for nothing" characterized the labor that joined the carceral and colonial spaces.[58] An initial source of tension was found in Japanese Americans who rejected their position vis-à-vis Native Americans and the adobe school-building project. While administrators claimed that the buildings were for educating Japanese American children, and then eventually Native Americans, the idea of working as a community to build school structures that "were unfamiliar and were looked upon as inferior" was off-putting for the prisoners.[59] The labor required to make the bricks, let alone build the schools, was arduous. Workers "dabble[d] in mud" in 124-degree weather in the sun, baked the bricks in large, hot ovens, and ruined good work clothes (which they paid for with their own cash advances) for twelve dollars a month (supervisors promised them sixteen dollars). Women as old as seventy years mixed the materials and formed the bricks, relishing the days when the temperature remained under one hundred degrees and taking frequent rests (to the dismay of Mr. Popkins, head of the construction department).[60] In August 1942, laborers responded to these conditions with a strike, resulting in little enthusiasm from other Japanese Americans for the adobe work. Protests from Japanese Americans disappointed the project supervisors, particularly when their hopes of making five hundred thousand adobe bricks by the end of the summer of 1942 were dashed.[61] The OIA and WRA continued a project of colonization by tapping into a system of coerced work brought about by the war. In protesting their self-identified use as "slaves" for Native American–centered improvements, Japanese Americans rejected their exploitation but also attempted to leverage their status as free laborers as compared to Native Americans.[62]

From Desert to Farm: Japanese Americans, Agricultural Work, and Growing Unrest

Between June and August 1942, the Agricultural Departments for all three units of Poston were formed, and active members of the Work Corps were able to proceed with their mission of turning the dry desert into a flourishing agricultural paradise. Each agricultural department consisted of three divisions: farming, stock raising, and landscaping work. Each of these divisions—staffed by Japanese American members of the Work Corps, their immediate Japanese American supervisors, and white foremen and administrators in charge of each department—were also further subdivided into units such as those dedicated to truck farming or those focused on testing different crops and gardening.

The administrators embraced the idea that Japanese Americans were innately skilled at farming. The WRA drew up a list of a variety of crops, including carrots, beets, onions, and cabbage (separate from more specialized and difficult crops like daikon and soy beans), for the Agricultural Departments to produce and predicted that Poston alone would be able to produce more than two million pounds of food to feed twenty thousand Japanese Americans for the year. In order to achieve this goal, both Collier and Eisenhower decided that Japanese Americans would subjugate twenty thousand acres of the eighty thousand acres of "waste land" in the area and complete an extensive irrigation system. Such ambitious goals required an extensive work force and demanded an astronomical amount of labor in an inhospitable environment.[63]

While the imprisoned Japanese Americans were unaware of the specific quotas that the WRA expected them to fulfill, they had their doubts for why they were being asked to complete such extensive work on the reservation. There had to be an explanation beyond self-sufficiency. The prisoners repeatedly questioned WRA administrators and supervisors on the purpose of the Agricultural Departments. The WRA eventually did reveal to the Japanese

Americans that the fruits of their labor would potentially go to other sources if needed, but questions still abounded. "How would the agricultural products be marketed? How much food was stored ahead in the warehouse?"[64] Japanese Americans were rightfully concerned that the emphasis on farm labor would benefit others more than it would themselves.[65]

Ben Sakamoto, a twenty-three-year-old Nisei prisoner who lived in Block 53 in Poston I, also objected to the agricultural schemes of the Poston administrators. Ever since he was a small child, Sakamoto had farmed California's Coachella Valley, but he was less than motivated to continue the family business at Poston. Sakamoto instead opted for a clerk position in one of the warehouses at Poston I. When he was interviewed by Leighton's sociological assistants, Sakamoto argued that the experienced farmers (including himself) declined to work in the Agricultural Departments because "there was no percentage in it . . . back home, people made money, but here there is no future in it."[66]

Local farmers, businessmen, and the OIA had long hoped to make the land of the Parker Valley and the Colorado River Indian Reservation arable. In 1865, after the OIA established the reservation, Charles Poston (namesake of the prison and colony) received $120,000 from the federal government to build an efficient irrigation system. By 1875, the ʾAha Makhav people who lived on the reservation had completed an irrigation canal; however, the poor quality of the headwaters from the Parker Dam as well as the instability of the sandy soil prevented the canal from diverting water to the reservation. As a result, the ʾAha Makhav turned to hand watering meager crops or relying on rare floodwaters, leading to a significant decline in food production and an increased dependence on resources from the OIA. In 1910, Congress provided $50,000 to the OIA to yet again try to build an effective irrigation canal on the site. While the ʾAha Makhav installed a successful water-pumping plant on the reservation, the promised irrigation canal never materialized. The OIA became so desperate to make good on Congress's one-million-dollar project that they leased land on reservation territory to non–Native Americans in vain hopes that they would be inclined to establish an irrigation system.[67] The history of OIA's irrigation ambitions at Poston was characterized by decades of futility, but despite all of these setbacks, William C. Sharp (Poston's farm supervisor) argued that "the land of this valley is as good an area for farming as that which exists anywhere in the southwestern United States."[68] All that was required was the now readily available labor found among the imprisoned Japanese Americans.

Poston I served as the initial focus for the completion of the irrigation canal. The groundwork already existed for the venture from the work completed by the 'Aha Makhav in previous decades but required more ditch-digging and "landscaping" around the blocks and barracks. An Engineering Department established multiple crews to complete the canal and install a pump system and drains to divert water from the main source—wells and dam—to the various agricultural plots at the prison camp, which included both larger areas for subsistence farming and smaller plots for truck farming and other experimental crops.[69] The Public Works Department of the WRA, including the Engineering, Construction, Survey and Plans, and Excavation and Subjugation Divisions, oversaw the operations. By the fall of 1942, other related prisoner labor groups, such as those involved in road construction and public works crews devoted to diverting water for agriculture and animal husbandry, were established in all Poston camps.[70] Once the projects were completed, it would fall to the Engineering and Agricultural Departments to perform maintenance, and the canals could be continuously extended as more land became subjugated and available for farming.[71] By the end of 1944, Japanese American prisoners had completed more than forty miles of irrigation canals and supporting laterals across all three camps at Poston.[72]

Despite the end result, Leighton provided other glimpses of the struggling irrigation and agricultural programs. Upon completing a report on the conditions of Poston by the end of 1942, Leighton wrote to project director Wade Head and Collier (in a tone reminiscent of Eisenhower's earlier visit to the prison in May) to express his disappointment with the state of agriculture and other projects. At the time, the water irrigation system only reached Poston I, animal husbandry was failing, and only a few lonely patches of cucumbers, tomatoes, and daikon grew on personal lots and in individual block gardens. "In making these observations, it is not our desire to blame any individual or department," Leighton assured, "but rather to learn from past experience what may be helpful in the future."[73] He offered a series of explanations for the failure of the agricultural program but highlighted two, which he termed "outside" and "internal" forces: "trouble getting supplies and equipment—the result of outside forces"; and "trouble securing full cooperative work effort by the residents—the result of internal forces."[74]

The two were related, as the prisoners employed on the project keenly felt the "external forces" that hindered supply procurement. Henry Suzuki, a Nisei member of the truck crops crew, complained in a weekly report from August that his crew lacked long hoes to plant celery (leaving them to do it in the "primitive" manner by hand, which slowed down the process considerably) and were forced to use old milk jugs and pieces of crates to fix certain parts of the irrigation system in an attempt to save and maintain the crops they had planted.[75] Meanwhile, Leighton credited the "internal forces" at work in preventing the prisoners from pulling together to complete the irrigation system to "a present, widespread feeling of apathy among the evacuees," which increased within the first six months of their time at Poston.[76] Some Nisei called it "the WPA feeling," while one Issei Leighton interviewed retorted, "Of course we should work, but for $12 and $16 a month, we should not work very hard."[77] Far from seeing themselves as pioneers in a colony, many of the imprisoned Japanese Americans viewed themselves as "slaves" who worked for little or no benefit to themselves. In fact, as one prisoner noted, "the old notion of building a community went out the window when we saw how we were to work and what we were to be paid . . . for the welfare of the Indians and the government, not for ourselves."[78]

In tandem with the construction of the irrigation canal, crews in all units of the camps cleared trees, rocks, and other obstacles for both irrigation and general cultivation. Through the summer and early fall of 1942, these crews typically consisted of twenty to thirty members of the Work Corps (laboring for the twelve- or sixteen-dollar-a-month wage) overseen by either Issei or Nisei supervisors and a white manager. The work required shoveling and hauling large amounts of soil, felling trees, and moving required materials in the sweltering heat. A primary nuisance for many of the crews was the unyielding soil, which often necessitated multiple attempts at digging up the roots of hardy mesquite trees, proving difficult for both land improvement and cultivation.[79] Other factors including the seemingly never-ending need for materials and supplies that were always late in arriving, as well as environmental and climatic conditions that made land subjugation a challenging and often unrewarding job as well as one defined by exploitation and unrest.

Richard Nishimoto left a detailed account of his work on a land subjugation crew, illustrating not only the harsh conditions and challenges but also the views of his fellow laborers at Poston. Nishimoto was both a member of the subjugation crew at Poston I and a research assistant for the Japanese American Evacuation and Resettlement Study, a sociological project directed by University of California, Berkeley, anthropologist Dorothy Swaine Thomas and composed of various Nisei and Issei research assistants, which operated independently from the Sociological Bureau. While at Poston I, Nishimoto became a foreman of a group of thirty men employed on a firebreak gang.

Figure 10. A Japanese American crew clears sagebrush at the Topaz prison camp in preparation for constructing irrigation ditches. Photo by Tom Parker, October 18, 1942. Workers at Poston engaged in similar work. Courtesy of the Bancroft Library.

Although firebreaks—large tracts of cleared and leveled land—are typically created in order to prevent the spread of wildfires, at Poston they doubled as cleared areas for irrigation canals and, if needed, additional plots of land for agricultural production.

In the fall of 1942, while Nishimoto was serving as a research assistant (or "informant") for University of California, Berkeley, anthropology PhD student Tamie Tsuchiyama (another Poston-based sociological researcher interested in the "exodus" of Japanese Americans and their later life at relocation centers), he decided to write of his experiences as foreman of the firebreak gang between June 27, 1942, and September 14, 1942.[80] Nishimoto's desire to understand and even influence the political landscape of Poston encouraged him to use his unassuming manner to buddy up to the Issei and others in the prison, and so resulted in an unusually descriptive and well-informed firsthand account of daily life.[81] As a result of Nishimoto's language skills (many of the men who initially labored as part of the firebreak gang were Issei) and his engineering degree, John Evans, the head supervisor of the project, appointed him as foreman of the group. In exchange, Nishimoto was responsible for "supervising and directing his fellow-prisoners on the field, having full responsibility for maintaining order and harmony among them and keeping in contact with the administrative branches or the Engineering Department for coordination."[82] Nishimoto described the firebreak gang as "a typical group of men who were engaged in outdoor labor of unskilled variety in this project," with "characteristics . . . either similar or identical with those of other outdoor labor groups such as the poultry crew, the fish culture crew, the farm gang, etc."[83]

The firebreak gang's work was divided into two phases. The first consisted of cleaning up piles of scrap lumber lying about the camp that were remnants of the contractors' attempts to hastily prepare the prison for its inhabitants. The workers would then separate the lumber that was still useable and haul it away before burning the remaining trash. During the second phase, workers felled trees and attacked the stumps before leveling the ground for irrigation and cultivation using tractors, axes, shovels, rakes, and pitchforks. Even considering the arduous tasks, Nishimoto generally described the workers he oversaw as "willing to cooperate with each other and obedient to the leader," with "neither friction nor quarrel among them" and "without antagonistic feeling." Nishimoto noted that "there was neither a trace of sentiment nor an occasion to resort to such a concerted collective action as a strike," but also that he did not wish to give the reader the impression that work on the firebreak gang was without problems. On the contrary, his account—written in more of a memoir or novel form—reveals a troubled work environment and consistent grievances relating to the larger goals of the crew and their exploitation.[84]

From the beginning, getting men to sign up for the firebreak gang proved difficult. In late May 1942, John Evans (supervisor of the firebreak gang for Poston I and an associate engineer) was tasked by the Engineering Department with finding at least 250 Japanese Americans to work in clearing the land for the irrigation canal. Evans urged all of the block managers to "get all [their] idle men out" and directly contact the men without employment and persuade them to join the gang. During a meeting with all of the unemployed men on June 6, Evans pointed out that "the whole community would be benefitted by [their labor]," as the sooner they worked to complete the canal, "the quicker [they] will have water for vegetables and dust control." Also, "if water was brought into Poston I, it would have a cooling effect" and few would suffer from the intense heat. Finally, Evans also promised the prisoners that "they would be compensated for the public-spirited service."[85] Tom Ito, a Nisei assistant to Evans, also appealed to the men by asking them to "help the country" during the war. Ito's message worked on Nishimoto, who joined the crew the next day. However, rather than 250, only about one hundred men reported for work on the firebreak gang, proving that Evans and the rest of the administration were overly optimistic in thinking that hundreds of Japanese Americans would willingly sign up for uncompensated work.

When Nishimoto reported for work at Block 44's firebreak on the morning of June 7, he found "one big mess": one hundred mainly Issei men "excitedly picking up lumber off the ground and energetically throwing them on trucks and trailers scattered all over" the site. The men seemed to be doing this work with wild abandon, creating "commotion and confusion all over the field." Another white assistant to Evans who was supervising until Nishimoto arrived told him that he was working them as quickly as he could and advised Nishimoto, "Don't let them ease up. Keep 'em busy."[86] They continued at this pace for about two hours, until the temperature began to rise by late morning. "How do they expect us to work without any drinking water around?" one man asked while throwing his pile of lumber to the ground and grabbing a handkerchief to wipe his face. Others began to grumble about the heat: "It's too hot. No use working! We're getting only six cents an hour anyway!" Nishimoto kept track of the temperatures throughout his days with the crew, noting that it was a scorching 113 that day. A man in another group began to shout, "Who do they think we are? Hell, we're no slaves. We don't have to work if we don't want to!" Nishimoto tried to reason with them in his new capacity as supervisor, but the "damage was done" and they "resented that [he] was trying to get the most out of them in the shortest time."

Nishimoto initially believed—like many of the sociological team he would come to work with—that the reactions of the group to their work was the result of psychological complications and a need for personality adjustments to their new surroundings. "I could sense uneasiness and unrest among the men," Nishimoto recalled. "They are not like the Isseis [sic] I had known before the evacuation," recalling members of the first generation who "were all industrious, diligent, obedient, and courteous people." In contrast, "these men . . . were suspicious, ill-humored, discourteous, irritable people." Calling up well-worn tropes of the older generation of Japanese Americans as peaceful and passive and the Nisei and Kibei as the "trouble makers," Nishimoto was dumbfounded by the recalcitrance he faced from his crew. But he "calculated that they were under severe strain and in an abnormal state of mind resulting from the evacuation . . . and had not adjusted themselves to the new environment," making them think of Nishimoto as "a white man's stooge." Consequently, Nishimoto also "suspected that they were not working there entirely from their own free will, but instead some kind of pressure or coercion was exercised upon them."[87] Bearing all of this in mind, Nishimoto made adjustments to the work schedule that day. He abandoned the supervisor's charge that he work the crew as hard as possible and instead sent a number of teenage boys in the area to fetch water from the nearby mess hall, ordered workers to rest between loadings, and advised the men to load at a slower speed so as not to strain themselves in the heat. Nishimoto's adjustments worked to a degree, as the number of complaints lessened over the course of the day and the next few weeks.

Nishimoto soon discovered, however, that deeper problems regarding the exploitative nature of the work often contributed to "grumblings" more than poor attitudes or mindsets. One day Nishimoto ran into a group of "bachelor Issei" having a conversation with each other in Japanese. As soon he approached, the men stared sharply at Nishimoto, immediately ceased their conversation, and went back to work. Nishimoto was eventually able to speak with one of the group members, and learned that the bachelors as well as others in the gang—both Issei and Nisei—believed that because they were "involuntary evacuees" (or forcibly removed), "no one could compel them to work," suggesting that under the Geneva Convention protocols, they could not be made to work.[88] Furthermore, they doubted that they would be compensated for their services based on the poor track record of payment for members of the Work Corps earlier at Poston and elsewhere. They also indicated that they had been "tricked" into working because the recruiter initially told them that the work would only last a day or two (they were on day ten of the job).

Nishimoto's own run-ins with his white supervisors did little to convince him that his crew's beliefs were unfounded. Although he repeatedly attempted to persuade his men that the "white men were not there to hurt" but to help them form a cooperative community, this mantra became more difficult for Nishimoto to accept as he witnessed firsthand the white supervisors' calloused responses to grievances.

A few weeks into the job, Nishimoto noticed that more white supervisors began to arrive to check up on the gang and ensure that Nishimoto was doing his job—an increasingly unwelcome turn of events for both Nishimoto and his workers. In addition to being criticized by a manager for allowing his workers to take breaks, Nishimoto was also reprimanded for not drumming up enough workers for the project, as if the working conditions were not reasons for people choosing not to join or remain on the job. A "Mr. Barbour," one of many assistant supervisors for the Engineering Department, pulled up to observe the progress at Poston I and noticed that there were far fewer men working than what he had hoped for. *Now, what does he want?* Nishimoto grumbled to himself.[89]

"Well, how many men you got here working?" Barbour asked.

"Nineteen, sir."

"Nineteen? Why don't you get more men? There are lots of men sitting on their asses all over camp. Why don't you get 'em? You should have at least a couple hundred out here," he replied.[90]

A couple of hundred! Nishimoto again thought to himself. *Like hell! Just try and get them to work for this little money and in this heat!* Of course, Nishimoto checked himself and replied more respectfully, but the implications from Barbour that Nishimoto was not doing his job properly and that the men of the camp refused to work because they were lazy were too much for even this typically pro-administration prisoner to take.[91]

Nishimoto became more defiant in his role as supervisor as the months dragged on. On one occasion, Evans admonished Nishimoto for allowing all of his men to take a break and sit down at the same time. "If you let them all sit down at once, it will look like a sit-down strike," Evans pointed out. *So what! Let it look like sit down strike!* Nishimoto thought, and while he explained more politely to Evans that he was the foreman and direct supervisor and therefore he would be the one to issue breaks, he told his crew that if they were resting and saw another supervisor to "never mind the white man and stay resting on your break."[92]

It would ultimately be the poor pay and exploitative nature of the work that would destroy Nishimoto's respect for many of the white supervisors and administrators. By mid-August, Nishimoto wrote that the gang was operating rather smoothly as more land was cleared and subjugated. With temperatures "easing" into the low nineties, the men on his crew were apt to work more efficiently, "with better speed and steadier constancy in swinging axes and digging shovels." They were able to subjugate between five and seven acres of land a day, which pleased Nishimoto and led him to believe that they "would have compared favorably, if not better, with that of any group of men employed elsewhere in the country at higher wartime wages." The reward for their work finally came on August 27, when the paymaster announced that the men of the firebreak gang would receive their checks.

This was a momentous day as most of the men had never received wages at Poston for their work before. Even Nishimoto would have money for the first time since he was removed from his home. Nishimoto playfully ribbed some of his workers before they got their checks, telling them they were excused for the morning because of receiving their pay and asking them, "What are you going to do with all the dough?" His men chuckled and one cynically replied, "Let's see what the government money looks like, when we get it," but his men beamed with the thought of receiving their first cash advances.[93]

But when they returned later that afternoon, the men were furious as they marched up to Nishimoto while brandishing their pay stubs. Seemingly all of the members of his crew had been "cheated" of their pay in some capacity as they were supposed to receive the standard monthly wage, yet their checks were for arbitrary amounts far below that. Two men received only $7.83 for the month (and they calculated they had worked 196 hours for the month of July), another received $10.81, and others received not a single cent because their names were not on the payroll. Others were nervous because they had obtained payday "loans" from Evans to purchase work clothes from the prison store which far exceeded what they had received in pay. Some called those in the accounting department a "bunch of imbeciles," and others speculated that their low pay was the result of administrators' "manipulating the paybook" and overcharging for advances for clothes and supplies. Nishimoto was disappointed in the administration for making his attempts to try to maintain peace and order look foolish, as well as mistreating his workers. A few days later Nishimoto received his own check: $9.28 instead of the promised $12 a month.[94] Another worker advised Nishimoto that he and the crew should "fight," and rather than resisting, Nishimoto thought to himself, *Fight? Why not?* He marched over to see Walter Palmer, the head of the payroll department for Poston I.

Palmer was less than sympathetic when Nishimoto stormed into his office and demanded an explanation for why he and his workers received so little pay. After examining the paychecks and the time cards for the men, Palmer explained that the checks were small, but such amounts were necessary considering deductions for work supplies as well as damages to some vehicles operated by the crew. Also, money had been deducted for the frequent breaks that many had taken in defiance of the wishes of the upper administration. When Nishimoto pushed back, suggesting that some of the jobs of the men should be considered eligible for the higher monthly rate of sixteen dollars instead of twelve dollars since they were doing skilled manual labor, Palmer replied that such a request was ridiculous because "they were just common laborers pulling stumps out." Seeing as how he was getting nowhere with Palmer, Nishimoto stormed out—seething—and back to his room.

Bastard! So we are common laborers, eh? he silently fumed.

Ever the sociologist, Nishimoto spent the rest of the night poring over pay stubs and time cards from his men, authoring a critical report to pass along to Evans and other members of the administration.[95]

Nishimoto's dealings with Palmer were representative of larger issues between Japanese American laborers and their (often white) supervisors. Numerous reported incidents and grievances of Japanese Americans against their white supervisors serve as evidence of the racialized work conditions the prisoners encountered. Sociological researchers stationed at Poston were quick to compose their own studies of the project directors, their assistants, and the white supervisors which corroborated Nishimoto's often callous interactions with men like Palmer and Barbour. Leighton differentiated between the "people-minded staff members" and the "stereotyped-staff members." The former worked for Poston and viewed "the evacuees as people first and Japanese secondarily," as if the two could be separated. They "on the whole established effective relationships with the evacuees pertinent to the accomplishment of their various jobs" and "respected the policies of self-government and self-management . . . as both practical and desirable."[96] Men like Wade Head, project director of Poston, his assistant and associate directors, and others who oversaw more of the professional operations of the prison were characterized by Leighton as possessing "practical ability and calm good sense." These men had previously held positions in the OIA or other agencies and were "anxious to promote the policies of community building as laid down by their superiors.[97]

Opposite of the "people-minded staff members" were the "stereotype-minded" staff who tended to hold lower-level administrative or supervisory positions and, unfortunately, had more direct contact with Japanese Americans. These employees—supervisors in construction as well as those employed in accounting (like Palmer), fiscal matters, timekeeping, procurement, transportation and supply, land subjugation, irrigation, and utility management as well as some members of the Army Corps of Engineers and post office employees—viewed the prisoners as "Japanese first and people secondarily." These were often positions which required less skill and, in general, "the amount of education they [the stereo-type minded] had received was gener-ally less than in the case of those who were people-minded."[98] Unlike the "high-minded" and more educated administrators, Leighton suggested that these staffers were less interested in the overall goals of the colony than in receiving a paycheck. In fact, "self-government and self-management of eco-nomic enterprises on the whole [were] regarded as visionary and impracti-cal" because the white supervisors viewed employing Japanese Americans as little more than "giving some of those Japs white men's jobs." Although Leighton did not immediately identify the "stereotype-minded staff" as rac-ist or even prejudiced (to use the more common term at the time), it was clear in his descriptions that these men were obstacles because they viewed Japanese Americans as "culturally deficient" and possessing inherently negative characteristics.[99] As a result, "among many of those who were stereotype-minded was a conviction that the Center was or ought to be a concentration camp" meant to ensure discipline and mete out punishments as necessary for the characteristically treacherous Japanese Americans. These administrators and supervisors functioned more as wardens in a prison than employers or staff when it came to their interactions with Japanese Americans.

Another test of Nishimoto's patience and trust came a few weeks later when some of the men were not payed. As the work went on through the end of August, there were men who wanted to sign up for the firebreak crew on a temporary basis simply to help get water to their camp, but Nishimoto was unsure of how this would work in practice. Confused, he went to Evans, who informed him to have the men work for three days as "volunteers," and then the administration would figure out a way to compensate them for their labor and possibly work them into a permanent job if they so desired. Approxi-mately thirty men volunteered in exchange for access to water for their own gardening and personal needs as well as the promise of a small cash advance for temporary work. However, come payday, another supervisor, Meecham, came over with the time cards from the volunteers and said that they were not valid as the men were not formally assigned to the project. Nishimoto was flabbergasted and tried to explain the agreement made with Evans, but Meecham simply informed him to go see Palmer (again).

Remembering his last run-in with the paymaster, Nishimoto begrudg-ingly walked over to his nemesis's office and prepared to do battle for the volunteers. As expected, Palmer was quick to respond that "the Japs worked as volunteers" and didn't have work cards. "We can't pay wages to guys who don't have work cards," Palmer insisted. "That's the rule here and I can't do anything about it." It was difficult for Nishimoto to maintain whatever composure he had left, so he gritted his teeth and explained, "Mr. Evans promised us that we are going to be paid for what we were doing, although we don't have work cards." Palmer immediately snapped, "Mr. Evans doesn't set the policy of this department. He can't make promises like that without our knowledge." Nishimoto eventually marched out again and over to another office of lower-level administrators and was able to secure the help of one accountant in getting some pay for three of the older Issei men (mainly because she felt terrible that such elderly men had worked for nothing), but the others never received compensation for their work; only access to the most basic of human rights—water.[100]

While Nishimoto was able to intervene in this instance, his internal wrestling with what had happened led to disillusionment with the goals of Poston. "I was angry," Nishimoto wrote in his account of his time on the firebreak gang. "My men were tricked into working by a false promise of financial return." Nishimoto thought of the "treachery" his men had faced, coming to terms with the fact that the supervisors "just wanted my men to work for nothing" and "just wanted to exploit them without any intention of paying wages." Although Nishimoto focused explicitly on his crew, he was not incorrect in his earlier statement that their experiences were similar to those of other workers across all three camps of Poston. An attempt to use Japanese Americans from Poston to harvest cotton under the supervision of the WRA and the army on nearby farms in Arizona resulted in many of the volunteers from the Work Corps going weeks without pay. Meanwhile, a camouflage net factory set up at Poston III produced conflict as well as netting when Japanese Americans attempted to pool their wages for redistribution to have more control over their pay free of WRA oversight. But only being immediately aware of the challenges his crew faced under exploitative labor was enough to make Nishimoto question the true motives of what the Poston administration was up to and their true feelings about the laborers who worked for them, against their will, without pay, and wrongfully imprisoned. *God damn it!! So we are Japs are we? Ignorant bastards!* Nishimoto raged as he worried how many more men "would be working for nothing" if things were allowed to continue like this. He did not know to whom or where to turn beyond Palmer, Evans, and the low-level accountant who helped him; however, he knew that this was about more than community building. He was beginning to come around to his men's cries of working for nothing.[101]

The "Poston Incident"

Nishimoto's growing dissatisfaction with exploitative labor conditions and his feelings of helplessness in addressing them demonstrated the weaknesses of one of Poston's most prized assets: an organized system of self-government for Japanese Americans. While all of the prison camps had a form of self-government, Collier and the administrators of Poston celebrated their version for its expansiveness, experimental nature, and contribution to the study of democratic institutions. But no matter their intentions, the reality was that Poston was still a prison work camp.

The temporary council structure was carried over to Poston and resembled that of the other camps. Each residential block was represented by a block manager, and many of the Nisei volunteer workers who arrived earlier obtained these positions (though later Issei held them as well).[102] The block managers focused on "block welfare, block problems, block morale, and block matters of all kinds," with some elected and others serving as co-leaders with members of work units. The block managers could then meet with those of the larger residential units (I, II, and III) at Poston to discuss general prison-wide matters. At the community council level, however, only Nisei could stand to represent their communities, on the basis of their supposed loyalty to the country and the administration.

As Poston consisted of three distinct subcamps (or units), the governing structure differed slightly from some of the other prisons. A unit council existed as a separate body between the block councils and overall community council. Director Wade Head approved the election of Nisei local councils for each residential unit and then charged those unit councils with electing representatives to serve as part of the general community council.[103] The community council members were all Nisei, with an average age of thirty-one and little to no experience in government or community leadership before removal. The camp administration charged the community council with issuing a charter encoding community-wide regulations and policies ranging from punishment for petty crimes to establishing and regulating leisure activities. The community council completed the charter in the fall of 1942.[104]

Despite the representative nature of self-government at Poston, the WRA, DeWitt, and Bendetsen hesitated to hand over too much power to the prisoners. In August 1942, WRA administrators agreed that responsibility for day-to-day activities and immediate policy making would rest with the prisoners, but the assistant project director for each prison would hold the power to veto all and any decisions made by the prisoners. At Poston, the individual unit directors for Poston I, II, and III (Len Nelson, James Crawford, and Morris Burge, respectively) held veto power in their respective units.[105] Self-governance was hardly self-governance at all, since all important matters were ultimately handled by the administration and, in practice, prisoners were not always consulted or deferred to despite the veneer of communal democracy.

The limitations on self-government imposed by the administrators at Poston, as well as the exclusion of Issei from any positions of authority, practically set the experiment up for failure. Even the WRA acknowledged that "the early problems of center management were largely beyond the effective responsibility of a politically organized evacuee group."[106] From the earliest days at Poston, block managers shouldered the heavy burdens of attempting to deal with the day-to-day trials and tribulations of living in a prison that was barely up and running. Over time, more Issei were elected block managers as they tended to garner respect among the new communities. Their constituents came to them requesting more food, water, building materials, and medicine, and presented a variety of other concerns and complaints. Unfortunately, the block managers often found these problems insurmountable. Nevertheless, the block managers did know their residents and were able to build a rapport with them and assure them that they were doing their best. But their best was limited as they were granted few political privileges by the administration and basically served to make sure that whatever daily supplies existed were distributed efficiently and that daily work assignments were completed. Block managers were also expected to work alongside white supervisors to sort out labor issues, problems that would soon become far too unruly for any one block manager to adequately address.

The unit- and prison-wide community councils, however, were, in the eyes of the prisoners, less effective still. First, as only Nisei could serve in these positions, the councils were often referred to as "the children councils" by older Issei or Kibei. Second, the positions did not require as much day-to-day interaction with the units, and their power was constrained by the whims of the administration. While the community councils handled some of the larger affairs, the Issei imprisoned in Poston attempted to address their own displeasure in being left out of any substantive political role. This was a position that many were unaccustomed to in their former communities. Block managers handled most of the work and resolved complaints, but received no formal recognition in return. Moreover, Issei were not initially allowed to vote in council elections (although this was later amended). Barred from holding political positions, some of the Issei created their own representative bodies, the Issei advisory councils, which served similar functions as the community councils but catered more to the needs of the older generations and the Kibei. The administration did not formally recognize the advisory councils, but the advisory councils worked informally with the community councils in a variety of matters concerning supplies, labor, and regulations. Despite this initiative, tensions would still rise as the administration failed to recognize the Issei, particularly when more Nisei would leave Poston for outside employment and to return to school, leaving the Issei to manage and work the prisons. This tension soon boiled over when mixed with labor issues.

The cooperative spirit among the Japanese Americans that both the sociological researchers and the camp administration were waiting for finally emerged on November 18, 1942, but in the form of a labor strike. The immediate causes of the Poston strike were similar to those at Manzanar. Tensions among Issei, Kibei, and Nisei fomented suspicions that prisoners (particularly Nisei) cooperating closely with the administration were acting as "informants" for both Head and the FBI. A community analysis of Poston detailed "a series of gang beatings in Poston I" in the previous three to four months before the strike, with "a gang of six to twelve unidentified men [attacking]" alleged "stool pigeons" and informers with clubs at night and fleeing before they could be apprehended.[107] No witnesses came forward in any of the reported cases, allegedly because they and their families had been threatened with reprisals if they betrayed their fellow incarcerees.

In the fall of 1942, two violent attacks resulted in the controversial detention of two suspects, which roiled the camp. On October 18, Nisei Joseph Seto was attacked in his barracks, and later, on November 14, Kibei Kay Nishimura suffered a similar fate. Little is known about Seto, but the community analysis reported that Nishimura was "generally disliked by the community because of alleged improper moral conduct" and suspicions that he was serving as an informant.[108] Based on circumstantial evidence gathered by camp police from other prisoners, the director of internal security, Ernest

Miller, and Wade Head arrested Isamu Uchida for the Seto attack and Nisei George Fujii for his membership in the gang of approximately ten who attacked Nishimura. While Uchida and Fujii were not charged with any crime, they were arrested and held for further questioning.

Unknown to Head and the Internal Security Department was the fact that both Uchida and Fujii were beloved members of the community. Within the first three days that the men were held for questioning, family and friends of both Uchida and Fujii visited them in the prison, fearing that they would be taken out of Poston and tried in Parker, Arizona, where they would not receive a fair hearing, considering the hostile public sentiment toward Japanese Americans. Once Head, fearing that the beatings indicated some form of mass sabotage effort, involved the FBI, those close to the two men and the larger community of Poston I grew more concerned for their well-being. Rumors that the cross-examination methods used by the FBI were particularly harsh, as well as the perceived threat that "if the suspects did not talk, it might result in internment of their parents," only fueled the growing fear and resentment over the arrests and detainment, regardless of the suspects' actual involvement in the assaults.[109]

Witnesses described what happened next as either a spontaneous movement brought on by the anxieties of the prisoners or manifestations of pro-Axis and anti-administration agitators, depending on the report. On November 17, friends and family members as well as fellow inhabitants of the block where Uchida and Fujii lived met with a group of Issei who were granted permission by Wade Head to visit him and discuss their views on the situation. The Issei representatives of the block "attested to the good character of both of the suspects," offered to show evidence in support of their conclusion in the form of character testimonies and others who would speak on behalf of the men, and asked that the two might be released.[110] Head referred the group to the FBI, which, unsurprisingly, refused to either listen to the delegation or release the suspects.

Unhappy with their treatment, the group returned to Poston I and relayed their unsatisfactory dealings with Head and the FBI, gathering in meetings in six different blocks to plan their next moves. Rumors circulated throughout the camp that Fujii was to be charged with murder and that Uchida's fate was unknown.[111] Some residents (including members of the delegation) called for a demonstration in front of the jail to prevent the removal of Fujii and Uchida from the camp. Vague plans were already in place for a strike if their wishes were not respected. The next morning, Wednesday, November 18, another delegation of residents familiar with Fujii and Uchida approached Head to plead for the release of the prisoners. This time, however, they brought a petition containing the names of 110 residents of their block "respectfully requesting the release of the prisoners on the ground that they were innocent—and again offering to show evidence to prove it." Just as before, Head brushed them off and referred them to the FBI, where the agents all but slammed the door in their faces.

Rebuffed a second time, the delegation returned again to Poston I. In response to this news, however, many prisoners seriously discussed the idea of a work strike to protest their treatment by both the project director and the FBI agents. At noon, prisoners from Unit I congregated outside the jail where Uchida and Fujii were held. Depending on the source, the size of the crowd ranged from a few hundred (according to Leighton's account) to "a mob" of one thousand to fifteen hundred Japanese Americans (according to official camp reports).[112] Once gathered, a number of those in attendance delivered speeches to the effect that they were prepared to prevent the removal of Uchida and Fujii by any means necessary, including "turning over the FBI car when it came and to spirit the prisoners out of the jail."[113] Someone rang a bell, calling attention to the crowd and urging others to join, while other Issei men went block to block to announce that a general work strike might be in the offing if the prisoners were not released. Noting the size of the crowd, the chairman of the Issei advisory board took the opportunity to declare the demonstration a "mass meeting," scribbled down a declaration, and climbed on a nearby tank to "make a speech stressing the demand for release." More prisoners made their way down to the jail, with many walking off their jobs to simply investigate the commotion after hearing the word "strike." One participant admitted that he was not really aware of what was going on with Fujii and Uchida. "I don't know what the issues were and I don't imagine anyone else did either," he explained. "There were so many conflicting issues. Everyone took up the torch in defense of his own particular peeve."[114] Although the immediate cause for the gathering of the mob was the arrests of Uchida and Fujii and the consensus that their detention by the FBI was unwarranted, as the individual above attested, it quickly morphed into a protest using labor as a weapon to lash out against the general conditions of Poston.

Although the strike was contained to Poston I, those employed on various works projects in other units walked off their jobs on Wednesday, November 18. The protest on behalf of Uchida and Fujii grew "until their plight became a symbol of everybody's grievance," creating momentum for the movement and "sweeping up into its form many other issues." From members of the agricultural crew to those working in the mess halls, employees left work to stand in the picket lines in eight-hour shifts in front of the jail. Every block in Poston I also sent representatives to join the march, replete with flags bearing their unit number. Women cooked over open bonfires in order to keep the mess hall closed, giving an air of "carnival" to the strike as the prisoners commandeered speakers and broadcast Japanese music and sang songs in both English and Japanese. Reports were sure to mention that "there were no indications of any organized, premeditated acts of violence during the strike," nor "acts of organized sabotage" save for some "unauthorized opening and closing of valves" in the hospital, but these could not be proven as acts of sabotage.[115] Although one area engineer from the Work Corps had noticed an increase in damages to equipment in the two months prior to the strike, he could not say for sure that it wasn't merely the result of carelessness in performing maintenance.[116]

Support for and participation in the strike spanned class and generational divides. While members of Poston II and III were not as quick to join the strike as they did not have any direct relationship to the two men arrested and were hesitant to anger the administration with the FBI in town, others were sympathetic even if they stayed on the sidelines.[117] Representatives from Poston II issued a statement to the administration and those on strike at Poston I on November 20, linking the work stoppage to broader issues of democratic self-governance, writing, "The issue is not 'strike or not strike,' but whether we Poston residents believe in, are capable of and shall maintain law and order under a democratic form of government!"[118]

Poston II representatives were disappointed that the administration was not living up to its promise of allowing the community to tend to its own affairs in policing matters. They assured the strikers that they were "in active sympathy with the problem of [their] fellow evacuee residents."[119] Many Nisei supported the strike and walked out of their duties as well, but the leadership coalesced around the Issei and Kibei who organized meetings on how next to proceed. Those who worked in the hospital at Poston I were exempted from the strike as they were considered "necessary employees," but they developed resentful attitudes toward the strikers as they feared their recklessness jeopardized their careers both within and eventually outside Poston. Overall, however, the strike grew with both explicit and implied support for using labor to fight back against the broader structural issues in the camps. Leighton and others later characterized the strike as without leadership and not representative of the prisoners. Not all of Poston participated, but the role of various committees and the community council in the strike undermines these claims. The administration's interpretation of the strike as a disorganized, chaotic, and unrepresentative affair reinforced the notion of saboteurs and disloyal Issei and Kibei as the sole catalyst of the uprising.

The absence of many of Poston's administrators left most of the negotiating initially in the hands of the prisoners' committees and assistant-level administration. On the morning of November 18 (when the second delegation presented their petition to the FBI directors), Head and his associate director left to attend a meeting with Dillon Myer and other prison directors in Salt Lake City. Project attorney Theodore Haas was away on a business trip. John Maeno—a member of the legal department at Poston as well as a community council leader—was also out of the camp, attending a national conference of the JACL, leaving the Issei to deal with the mounting tensions among the prisoners, and assistant project director John Evans to deal with the growing strike. At one o'clock in the afternoon, the community council (sans its director) and the Issei advisory board met to hold a regularly scheduled meeting, but instead of following the out-of-date agenda they turned their attention to the strike and the protests in front of the jail. During the meeting, assistant director Evans appeared—now having been thrust into a position of leadership—and attempted to assure the crowd that the project director would do what needed to be done upon his return and "to trust the properly constituted authorities to do the job for which they are equipped."[120] His speech did little to assuage the prisoners. As a concession, he agreed to let the council draw up and submit a written explanation so that he could have it ready for when Head returned (unaware of the fact that the two delegations had already twice attempted to file such reports with Head and the FBI directors).

In turn, the council submitted a petition detailing that "the residents of Poston feeling aggrieved and indignant of this unjust action taken against these two people have demonstrated in numbers their feelings in open meeting," and demanded that the two men be released immediately. The council also clarified that they did not believe that the investigation should be halted but rather that the men not be held for more than seventy-two hours since they were not formally under arrest per Arizona state law. Evans refused to turn over the prisoners, citing the need to maintain law and order and angering the council and crowd. The acting chairman of the council, a "very Americanized Nisei," appealed to the oft-repeated ethos of the administration in his reply: "If you cannot trust us, then we have nothing more to do. We feel you should give us self-government."[121] Their strategy had no effect on Evans, and in retaliation, the council members resigned their positions in protest, as did the Issei advisors and the block managers. The hurt and disappointed members of the government of Poston I marched out of the meeting hall and down to the jail to inform the protestors that the mass strike would continue.

Although the community council and advisory board dissolved themselves, the prisoners of Poston I recognized the need for an official representative body to negotiate with Evans. In response, ex-members of the advisory boards formed an "Emergency Executive Council" of twelve, consisting of a mix of representatives from all four blocks and three additional members—all Issei and Kibei. Other representatives from Units II and III joined in to serve as mediators and assist with the negotiations. At this point, Evans was wrestling with the idea of whether or not he should call in the army to provide additional support to the military police should matters escalate to violence and the safety of prisoners and government property be put at risk. Some members of the administration (those Leighton described as "stereotype minded") argued that Evans "coddled" the prisoners.[122] Both the supply officer and the fiscal officer, known for their anti-Japanese attitudes, fled the camp in a government car and refused to return until the strike ended when Evans declined to call in the army.[123] But Evans hesitated to ask for more men from the military for fear that violence would be the end result. Making matters worse was the continued absence of Head, whom Evans repeatedly attempted to reach. In search of a resolution to the crisis, the assistant director contacted the Indiana branch of the WRA, where representatives advised that, if he desired, he could release Uchida and Fujii, but the choice was his. In the meantime, Evans requested more military police guards from DeWitt. Between November 19 and November 20, prisoner representatives and Evans held additional meetings, with little success. The growing frustrations of the prisoners reached a fever pitch. "Either give us self-government or call in the Army and get it over with," one in attendance said.[124]

A turning point in the strike developed when Head returned from his trip on November 24 to assess the situation. A meeting with the emergency executive council indicated a possible easing of positions on both sides. One member of the emergency executive council suggested that all of the residents of Poston should sign an affidavit confirming Uchida's innocence, but ultimately agreed that the prisoner could be released so long as the community judicial committee would agree to hold a trial. In return for the release of the prisoner, Head demanded that the emergency council and other committees work to prevent beatings and further assaults as well as "work to improve the low level of work efficiency in the Community." Even during times of unrest and protest, the administration was as concerned with productivity as it was with general order. In response, the council agreed to establish multiple subcommittees to deal with issues of labor, judicial matters, and public relations, while the administration insisted on having more administrative members serve on some of the committees, and that come January, elections would be held for new community leaders. Although some administrators were displeased with Head's decision and suggested that he should have simply refused to recognize the legitimacy of the executive council altogether, Head approved of the negotiations.

The strike therefore formally ended on November 24, and on January 30, 1943, the prisoners of Poston formed a new governing body consisting of a city planning board (which would eventually give way to the central executive council), an honors council, and a labor relations board (a union-esque body). The new representatives then set about rehiring new employees for a fresh start. The emergency council agreed to the administration's demand that "the work stoppage be treated as a cessation of all previous employment on the project, and reemployment will be carried on through the Employment Office under strict WRA employment regulations."[125] Head was satisfied with the results because the strike ended and camp life stabilized. The prisoners viewed the negotiation as a limited victory as they were able to still hold on to the idea of self-government and bargain for the release of Uchida.

The outcome of the negotiations ended the strike and managed to preserve the idea of self-government but left many important matters unresolved. The new, fragmented system of self-government did little to encourage cooperation from all of the prisoners and fostered further tensions and disunity among them. Although the labor relations board was charged with mediating all labor disputes, studying labor conditions, and making recommendations to the administration as well as serving as spokesmen for the prison workers—all responsibilities and rights of unions—the much-resented working conditions were not addressed. While Collier viewed Poston as an experimental colony, the WRA administrators viewed it as just another prison for Japanese Americans that relied on the efficient use of labor to ensure that the institution was self-sustaining. Prisoners at Poston were angry over both their exploitation and the limitations of the vaunted self-democracy program which, they were repeatedly told, made Poston unique. Collier and some administrators viewed colonial self-government as a form of cooperative democracy, while the prisoners viewed it as a means of seeking redress from an otherwise adversarial administration. And when those methods were not respected, they resorted to the one form of action they knew would get attention and over which they enjoyed control: ceasing their labor. The protests exposed the myth of Poston as a cooperative, self-governing colonial space, revealing that the administrators were more concerned with work efficiency than they were with self-government. Employment Division administrator Vernon Kennedy would eventually declare that the strike "was political and not industrial." The historical record, as well as the flurry of reports and analyses from the administrators and sociologists, however, reveals a different picture.[126]

Explaining the Strike

The labor situation at Poston provided much fodder for the Bureau of Sociological Research in determining what had caused the strike and what lessons should be learned. Sociologists offered multiple explanations, yet dissatisfaction with working conditions was at the root of the analysis. Although the immediate cause was the arrest of Uchida and Fujii, the administration and the bureau developed different theories on the factors contributing to the protest. Wade Head issued an official statement to the WRA and the public that listed growing "pro-Axis" sentiment among some members of Poston I as the underlying factor. He acknowledged that the attacks and resulting arrests were the initial causes but also suggested that "a small, but well-organized pro-Axis group took advantage of the situation to seize control of the largest of the three Poston units and create a general strike."[127] Describing the mass strike as a "walkout," Head continued by explaining that it was "the strategy of the pro-Axis group . . . to deliberately attempt to destroy the administration of the American-born Japanese."[128] The fact that the strikers flew Japanese flags at some points and also hung effigies of "dogs" (*inu*, or informers) by the bonfires contributed to Head's perceptions even if they did not directly indicate a pro-Axis uprising. By emphasizing the work of pro-Axis forces and the control that was maintained and reestablished at Poston, Head hoped to convince others that this was the work of a small group of prisoners and not indicative of deeper problems in the camp. Head's framing of the strike as "pro-Axis" angered the Issei and others in the camp, because such a label "merely avoided the true issues."[129]

Other members of the administration touted labor conditions or unrest more than others. Project attorney Theodore Haas wrote to the WRA's solicitor, Phillip M. Glick, in January 1943 and looked to systematic pressures and day-to-day aggravations as the deeper causes of the strike. "The immediate cause of the incident," Haas began, "was like the immediate cause of the recent disturbance in Manzanar and certain other relocation centers—law and order."[130] But Haas also believed that "once or perhaps twice before during a controversy with the administration, a demonstration had been planned." He was not wrong; workers in the adobe project and later the mess hall kitchen did go on strike in protest of their working conditions.[131]

Reports indicated that the contradictions between Collier's view of Poston as a cooperative colony and the WRA administrators' view of the camp as one in a larger system of prisons where labor and harsh conditions were the norm contributed to the strike. Edward Spicer (another member of the sociological bureau) and Leighton composed a "Brief History of Poston" to submit along with their required reports to the WRA and the OIA and noted that the strike "became a symbol around which everybody could rally." The issue of civil liberty—or "holding men without trial and without access to habeas corpus"—served as "a goal and a slogan . . . for the scattered fragments of the community to become organized for the first time" since their arrival.[132]

"Conflicting polices" between the OIA and the WRA were also confusing and frustrating for the incarcerated. In early November Collier again explained to Japanese Americans in Poston that they should view their time in the prison as a long-term "experiment in colonial administration," or a group project. But later that month, WRA director Dillon Myer arrived at Poston and delivered the opposite message. Myers "spoke of all relocation centers as merely way stations on a road between evacuated California homes and more secure places in American agriculture and industry." In this speech, "Poston was pictured as soon sending its members out in a steady stream to supply the expanding needs of wartime America," a statement which "made little impression on a community that had been told to count on five or ten years here."[133]

Were the prisoners to focus on settling in, working to make their community the best that it could be while wrongfully imprisoned, and trying to save the meager wages they made? Or should they be ready to be released into the larger outside world and continue to prove their worth through their work in unfamiliar industries beyond the Rocky Mountains?

While it was Myers's goal to get as many Japanese Americans out of the prisons as soon as possible—particularly those who were deemed loyal and could be released for work or school—this idea was unfamiliar to the prisoners and new to Collier, who often quarreled with Myers during the late fall.[134] The two agencies' conflicting visions caught Japanese Americans in the crosshairs, as did delays "in completing development of National WRA policies for project operation and relocation, and subsequent radical changes in these policies."[135]

Living and working conditions were also highlighted in reports of the strike. A "Summary of Preliminary Observations" from late November listed "delays in payments" as well as a "lack of understanding on the part of a few of our personnel in how to handle Japanese evacuee labor" at the top of the reasons for the strike. A standard monthly report offered that the "extreme heat, dust, and crowded living quarters" that the workers returned home to did little to bolster support for the administration and its litany of broken promises. Prisoners were running out of clothing, and by November no stoves had been installed in living units, prompting the reports officer to speculate that "perhaps one reason the picket fires were so well attended at night was due to their being the most comfortable place to camp."[136] Conversely, in the early summer, "a number of babies died in the hospital" at Poston I, and it was "believed by most of the evacuee doctors and the greater part of the community that they died from dehydration and that this could have been avoided had coolers been placed in the children's ward."[137]

The reactions of the prisoners themselves to the strike were mixed. While many interviewed by Leighton offered similar explanations as the administrators, others detailed more specific reasons for why the strike began and continued. For instance, when asked "What was the objective of this strike?," one Issei interviewed by Leighton's team explained that "the release of Mr. Fujii and Mr. Uchida were a minor case, and the major case was still in the background." Instead, "the right to have a self-forming government was in the mind of many Isseis [sic]" who both directly and indirectly supported the strike and protests. According to this man, Nisei either supported this goal or they didn't—with the more administrative-minded ones choosing to sit on the sidelines so as not to anger any of the higher-ups, as they had "a lot at stake to lose in the protest" compared to the Issei.[138]

With the reports submitted and the damage totaled, administrators as well as the sociological bureau offered their solutions to some of the underlying factors. After all, this was what Poston was designed to be—an experimental center to analyze working relationships and democracy and apply socio-logical and practical solutions to problems. Theodore Haas, who also high-lighted the weakness of the organization of Poston, suggested that "more rather than less freedom should be granted to the vast majority" at Poston.[139] "Some in the staff, I fear, perhaps some in Washington would draw conclu-sions from incidents like those in Manzanar and Poston that greater control is necessary," he lamented. "Opportunities to them should be opened up," so long as there was "the planning of more definiteness and the continuity of policy," and "more rather than less self government as it was largely due to this that the disturbance was localized to Unit I," where many Issei lived.[140]

Still others suggested that the problems that contributed to the strike were related to work and economics and provided a number of solutions that re-lied on the more efficient extraction of labor from the prisoners. They noted that underlying causes of the strike could be found in what they described as Japanese American "inefficiencies" and lack of motivation to work hard. Mary Ellicott Arnold and Lionel Perkins, a team of sociologists from the Rochdale Institute who briefly visited Poston during August and September, had already identified potential problems and suggested that "cooperative enterprises" among the prisoners were the solution. "The situation at Poston reflects a serious war emergency," they explained. "The evacuees are wards of the Government. Food and lodging are supplied them. They have medical attendance. They have a cash relief or dole which goes by the name of 'cash advance.'"[141] However, "the evacuees are expected to perform certain duties or services. But the cash advances they receive bear little or no relation to the kind of character of the service they give." Although this economic setup based on make-believe wages was perhaps necessary during the early days of Poston, it undermined the whole goal of the prison project and created re-sentment among the prisoners.

To solve this problem, the inmates should be encouraged to form coop-erative businesses and farms where they could earn wages for selling their products to outside markets. Cooperatives (or co-op stores) were later estab-lished at Poston but with mixed results as prisoners clashed over what to do with the proceeds. A private contractor also established a camouflage net fac-tory at Poston in the spring of 1942, which was meant to function as a coop-erative. Japanese Americans, however, voted against the cooperative because they could not develop an adequate plan for dividing the profits. (The camo net factory was eventually shut down by the army in May 1943 due to a lack of interest by prisoners as well as disputes with the contractor).[142] Collier himself began to look toward economic incentives for making his experiment work beyond simply "community effort," and suggested that the "WRA could be persuaded to [return] to its original policy of producing surplus food" to give Japanese Americans something to strive for. By September 1942, Poston had moved from requiring Japanese Americans to produce extra food for other camps, the military, and the market toward focusing only on self-sufficiency, as more work was needed in land subjugation and irrigation at Poston.

Following the strike, however, Collier questioned his model community, wondering if perhaps Japanese Americans lacked incentives to work at all. Perhaps using Japanese American labor for its supposed cost-effectiveness was not a wise policy, and building an experimental colony on the principle of self-sufficiency was neither appealing nor realistic. Collier also identified a "need to restore economic motivation to Japanese workers" by "abandoning the present cash advance wage scale and substituting prevailing wages or permitting cooperative programs for Japanese to share in the benefits of the increased production." After all, Collier reiterated, the Japanese Americans "were not kept in the relocation centers for punitive reasons. . . . There is no rationale in asking them to work hard in absence of any kind of economic motivation."[143]

Similarly, WRA administrator Albert Wathan visited Poston in the spring of 1943 and was unhappy with what he discovered. It seemed to him "that we have missed the boat at Poston, and the WRA had adopted a very short-sighted policy toward the whole Jap problem . . . in fact, calling it shortsighted is in my opinion leaning over backward toward charity." Wathan found the state of Poston to be a mess, with Japanese Americans unmotivated and, more importantly, a drain on the resources of both the OIA and the WRA. He suggested that along with infrastructure improvements, Japanese Americans should also be used on construction programs such as landscaping, the building of swimming pools, and roads outside of the camp in addition to an agricultural surplus program so that they would be paid a prevailing wage. In doing so, the OIA and the WRA would be able to increase the charges of subsistence from the prisoners, which "should result in making the Japs become entirely self-supporting within a short time," eliminating "this drain on the nation's food supply" and transforming Poston "from an importing to an exporting community." Under Wathan's plan, Poston would still remain a colony, although a self-sustaining one built on the backs of prison labor.[144]

E. J. Utz, a former Farm Security Administration member and then director of agriculture for the WRA, also paid a visit to Poston to speak with

Head; he suggested that "single, large scale, and commercial agricultural units" be established at Poston rather than focusing on smaller plots. Utz explained that the "WRA is committed, under the terms of its grant of power, to turning the lands reclaimed and developed by the evacuees back to public ownership," thus "the Japanese are to make their contributions to the war in opening such lands and in readying them for occupation by someone else after the war." In other words, the poor conditions that contributed to the strike at Poston were the result of a lack of clear economic motivation for the prisoners. Utz's proposal was to run Poston like an economic venture to benefit the public, those who would live on the land after incarceration (which he suggested was to be "the public"—not necessarily referring to Native Americans), and the military.[145] The problem was not that Japanese Americans were coerced to work but that the concept of working to maintain a self-sufficient colony was not motivating for the community. Making Poston a capitalistic venture—run and administered by the state—required an obedient yet inspired group of laborers. The WRA attempted to create a new status of labor under incarceration, one that rewarded laborers with wages but also limited their rights through imprisonment.

The Beginning of the End for the WRA and the Dies Committee Investigation

Despite the WRA's effort to minimize public knowledge of the strike, nearby communities eventually heard of the unrest and responded critically to both the overall Poston project and the WRA's and OIA's inability to maintain it. Sensational media coverage of the "riots" only increased locals' doubts about the viability of operating Poston like a "colony" rather than a prison camp. On November 21, the *Los Angeles Times* reported on the strike before an official statement was released by the WRA, describing it (incorrectly) as the "first mass defiance of authority since the War Relocation Authority began the task of removing over 160,000 Japanese" from the West Coast, and listing the cause of the strike as stemming "from the filing of charges of attempted murder against a wrestler following an unpublicized series of gang fights."[146] More alarmist was the *San Francisco Examiner*'s report, titled "Evacuee Camp Terrorized by Pro-Axis Japs." This article declared that a "foreign-born clique" seized control of the community government and forced the resignation of the loyal council, meanwhile forcing "6,500 workers, most of them youths and women, to quit their jobs" in an unchecked "reign of terror."[147]

The strike at Poston also made the WRA and OIA more vulnerable to general attacks on their laxity and "wide open" policy. An article from the *San Francisco Examiner* featured an investigative story on Poston criticizing its system of self-government and what the article described as luxuries, including being able to operate cars on prison property and enjoying "unlimited and uncensored telephonic liberties" for those who wanted to make calls to friends and family. The fact that "one Jap volunteered the information that he was going to visit his wife at San Diego, one of our most important naval bases, . . . and had a pass from the WRA" was the final straw.[148] For the media and the public, the problem was not one of economics, labor, or self-government but rather an inefficient and weak agency treating Japanese Americans as members of society rather than potential enemies—the proof being the strike at Poston.

The first half of 1943 proved to be a challenging period for the WRA, particularly when Congress became interested in its operations following the highly publicized strikes and riots at Poston and in other camps. Myer was proud of the fact that the administration at Poston did not resort to "punitive measures" to enforce Japanese American compliance, since the centers "were not prison camps."[149] Others, however, were not convinced that operating Poston as a self-governing colony rather than a prison camp was the appropriate course of action. Later, Myer noted that despite rotating project directors and replacing them with individuals who were committed to the goal of the camps (Americanization and resettlement, but not without order and authority) as well as allowing the FBI to investigate all the prison camps for sabotage in early 1943, "the first two years of our operation were the worst. . . . With centers in turmoil . . . and the continued and intensive hounding by our detractors, we were kept busy."[150]

Much to Myer's annoyance, to welcome in the New Year, a subcommittee of the Committee on Military Affairs of the US Senate held a number of hearings on a proposed bill (S. 444) which would transfer responsibility of the prison camps from the WRA to the War Department. Supported by West Coast chapters of the American Legion, the bill represented a loss of confidence in the WRA to handle the strikes, riots, and uprisings in a responsible and orderly fashion. Subsequent prisoner protests against the use of a loyalty questionnaire for relocation purposes also contributed to concerns from the military and the government about the WRA's competence.[151] The Senate held hearings throughout January, and a number of negative reports on the presence of potential saboteurs in the camps were submitted by antagonists of both the WRA and Japanese Americans more generally. However, the final report of the committee only mildly rebuked the WRA, advising it to initiate a segregation program to remove the troublemakers and place them in a separate facility (Tule Lake become a large segregation center) and, separately, to allow Nisei to be drafted into the military.[152]

Myer no sooner breathed a sigh of relief when two men who "identified themselves as investigators of the Dies Committee" appeared unannounced at the Manzanar prison camp in May 1943. The Dies Committee (or the House Committee on Un-American Activities, named for its chairman, Texas Democratic House member Martin Dies Jr.) was originally established in 1938 to investigate Americans with communist or fascist ties. Concerned that the number of strikes and riots at Manzanar, Poston, and elsewhere indicated that there were growing pro-Axis sentiments in the camps, Dies appointed a three-man subcommittee consisting of John Costello of California, Karle E. Mundt of South Dakota, and Herman P. Eberharter of Pennsylvania to conduct investigations into the WRA camps. Myer, caught off guard, scrambled to rally his troops, get all of his project directors on board, and ensure proper order in the camps in advance of the new investigations.

In early June 1943, Eberharter and Costello made their way to Poston to conduct their inspection and interview various members of the administration and to view the conditions themselves. Fortunately for Myer, the overall mood of the visit of the two congressmen was amicable. On June 8, Head met with the two; they began by cracking jokes about some of the information floating around about Poston and its supposed reputation for being a hotbed of saboteur activity. Referencing damaging testimony provided to the committee by Congressman J. Parnell of New Jersey (a member of the full committee but not the subcommittee), who made a trip to Los Angeles to speak on the WRA's policy of "releasing disloyal Japs," both Costello and Eberharter "joked about the testimony given" and realized that "it's absolutely false."[153] After touring the grounds, Eberharter in particular "personally seemed to be touched by the fact that the people seemed to be living under very crowded conditions and that certainly they were not being pampered," a common criticism from the media. Visits to the work sites followed, as well as to the jail and adobe projects, where the investigators were able to view Japanese Americans working diligently. The two men even mugged for the cameras by posing with the prisoners and pretending to work or serve meals in the mess hall (to Head's disgust). A more thorough investigation conducted by military police only found one flag that appeared to be "suspicious," but it turned out to be an emblem of the Red Cross flag rather than a Japanese flag.

Following the tour around Poston, Head, a few other administrators, and Eberharter and Costello went to town for dinner and a few drinks, where Eberharter had one too many cocktails, became weepy and "maudlin" about the poor conditions of the Japanese Americans in the prisons, and blacked out. Costello had to carry him to the train for their trip home.[154] All in all, it was a rather successful visit. Reports from R. N. Parnell (no relation to J. Parnell above), the associate engineer hired for the Dies Committee, based on information from the inspection confirmed that, although not as efficient as he may have liked, the prisoners were making good progress on the irrigation project and saving the government millions of dollars, further supporting the idea that everything was well at Poston.[155]

Testimony before the committee in Washington, DC, commenced in June, and Myer appeared to testify in July. Myer, armed with reports and memoranda, appeared ready to do battle on behalf of Poston's mission and the WRA. Myer focused much of his statement on undermining the previous and largely negative testimony by Harold Townsend, former chief supply and transportation officer at Poston, who had fled the camp in a motor pool vehicle when he realized the army would not be called in to quell the strikers. Townsend provided statements to the committee in early June emphasizing the disorganized nature of Poston, theft and other crime among its residents, and—most importantly—the laxity of the prison administration. He described the "insolence, double-crossing, and viciousness" of the Japanese Americans who were rearing "scores" of children out of wedlock "by orders from Tokyo" as a deviant plan for subversion and sabotage.[156] Townsend also significantly exaggerated the danger of the strike, while others, such as Father Clement, a Maryknoll missionary stationed at Poston, testified that he had never seen any such displays of pro-Axis sentiment nor even heard Japanese music nor seen Japanese flags.[157]

While the media clamored to publish Townsend's testimony, few in Congress accepted it as the gospel truth, and Leighton referred to Townsend as "insane" after reading and hearing his racist remarks. Myer also emphasized the "grave international implications" of the investigations, "providing the enemy with material which can be used to convince the peoples of the Orient that the United States is undemocratic and is fighting a racial war."[158] In the end, the subcommittee's final report, issued on September 30, 1943, recommended that the WRA remain in charge of Poston, but only if the agency expedited the leave program in place, created a "board composed of representatives of the WRA and the various intelligence agencies of the federal government . . . to investigate evacuees who apply for release and to pass finally upon their application," and inaugurated a "thoroughgoing program of Americanization for those Japanese who remain in the centers."[159] The WRA, as the overseeing agency of the prison camps, would live to see another day.

But the OIA and its dedication to viewing Poston as a colony rather than a prison work camp would face more challenges. Mounting pressure from the WRA to move Japanese Americans out of the prisons and back into society disrupted the work patterns established at Poston and increased concerns that operating Poston in such a unique manner was hindering rather than helping productivity, the war effort, and the self-sufficiency of the prison. Harold Ickes was already pushing for the OIA and the Department of the Interior to withdraw its support and supervision of Poston, and, by the early summer of 1943, the WRA assumed sole control of the prison camp.[160] Others suggested that the best solution for the problems at Poston was for the OIA to simply abandon the project.

As more Nisei left to pursue work outside the camp in agriculture, beet labor, and other ventures, there was a noticeable labor shortage at the prison. Layoffs and closures of certain departments (including landscaping) became necessary for the WRA to work within its budget, and a Manpower Commission was even established among the Japanese Americans as part of the new self-government structure after the strike, to address the problems of labor and jobs.[161] And, with fewer jobs to go around, one of the main organizing tactics of incarceration—work—was more difficult to maintain, forcing the WRA and the Department of the Interior to question the need for the OIA to continue to be part of Poston. In a report from June 10, 1943, an administrator noted, "It becomes evident that it is not sufficient to offer a group of people self-government, and that giving them a plan for organization is a long way from having a relatively self-sufficient and self-responsible community come into existence." Even the solicitor for the DOI doubted the purpose of trying to operate Poston in a unique way. "Only fair and possibly poor results in the use of evacuee labor have been obtained in certain land leveling operations and certain phases of the road construction program," he pointed out in a memo to Collier.

If the labor program was failing, then the point of the OIA remaining in joint custody of the prison no longer existed, challenging Collier's idea of an experimental, democratic colony that would also be profitable. Also, challenges such as the strike were too much for the OIA, which had other jobs to do pertaining to Native Americans. As a result, "unless the Interior Department were to take over the entire relocation program" and not share duties with the WRA, "it is suggested that the existing agreement be revised to limit Interior's participation to control over the construction program as to irrigation facilities, over land subjugation work, and over irrigation practices." More specifically, the report "suggested that the Interior withdraw as the operating agency of the Poston Project" save for making sure that the infrastructure programs were completed.[162] In the spring of 1943, Collier and the OIA faced enough pressure that the WRA took over operations and became the sole agency in charge of Poston.

After the negotiations of the strike at Poston in November, Vernon Kennedy, chief of the Employment Division at Poston, observed the end of the affair in what was one of the more bizarre acts committed by a member of the administration. Another administrator recounted in a report that he, along with a member of the employment division, met with Kennedy in his room at about one in the morning on November 25, 1942. When Edward Spicer arrived, he found Kennedy and the other administrator drinking and talking excitedly about the end of the strike and what was to come next for Poston. More specifically, Kennedy announced that earlier in the night, he and the other administrator had been holding "a wake on Poston," placing candles around the "dead body" (nothing) in the middle of the floor of the other administrator's room and crossing themselves in front of it as Poston was now "dead." "It's capitulation to gangsters. That's all," Kennedy quipped, while assistant project director John Evans looked down at the floor and mumbled, "Wade Head is a good fellow." Obviously, Kennedy did not think highly of Head's handling of the strike and suggested that his "capitulation" to the council members not only shifted the balance of power from the administration to the prisoners but also marked the end to a potentially profitable and certainly worthwhile labor program.[163]

The Poston strike was a prisoner-led event that challenged the core and structure of the compound. More importantly, it called attention to the conflicting goals of the various agencies vying for control for center. Was Poston to be a self-sufficient, permanent colony, or a prison work camp similar to the others in the system of Japanese American incarceration? What the prisoners proved, from the earliest days of Poston, was that because their labor was the key ingredient designed to make the prison function through self-sufficiency and to complete infrastructure programs, there really was no choice. Poston, regardless of Collier's lofty goals, was an inherently carceral space on colonized land. It was a prison camp where Japanese Americans labored on behalf of the government for low or often no pay and with circumscribed self-governing rights. And in the end, the chaos of the administration of Poston and the overly ambitious goals for the camp would lead many to question the purpose of incarceration and whether or not Japanese Americans would be more resourceful and productive outside than inside the camps.

CHAPTER 5

Redemptive Labor

Japanese American Resettlement

From the Minidoka prison to the desert of Poston, imprisoned Japanese Americans of all generations stared fixedly at the loyalty questionnaire provided by their camp administration during the summer of 1943. Their pens and pencils hovered above the sheet, puzzled looks on their faces. The answers they provided for some of the questions would either send them to a maximum-security segregation center or indicate they were worthy of leaving the prisons indefinitely. Many of the questions on the form were fairly routine, inquiring about marital status, sex, education, language abilities, and hobbies. But questions 27 and 28 posed conundrums to all prisoners aged seventeen and older, who were forced to answer them, in spite of their apparent yes/no simplicity:

> Question 27: "Are you willing to serve in the armed forces of the
> United states on combat duty, wherever ordered?"
> Question 28: "Will you swear unqualified allegiance to the United
> States of America and faithfully defend the United States from
> any or all attacks by foreign and domestic forces, and forswear any
> form of allegiance or obedience to the Japanese emperor, or any
> other form of government, power, or organization?"

The first question reflected Assistant Secretary of War John J. McCloy's support for the new policy that Nisei register for the draft and serve in the military (as hundreds would under the 100th Infantry Battalion and later the decorated 442nd Infantry Regiment of the Army).[1] Despite protests from

General DeWitt and other army officers who argued that the "loyal" Japanese Americans could not be separated from the "disloyal" by a mere questionnaire, recruiters traveled to different camps to distribute the form and enlist Nisei men as well as Nisei women who might be willing to serve as nurses or secretaries.[2]

The implications of question 28 were numerous. Pledging loyalty to the United States by answering yes might indicate that those surveyed *did* harbor feelings of loyalty to Japan. A yes could (and did) result in punishment or retaliation. Issei who answered in the affirmative were also at risk for becoming stateless persons. Worse still, answering no to the second question could be (and was) interpreted as a willingness to renounce US citizenship.

In an act of rebellion, approximately 5,300 young men and women answered no to both questions. One "No-No Boy"—as those who chose this course action became known—explained, "I answered both questions in the negative, not because of disloyalty but due to the disgusting and shabby treatment given us."[3] The army was the organization placed in charge of forcibly removing Japanese Americans from their home and imprisoning them. In some camps including Poston and Tule Lake, entire blocks voted to either refuse to answer the questionnaire or answer no-no as an act of defiance, often creating friction with family members and others in their communities that lasted for decades afterward. Others chose to answer negatively because they were frightened of being separated from their families.

The War Department and WRA deemed those who chose the path of no-no to be disloyal, and they were given the "opportunity" to renounce their citizenship or repatriate to Japan. They were also transferred to Tule Lake, where three thousand prisoners refused to answer "correctly," making the camp a prison within a prison for disloyal Japanese Americans. The complicated acts of protest among Japanese American men who answered in the negative for questions 27 and 28 and refused military service—indicating resistance—have been heralded in many scholarly and literary works. The importance of the loyalty questionnaire for determining fitness for military service or subversion, however, does not tell the entire story.[4]

WRA administrators also used the loyalty questionnaire for the "leave clearance" program. This initiative granted imprisoned Japanese Americans their freedom so long as they were "not suspected of disloyalty," could "maintain employment or secure other means of support outside the West Coast," find placement "within a community in which [they would] be accepted without incident," and "keep the Authority informed of [their] places of residence and employment."⁵ Although the WRA and WCCA approved leave clearances as early as the summer of 1942 for agricultural labor, the process accelerated (much to the dismay of the army, which accused the WRA of threatening internal security) after the investigation of the agency and the prisons by the Dies Committee. The growing unpopularity of the WRA and the hypocrisy of allowing some Japanese Americans to serve in the military while others remained in the camps, draining valuable taxpayer dollars away from the more pressing needs of the war effort, contributed to the WRA's notion that perhaps releasing Japanese Americans was the next logical step. When granting leave clearance to Japanese Americans for private employment or work in wartime industries, question 28 on the loyalty questionnaire was scrutinized for any inkling of subversion. As a result, the WRA expected thousands of Japanese Americans to prove their loyalty to the war effort through their labor, demonstrating that they could function in communities beyond the West Coast.

Loyalty and work were connected for incarcerated Japanese Americans and continued to be for those who left the prisons and resettled with the assistance of various agencies beyond the military areas on the West Coast. Treated and sometimes referred to informally by the public as "parolees" (indicating that Japanese Americans were interned like enemy aliens), released Japanese Americans were forcibly removed again as jobs which were once plentiful in the prisons were eliminated due to WRA budget cuts, leaving many struggling to save money or even purchase necessary items from the canteens. Their resettlement was dictated by their employment status and depended on locating to a community willing to accommodate them. The WRA and labor demands circumscribed the freedom of Japanese Americans to choose where they went after being released from the camps. Numerous attempts by state legislatures to curtail property rights and even voting rights for Japanese American citizens, as well as virulent anti-Japanese sentiment in communities along the West Coast, also made returning to their homes challenging if not impossible, even after Major General Henry Pratt (then in charge of the Western Defense Command) lifted the exclusion orders in December 1944.⁶

The government and the public suggested that continuing to work where needed was the way for Japanese Americans to "prove" their willingness to reintegrate into American communities as well as their loyalty and dedication to the war effort. Here, Japanese Americans were forced to perform their loyalty and prove their worth in order to be released, signaling a transformation from the "yellow peril" to the "model minority" in the eyes of many of their fellow citizens.[7] The catalyst for this transformation was labor; supporting the war effort through labor was redemptive. Work shortages in wartime industries and agriculture continued to shape the experiences of Japanese Americans even beyond the camps and continued to limit their options in resettlement. Administrators argued that their time in the prison camps had allowed them to continue to sharpen their labor skills and adaptability for the outside world. The incarceration of Japanese Americans was seen as a redemptive and rehabilitative prison program that served the nation's needs for security while also turning Japanese Americans into ready workers during their parole period.

But the often exploitative working conditions Japanese Americans faced beyond the camps proved that their labor was rarely redemptive. Their identities as former prisoners of the state and in need of "rehabilitation" as suspects challenged their status as free laborers, making the redemptive goals of the WRA difficult to put into practice. Post-prison work resembled a parolee system rather than a truly free—or redemptive—labor arrangement.

"Starvation Time": Labor Crises in the Camps and the WRA's Plan for Resettlement

Things looked grim for Poston by the spring of 1943. Despite able-bodied and of-age Japanese Americans working to make the prison self-sufficient, it was becoming more difficult for both the prisoners and the administrators to ignore the fact that there was a severe labor shortage in the camp. Coerced labor had become so crucial and the emphasis on all participating in the community projects and on self-sufficiency so pronounced that as the population dwindled, it became virtually impossible to continue operating the prison camps at full capacity. The WRA's decision to grant more leave clearances to Nisei, either for the purpose of outside employment or to resume education, resulted in an overall decrease in the number of Japanese American prisoners—leaving older Issei to work.

T. S. Takahashi, a supervisor in the Agricultural Department, lamented the plight of his workers and those who were left behind during an interview with a member of the Bureau of Sociological Research. The interviewer made the mistake of asking how the Agricultural Department was faring. For an

hour and a half, he was engaged in a "conversation which was more of a mono-
logue centered around agriculture . . . and manpower shortages" with Takahashi. "I'll tell you what is wrong with the agricultural situation," Takahashi
said. "You should study the administration." Yet despite directing the interviewer to an administrator, Takahashi launched into his views on the labor
shortage and the crippling effects it was having on the ability of his crew and
others at Poston. He mocked the Manpower Commission (the branch of self-
government established after the Poston strike to evaluate labor issues) and
its "impractical" solution of establishing a labor pool to round up those who
were unemployed or those spending too much time working in camouflage
netting and not contributing to the good of the community. (Ironically, Takahashi echoed the calls of John Collier and others who urged cooperative
community support for the success of the prison colony.) Referencing the extra work men in the Agriculture Department shouldered, including building slaughterhouses, raising and butchering more hogs with fewer men, and
garbage duties, Takahashi worried that "if any more of the men leave, we
won't even be able to leave the project with anything for these Isseis [sic]."
Not only were Japanese Americans forced to labor for self-sufficiency or to
boost morale; they were forced to labor for sheer survival. Takahashi also
scoffed at the plan suggested by the interviewer of having each family grow
their own food on small plots of land both in the prison and in closely guarded
areas outside. "That problem seems pretty obvious," Takahashi quipped—
there was no machinery available and not enough materials for everyone
who wanted to farm their own plots of land. At this point, Takahashi was
interested in getting by with increasingly smaller crews to "raise enough food
to keep . . . from starving."[8]

Despite the acute nature of Takahashi's complaints of being forced to do
more work with fewer workers, the administration's granting of leave clearances to imprisoned Japanese Americans was not a recently established process at the time. The WRA and the army had granted the first leave permissions
during the summer of 1942 for agricultural work on a "retail basis," which
meant that each application was processed carefully and individually at each
detention center.[9] This turned out to be a tedious undertaking. When Dillon
Myer assumed control of the WRA in the summer of 1942, his primary goal
became moving as many Nisei out of the prisons as possible, arguing that
imprisoning Japanese Americans was no longer necessary and only contributed to malaise and the potential for subversion. Myer later explained
that he agreed to release more Japanese Americans because administrators

"recognized that loyalty could not flourish in an atmosphere of restriction and discriminatory segregation." The abnormal conditions of the prisons also limited the ability of the WRA to restore Japanese Americans as "loyal citizens and law-abiding aliens to a normal useful American life."[10]

There were also labor demands outside the camps.

By mid-August 1942, the WRA hammered out a more comprehensive leave plan approved by the Department of Justice in September, contributing to the sharp increase in the number of prisoners leaving to work in beet harvesting and other agricultural labor. The new leave policy consisted of a variety of types of leave including those for short-term passes for medical needs and tending to property issues; seasonal passes for agricultural labor; and indefinite leave for those deemed loyal who had secured "a definite job or some other means of support."[11] To expedite leave clearances, Myer closed all of the regional WRA offices responsible for the prisons and refashioned them as "relocation field offices" overseen by Tom Holland (employment chief for the WRA). By the winter and spring of 1943, regional relocation offices tasked with resettling Japanese Americans opened in Chicago, Cleveland, Minneapolis, Des Moines, New York, Salt Lake City, Kansas City, Little Rock, and Boston. Regional administrators were responsible for both identifying potential employers and serving as public relations outlets to promote acceptance and good will toward Japanese Americans.[12]

The WRA accelerated its leave clearance program in March 1943, a month before Takahashi described the effects of a dwindling work population at Poston. The increase in the number of prisoners released from the camps occurred almost in spite of rather than because of the involvement of General DeWitt and Colonel Bendetsen in the process. As leaders of the Western Defense Command, both men had their reservations about releasing so many Japanese Americans, particularly those looking to return to the West Coast. DeWitt was an outspoken opponent of the loyalty questionnaire and distrusted the ability of a piece of paper to separate the loyal from the disloyal. As there was no easy way to confirm that they had filled out the questionnaire truthfully, DeWitt argued that Japanese Americans should remain in the prisons indefinitely. DeWitt and Bendetsen specifically took issue with what they argued was the WRA's laxity in handling leave clearances in the summer and fall of 1942. In order for a prisoner to be paroled, he or she required both "clearance" from the Washington, DC, office of the WRA (a process initiated in the prison camps) proving they were not a security risk and a "permit" issued jointly by the military and the WRA if employment and

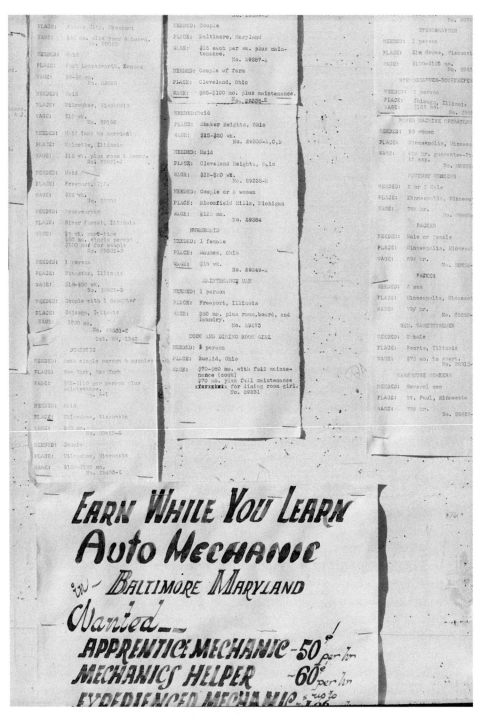

Figure 11. Work-offer board at the Manzanar prison camp. Photo by Ansel Adams, 1943.
Courtesy of the Library of Congress.

resettlement plans (established with assistance of regional WRA offices) were viable.[13] The process was rather lengthy but not nearly as thorough as De-Witt and Bendetsen would have liked to prevent subversion and security risks.

But even the army had to face the fact that Japanese American labor was in high demand in the Midwest and the Eastern Defense Command. Beginning in late 1942, the army and War Department received multiple requests from manufacturers for Japanese Americans to meet labor demands in industrial plants. Considering that Japanese Americans would be working in munitions and around crucial defense operations, DeWitt and Bendetsen as well as other members of the Western Defense Command argued that additional investigative measures into the loyalty of potential parolees were needed to avoid sabotage. For them, answering question 28 on the form was not enough; a more extensive process was required to determine the eligibility of Japanese Americans for indefinite leave as opposed to the "slipshod" WRA procedures. The Western Defense Command began its own preemployment investigations, which focused on any subversive organizations or publications associated with a potential parolee as well as how many times they had traveled to Japan. This investigative undertaking proved to be time-consuming and did not yield any concrete evidence of loyalty or disloyalty.

In January 1943, the War Department established the Japanese American Joint Board (JAJB) as an extra layer of bureaucracy for the leave clearance process. Although the WRA would still maintain ultimate authority in the decision to clear and release prisoners, the JAJB, composed of representatives from the WRA and the Offices of Naval Intelligence, Army Intelligence, and the Provost Marshal General, "would help in identifying pro-Japanese individuals and especially in determining eligibility of Japanese American citizens for work in war plants."[14] The JAJB existed to make recommendations to the WRA in cases where the military expressed concern, although the WRA could choose to investigate further or not—the recommendations of the JAJB were nonbinding.

The effectiveness of the JAJB was questionable and the board itself was short-lived, functioning for approximately a year. Conflicts between members of the military as well as increasing pressure from the WRA and manufacturers for Japanese Americans to be released rendered the JAJB a nuisance to those looking to rapidly move Japanese Americans out of the prisons and into war work. Initially, General Hugh Drum (DeWitt's counterpart for the Eastern Defense Command) refused to have any Japanese Americans cleared for resettlement and work in the eastern part of the country. Assistant Secretary of War McCloy later overruled him and insisted that any Japanese Americans cleared by the JAJB be accepted for resettlement and employment in the Eastern Defense Command. Despite this relaxation, the review process on behalf of the JAJB was so slow that valuable opportunities for Japanese Americans to be paroled and released were lost, including over ten thousand requests for Japanese American workers from employers in Chicago alone. Japanese Americans who were desperate to get out of prison but were held up by the JAJB investigations grew angry with the WRA and the government. According to Myer, they came to believe that this was just one more incident of discrimination and racism against a group of people who had already suffered enough and were repeatedly required to prove their loyalty.[15] By the time the JAJB dissolved in January 1944, the board had heard 39,000 cases for leave, recommending to the WRA that 12,600 be denied. The WRA ignored many of the recommendations and released half of those rejected by the JAJB on indefinite leave for employment in plants east of the Rockies.[16]

Even before the JAJB was dissolved, however, the WRA decentralized the leave process by March 1943, allowing for more parolees to be cleared and resettled throughout the United States. Rather than requiring that all requests for leave be approved by the WRA office in Washington, DC, Myer granted permission to each camp director to approve Japanese Americans for release. WRA headquarters also gave more authority to each field office in judging the suitability of "community attitudes" in cities and towns toward Japanese Americans. Additionally, the WRA established a financial aid program for released prisoners who lacked any form of savings or "independent means." Those without dependents received fifty dollars while seventy-five or one hundred dollars were provided for those with one or two or more dependents, respectively. The WRA later granted twenty-five dollars per person regardless of family size, plus three dollars per diem and coach train fare to their final destination.[17] By the summer of 1943, thousands of Japanese Americans resettled in far-flung places across the country, building their new lives while making the best of their newfound parolee status.

But life became more challenging for those who remained in the prisons, as the WRA attempted to do more with fewer workers while shutting down projects and departments that once employed a large number of prisoners. Particularly at Poston, where cooperative work was stressed by the administration, Issei and Nisei who remained worried that there would not be enough workers to help run the prison. And they were not alone.

On July 8, 1943, head of agriculture H. A. Mathiesen was present at a special meeting of Block 37 in Poston I to discuss the increasingly dire food situation. Mathiesen addressed the dwindling group and noted the many changes in the prison over the past year. "Young people are leaving daily to settle on the outside," and as a result, "the burden is thrown upon the Isseis [*sic*] more and more in [the] Agricultural program."[18] The decreasing number of able-bodied men meant that only a small portion of the original plan to cultivate forty thousand acres of land could realistically be achieved, resulting in a decrease in workers needed—only 1 percent of the original personnel and crew. But the administration cut more projects than necessary, challenging the notion of self-sufficiency at Poston. Nonetheless, the prison administrators placed the responsibility of ensuring that the fourteen-cents-per-day shortage in costs for food allotment on the Agricultural Department was met with prisoner-produced crops and slaughtered animals.

Further complicating matters was the fact that there was increasing miscommunication between the Agricultural Department and those in charge of the budget at Poston. Somehow, the prisoners were expected to produce enough food for those who remained, but with fewer resources and smaller crews. Materials needed to do repair work on the irrigation canals so that water could reach the different units were not available, and the seven thousand dollars for fertilizer to grow crops was also "requisitioned" by the administration.[19] Mathiesen was well aware of these setbacks but offered little assurance or hope for those who remained, only suggesting that the prisoners make do with what they had and come together in the familiar Poston cooperative spirit. Although administrators at Poston limited the number of leave clearances to ten temporary permits per day for those with "urgent" job offers in manufacturing and those reuniting with families, many administrators and prisoners predicted a camp-wide subsistence "crisis" by the fall.[20] Labor became a crucial component of the operation of the camps, and when the labor force declined, day-to-day functions fell into disarray.

Alexander Leighton and other members of the Bureau of Sociological Research also expressed their disillusionment with the incarceration project as more prisoners left Poston. The social scientists who reported on the conditions of Poston at times indirectly argued that imprisonment had created an abnormal situation for those who remained in the work camps—one with apparently no easy or straightforward solutions. Closing the camps created problems for the incarcerees who would be released, but keeping Japanese Americans imprisoned who could not be approved for leave also proved deleterious to their physical and mental health. Others who chose to remain out of fear for what awaited them on the outside, potential (and real) violence directed toward Japanese Americans, and uncertainty of their financial future were also affected.

Monthly reports described chaotic situations in Poston and contained dire predictions for "an approaching crisis" within the next year. "Prediction has fallen into disrepute among many scientists, especially social scientists," the July monthly report for Poston began, yet it did not shy away from prognostication when it came to the plight of Japanese Americans in the prison.[21] "Assuming that the policy of the War Relocation Authority continues in its present form, that is, emphasis on mass resettlement . . . and assuming that no drastic and unexpected changes occur in national life due to the war or other causes . . . the following is likely to occur," turning to a detailed list of gloomy predictions.[22] The social scientists doubted that "it would be possible to close the relocation centers or even a portion of them" and would instead result in a shifting of the largely Issei remaining populations from one prison to another, leading to instability and further disillusionment.[23] "Inside the centers, the standard of living and morale will drop," and while Japanese Americans were widely known in sociological circles as law-abiding and adverse to crime, the conditions in the prisons would increase instances of stealing, "gangsterism," and "demands on the government for assistance." If no assistance was provided, prisoners would turn to "illicit private industries" and lose their will to work. The authors went so far as to suggest that Japanese American prisoners, if left to their own devices in the current conditions of the prisons, "would show the signs and symptoms of a demoralized community just as the 'Okies' and the 'Arkies' showed them in California when they were vainly seeking some security after the drought."[24] Here, the social scientists likened the Issei and Nisei who remained in the camps—those who were not deemed loyal enough to leave the centers—to the stereotypes of other classes of Americans. As more Japanese Americans turned to illegal means of support to get what they needed, "most of the community will be apathetic, but there will be struggles for power between small rival gangs who will agitate against cooperation with the administration in agriculture and other programs," making it increasingly difficult to grow food and provide subsistence for those who remained, let alone administer the camp.[25]

Without the loyal Nisei, who left the camp in droves, social scientists feared that the idea of self-governance at Poston would also be in shambles, undercutting the original purpose of the "colony." As a result, prisoners might ask for more of the administrators, or worse, might appeal to the Spanish Consul (an avenue of redress which other prisoners at Tule Lake and elsewhere had taken to make demands for better treatment) for more food and resources. "Thus, while the evacuees are giving less and less, the Government may find itself in a position in which it is advisable for the sake of American prisoners to give more and more."[26] As camp order broke down, the prisoners might once again go on strike, forcing the administration to "give-in" while the prisoners performed even less labor. More problematic, as administrators also left the prison when their services were either no longer needed or no longer affordable, those who remained might be forced to assume administrative positions once held by whites and Nisei, making them also vulnerable to the demands of the rowdier and less pliable members of the Japanese American prison population.

Other social scientists, including Leighton, charged the WRA with a particularly despicable and underhanded plan addressing the conditions in the prisons: purposefully making the lives of the prisoners so miserable that they would have no other choice but to leave. The Bureau of Sociological Research charged that although "it has been stated from time to time, that nobody will be forced out of the relocation centers," this was "only true in a literal sense" as "measures are being applied which amount to coercion."[27] This was certainly a weighty charge against the WRA, which proclaimed itself the ward of the Japanese Americans during the war, doing everything in its power to care for their welfare.

"Life in the relocation centers is being kept at a bare subsistence level," Leighton suggested, adding that in this case "a bare subsistence level is lower than a slum level."[28] "The amount of employment available to evacuees is being cut, creating thereby over two thousand unemployed in [Poston] alone," a curious development given Poston's mission and the centrality of work to the camp experience. As many prisoners came to depend on cash advances to purchase items like clothing and special dietary supplements from the canteens and cooperative stores, the loss of employment options directly affected more than morale; it had the potential for severely affect prisoner health and general well-being. Unemployment pay ($1.50 to $3.75 depending on the job and as long as unemployment was not the fault of the worker) was part of the WRA's work policy, but distribution was often haphazard and incomplete, more so in the last days of the Poston camp. Leighton also noted that "at the same time, private industry and agriculture are forbidden" in Poston, referencing the decision among administrators in the fall of 1942 to focus the prisoners on self-sufficiency rather than the production of marketable surplus goods. Unemployment compensation was only made available for prisoners who were ill, not those who lost their jobs and, while all of these changes occurred, "the allowance for food is being reduced from 45 cents per capita per day to 31 cents, with the idea that the people will either grow their own food or do without, or get out of the centers."[29] Leighton also explained that "no funds are provided for recreation, athletics or community improvements," demonstrating that Poston had firmly abandoned its original purpose of serving as a self-sufficient, self-governing community.[30]

Dillon Myer naturally disagreed with Leighton's assessments and told the Bureau of Sociological Research so directly in a letter. He contested a number of Leighton's points, particularly the notion that the WRA and individual camps directors purposefully starved Japanese Americans and made their lives miserable in order to force them out of the prisons. "You have pointed out that the employment policy and the reduction in food costs are indicative of indirect coercive methods being utilized by WRA to force relocation," Myer indicated, but he denied that these were the ulterior goals of the agency.[31] He maintained that "never at any time has there been any thought of utilizing the food policy in order to gain relocation."[32] Forcing the prisoners at Poston to grow more food with fewer laborers and resources was a result of "transportation problems and the lack of certain types of foods on many markets," making it "essential to produce as many vegetables and as much meat and animal products at all centers where possible in order to maintain an adequate diet which would include the proper varieties of food."[33]

As far as cutting jobs to encourage Japanese Americans to transition to life outside, Myer understood "how this assumption might be made," but argued that "employment at the projects had been a real problem right from the start" because of overstaffing of both administrative and prison labor positions.[34] Also, Myer insisted that limiting positions was a way "to make certain that every individual made his contributions to the center" rather than doubling up on key jobs; to "assist them in maintaining self-respect by insisting on a full day's work" instead of allowing only partial employment and making up shortfalls in cash advances and wages with government benefits; and "to assure that government funds were properly expended only for services rendered."[35] He held steadfastly to the idea that "it is not our intention to reduce permanently the total employment at the projects if there are people who wish to work," in order to force people out of the prisons, but that "it will make for a healthier situation if we always have a few people looking for employment."[36] Leighton did not elaborate on this point, but it was implied that imbuing Poston with a spirit of healthy competition for jobs would spur better work performance and increase morale in the prisons. As more Japanese Americans left the camp, the mission of Poston had transitioned from one of a communal and cooperative spirit to implementing incentives for participation in a more capitalistic venture through job competition, wages, and purchasing power at the canteens.

Japanese Americans imprisoned in Poston and elsewhere certainly took note of the changes in policies and voiced their concerns. During an interview in April 1943, one prisoner explained that he replied no to both questions 27 and 28 and ultimately refused to join up for military service, citing the way he and others had been treated by the military and the government during the war. But the young man went one step further in his protests. He noted changes in food quality and quantity, explaining that while the food isn't the best, it was something, but he knew he was "not getting what it takes, because the minute [he] [exerted] himself, he would get pretty tired," indicating that he was working hard but not receiving enough food. His solution? "Hell, I'm going to stay in here until they drive me out." He argued, "It is the obligation of the government to see that we are taken care of. They put us in here." After all, if he did resettle with his wife and kids, he would "rob [and] murder" for food if he had to.[37]

Not long after the interview above took place, Poston incarceree Bob Kazaki wrote an impassioned letter to director Wade Head decrying the process of what he called "re-evacuation." He recounted the fact that voluntarily evacuating their homes in California was extolled as the "patriotic thing to do" on behalf of the Japanese Americans, yet "now that we are settled here, and neurotic congressmen are raving about the 'terrific cost' of these projects, a voice exhorts us to relecate [sic], it is the patriotic thing to do."[38] Similar to the ways in which Japanese Americans were encouraged to prove their loyalty while laboring inside the prisons, now they were being coerced to leave and find jobs to redeem themselves once again. Even though the WRA did offer to pay for the transportation of those looking to leave, Kazaki said, "I think I'll wait a little longer. There may come a time when we will be given a 'bonus' and a new suit of clothes . . . and a job if we get the hell out of here."[39]

What Kazaki wanted more than anything else was to be able to go home to California where he "had a good job and was satisfied with life and the best climate in the world."[40] He compared the instructions given to Japanese

Americans leaving the prisons to not "gather together in groups such as Little Tokyo" while making "no mention of the Chinatowns, the Ghettos, the Lithuanian Colonies, the Slovakian Villages, the Amish, and [a] hundred and one other foreign groupings."[41] Between being forced to resettle to a place he did not want to and take a job that was not as stable and well paying as the one he had before, Kazaki highlighted similar feelings among other prisoners who were transitioning to the status of "parolees" as they left the prisons. Resettlement appeared to be more of a dispersal that benefited the WRA and white Americans along the West Coast. Japanese Americans' choices in where they went and the jobs they acquired were circumscribed, so just as they had during previous strikes at Santa Anita, Manzanar, and Poston, Japanese Americans turned to using their labor as a weapon, this time refusing to leave and take outside jobs. As some WRA administrators wondered, what loyal American dedicated to the war effort would willingly choose to remain in a prison when freedom and wages waited for them on the outside? With conditions being what they were in the prisons by the spring and summer of 1943, choosing to continue to live in them spoke volumes and forced the WRA and the federal government to look at what forced removal had done to Japanese Americans. Remaining and protesting the conditions inside and outside the prisons may have appeared counterproductive or nonsensical, but a reaction such as a statement on behalf of prisoners like Kazaki's was a way to exercise control over his labor and his life in a situation where both were largely out of his control.

Ex parte Mitsuye Endo: Rereading the Case Through the Lens of Labor

Another Nisei incarceree, Mitsuye Endo, whose name would forever be attached to one of the Supreme Court cases centered on the constitutionality of wartime incarceration, fought for agency in her employment opportunities through the legal system by filing a writ of habeas corpus. After forced removal, Endo lost her job with the California state government and was unable to reclaim it, as exclusion orders prohibited her from returning to her home in Sacramento in 1943. Although the WRA was resettling Japanese Americans based on labor needs for the war effort, Endo had her own ideas on where her skills were most suited. Endo's case was a limited success as the court ruled in 1944 that imprisoning loyal Japanese Americans was a violation of their constitutional rights as American citizens. However, a rereading of this well-known legal battle also highlights the importance of employment in the case as well as the challenges the WRA faced in promoting the idea of redemptive labor.[42]

Endo, born in Sacramento, California, to Issei parents in 1920, initially felt the first pang of discrimination following America's entry in World War II with the loss of her stable and well-paying job. She graduated high school in 1938 and then immediately enrolled in a nearby clerical school, where she excelled in her studies. She secured a job as a clerical worker for the California Department of Employment and was well on her way to establishing a career when the Japanese attacked Pearl Harbor and she, like other Japanese Americans, had her life turned upside down. By the spring of 1942, the California State Personnel Board dismissed all Nisei employees, arguing that retaining them was a potential security risk and liability. Out of the approximately three hundred to five hundred Japanese American employees who worked for the state (most for the Department of Motor Vehicles), Endo was one of sixty-three who joined in litigation against California with the assistance of attorney James Purcell, who previously worked with the Japanese American Citizens League (JACL) on other discrimination cases.[43]

Purcell found, however, that the forced removal of Japanese Americans from the West Coast made the firings more difficult to challenge. Rather than a vague argument that Japanese Americans could no longer work for the state because their loyalty was in question as a result of Executive Order 9066, the state could now claim that Japanese Americans were unable to perform their duties because of their incarceration. Additionally, because Nisei born in the United States before 1924 were dual citizens of both the United States and Japan, the administrators for the state declared that all Nisei had lied on their application forms when they initially applied for their jobs by falsely claiming American citizenship. While Japanese Americans were incarcerated, the State Personnel Board agreed to hold trials for the former employees in Sacramento, knowing full well that it would be impossible for the now-imprisoned Japanese Americans to appear in court. Purcell was able to convince the board to postpone the hearings until after the exclusion orders were lifted if the former employees still wanted their former jobs.

In the early summer of 1942, Purcell arrived at the Tanforan detention center in California to obtain the signatures of two former employees of the California Department of Motor Vehicles who wanted to be part of the suit against California and was immediately shocked at the conditions in the camp. Purcell wanted more for his clients than the mere return of their jobs. The "youthful, hard-hitting" lawyer saw the loss of jobs as part of the larger threat to liberty and civil rights inherent in incarceration.[44] He wanted a showdown with the Supreme Court and brought a habeas corpus case against the government, allowing his clients to fight for their civil rights as well as their employment.

Mitsuye Endo was an ideal candidate for such a lawsuit. By June 1942, Endo was held with her family at the Sacramento Detention Center, awaiting transfer to the Tule Lake prison camp. By the time Purcell initiated his proceedings, Endo had been transferred to Tule Lake, where she received a questionnaire from Purcell designed to obtain basic information on potential candidates for his habeas corpus case. He gathered data on each former employee's education background, language skills, general character, and their travel history to Japan. While few of the files on the sixty-three former Nisei employees contained anything incriminating, Endo was ideal, as Purcell prioritized respectability politics for his case.[45] Not only was Endo a young woman with a career that the state and federal governments had cut short, but she was also a practicing Methodist, generally well-behaved (an important quality to note as to distinguish her from other "troublemakers" at Tule Lake later on), had a brother serving in the military, and—even better—had never been to Japan and spoke minimal Japanese.

Endo, however, was not immediately on board with Purcell's plan and was initially hesitant to become part of a larger court case that would directly attack the constitutional foundation of incarceration. For imprisoned minorities, attacking the United States government was a terrifying prospect. Uncertainty and fear prompted many imprisoned Japanese Americans to focus on survival and maintaining their mental and physical well-being, acts of resistance in and of themselves. Others actively protested, including Gordon Hirabayashi, a student at the University of Washington who resisted the 7 P.M. curfew placed on those of Japanese descent after EO 9066 and later appealed his case to the Supreme Court; but as Endo demonstrated, protest assumed a variety of forms.[46] Unlike Hirabayashi, though, Endo had no broad activist goals for working with Purcell. Endo had only signed up for a lawsuit against her former employer; she wanted the possibility to have her job back after incarceration. Removal and incarceration forced Endo and her co-plaintiffs to take lower-paying and less secure jobs against their will and without cause. Despite her initial hesitancy, however, Endo reluctantly agreed to join in Purcell's case, stating, "I agreed to do it at that moment because they said it's for the good of everybody, and so I said, well if that's it, I'll go ahead and do it."[47] Endo's fight against job discrimination became a fight against wrongful imprisonment.

On July 13, 1942, while Endo was imprisoned with her family at Tule Lake, Purcell filed a habeas corpus petition on her behalf. Purcell claimed that Endo was indeed a prisoner and had been detained without proper trial or due process. Public Law 503 (the provision that made it illegal to obstruct Executive Order 9066—including going on strike) had not granted the military authority to detain Japanese Americans since martial law was never declared in the Western Defense Command. Therefore, Endo's imprisonment was illegal and unconstitutional. Because no martial law existed under Executive Order 9066, the legislative system functioned as normal, meaning that Endo was entitled to a trial for her supposed crimes.[48] Judge Michael Roche of the United States District Court for the Northern District of California received the petition but did not make a ruling on it for well over a year, eventually choosing to dismiss it in July 1943 with no explanation. Purcell appealed the case to the Ninth Circuit Court of Appeals in April 1944, where Judge William Denman (who would later describe his disgust with the prisonlike conditions of the "relocation centers" in the 1949) passed the case to the federal Supreme Court rather than make a ruling.[49]

While Purcell prepared for his long-awaited argument before the Supreme Court, Endo was transferred to the Topaz prison in Utah, and labor assumed a prominent position in her case. By the summer of 1944, the WRA's program of "all-out relocation," or encouraging as many Japanese Americans to leave as possible, was in full swing. Similar to others at Topaz, Endo had successfully navigated the leave clearance process, proving that she was loyal and that "no security reason bars the grant to her of indefinite leave," or resettlement in a community beyond the camp.[50] The WRA granted Endo her leave clearance on August 23, 1943 (while she was still at Tule Lake) and deemed her "eligible for indefinite leave for the purpose of employment or residence in the Eastern Defense Command, as well as in other areas."[51]

Her leave clearance based on her loyalty, however, "did not authorize her departure from the relocation center." The WRA required that she, like all other prisoners looking to resettle, follow up with additional information on her proposed whereabouts and employment situation after her release. This involved a requirement to "notify [a WRA relocation official] of change of address" (which the WRA argued was "reasonable for administrative reasons—not for surveillance"), and to prove that she "had the ability to support herself" and would be able to relocate indefinitely to a community which the WRA deemed accepting and friendly for their protection as well as to lessen racial conflict.[52] Nothing, as Solicitor General Charles Fahy would later remark, stood in "the way of her liberty," except, of course, her inability to return to the West Coast.[53] This was a nonnegotiable point for Endo, who, pursuant to her previous employment battle, wanted to return to her job in California. Employment in the Eastern Defense Command (or anywhere east of the Rockies) based on her skill set and loyalty was certainly an option. But this was a fight based on the right to freely seek employment regardless of location. Because of the restrictions placed on her entry into military defense areas, Endo was unable to resume the job she once held. Furthermore, her ineligibility to return to California meant that she was unable to seek redress for either the termination of her employment or her unlawful imprisonment. Because of these conditions, and with the guidance of Purcell, Endo refused to submit an application for indefinite leave. In September 1943, rather than relocating to a community outside the prison system, she chose to transfer to Topaz and rejected a forced second removal and the life of a parolee.

Endo's case, *Ex parte Endo*, rested on proving that she was wrongfully imprisoned or detained and, therefore, that the leave clearance process—heavily dependent on employment—did not apply to her. Endo argued that if she had received proper due process and therefore been designated a loyal citizen, she would not "be required to meet [the] conditions" set forth by the WRA in order for her to receive indefinite leave. Endo maintained that "no charge justifying her imprisonment [had] ever been made against her; that she [was] confined solely because she [was] of Japanese ancestry; . . . that she [was] not subject to military law," and that her detainment was entirely unconstitutional.[54] Furthermore, based on the amended argument from the state of California that the Japanese American employees had been fired because they were no longer able to work, Endo argued that she "had been suspended from her position as a permanent Civil Service employee because she [was] unable to perform her duties as such employee due to her imprisonment." Her standing as a civil service employee constituted "a vested property right" which was "imperiled by her confinement."[55]

Legal representatives for the WRA were quick to fight back. Solicitor General Fahy, who argued on behalf of the government in this case, doubted Endo's claims. Endo was not denied due process because there was nothing that stood in the way of ending her so-called imprisonment "except her refusal to apply for leave" and abide by the requirements stated.[56] Endo was "not by any means in prison, or in any sense irrevocably confined," nor was she "interned as an enemy or detained as disloyal."[57] She was "in practical fact not detained against her will, except against her will not to cooperate in the leave regulation requirements under which 28,000 in like circumstances had already obtained indefinite leave" and others were in the process of doing so "at the rate of several hundred per week." Granted, "in ordinary times, under ordinary circumstances, clearly she would be right; but no such conditions would ever exist in ordinary times or circumstances."[58]

When the case reached the Supreme Court in October 1944 (heard consecutively with *Korematsu v. United States*, dealing with the racial implications of exclusion and forced removal), the justices faced the question of whether or not Endo's detention was valid and/or constitutional even if she declined to follow the regulations for securing indefinite leave. In an affidavit filed by Purcell on February 19, 1943, Endo maintained that the WRA "made no provision for the return of the appellant to her former place of residence and employment in the State of California." Her decision to refuse to apply for indefinite leave was based on the idea that such an application "would be a useless act" as she would not be able to return to the West Coast." Furthermore, she was "confined and detained against her will," meaning that she was "refused the right to return to her previous place of residence and employment."[59]

Although whether or not Endo had been unlawfully detained in the first place was a central point in the case, Frank Hennessy, the United States attorney for the Northern District of California, and Edward J. Ennis, director of the Alien Enemy Control Unit for the Department of Justice, focused exclusively on whether or not denying her permission to return to the West Coast and resume her employment constituted unlawful detainment. Like Fahy, Hennessy and Ennis argued that Endo was not unlawfully detained because she was able to leave Topaz whenever she wished. She just could not return to the West Coast when she left. In response to Endo's criticisms of the requirements of the WRA that she "agree to make reports as to her arrival at her proposed destination and as to any subsequent changes in her employment or residence," Hennessy and Ennis believed "that this condition is reasonable and valid" and that "the courts would not grant release without her compliance with this conditions."[60]

In December 1944, the Supreme Court justices unanimously ruled on Endo's case. They decided that detention itself was not unconstitutional as the act which created the WRA in March 1942 as well as the executive orders made no specific mention of detentions.[61] However, when it came to loyal citizens (as the court decided Endo was), "the authority to detain a citizen or to grant him a conditional release as protection against espionage or sabotage is exhausted at least when his loyalty is conceded." "If we held that the authority to detain continued thereafter," Justice Douglas continued in his opinion, "we would transform an espionage or sabotage measure into something else," which was not done by EO 9066 nor any other congressional act. Seeing as how Endo was loyal, the court reversed the previous decision against the writ of habeas corpus and declared that she was "entitled to an unconditional release by the War Relocation Authority." The court decided that detaining loyal American citizens, even in times of war, was unconstitutional, even if not inherently racist. Endo was, by order from the highest court, free to leave Topaz.[62]

But she was not free to leave on her terms, as she was still barred from returning to the West Coast to resume her employment. The court made no decision on the West Coast exclusion orders and, in fact, supported the original decision of forced removal. Specifically relating to Endo and her ability to now leave Topaz, Justice Frank Murphy (who had passionately voiced his dissent in the *Korematsu v. United States* ruling when the justices upheld exclusion under EO 9066) questioned whether or not her unconditional release was truly unconditional. "It would seem to me that the 'unconditional' release given to Miss Endo necessarily implies 'the right to pass freely from state to state' including the right to move freely to California," Murphy stated.[63] Though the Endo decision granted the plaintiff her freedom, the decision did not challenge the exclusion orders from the West Coast nor the prohibition on her employment in California.

Ironically, the decision of the court in the Endo case as it related to her ability to return to the West Coast had already been decided by the military. As early as the winter of 1943, Lieutenant General Delos Emmons (who had replaced DeWitt as Western Defense commander earlier in September) began to make individual exemptions to loyal Nisei seeking to return to the West Coast after Nisei soldiers were allowed to do the same on furlough, indicating changing attitudes on the necessity of exclusion. On December 17, 1944, one day before the Supreme Court ruled on the case, Western Defense commander Charles Bonesteel (who assumed the position after Emmons) issued Public Proclamation 21, which granted permission for Japanese Americans cleared for leave to return to the West Coast, nullifying the exclusion orders from 1942. Beginning on January 2, 1945, Japanese Americans such as Endo would be allowed to return home and attempt to begin the process of rebuilding their lives. Ever knowing which way the political winds were blowing, Roosevelt supported the proclamation.

The Endo case was instrumental in restoring the ability of loyal Japanese Americans to leave the prisons without the intrusive oversight of the WRA. However, the case did not rule on the constitutionality of the broader program of removal and incarceration, nor did the case directly challenge the WRA leave procedures or assist those like Endo with resuming their former jobs. Rather, the court's decision on *Endo* allowed the WRA to continue its policy of requiring employment as a condition of release—potentially employment that did not replicate the types the prisoners held before incarceration and coercing them into accepting whatever jobs were available in a community that would welcome them.

Camp newspapers had quite a time reporting on Ms. Mitsuye Endo's resettlement following her legal "victory." Interestingly, her residence would not be in California. The *Minidoka Irrigator* reported that Endo "will make her home in Chicago instead of in California" and that "authorities of the Topaz relocation center said Miss Endow [*sic*] left recently to live with her sister, Mrs. George Yamamoto, in Chicago."[64] The *Colorado Times* even reported on Endo's decision to "spurn her California home" and "seek [a] job in [the] Windy City."[65] The "determined little Japanese American girl" arrived in Chicago in May 1945 to live with her two sisters, who had previously resettled and apparently "had words of praise for Chicago." Endo, "the darkhaired stenographer," reportedly decided on Chicago not only for familial reasons but also because she understood that "Chicago people hold no resentment against Americans of Japanese ancestry." Endo had read and heard that this "was not the situation on the West Coast," including her hometown of Sacramento. "Maybe after the war, we'll all move back to Sacramento," Endo explained, planning on bringing the rest of her family from Topaz to Chicago.[66]

The "Second Forced Removal": Resettlement on the Outside

Endo's concerns about returning to California appeared justified, despite the lifting of the exclusion orders earlier that year. An article in the *Colorado Times* titled "Burning Nisei Home Draws $1,000 Fine" detailed the exploits

Figure 12. Mitsuye Endo leaving the Topaz prison camp in 1945 (January 1, 1945).
Used by permission, Utah State Historical Society.

of a twenty-two-year-old farmer from Vashon Island, Washington, who pleaded guilty to second-degree arson after being arrested for "burning homes of evacuated Japanese" in an effort to "prevent return of the Japanese to the Puget Sound Island."[67] Another report described recent acts of "terrorism" against returning Japanese Americans to the Fresno, California, area, where two men held vigil outside the home of the recently returned Mimura family and opened fire on the house, nearly killing the couple's six-year-old son while he was taking a bath.[68] The local sheriff said that the attacks on the Mimura family were similar to others in California's San Joaquin Valley, prompting state law enforcement officials to seek "a coordinated plan for halting the attacks" despite district attorney James M. Thuesen's claim that "persons who make an issue of sympathizing with returning Japanese are partially to blame for the series of attacks upon the homes of returned evacuees."[69] These developments were all chronicled on the front page of just one regional newspaper. With such virulent threats and attacks on Japanese American lives and property, it remained questionable if former prisoners (now essentially parolees) actually did have the freedom to return to the West Coast and attempt to rebuild their lives.[70]

Scores of proposed (and passed) state-level and local legislation targeting Japanese Americans also resulted in unwelcoming and downright hostile environments. Legislative measures designed to limit the rights of Nisei were similar to the anti-alien land laws of the early twentieth century. West Coast state legislatures passed laws preventing foreign-born Asians from owning property to discourage Japanese immigrants from settling on the West Coast when the federal government did not respond to the "yellow invasion" the way politicians and their constituents had hoped.[71] During and after World War II this legislative trend continued. Texas, for example, sought to limit the employment opportunities of white-collar Issei looking to resettle. In 1943, three bills were proposed and passed requiring a person to be a US citizen in order to obtain state licenses for selling liquor and practicing dentistry.[72] Meanwhile, Pennsylvania prohibited any government money to be spent on facilities that would employ, educate, or house Japanese Americans.[73]

In other states, prejudice limited employment opportunities for the recently released and soon-to-be released prisoners. Governor Carville of Nevada openly opposed "importation of evacuees for labor," and the county commissioners of Washoe, Nevada, "denied dude ranchers [the] right to employ evacuees."[74] These measures were not justified in the language of unfair competition, wages, or other such factors—only on the notion of not want-ing "enemy aliens" within the state. Similarly, many farm and labor organ-izations that represented agricultural employers openly protested the hiring of Japanese Americans, limiting what had been a prominent occupation for the prisoners prior to forced removal. In the Bitterroot Valley of Montana, farmers organized against Japanese American land acquisition, while the Ar-izona Farm Bureau recommended "duration confinement" for prisoners throughout the war. Such proclamations intimidated Japanese Americans and discouraged WRA administrators from resettling Japanese Americans on the West Coast.[75] Escheat suits on behalf of the state of California initi-ated against Issei who had purchased, owned, and operated land through loopholes in anti-alien land laws also further victimized those who had been imprisoned and limited their opportunities for voluntary self-sufficiency.[76]

Local and state-level resistance to Japanese American resettlement did not stop the WRA from clearing thousands of Issei and Nisei for indefinite leave in 1943 and 1944, particularly for war industry–related work. Even follow-ing the disbanding of the Japanese American Joint Board in 1944, the army continued to be involved in the leave clearance process as questions about Japanese American loyalty and fitness for high-security wartime work (which ranged from working in munitions plants to—ironically—handling dyna-mite) pervaded the American public.

As with the early phases of removal and detention, army officials initially attempted to remain as distant from the entire process as possible, not want-ing to become weighed down with excessive administrative tasks and pub-licity problems in the middle of a war. A memo from Calvert L. Dedrick, the chief economist hired on as a consultant for the joint board, to the leaders of the Western Defense Command assured them that "there appears to be no grounds for apprehension that this office will become involved in the politi-cal controversy over the release of Japanese-Americans from War Relocation Projects."[77] Furthermore, the Provost Marshal General's Office "is not now, never has been, and never should be in the business of passing final judgment on the release, relocation, or retention of any Japanese evacuee as long as the War Relocation Authority has this responsibility"; however, the military "can indicate whether there is any objection to the employment of a Japanese in a plant or facility important to the War effort."[78] Since Japanese Americans, according to Dedrick, were willing to take high-paying jobs no matter the location or the type of employment, this included wartime industrial work, making it necessary for the joint board to "remove the individual from such

employment" if there were concerns about their loyalty.[79] The army participated in both the approval of Japanese Americans for work in war industries
and the recall of these parolees. This authority further emphasized that although Japanese Americans were technically cleared for indefinite leave and
even approved to work in what would otherwise be considered highly sensitive areas, the freedom in choosing and maintaining employment was always
tenuous and circumspect.[80]

During the summer of 1944, a group of fifty-nine Issei and Nisei employed
at the Illinois Central Railroad raised the sensitive issue of Japanese American employment in "high-security" jobs outside the prison camps. From 1943
on, many industries, including railroads, continued to experience labor shortages similar to those faced by the agricultural sector earlier in the war. The
Illinois Central Railroad connected various major cities and economic centers of manufacturing from the Midwest to the Gulf Coast and was often referred to as the "Mainline of Mid-America," but management reported a
continued shortage of labor. "We have been, and still are, desperately short
of workmen to perform the necessary work of our railroad," C. R. Young,
manager of personnel for Illinois Central, lamented in July 1944.[81] Like Midwest and West Coast farmers, Young described shortages caused by "large
and continuous turnover due to losses to armed forces . . . death, retirement,
resignation . . . competition among all industries for new employees, loss of
productivity due to new, inexperienced and physically handicapped workmen, and virtual disappearance of any surplus labor," particularly on the
Chicago Terminal portion of the line.[82] By June 1944, Illinois Central faced
a shortage of 2,099 workers, including 177 freight house clerks and laborers
and 828 section laborers.

Fortunately for Young, the WRA's Chicago office was in search of employment opportunities in the summer of 1944 for a group of Japanese
Americans from the Heart Mountain prison camp in Wyoming. The leave
clearance policy for any form of employment crucial to the war effort was
similar to the leave processes for agriculture. The exception was government
work or war industry work, which required special permission from the Provost Marshal General's Office and investigation by the FBI. Regardless, any
Japanese American employed in defense industries was supposedly thoroughly vetted for such work, including the fifty-nine Nisei and Issei who
went to work on the Chicago Terminal of the Illinois Central line in July 1944,
living in boxcars near the work site. The acting director of the Chicago WRA
Office, M. Jacoby, and C. C. Gilmore, representative of the WRA from Heart

Mountain, visited various work stations at the Chicago Terminal of the Illinois Central line on June 28, 1944, accompanied by an employment agent from Illinois Central, Mr. J. C. Conley, to assess the working conditions and determine if there was indeed a labor shortage. Once the WRA representatives were satisfied, Conley left for Heart Mountain, where he recruited the fifty-nine workers and returned with them to Chicago on July 20.[83] These were all "loyal" and "obedient" men who were eager to leave the prison as much as Illinois Central was eager to have their assistance. But this labor agreement would not be as seamlessly implemented as all parties had hoped.

The problems for the Japanese Americans who arrived in Chicago began almost immediately. The local Brotherhood of Railway Clerks (BRC), the American Federation of Labor (AFL)–affiliated union representing the rail workers, was less than enthusiastic about Illinois Central enlisting the "enemy" to work alongside loyal Americans, and the union expressed its discontent in writing. While concerns about defense, safety, and unfair labor competition peppered a resolution submitted to management, the union leadership emphasized that Illinois Central did not consult them as to whether or not they wanted to labor alongside Japanese Americans. As representatives of the workers, the union claimed it should have been included in the decision-making process along with the WRA and the employers on whether or not to bring in Japanese American workers.[84]

WRA administrators attempted to take into consideration unions' negative attitudes toward Japanese Americans. WRA administrators at Poston warned during a block meeting that "some unions are very much interested [in Japanese American labor]," but "some and most of them are not."[85] Limiting the union-directed hostility faced by Japanese American resettled workers was a top priority among WRA field officers and administrators. At the same time, however, working with unions directly to prevent such issues was not something that interested the WRA, restricting some employment options that otherwise would have been available to the resettled Japanese Americans. When one Japanese American man at Poston asked Thomas Holland (then chief of the Employment Division of the WRA at the Washington, DC, office) during a block meeting how the protests at Poston and Manzanar may have affected the views of unions toward Japanese Americans, Holland replied, "That sort of thing will make it more difficult to relocate people. . . . It will hamper to some extent our efforts." He admitted that in the process of resettlement, "there will be plenty of unfortunate incidents" involving resettled Japanese Americans and unions.[86]

The BRC's response to the Japanese American workers who arrived in Chicago in July 1944 confirmed Holland's predictions. Correspondence between the union leaders and personnel manager C. R. Young revealed that the union was opposed to the plan to use Japanese American labor from its inception. "Short over one hundred section laborers Chicago Terminal today. Unable to employ sufficient force to keep up important work," Young began in a pleading telegram to Elmer E. Milliman, president of the Brotherhood of Maintenance of Way Employees, an organization that was aligned with the BRC and represented the men employed on the Chicago Terminal specifically.[87] "Understand only men approved by FBI will be released. These men not prisoners of war but first and second generation Japanese in same category as many orientals [*sic*] here," referring to Chinese and Filipinos employed on the lines and in Illinois Central.[88] "There should be no discrimination in working these individuals under prevailing rules agreement under precedented [*sic*] war conditions," Young reminded Milliman, referencing FDR's Executive Order 8802 prohibiting employment discrimination in wartime defense industries.[89] Young was not seeking approval from the union for the new policy so much as its support in ensuring that there would be no trouble from the workers.

Milliman dashed Young's hopes when he replied via telegram the next day. "Our organization is opposed to employment of Japanese Internees [*sic*] because our people and other railroad employees are opposed to working with them under existing war circumstances," referencing statements made earlier that summer by F. L. Noakes, general chairman of the union.[90] "If you have exhausted every effort to obtain sufficient domestic workers to meet your needs, why don't you endeavor to meet your shortage as other railroads have done, by employing Mexicans," Milliman asked, offering assistance on behalf of the railroad retirement board in working with the War Manpower Commission to get "Mexican nationals" to Chicago.[91] Using Mexican migrant labor was not only a desired wartime option among agriculturalists; industrialists also looked to capitalize on the Bracero program in railroad maintenance.[92] Following the telegram, Young requested a meeting with Noakes to further discuss the matter, but Noakes was hospitalized from July 8 through the 19th (the day before the Japanese Americans from Heart Mountain arrived) and was unable to comply with his wishes.[93]

When the Japanese American men from Heart Mountain arrived, the response from the unionized workers was swift. On July 20, local representatives of the BRC met with representatives from the Chicago resettlement branch of the WRA and personnel managers from Illinois Central and stated that "if these Japanese-Americans were put to work, all other freight house employees would stop work."[94] Young tried to assure the representatives that all of the Japanese Americans were cleared and loyal, but to no avail. On July 25, Noakes followed up on the threat and announced that he was "personnaly [sic] opposed to the employment of Japanese-Americans, regardless of their citizenship status and that he would oppose their employment with all the resources at his command." When Illinois Central warned that such an act would be a violation of FDR's executive order and the Railway Labor Act (passed in 1936 to promote negotiations through arbitration rather than strikes), Noakes replied that this action "would not be a strike, but a mass vacation or sick leave, the men would merely stop working."[95]

Still, Young urged George Harrison (grand president of the Brotherhood of Railway Clerks) to reconsider his position, as the union was unable to drum up extra employees to help with the manpower shortage, and because the Japanese Americans employed at Illinois Central were "not prisoners of war and are wards of the Federal Government" posing no threat.[96] But Young's pleas failed. During a meeting of sixteen unions representing employees in the railroad industry, the labor organizers expressed support for the views of their leaders: "It is our profound and unanimous conviction that the injection of Japanese Evacuees at this time would profoundly disturb the morale of the employes [sic] and would in all probability precipitate a condition for which neither of the organizations could assume responsibility and which they would be wholly unable to control," referencing strikes or perhaps worse.[97] The gauntlet was thrown. The Brotherhood of Maintenance of Way Employees established a deadline of 11:00 A.M. on Sunday, July 30, for the Japanese American men to be removed, or the workers would go on strike.

While Young and the other personnel managers at Illinois Central were frustrated by the union's display, the army was not amused when it caught wind of the growing unrest. A strike threatened productivity, while conflicts between the Illinois Central workers and the Japanese American employees would highlight the army's inability to handle its affairs. As much as the army desired to remain removed from the resettlement program in favor of keeping the process in the hands of civilian agencies, the unions' charges of Japanese American disloyalty could not go unanswered. Major E. C. Millstead (chief of the Intelligence and Personnel Security Branch of the Central Defense Command of the Army) informed the commanding general of the Central Defense Command, Lieutenant General Ben Lear, that Illinois Central assigned Japanese

Americans hired as freight handlers to tasks located near "crates and cartons containing materials consigned to the Army Air Forces, the Navy, the Signal Corps and Infantry Drill Manuals to be shipped to the West Coast." Furthermore, "approximately 50% of the crates and cartons inspected contained materials important to the war effort" including dynamite, and "this freight house is considered to be one of the largest in the United States."[98] Japanese Americans would "be in a position to do damage to the war effort."[99] Worse yet, the discovery that twenty-five of the fifty-nine Japanese Americans employed were "aliens" with incomplete background checks enraged the army directors in charge of providing special clearance for war work.

How did these Japanese American men with "questionable backgrounds" and only partial background checks end up working at such a sensitive area for defense? The answer was miscommunication and confusion in the clearance process. When army officers working for the Provost Marshal General's Office investigated the matter, they found that the WRA cleared the Japanese American men without first receiving approval from the FBI. While common in order to increase the pace of all-out relocation, this shortcut applied primarily to work outside the defense industries, not to jobs that included handling sensitive materials on main transportation lines. In response, Lieutenant Colonel Hoopes (deputy director of the Internal Security Division) advised the railroad to consider terminating the employment of the Japanese Americans until the War Department could further investigate the matter.[100]

In the middle of the confusion were the Japanese American men who found themselves in Chicago—unfamiliar territory—with their jobs and well-being at the mercy of the government and their new employer. Although the Provost Marshal General's Office determined that the solution to the problem was to place the clearance of the fifty-nine Japanese American employees at Illinois Central at the top of their priority list to prevent a labor strike, Illinois Central bowed to the whims of the union to remove the men from employment and "keep them off the work until they have been cleared."[101] The workers sat idly and "remained in their boxcars which [were] their homes while they are on the job."[102] Illinois Central provided food for the men, but their future was uncertain. Having agreed to work for Illinois Central and relocated with aid from the WRA, they now lacked control over their employment situation. Although resettled and freed from the Heart Mountain prison, their choices were circumscribed in terms of living and working conditions, and their ability to redeem themselves through labor was denied.

Ultimately, the situation was resolved following a more thorough investigation. On a second look, the Provost Marshal General's Office, with the
cooperation of the FBI, discovered that eighteen of the fifty-nine security
questionnaires revealed that "five of the workers of Japanese ancestry were
undesirable and [would] be excluded from continuing their duties," while four
others "received limited approval and would not be permitted access to classi-
fied material." Nine were fully approved and would be relocated to other parts
of the line. These solutions appeared to appease the union, which called off the
strike, and newspapers in the area reported that the "Japanese problem" at Illinois Central was solved when "the railroad announced the dismissal of 59
Japanese American trackmen over whose employment the other workers had
threatened to strike."[103] The Japanese Americans were eventually reemployed
and placed in another work area, but the threatened strike and the reactions of
the army, the WRA, and Illinois Central demonstrated that many parolees
still depended on the government for employment. Although the resettled
Japanese Americans could turn to the WRA for protection, they were also
heavily dependent on private employers who in turn were beholden to appeasing workers and unions. The performance of redemptive labor was complicated and largely shaped by forces beyond the control of the former prisoners.

Community Resettlement and Redemptive Labor

Resettlement for Japanese Americans was often a mixed experience and illus-
trates the complicated intersections of freedom of choice and labor restrictions. Regardless of where Japanese Americans ultimately settled, all-out
relocation essentially forced them out of the prisons. Yet steady employment
was a requirement for leaving (unless they could prove that they had alternate
forms of support—which was nearly impossible for many who lost their livelihood, jobs, and property during incarceration). As seen earlier, Japanese
Americans were cleared to return to the West Coast after December 1944,
when the exclusion orders were lifted, but their reception was in many cases
less than welcoming. Collaborations as well as conflicts with African Americans and other minority groups over issues of discrimination in employment
and housing shortages also created a need for both white and Japanese
American groups (such as the JACL) to assist with resettlement in California
and elsewhere.[104] Organizations including the Fair Play Committee and its
chapters in Oregon, Washington, and California worked with Quakers and

other Christian organizations to find "sponsors" for Japanese American families returning to the West Coast and communities that welcomed their resettlement.[105]

However, Japanese Americans did not always have a say in their sites of resettlement. If a Japanese American released from Tule Lake or Manzanar who was originally a business owner in southern California could only find sponsored employment as a machinist in Chicago, did their resettlement represent free choice or the strictures of a labor-driven relocation program? Did Japanese Americans have freedom of movement and choice of employment in this context? Within a system of capitalism, one could argue that any employee was often forced to follow jobs as they became available, particularly during a regimented war economy and in the prior Great Depression, when choices were few. However, the experience of incarceration made the Japanese American processes of seeking employment and resettlement unique, in that their status as free laborers was circumscribed by their identities as former prisoners of the state and by their need for redemption and rehabilitation as "enemy others."

At many points and in many settings, the WRA and social scientists argued that a goal of incarceration was to assist Japanese Americans in reentering American society and assimilating to a greater degree than before. In practice, this meant scattering Japanese Americans throughout the Midwest and along the East Coast and breaking up any potential for the formation of new "Little Tokyos."[106] For many social scientists and camp administrators, labor programs in the camps were an essential means to the end of Japanese American rehabilitation, an opportunity for Japanese Americans to either hone existing skills or learn new ones that would apply to coveted manufacturing jobs. These new skills would help meet wartime labor demands, which often dictated the resettlement patterns of Japanese Americans while also encouraging diffusion and assimilation of the Japanese American population. Both during and after incarceration, the WRA sold the incarceration program as a rehabilitative undertaking. Administrators helped minorities previously on the margins of American society to learn the proper skills (primarily labor related) to fully reintegrate and adapt better than they had before. Here, the imprisonment of Japanese Americans was rehabilitative rather than punitive. The redemptive power of labor as the mechanism for Japanese American cultural rehabilitation was a central component of resettlement.

"Where do we go from here?" an article in the *Poston Chronicle* asked in March 1945.

For many Japanese Americans, the answer depended on the availability of work.[107] For employment not directly connected with military or defense plants, the process of resettlement often began in the prisons with the perusal of job ads from the Office of Outside Employment. Positions varied by skill level and experience and, as soon the employment office posted them, the ads were good for only ten days before they were passed on to another prison.[108]

Industrial positions were some of the most sought-after jobs among the prisoners, and employer demands for laborers were high. In June 1943, the Office of Outside Employment advertised positions for men and women operating sewing machines in a Chicago plant that paid twenty-five to thirty-five dollars for forty to forty-five hours of work per week. A Toledo monument company also requested one man or woman "to design, lay-out and stencil tombstones" with "wages to be arranged." Many of the jobs, including the aforementioned sewing machine operator posting, promised under one dollar per hour to begin, with the potential to advance to higher-paying positions within a few weeks or months. Some jobs required previous experience, while many were simply eager to get warm bodies in to help meet the demands of the booming war economy.[109]

Many of the industrial jobs were located in the Midwest, with Chicago, Indiana, and Cleveland receiving large numbers of Japanese Americans from the camps. Compared to some cities on the East Coast, the Midwest was a haven for refugees from the prisons who could not return to the West. While hostels run by Christian groups or the WRA offering affordable and friendly accommodations to relocating Japanese Americans popped up in New York City during all-out relocation, some residents—including Mayor Fiorello H. La Guardia—openly opposed the resettlement of "enemy aliens." La Guardia claimed Japanese Americans jeopardized the safety of the city and encouraged protests among the city's large Chinese American community in response to heightened ethnic tensions between Japan and China during the war.[110] Midwestern cities were not without discriminatory reactions among residents to newly settled Japanese Americans. The WRA regional offices charged with assisting the new arrivals were easy targets for public protests against the resettlement program. Chicagoans, for example, protested against Japanese Americans looking to purchase homes in the Windy City.[111]

Overall, however, Japanese Americans who left the prisons for the Midwest often reported favorably on the economic opportunities and their reception there. Even though Chicago posed racial problems for Japanese Americans, who would compete with African Americans and whites for jobs and housing, the *Chicago Sun* attempted to encourage Japanese Americans looking for a place to resettle to consider Evanston. The Chicago suburb, with easy access to job opportunities and employers looking to meet labor demands, was a good option for Japanese Americans looking for a new home. "In the Middle West are thousands of people of Japanese ancestry, uprooted from their West Coast homes and compelled, by exigence of war, to make new lives for themselves in strange communities," the article began. Noting some of the struggles faced by Japanese Americans looking to purchase homes in Evanston, the author assured readers that these were minor occurrences and undoubtedly, as more stories of the Japanese American 442nd Infantry Regiment's courage and combat in Italy reached the nationwide news, "Evanston . . . will still be a safe and pleasant place to live."[112]

Cleveland, in particular, provided both economic opportunities and a welcoming environment for Nisei, who assisted the city with meeting its severe labor shortage in wartime manufacturing. Prior to the 1940s, only a small community of Japanese Americans had found their way to northeast Ohio. Once the war began, many Cleveland manufacturers, including those who made glass, steel, rubber, and other consumer and military products, found themselves short of workers as more men went overseas to fight—a familiar story unfolding in many cities across the country. Desperate for a workforce to support military contracts, employers turned to the imprisoned Japanese Americans.

What set Cleveland apart in the resettlement and parole process was its long-standing network of civic agencies and religious organizations that assisted incoming Japanese Americans. As a city that prospered and grew during the Gilded Age thanks to men like oil baron John D. Rockefeller, Cleveland also experienced social and economic ills as a result of its heavy and rapid industrialization. Housing shortages, poverty, illness, and the struggles of the working class and the city's newly arriving Eastern European immigrants, and later African Americans from the South moving north during the Great Migration, prompted responses from Progressive Era reformers. A network of settlement houses aimed at providing social services in the form of childcare, English language classes, and other cultural and educational opportunities became hallmarks of the city, as did religious organizations and agencies such as the Federation for Charity and Philanthropy. With a reputation for social services and a central location in the Midwest near social and economic opportunities, Cleveland was the nation's sixth largest city at the time. The WRA established a regional office there under the direction of Robert Cullum and Dorothy Barber following visits to the area by George Rundquist (executive secretary on the resettlement of Japanese Americans) in late 1942. Cleveland eventually became the third largest city, after Chicago and Denver, to receive resettled Japanese Americans, approximately three thousand by 1945. With opportunities for employment and a history of immigrant communities and philanthropy, Cleveland was a model city for Japanese American redemptive labor.[113]

One of Cleveland's most active boosters for Japanese American resettlement in the city and surrounding region was engineer George S. Trundle Jr. Trundle was a well-known and well-liked figure in northeast Ohio, as devoted to social problems and philanthropy as he was to overseeing his engineering consulting firm, the Trundle Engineering Company of Cleveland. Trundle and his corporation witnessed a windfall during the war when it served as a consultant to the Quartermaster of the Army for production analysis and testing, but Trundle was also associated with the various manufacturers and industrialists of Cleveland who worked on government and military contracts. Cleveland Steel, Master Chrome, and the Taylor-Boggis Foundry in Euclid, Ohio (an eastern suburb of the city) all reaped the economic benefits of military contracts but struggled to maintain a robust labor force by the final years of the war. These corporations were clients of Trundle, who determined that if all-out relocation was a goal of the WRA, then the labor-starved industrialists of Cleveland could help with the program.[114]

In early 1943, Trundle, with the assistance of other agencies in Cleveland, formed the Cleveland Resettlement Committee for Japanese Americans (CRC). Trundle had served as a consultant on employment for the WRA during the early years of all-out relocation, making him a prime choice to serve as chairman of the new agency. He quickly went to work enlisting the help of religious organizations including Catholic Charities, the Cleveland Church Federation, the Jewish Social Service Bureau, and the Baptist Church, as well as public agencies including the Urban League of Cleveland, the Consumer League of Cleveland, the United States Employment Service, and the Cleveland Public Library, in the formation of subcommittees to address different aspects of resettlement—including housing, education, cultural opportunities, and more.[115]

Throughout 1943, Trundle made visits to various WRA camps and worked with the agency to promote Cleveland as a potential site of resettlement for Japanese Americans. Many of the selling points for Cleveland focused on the city's economic opportunities. Cleveland Steel Products pushed hard for Trundle and WRA representatives to recruit Japanese Americans to join their thinning production lines. Cleveland Steel specialized in making windshield wipers, propeller shafts, universal joints, and drive shafts for airplane parts and armor plates under military contract, but in 1943, they were "approximately 20% behind schedule" and faced the risk of losing lucrative military contracts.[116] Trundle was initially able to recruit a trial group of eighteen Nisei men between the ages of eighteen and twenty-two to travel to Cleveland to work for the steel company once they were cleared for leave.

The response of the management of Cleveland Steel to the new workers was glowing. The Army's Fifth Service Command received reports from the company that as a result of even just eighteen additional Japanese American workers, "the company is now caught up completely to its production schedule." The company praised the work ethic of the men as they "set an example by their application and industry, remaining almost constantly at their machines" and rarely called out from work, a problem that previously plagued the plant. Although there were initial negative reactions among some workers at Cleveland Steel to the hiring of the men that mirrored the hostile reception afforded to Japanese American workers in Chicago, the situation was quickly resolved and the company reported that the effect of employing Japanese Americans "has been to stimulate the whites or Caucasians into real production."[117] Cleveland Steel and other manufacturing companies called on Trundle to drum up more workers, and the WRA even published a pamphlet, *Facts on Cleveland*, which listed numerous economic opportunities for those looking to relocate.[118]

Trundle also worked with other employers in the region to place ads in prison newspapers for clerical and domestic work for women. Combined with the establishment of religious and WRA-run hostels in Cleveland and a general level of reported acceptance among the resettled Nisei (despite later pushback in looking for housing from some white residents who resented their presence and lobbied for government intervention), the city became an attractive spot for those looking to leave the camps.[119]

The military and WRA officials used Cleveland as a showcase for demonstrating how quickly Japanese Americans adapted to their new environment and how crucial they were to the war effort. The Provost Marshal General's Office gathered favorable reports from employers and media outlets to compose a file of "good publicity" for the resettlement program. A newspaper clipping from the *Cleveland Plain Dealer* featuring Cleveland Steel Product's general manager W. J. Smith boasting of his Japanese American employees and describing them as "very adept" in learning new skills and assisting with production goals was filed away for future reference. Another section of the same article showcased an elderly Japanese American couple who not only worked hard at a Cleveland bakery but also seemed "thoroughly at home in their surroundings" and "enter[ed] with almost a pathetic gratitude into the banter of their fellow workers." The *Plain Dealer* proclaimed that the couple and the other Japanese Americans who came to Cleveland had "earned their right to belong" through their good spirits and hard work.[120]

The employment of Japanese Americans in Cleveland, however, was not without its problems. Cleveland Metal Products Company requested a group of Nisei for work but reported that they slowed their initially high rate of production after threats from their white coworkers, who chastised them for working too hard. The Department of the Interior (now custodian for the WRA) had desired to use some examples of successfully resettled and employed Japanese Americans to raise public support for all-out relocation and turned to Cleveland as a source. Cleveland Metal Products was initially a solid option as managers had nothing but good things to say about the Japanese American employees, but the recent news of racial conflict and slow production concerned the Provost Marshal General's Office (PMO). Major Joseph Hughes (executive of the Personnel Security Division of the PMO) warned against focusing on Cleveland Metal Products as the Department of the Interior was "interested in a newspaper release to the effect that labor problems are solved through the utilization of Japanese-Americans," while the PMO wanted "the facts to be accurate and not place the Army in the position of obstructing full utilization of labor, which might be charged if we thereafter remove the Japanese-Americans under our program." While in this case the PMO and Department of Interior chose to highlight a corporation based in Chicago that hired Japanese Americans, Cleveland continued to be a bright spot for the WRA and the PMO as an example of a city that proved that Japanese Americans were productive members of society willing to use their labor to adapt and assist with the war effort.[121]

The Road to Seabrook Farms

By May 1944, the WRA relocated approximately 21,400 Japanese American former prisoners. Those with experience in clerical or sales work had secured employment most efficiently. An Occupational Study of Relocation by the

WRA reported that 7,100 Japanese Americans were employed in clerical, sales, or "managerial work" in cities from Salt Lake City to Philadelphia.[122]

Those who had the most difficult time securing steady employment were those whose only previous experience was in agriculture, approximately 20 percent of the resettled population. Perhaps due to the transitory and temporary nature of agricultural employment, those who were released for work in agriculture frequently changed jobs. Another factor was the background of many who had previous agricultural experience. These were men and women who were perhaps more skilled in running farms, truck farming, and horticulture than migratory agricultural work, yet were not previously at the mercy of agribusiness and larger private farmers for their well-being during their former lives on the West Coast.[123]

Japanese Americans who sought work in agriculture faced the greatest potential for exploitation, underpayment, and poor living and working conditions. While industrialists tended to be more mindful of pay and work environment for Japanese Americans due to more oversight from the government and the military, agriculturalists had more opportunities for coercion and exploitation with less regulation.

Plenty of private employers took advantage of the WRA's all-out relocation policy to look for laborers to help meet shortages. In July 1945, George Kamacho, a representative from the Utah Cannery Association, arrived at Poston seeking two hundred young Japanese American women (single or married) to travel to southern California for work in canning plants making thirty-five cents an hour or twelve cents per pound canning string beans and tomatoes. Kamacho agreed to pay the transportation costs from Poston as well as charge only twenty-five cents a week for a room and an additional $1.10 a week for meals at the labor camp. The job, however, would only last from July through the end of November, leaving the young women to look for other work at that point.[124] Another farmer near Delray Beach in Florida advertised through the New Orleans WRA office for thirty incarcerees (either Issei or Nisei) who would travel to his flower and vegetable farm to pick beans for fifty cents an hour for ten to twelve hours a day, with housing included. R. E. Arne, a bamboo farmer near New Orleans, came to the Topaz prison looking to recruit "a large number" of workers to "do something" with the bamboo forest on his property.[125] "The South is a pioneer area where a person can start over again," Arne explained, and encouraged Japanese American prisoners to sign up to work the land or serve as cooks and other domestic laborers. Even Henry Ford sought prison laborers for his eighty-five-thousand-acre

Richmond Farm plantation in Georgia and sent representatives to Jerome and
Rohwer camps to recruit workers.[126] Many of these agricultural jobs were
opportunities to leave the prisons and resettle (particularly for women, who
in some cases could theoretically earn more money than before removal
and incarceration), but their locations were often rural, far from oversight and
regulation by the WRA. These jobs were also temporary as they ebbed and
flowed with the planting and harvesting seasons. And while larger landowners looked to Japanese Americans to fill labor needs, not all smaller farmers
agreed with this plan. In Great Meadows, New Jersey, five hundred "farm
folk" packed an auditorium in April 1944 to protest five Japanese American
farmers who had been invited by members of the state legislature to come
and help harvest Edward Kowalick's crops, citing this as proof of a "yellow
peril" that would soon sweep the state.[127] Additionally, while the WRA and
the federal government provided assistance with initial resettlement, many
Japanese Americans had to take matters into their own hands to find more
stable employment.

One company that recruited a large number of Japanese Americans with
the assistance of the WRA and serves as an example of the exploitative work
environment created by incarceration was Seabrook Farms of New Jersey. Located in the southern portion of the state approximately thirty-five miles
from the Delaware Bay, Seabrook Farms—owned and operated by Charles
Franklin Seabrook, who assumed operation of the business after his father's
death during World War I—capitalized on irrigation and production tech-
nology to become the "Henry Ford of Agriculture." Seabrook also constructed
a number of roads (including State Highway 77, which served as a major
transportation route to Philadelphia and points beyond) as well as housing
for a growing number of employees who came to work in planting and harvesting crops by the 1930s. Seabrook received a windfall when General Foods
purchased the Birdseye patent for frozen food in 1929 following the stock
market crash. General Foods struck an agreement with Seabrook for access
to crops, and the southern New Jersey farm quickly expanded into Pennsylvania and Delaware to become a major truck-farming corporation.[128]

But with greater demand came a greater need for labor. While the corporation had an ample number of engineers and scientists to perfect crops
and freezing mechanisms to produce one-fifth of the country's agricultural
demands (including for the government), it lacked a steady supply of manual
labor during the war. Seabrook Farms hired immigrants, children, students,
those who were unable to be drafted into the military, African American

migrant workers from the South, and Jamaican migrants from Florida, yet still struggled to keep up with demand. Until, that is, the WRA announced its all-out relocation program.[129]

Throughout 1944, Seabrook Farms heavily recruited Japanese Americans from the camps. The corporation held trial runs with approximately ninety Japanese Americans in the summer of 1944, and, by October, the business sent Japanese Americans who worked at the farm back to the prisons as labor recruiters. Three arrived at Topaz in late October looking to sign up interested prisoners for work in the corporation's dehydration and packing plant in New Jersey. The recruiters advertised the positions as paying men sixty cents and women forty cents per hour. Approximately forty interested prisoners who attended an informative meeting also learned from the recruiters that in addition to an hourly wage, they would receive "furnished apartments which included a kitchenette, living room, bathroom, and one or more bedrooms" for families, and dormitory-style accommodations for single workers. Seabrook would provide workers with meals from an on-site mess hall, in addition to schools for Japanese American children and Buddhist as well as Christian worship services in what came to resemble a company town in rural New Jersey.[130] Certainly, the living facilities sounded better than the cramped conditions of Topaz. Moreover, the corporation promised to cover transportation costs either to Philadelphia if a critical mass of interested workers signed up by October 30, or as far as Chicago if fewer than the desired number answered the recruitment call. Those who agreed to work at Seabrook received rushed processing and were released on a "trial indefinite leave" status, meaning that they could be recalled at any moment.[131] This made Seabrook's offer for transportation cost "unusual" since typically those on a trial leave covered their own travel.[132]

Seabrook's recruitment efforts paid off. By the end of the year, there were 831 Japanese Americans working at the New Jersey plant, including 178 Japanese Latin Americans who were released from the Crystal City internment camp in Texas.[133] All of the prisoners who signed up to work at Seabrook Farms hoped to engage in the same form of redemptive labor as the others who resettled.

But all was not as it seemed. Once the employees arrived at Seabrook Farms, there were strong reactions to the work, the living conditions, and the general environment of the farm. Oral histories abound of the experiences of the Japanese Americans who attempted to start their lives anew at the processing plants in New Jersey, far from their homes on the West Coast.

Shigeo Kihara remembered arriving at Seabrook farms with his mother and father after his aunt and uncle went to work at the plant and then wrote of the job opportunities available. Kihara and his family were cleared to leave Manzanar in 1944 and initially returned to their original home in Gardenia, California, in an attempt to rebuild their lives, but found no opportunities there. Their other option was to move to Oregon for farm work, but they ultimately decided to follow their family to New Jersey. Kihara described Seabrook Farms as a community "setup like a military barracks" similar to Manzanar, but made out of cinder blocks instead of lumber and with about five families to each barrack. The living conditions were exactly as they were described by the recruiters in terms of kitchenettes and rooms, and within the barracks were community centers with schools and "shoe repair shops," among other small service buildings. Kihara disliked the East Coast humidity in the summer, but there was "no comparison" in quality between Manzanar and the upgraded lodging at Seabrook Farms.[134]

All in all, Kihara described an "easy" transition to life at Seabrook Farms for his family and a "real good beginning" with "fair wages, a decent living area, and everything." "I think it was a real good beginning for a lot of people that were . . . well, you could look at it in a sense that they lost everything during the war," Kihara began. "They didn't have anything to come back to here in California or they didn't have anything to look forward to in California. And so they went to New Jersey, and they had a new beginning." Kihara remembered boarding buses for transport to the fields and the processing plants (he picked vegetables by the basket and was paid by the bushel rather than hourly because he was a teenager at the time). Apart from having sore knees from kneeling most of the day, he did not recall any particularly poor working or living conditions. Kihara viewed laboring in the fields at Seabrook as a means of fun where he got to meet other Japanese Americans his age.[135]

He and his family would eventually return to the West Coast and settle in Sacramento, but he admitted that he "didn't really look forward to coming back." Kihara's father had some mechanical engineering experience and was able to secure a better-paying job on the assembly line in New Jersey, which may explain his overall positive experience at Seabrook Farms. Or perhaps Seabrook Farms was indeed a fresh start and a promise of a new life outside the prisons. "I think all of us kids were happy over there [New Jersey]. We were adjusted, we had our friends, we had everything we needed, so we didn't know what we were coming back to over here [California]."[136]

Sumiko Yamauchi, however, had a much different experience. She and her four other family members left Manzanar in June 1944 to work at Seabrook Farms after listening to recruiters who visited the prison in the spring. The reason for leaving to work at Seabrook was simple: she and her family had few other options, and "Seabrook Farm would pay our way from Manzanar all the way to New Jersey, and they would have housing for us." The opportunity for cost-free transportation and housing was simply too good to pass up for those with few financial resources and employment options. But when Yamauchi and her family arrived at New Jersey, the reality was far below their expectations. Yamauchi described the housing as "horrible," so horrible in fact that they immediately "wanted to come back to camp." They were told that they would be living in a "bungalow," but what they found were ramshackle structures "worse than shacks." "The doors wouldn't close, we had to pick the door up and fit it in. The house was leaning, and you had to push against the wall in order to get the door in." Yamauchi described the barrack she lived in while at Manzanar as "the Hilton hotel" compared to the lodging at Seabrook Farms.[137]

How did Yamauchi's experience with living conditions differ so much from Kihara's? Yamauchi's family arrived before the Kiharas, which meant that some of the earlier arrivals were placed in substandard housing units previously used to house the German prisoners of war who also worked the land at Seabrook. Later she and her mother were able to move into better bungalows where other migrant workers lived, but initially she and her family lived where they could.

Yamauchi described the work in equally negative terms. "Because you're working six days a week, and the only time you had a day off was Sunday, and that was if you got off work at all ... you worked eleven hours a day." Workers were "dirty and tired" and "stuck in New Jersey" because Seabrook owned so much property in southern New Jersey that the nearest town with a store was forty-five minutes away. Workers were able take a bus to the store, but they had few opportunities to take advantage of the trip because of the constant work in the fields and in the processing plants. Yamauchi also described Seabrook Farms as a company town. Workers were able to eat at the cafeteria and purchase additional goods from an on-site dry goods store, and workers often "[bought] all of their dry goods there." They purchased goods on a credit system with the costs deducted from their paychecks, often leaving them with little at the end of the month. Yamauchi and her family eventually returned to the West Coast, but she and her family's opportunities to leave Seabrook were limited as her parents did not speak English well.[138]

Life at Seabrook Farms was worse still for the Japanese Latin Americans who arrived in New Jersey from Crystal City. These internees were some of the most vulnerable. Similar to Canada, Mexico, and the United States, South American nations also removed and detained Nikkei (emigrants from Japan and their descendants who settled around the world) living within their borders. The Japanese diaspora resulted in migrants living far and wide across the globe for employment and economic opportunities, including in Brazil and Peru, where they found work in mining and sugar production as well as in entrepreneurial ventures. But when war broke out and Peru joined the allied nations in the struggle against Japan and Germany, the Peruvian government interned its Japanese population. The FBI took a special interest in this population and agreed to transport and intern Japanese Peruvians at Crystal City. However, the status of these detainees was complicated.[139] They were considered "stateless" and, as one Japanese Peruvian woman discovered, also branded as "illegal" when they were released from the internment camps for work.

Elsa Kudo, a Japanese Peruvian who found herself in Crystal City with her family, was desperate to leave the internment camp and accepted an offer of employment from Seabrook Farms in 1944. By that point, the FBI was eager to close the internment camps and practically forced the internees to accept any offer of employment that came their way. These internees had few options, so Seabrook offered to serve as a sponsor for a number of the families who would be willing to work and take the place of the recently vacated German POWs. Seabrook promised the standard package of housing, food, and good pay, but, when Kudo arrived, she and her family were as disappointed as Sumiko Yamauchi was and found housing with "no sink, no running water . . . a communal bath," and mud everywhere.[140]

The most shocking development for the Kudo family, however, was their new status as "illegals" once they arrived at Seabrook Farms. Even though the US government had brought Japanese Peruvians to the United States against their will, they were deemed stateless and therefore "illegal aliens," with neither an option to return back to their homeland nor any path to legal status in the United States. Kudo explained that this new status caused "untold misery," as she and her family and the other Japanese Peruvians who arrived were forced by Seabrook to pay extra "taxes" to the company because of their supposed illegal entry. Seabrook deducted 33 percent from the paychecks of the Japanese Peruvians, "so by the time they got their paycheck there was hardly anything left. And because there was so little left, they couldn't go to town to buy groceries, 'cause then you had to pay the bus which was like twenty or ten cents or whatever." This forced the workers to go to the company store, which afforded no opportunities to save money to leave Seabrook Farms. Kudo described her experience at Seabrook as "just poverty on poverty" with low wages, but she reflected, "I think you cannot help if you don't have any, you'll take anything." Kudo and her family were exploited by Seabrook Farms and had few options if they wanted to leave the internment detention center.[141]

Others who reflected on their time at Seabrook Farms described little in the way of exploitation and also revealed that the farm offered an opportunity when they often had few other options for leaving the prisons. Grace Seto and her family initially left Manzanar to work on a farm in Berlin, Maryland. Grace's father "had no experience as a farmer, but he was willing to do anything to get started again." She recalled that her father said, "There is no way to start life anew again, we just can't," as they did not have the financial means to go back to California. Strapped for cash and looking for jobs that would allow them to stay together, Grace and her family found themselves in Berlin, but only for nine months as "things did not work out as he had anticipated" on the basis of what he was told by recruiters while they were still held in Manzanar. From Berlin, Grace and her family traveled to Seabrook Farms to work in "the huge, huge frozen food processing plant there." Her father, who was employed in good-paying clerical work before incarceration, was not able to use his "office skills" at Seabrook Farms and was employed instead in "working in the company garage, mainly taking care of inventory and transportation and such." But still, she and her family found their way to Seabrook Farms because there was nothing for them to return to after being incarcerated.[142]

Agricultural work like that found at Seabrook Farms resembled in many ways the earlier experiences of Japanese Americans when they left the prisons in 1942 for beet labor. The decision to work was free and voluntary in the sense that there were contracts, and no individual prisoner was forced to enter into a labor agreement with any farmer or corporation. However, the living and working conditions as well as recruitment methods challenged the free nature of the agreements. The fact that so many Japanese Americans who worked at Seabrook Farms did so under a "trial leave clearance" in order to receive free transportation also spoke to coercion. The desperation to get out of the prisons in many cases meant that redemptive labor and post-prison work resembled a parolee system rather than a truly free labor agreement.

By late 1945, a majority of the imprisoned Japanese Americans had resettled in cities, regions, and communities across the United States following the end of the war (though camps were still operating as not all of the prisoners had been cleared for leave by the WRA or were able to leave for employment opportunities). Whether with the assistance of the WRA and social service agencies or through tapping into social networks of friends, families, and burgeoning Japanese American communities in Cleveland, Indianapolis, Detroit, and New York, Japanese Americans left the prisons, and the prisons, in turn, were permanently closed one by one. All-out relocation—encouraging (or coercing) Japanese Americans to leave and find employment on the outside—had proven a success.

The end of the war following the surrender of Germany and the bombing of Hiroshima and Nagasaki in August 1945 as well as the lifting of the exclusion orders in late 1944 resulted in Roosevelt's administration no longer seeing the prisons as necessary. Not only were the camps demoralizing, they were also a drain on valuable government resources. In December 1944, Myer identified the "lifting of the blanket exclusion orders by the Western Defense Command . . . [as] undoubtedly the most significant event since evacuation both in the lives of the evacuated people and in the program of the War Relocation Authority," signaling that Japanese Americans had received "full restoration of the freedom of movement which is enjoyed by all other loyal citizens and law-abiding aliens in the United States."[143] It was also, as Myer explained, the "beginning of the end" for the agency. Turning to the "prime objective" of the WRA, which "as always, is to restore the people residing in relocation centers to private life in normal communities," Myer praised all-out relocation and the closing of the prisons because "the evacuees as a group have more friends and supporters throughout the Nation than at any previous time." Moreover, public assistance through the WRA and agreements with state and local agencies were available to help prisoners transition into a welcoming nation with "good demand for workers in war plants, in civilian goods production, in service occupations, and on the farms." "Both from the standpoint of the national welfare and the evacuees' long-range economic security, it is highly important that the people now residing at the relocation centers make the transition back to private life at a time when employment opportunities are still plentiful," Myer stressed.[144]

Privately, in a separate memo, Myer explained the ideological and financial reasons for closing the prisons. "The WRA had realized for many months that it was most important that the relocation job be completed, if possible, while the war was still in progress, because jobs and housing would be much easier to secure." But "total liquidation" also became a necessity because "center living was bad" for a number of moral, physical, and social reasons; "the very fact that they were set apart tended to heighten the impression that their loyalty was in question," and the dispersal of Japanese Americans was necessary for their speedy acceptance into normal American life. From a practical standpoint, "Congress would undoubtedly question the necessity of appropriating funds to continue centers (and such questions were raised in connection with our last budget." Number two on the list was the fact that "the country, still at war, needed the skills and the manpower represented by the center population."[145] While their skills and labor were once needed at the prisons for self-sufficiency, Japanese Americans were now more useful on the outside.

However, there was pushback from many prisoners on being released, which surprised Myer. "In spite of our announcement of what seemed to us perfectly logical reasons for liquidation," he explained, "strong opposition continued to develop from evacuees and their friends and enemies outside of the center." Apart from the expected anti-Japanese sentiment along the West Coast and in other communities and regions, Myer also detailed some observations of why some prisoners were hesitant to leave, once he and social scientists investigated the matter. The reasons should not have shocked the director. On February 16, 1945, Myer attended a conference in Salt Lake City with thirty Japanese American representatives from seven of the prisons, out of which came a "statement of facts" which Myer relayed to other administrators in the WRA. "Mental suffering" from forced removal and incarceration was at the top of the list, indicating the long and potentially permanent impact of incarceration on Japanese Americans, followed by "an almost complete destruction of financial foundations built during over a half century" by the imprisoned Japanese Americans. Many of those who remained in the prisons were the elderly and Issei who feared resettlement because of reports of prejudice, violence, and discrimination as well as uncertainty over their precarious economic conditions. They "were forced to dispose of their personal and real properties, business and agricultural equipment at a mere trifle of their cost" and "drew leases for the 'duration' of the war," hence if they left before the war was officially over, they would have "nothing to return to."[146]

Nonetheless, by the winter of 1945, all but the Tule Lake prison (which remained open for the Department of Justice to address issues of repatriation and legal status for the "subversive" groups) were closed, and Issei, Nisei, and Kibei, young and old, resettled and attempted to build new lives, create an identity which would ensure economic survival, at times collaborate with other racial and ethnic minority groups to address issues of housing and discrimination, and return to the West Coast—which, by 1947, once again became the region with the largest Japanese American population.

In December 1945, the *McGehee Times*, the local paper of McGehee, Arkansas, reported on the last days of nearby Rohwer prison. The remaining 345 Japanese Americans "said good bye to life in Rohwer" as they boarded the last train to leave for the West Coast. Many of this group were older men who "displayed almost no emotion" as they left, perhaps indicating the uncertainty and hesitation about what, if anything, they were returning to. The reporter "toured the ghost center" and noted that "the once-teeming camp seemed deadly quiet with only small groups of impassive Japanese and baggage waiting for the cars to transport them to the train." "The war-born city is dead." The paper also noted a request left by the Japanese Americans once held there, "an earnest, simple plea engraved on a handsome concrete monument standing guard over a plot hallowed by Japanese Americans who once lived there: May the people of Arkansas keep in beauty and reverence forever this ground where our bodies sleep."[147]

The following year, the *McGehee Times* honored the last requests and remembered not so much the imprisoned but the beneficial economic changes that occurred in the area as a result of the labor of the Japanese Americans. Although Japanese Americans had since departed, "signs of the Japanese 'Green Thumb' were left in the center." "Strawberry patches, fall gardens, chrysanthemums and shrubbery were abundant around the tar-paper covered buildings"; and "in good condition and representing the greatest investment in the center's outlay are the water, electrical, and sewer systems." Later in January 1946, the newspaper again reported on the impact of Japanese Americans on developing new forms of agriculture beyond cotton in Desha County, Arkansas. "Sometimes progress goes on right under our noses and we aren't aware of it," the paper noted. "We are presently thinking about the success of the Japanese-American evacuees, late of Rohwer relocation center, in truck farming." The "cotton-conscious county" desperately needed diversification in crops following the Civil War and the depreciation of cotton's value as a result of the Great Depression and rising competition from synthetic fibers. Japanese Americans imprisoned in Arkansas "found the Delta soil extremely productive, especially for cucumbers and eggplants," but they also "discovered that the local land would respond well to almost any vegetable." Farmers in the Delta experimented with truck-farming, particularly vegetables and strawberries, with success. "Inspiration for a great future in truck farming for the county has been given by the Japanese-Americans," and "county farmers could take the hint."[148]

There were other indications that as all-out relocation hit its stride and the prisons closed, land developed by Japanese Americans would be available for use by other farmers and settlers. The *Topaz Times* reported in February that "approximately 13,300 acres of irrigated land within Central Utah Relocation project will be leased to farmers of this region this spring, Roscoe E. Bell, acting project Director, announced today." Invitations to bid on this land were sent via mail to communities nearby so that "prospective bidders may study descriptions of tracts offered," with bids being accepted for ten days following their announcement. Twenty-four tracts of land were up for grabs ranging from 30 to 1,800 acres and including "old alfalfa, new seeding of alfalfa, wheat and barley planted last fall, acreage nearby ready to plant, stubble fields, sweet clover, pasture seeded last spring, irrigated pasture, non-irrigated pasture, and range land." Work done in the name of self-sufficiency among the Japanese Americans held in the Topaz prison was now available for others to purchase.[149]

And what of Poston, the "colony" which was to benefit from Japanese American labor and improve living conditions for the Native Americans who shared the reservation space? On August 1, 1945, Duncan Willis, then director of Poston who took over after Wade Head moved on and the WRA was transferred to the Department of the Interior, announced that "the Office of Indian Affairs has been perfecting plans to colonize Parker Valley with Indians from various tribes from the Colorado River watershed," and "definite plans had been made to bring sixteen Hopi families into the Center on or about September 1 and to provide them with housing" in Unit II of the prison. The DOI selected September 1 for the move-in date as it would allow the new arrivals enough time to "start work on their fall planting." The OIA selected Unit II because it was in the best shape and needed the fewest repairs and was also located "on the edge of the Unit and the Indian families who are to live there will have easy access to farms."[150]

With Japanese Americans resettled and employed outside the prisons, the WRA unofficially declared that redemption through labor, which was a staple of incarceration and resettlement, was a success. WRA administrators applauded themselves for relocating Japanese Americans to communities (including those on the West Coast) where their labor was needed and their presence welcome or at least tolerated. The WRA-created labor force of Japanese Americans contributed to the war effort and proved their loyalty, while offering irrigated land complete with crops and structures for veterans, the general public, and Native Americans. The labor performed by imprisoned Japanese Americans was recognized and admired by those who benefited from their exploitation. The idea that this group of individuals, so wronged by their nation, could freely and willingly labor for their country during a time of war factored into a new identity for Japanese Americans, one which rested on their economic success and ability to recover from the trauma of incarceration. More importantly, their willingness to perform labor on their own accord was taken as proof of their loyalty and successful "assimilation." The Japanese American prisoners went into the camps as potentially "subversive enemy aliens" but emerged, through their work, as patriotic Americans. The WRA touted these accomplishments, which contributed to a "model minority" identity that media and politicians would bestow on Japanese Americans in the coming decades. In the process, the WRA obscured the challenges Japanese Americans faced as parolees and the limits of redemptive labor.

In celebrating the work of imprisoned Japanese Americans and their ability to redeem themselves through labor, the prison element of their experience faded. Many Japanese Americans, looking to refashion their lives and regroup after the tragedy of forced removal and incarceration, preferred not to speak of their painful experiences, including wretched living and working conditions and disillusionment while imprisoned. The labor was recognized, but the coercion of prison work was slowly erased.

CONCLUSION

By 1993, 82,219 Japanese American survivors of wartime incarceration each received $20,000 from the same government that had imprisoned them fifty-one years earlier. Under the Civil Liberties Act of 1988, Congress "recognized that a grave injustice was done to both citizens and permanent resident aliens of Japanese ancestry" during World War II and issued a formal apology along with approval for monetary redress. The act established both the Office of Redress Administration to distribute payments and the Civil Liberties Public Education Fund to prevent such a miscarriage of justice from reoccurring.[1]

Congress calculated the redress amount based on "intangible" aspects of suffering including pain and mental anguish as well as more concrete and easily quantifiable losses relating to property. After the Commission on Wartime Relocation and Internment of Civilians issued its findings, both those who opposed and those who supported redress testified before the House Judiciary Subcommittee in April 1986. Some, like Republican senator S. I. Hayakawa, were disgusted by Japanese American requests for monetary payments, suggesting that this smacked of opportunism. Others argued that monetary compensation for losses was the only remedy for an act committed by the government against its citizens and loyal Americans. Grace Yoshihara, then executive director of the Japanese American Citizens League (JACL), which voted at a national meeting to seek monetary redress, argued that the amount proposed should "not be trivial because the injury was not trivial."[2] Minori Yusui, director of the Education and Legislative Board of the JACL, proclaimed that individuals should be compensated with specific amounts because the losses were individual.[3]

Perhaps Yoshihara and Yusui had someone like Akiyo Deloyd in mind when speaking of individual losses. Deloyd was only nineteen when she was imprisoned with her family at Poston. Her beloved mother died in the prison camp at age fifty-two due to complications from diabetes. Deloyd believed that her mother's condition was exacerbated by the starchy and monotonous diet of macaroni and potatoes served at the camp, an unpalatable replacement of the fresh fruits and vegetables grown on her family farm. Losses like these could not be quantified, but an amount that was respectable was required in order for the government to acknowledge the pain of incarceration.[4]

The Civil Liberties Act would also address losses that were economic in nature yet difficult to quantify, namely losses in education and "job training." As a result of imprisonment, Japanese Americans were removed from colleges, universities, and other vocational training programs and lost valuable time in building up their careers and savings. While the WRA and other officials repeatedly argued during the war that Japanese Americans gained valuable work experience in the prisons, readying them to take their places in American society once released, Congress argued differently fifty years later. Not all Japanese Americans gained experience or training in the prison camps; their confinement and forced labor prevented them from reaching their full earning potential. Incarceration harmed Japanese Americans financially.

But what of those who testified before the commission like Akiyo Deloyd, who lost her mother, but also suffered under coerced labor? Deloyd recounted that while she was at Poston, she worked eight hours a day, seven days a week for sixteen dollars a month as a waitress in a dining hall because she was told that "one member of the family had to work in the kitchen in order for the family to eat."[5] This was not an official WRA policy, but someone at some point informed Deloyd that this was the case and, more importantly, no supervisor in charge of the dining hall corrected her. Or perhaps Deloyd was too frightened to ask about this purported policy or question this idea. There was an expectation in Poston that if one wanted to eat, they worked. Japanese Americans like Deloyd performed their tasks with little or no choice and for well less than prevailing wages.

The commission did not directly address wages as a tangible and quantifiable loss, but long before the Civil Liberties Act, the public, government officials, and even the WRA administrators supported the idea of compensating Japanese Americans for their wartime losses. As early as 1942, members of Congress argued while apportioning the budget to pay for Japanese American incarceration that monetary losses on account of forced removal should be accounted for sooner rather than later. The call for recompense from civil and human rights organizations grew throughout the war years, and even WRA director Dillon Myer quietly supported the idea of reparations. In the middle of a program of injustice masked as a military necessity, there was no shortage of those who believed Japanese Americans suffered great economic losses under Executive Order 9066.[6]

When Oscar Chapman assumed the position of temporary secretary of the Department of the Interior after Harold Ickes resigned and the prison camps were closing toward the end of the war, Chapman worked with attorneys and WRA administrators in 1946 to develop a plan for redress. The proposed bill called for the establishment of an Evacuations Claims Commission devoted to identifying and investigating Japanese American losses during removal and detainment. Despite President Harry Truman's urging members of Congress to support the work of the commission, the bill died in Congress after Democratic legislators from the West Coast grew concerned that their support would undermine their chances for midterm reelection.

The lack of support for the bill overshadowed its relative ineffectiveness and the limitations it placed on redress. Concrete and tangible property losses were covered, but claims that were "largely speculative and less definitely appraisable such as those for wages or profits that might have been accrued had not evacuation occurred, for deterioration of skills and earning capacity, and for physical hardships of mental suffering" were not eligible. The Department of the Interior agreed with these limitations and argued that losses like wages could not be measured. Calculations were possible with available data, but Congress, the DOI, and the WRA deemed such an undertaking far too complex and, after all, attempting to quantify exploitation was a daunting task.[7]

Nevertheless, after the 1946 elections, President Truman's focus on issues of civil rights prompted renewed interest in claims for Japanese Americans. Truman identified Japanese American incarceration as "the most striking mass interference with justice since slavery" and set about to address the wrongdoings of the program. He worked with the JACL and with Dillon Myer (who went on to have a controversial career with the Bureau of Indian Affairs and admitted to feeling ashamed of Japanese American incarceration) and sympathetic members of Congress throughout 1947 to create a new commission and craft a new claims bill. Disagreements between JACL president Mike Masaoka and Truman's civil rights advisors over what form redress should take created deep divisions within the Japanese American community. Masaoka, already a problematic figure as many Japanese Americans regarded him as a sellout for going along with incarceration so willingly, supported a lump sum payment of $1,000 to each survivor, but Myer and Attorney General Tom Clark balked at the high amount as well as the implication that this would be seen as an indemnity payment on behalf of the government. Masaoka eventually backed down from pushing for the lump sum payment (to the dismay of many JACL members), but also raised the possibility of the government paying lost wages. Once again, however, the idea of recovering lost wages went nowhere.[8] After all, the Supreme Court upheld incarceration as a legal government program and there was little congressional appetite for expensive new outlays given the context of the postwar budget cuts.

After testimony from witnesses on the necessity of redress, including that of Myer and John J. McCloy, in 1948 Congress passed (with backing from more Republicans than Democrats) and Truman signed the Japanese American Evacuation Claims Act. Congress allotted $25 million for Japanese Americans who filed claims for property losses as a result of forced removal (not imprisonment). Only property lost because of the hastiness of removal would be covered; property that was damaged or stolen during the period of incarceration was not eligible for the program. Government restitution also required no admittance or acknowledgement of wrongdoing under Executive Order 9066. Japanese Americans were required to swear that seeking claims at this point would be their final attempt to collect money from the government for wartime losses. Claimants could not file for lost wages, profits, pain, or suffering—only lost property. Extensive collections of receipts and paperwork documenting losses were required for every claim. Claims greater than $2,500 required a lawsuit against the federal government and the Department of Justice, which repeatedly contested and denied many of those claims. Of the 23,689 claims, almost 40 percent were greater than $2,500 and therefore went before the Department of Justice, where only 137 of those 8,969 claims were rewarded. Amendments to the bill over the next fifteen years arranged compromise settlements of claimants and later extended the coverage of the program to interned enemy aliens as well. But the Evacuations Claims Act, with its limits and denials, barely awarded recompense to many survivors. It would take the Civil Liberties Act of 1988 to extend redress to more survivors.[9]

The issue of lost wages remains unaddressed. Between 1942 and 1945 most imprisoned Japanese Americans worked for low pay. Even after their release for agricultural or manufacturing work, they were unable to maintain their previous standard of living because of the disruptions of incarceration (as in the case of Mitsuye Endo). Addressing the lost wages of Japanese Americans would require the government and the public to come to terms with the fact that Japanese Americans were exploited and forced to work while also suffering from the indignities of imprisonment.

Before the House Judiciary Subcommittee in 1986, Republican representative from California Daniel Lungren stated his opposition to reparations, lamenting that if the government agreed to issue payments to survivors of Japanese American incarceration, then there would be "untold consequences" in the future. "Should the Chinese be paid back for their unpaid role in helping to build railroads that opened the American West?" he asked. "What about compensation for the rights of German Americans violated during WWI, the enslaved, and Native Americans whose land was seized by the federal government?" It is telling that Lungren began with the issue of exploited Chinese railroad workers, demonstrating (likely unintentionally) the direct connections between Japanese American forced or coerced labor in the prisons and the labor practices used to extract work from other Asian American groups.[10]

Calculating lost wages for those who were forced to labor while imprisoned would be a large undertaking this far removed from Executive Order 9066, particularly considering that, with every passing year, fewer survivors remain. Twenty thousand dollars in 1993 was equivalent to $2,256 in 1942 and $2,491 in 1945 (by the end of the war and closing of the camps).[11] Both amounts were roughly equivalent to an average yearly salary for someone employed in manufacturing during the war. But Japanese Americans were held in prisons for years in many cases, and the focus on property losses in calculating the amount of reparations did not account for the fact that $20,000 was equivalent to one yearly salary during the war.

It would be difficult but not impossible to donate extra funding for the creation of reminders of the prison labor performed by incarcerated Japanese Americans. Markers noting roads and infrastructure projects completed by Japanese Americans would bring this history to the surface. Additionally, funding from the National Endowment for the Humanities for histories of employers who profited from this labor and GIS mapping to expose the proximity of camps to regions that grew as a result of incarceration would visualize and memorialize this aspect of World War II history.

The forced labor of Japanese Americans—the wages of war—are central to American history and the often invisible networks of prison labor that continue to benefit the public as well as private corporations. Prison labor programs today are often seen as rehabilitative, and prisoner laborers do learn skills that might open opportunities for them if and when they are released. But who benefits from exploitation? As news reports have shown of the prisoners in California who fought the wildfires that swept the state in 2018, another question is who suffers under the often unstable and dangerous working conditions?[12] Comparing the experiences of the incarcerated, be it in the twenty-first century or World War II, is challenging, but Japanese Americans shared the same historical space as the unnamed and exploited who labored for the state and private employers in myriad ways.

NOTES

Introduction

1. "Camouflage—Observations by G.Y.," March 23, 1943, folder 52, box 9, Japanese American Relocation Center Records, 1935–1953 (hereafter referred to as JARC), Collection Number 3830, Division of Rare and Manuscript Collections, Cornell University Library, Ithaca, New York, 4.

2. "Camouflage—Observations by G.Y.," 4.

3. The Japanese American National Museum held a special exhibit between 2016 and 2017 titled "Uprooted: Japanese American Farm Labor Campus During World War II," but photos can still be accessed at http://www.janm.org/exhibits/uprooted/. The online Densho Encyclopedia also features many photos and first-person accounts of laboring under incarceration and is available at https://encyclopedia.densho.org/.

4. "Images of Internment: The Incarceration of Japanese Americans During World War II," (2017), https://fdrlibrary.org/images-of-internment.

5. "'Parole' Plan Mapped for Interned Japanese," *Los Angeles Examiner*, August 1, 1942, 3.

6. See John Howard's *Concentration Camps on the American Home Front* (Chicago: University of Chicago Press, 2008), 174–98; Connie Y. Chiang, *Nature Behind Barbed Wire: An Environmental History of the Japanese American Incarceration* (New York: Oxford University Press, 2018); Louis Fiset, *Camp Harmony: Japanese American Internment and the Puyallup Assembly Center* (Urbana: University of Illinois Press, 2009); and Priscilla Wegars, *Imprisoned in Paradise: Japanese Internee Road Workers at the World War II Kooskia Internment Camp* (Caldwell, ID: Caxton Press, 2010), for more on labor and Japanese American incarceration in the different camps.

7. See National JACL Power of Words II Committee, "Power of Words Handbook: A Guide to Language About Japanese Americans in World War II; Understanding Euphemisms and Preferred Terminology," April 27, 2013, https://jacl.org/wordpress/wp-content/uploads/2015/08/Power-of-Words-Rev.-Term.-Handbook.pdf. See also Takeya Mizuno, "The Creation of the 'Free' Press in Japanese-American Camps: The War Relocation Authority's Planning and Making of the Camp Newspaper Policy," *Journal of Mass Communication Quarterly* 78, no. 3 (2001): 515; and Raymond Y. Okamura, "The American Concentration Camps: A Cover-Up Through Euphemistic Terminology," *Journal of Ethnic Studies* 10, no. 3 (1982): 95–109, for more on the decision to use more explicit terms. I deliberately do not use the terminology "concentration camp" to avoid inappropriate comparisons with acts of genocide or ethnic cleansing,

as relating to the historical experiences of Native Americans, various nineteenth-century European colonial subjects, or the Holocaust.

8. Edward H. Spicer, Asael T. Hansen, Katherine Luomala, and Marvin K. Opler, *Impounded People: Japanese Americans in the Relocation Centers* (Tucson: University of Arizona Press, 1969).

9. See Roger Lotchin, *Japanese American Relocation in World War II: A Reconsideration* (New York: Cambridge University Press, 2018).

10. Commission on Wartime Relocation and Internment of Citizens, Hearing Before the Subcommittee on Administrative Law and Governmental Relations of the Committee on the Judiciary House of Representatives, Ninety-sixth Congress, Second Session on H.R. 5499, June 2, 1980, 123.

11. Mitchell T. Maki, Harry H. L. Kitano, and S. Megan Berthold, *Achieving the Impossible Dream: How Japanese Americans Obtained Redress* (Urbana: University of Illinois Press, 1999), 191–95.

12. Commission on Wartime Relocation and Internment of Civilians, *Personal Justice Denied: Report of the Commission on Wartime Relocation and Internment of Civilians* (Seattle: University of Washington Press, and Washington, DC: Civil Liberties Public Education Fund, 1997), 459.

13. Commission on Wartime Relocation and Internment of Civilians, *Personal Justice Denied*, 459. On February 23, 1942, a Japanese submarine fired on the Ellwood oil field off the coast of Santa Barbara, doing minimal damage but feeding into fears of a potential second Japanese attack. Despite the navy's investigation into Japanese threats and its findings against an event in the Munson Report, the calls for removal and incarceration increased among West Coast politicians as well as members of the army. See Nigel Hamilton, *The Mantle of Command: FDR at War, 1941–1942* (New York: Houghton Mifflin Harcourt, 2014), 216.

14. James H. Rowe to Grace Tully, February 2, 1942, folder—Assistant to the Attorney General files, Alien Enemy Control Unit, box 33, James H. Rowe, Jr. Papers, Franklin D. Roosevelt Presidential Library (hereafter referred to as FDR Library), Hyde Park, New York.

15. See Roger Daniels, *Prisoners Without Trial: Japanese Americans in World War II* (New York: Hill and Wang, 2004); Valerie J. Matsumoto, *Farming the Home Place: A Japanese American Community in California, 1919–1982* (Ithaca, NY: Cornell University Press, 1993); and Alice Yang Murray, "The History of 'Military Necessity' and the Justification for Internment," in *The Japanese American Internment: Historical Memories of the Japanese American Internment and the Struggle for Redress*, ed. Alice Yang Murray (Stanford, CA: Stanford University Press, 2008), 15–51.

16. Brian M. Hayashi, *Democratizing the Enemy: The Japanese American Internment* (Princeton, NJ: Princeton University Press, 2004), 5–6. See also Greg Robinson, *A Tragedy of Democracy: Japanese Confinement in North America* (New York: Columbia University Press, 2009); and Jerry Garcia, *Looking Like the Enemy: Japanese Mexicans, the Mexican State, and U.S. Hegemony, 1897–1945* (Tucson: University of Arizona Press, 2014).

17. A. Naomi Paik, *Rightlessness: Testimony and Redress in U.S. Prison Camps Since World War II* (Urbana: University of Illinois Press, 2016), 22.

18. For more on whether or not the camps were "concentration" camps or relocation centers, see Roger Lotchin, *Japanese American Relocation in World War II: A Reconsideration* (Cambridge: Cambridge University Press, 2018), 154–55, 236–38. Lotchin is not the colleague mentioned here, but *A Reconsideration*'s arguments are similar.

19. See L. L. Martin and M. L. Mitchelson, "Geographies of Detention and Imprisonment: Interrogating Spatial Practices of Confinement, Discipline, Law, and State Power," *Geography Compass* 3, no. 1 (2009): 459–77; Oliver Razac, *Barbed Wire: A Political History*, trans. Jonathan Kneight (New York: New Press, 2003); Michel Foucault, *Discipline and Punish: The Birth of the Prison* (New York: Vintage Books, 1979); Marie Gottschalk, "Hiding in Plain Sight: American Politics and the Carceral State," *Annual Review of Political Science* 11 (June 2008): 235–60.

20. See Eric Walz, *Nikkei in the Interior West: Japanese Immigration and Community Building, 1882–1945* (Tucson: University of Arizona Press, 2012), 173–75.

21. Dillon S. Myer, *Uprooted Americans: The Japanese Americans and the War Relocation Authority During World War II* (Tucson: University of Arizona Press, 1971), 26.

22. See Roger Daniels, Sandra C. Taylor, and Harry H. L. Kitano, eds., *Japanese Americans: From Relocation to Redress* (Salt Lake City: University of Utah Press, 1986), for more on property and economic losses in California.

23. See Amy Rutenberg, *Rough Draft: Cold War Military Manpower and the Origins of the Vietnam-Era Draft Resistance* (Ithaca, NY: Cornell University Press, 2019), 27–28.

24. Matthew L. Basso, *Meet Joe Copper: Masculinity and Race on Montana's World War II Home Front* (Chicago: University of Chicago Press, 2013). See also Alan S. Milward, *War, Economy, and Society, 1939–1945* (Berkeley: University of California Press, 1980); Arthur Herman, *Freedom's Forge: How American Business Produced Victory in World War II* (New York: Random House, 2013); and Harold G. Vatter, *The U.S. Economy in World War II* (New York: Columbia University Press, 1985). For more on war work, see Andrew E. Kersten, *Labor's Home Front: The American Federation of Labor During World War II* (New York: New York University Press, 2006); Stephanie A. Carpenter, *On the Farm Front: The Women's Land Army in World War II* (DeKalb: Northern Illinois University Press, 2003); and Emily Yellin, *Our Mothers' War: American Women at Home and at the Front During World War II* (New York: Free Press, 2004).

25. For a concise overview of the history of prison labor in the United States, see Leroy D. Clark and Gwendolyn M. Parker, "The Labor Law Problems of the Prisoner," *Rutgers Law Review* 28 (1975): 841–45. Beyond this article, the scholarship is vast. For more general information on the history of prisons in the United States, see Caleb Smith, *The Prison and the American Imagination* (New Haven, CT: Yale University Press, 2011); Scott Christianson, *With Liberty for Some: 500 Years of Imprisonment in America* (Boston: Northeastern Press, 1998); and Asatar P. Bair, "An Economic Analysis of Prison Labor in the United States" (PhD diss., University of Massachusetts, Amherst, 2004).

26. Clark and Parker, "Labor Law Problems," 842.

27. See Mary Ellen Curtin, *Black Prisoners and Their World, Alabama, 1865–1900* (Charlottesville: University of Virginia Press, 2000); Daniel Pete, *The Shadow of Slavery: Peonage in the South* (Urbana: University of Illinois Press, 1990); Ruth Gilmore, *Golden Gulag: Prisons, Surplus, Crisis, and Opposition in Globalizing California* (Berkeley: University of California

Press, 2007); Alex Lichtenstein, *Twice the Work of Free Labor: The Political Economy of Convict Labor in the New South* (New York: Verso, 1996); Matthew Mancini, *One Dies, Get Another: Convict Leasing in the American South* (Chapel Hill: University of North Carolina Press, 1996); Martha Myers, *Race, Labor, and Punishment in the New South* (Columbus: Ohio State University Press, 1998); David Oshinsky, *Worse Than Slavery: Parchman Farm and the Ordeal of Jim Crow Justice* (New York: Free Press, 1997); Douglas A. Blackmon, *Slavery by Another Name: The Re-enslavement of Black Americans from the Civil War to World War II* (New York: Anchor, 2009); Talitha L. LeFlouria, *Chained in Silence: Black Women and Convict Labor in the New South* (Chapel Hill: University of North Carolina Press, 2016); Clarence Jefferson Hall Jr., "Prisonland: Environment, Society, and Mass Incarceration on New York's Northern Frontier, 1845–1999" (PhD diss., State University of New York, Stony Brook, 2014); Volker Janssen, "When the 'Jungle' Met the Forest: Public Work, Civil Defense, and Prison Camps in Postwar California," *Journal of American History* 96, no. 3 (2009): 702–26; and Rebecca M. McLennan, *Crisis of Imprisonment: Protest, Politics, and the Making of the American Penal State, 1776–1941* (New York: Cambridge University Press, 2008).

28. Kelly Hernandez, *City of Inmates: Conquest, Rebellion, and the Rise of Human Caging in Los Angeles, 1771–1965* (Chapel Hill: University of North Carolina Press, 2017), 2–4.

29. Jean Allain, *Slavery in International Law: Of Human Exploitation and Trafficking* (Leiden, Netherlands: Brill, 2012), 234.

30. Beginning in March 1943, POWs from Germany and Italy began to arrive in larger numbers to the United States and were placed under the care of the War Department. Soon after, Washington decided to turn to the use of POWs primarily in the southern and southwestern portions of the United States for both private and military base work (in accordance with the Geneva Convention of 1929). Work was not mandatory, and those who chose to labor were paid according to their rank in the military. Japanese POWs also arrived in the United States beginning in May 1943 and presented a particular problem to the US government as there were fears that any perceived poor treatment of Japanese in the United States would result in poor treatment of the American POWs in Japan. For this reason, Japanese POWs often chose not to work with few repercussions, but when they did work, they performed many of the same public/private forms of labor as the Japanese American incarcerees. For more discussions on POWs and labor in the United States during World War II, see Arnold Krammer, "Japanese Prisoners of War in America," *Pacific Historical Review* 52, no. 1 (1983): 67–91.

31. Chiang, *Nature Behind Barbed Wire*, 69, 97.

32. See Gerald Shenk, *Work or Fight! Race, Gender, and the Draft in World War I* (London: Palgrave Macmillan, 2008), for more on the "Work or Fight" act. This program was also frequently used to compel African Americans (particularly African American women) to labor for low wages and exploitation.

33. Qtd. in Chiang, *Nature Behind Barbed Wire*, 91. See Russell A. Bankson, "Labor Trouble in Topaz," November 5, 1945, Project Reports Division, Historical Section, Central Utah Project, FBD-WRA, Reel 7 (Chiang, *Nature Behind Barbed Wire*, 245 n. 6).

34. Siobhan McGrath and Kendra Strauss, "Unfreedom and Workers' Power," in *Handbook of International Political Economy of Production*, ed. Kees van der Pijl (London: Edward Elgar, 2015), 392; Robert J. Steinfeld and Stanley L. Engerman, "Labor—Free or Coerced? An

Historical Reassessment of Differences and Similarities," in *Free and Unfree Labor: The Debate Continues*, ed. Tom Brass and Marcel van der Linden (New York: Peter Lang, 1997), 108–10. Citing theorists and scholars of slavery and human trafficking by no means implies that I am making direct comparisons between the prison labor performed by Japanese Americans and victims of human trafficking, chattel slavery, or labor used during the Holocaust; the broad discussions and concepts serve as a structure for analyzing the unique qualities of Japanese American prison labor during World War II.

35. Magaly Rodriguez Garcia, "On the Legal Boundaries of Coerced Labor," in *On Coerced Labor: Work and Compulsion After Chattel Slavery*, ed. Garcia and Marcel van der Linden (Leiden: Brill, 2016), 13–14, 26–27.

36. See Gunther Peck, *Reinventing Free Labor: Padrones and Immigrant Workers in the North American West, 1885–1930* (Cambridge: Cambridge University Press, 2000).

37. Qtd. in Garcia, "On the Legal Boundaries," 19–20.

38. Sources on the Thirteenth Amendment are vast, but see the following for more on the specific relationship with free and unfree labor: Alexander Tsesis, ed., *The Promises of Liberty: The History and Contemporary Relevance of the Thirteenth Amendment* (New York: Columbia University Press, 2010); L. S. VanderVelde, "Labor Vision of the Thirteenth Amendment," *University of Pennsylvania Law Review* 138 (1989): 437–504; and Michelle Alexander, *The New Jim Crow: Mass Incarceration in the Age of Colorblindness* (New York: New Press, 2012).

39. "Forced" and "coerced" labor are generally used interchangeably here and elsewhere. See Free the Slaves, "Hidden Slaves: Forced Labor in the United States" (September 2004), https://www.law.berkeley.edu/files/hiddenslaves_report.pdf.

40. Erin Hatton, "'Either You Do It or You're Going to the Box': Coerced Labor in Contemporary America," *Critical Sociology* 28 (2018): 3–4.

41. See Aimee Chin, "Long-Run Labor Market Effects of Japanese American Internment During World War II on Working-Age Male Incarcerees" (MA thesis, University of Houston, 2004); Jaime Arellano-Bover, "Displacement, Diversity, and Mobility: Career Impacts of Japanese American Internment," IZA Discussion Papers, Institute of Labor Economics, November 19, 2018; and Molly Malloy Cooper, "Japanese American Wages, 1940–1990" (PhD diss., Ohio State University, 2003), for a quantitative approach to this topic.

42. Christian Heimburger, "Life Beyond Barbed Wire: The Significance of Japanese American Labor in the Mountain West, 1942–1944" (PhD diss., University of Colorado, Boulder, 2012).

43. See Mary Dudziak, *Wartime: An Idea, Its History, and Its Consequences* (New York: Oxford University Press, 2013), for more on the idea of wartime and its impact extending long after official war has ended.

44. See Ujo Nakano, *Within the Barbed Wire Fence: A Japanese Man's Account of His Internment in Canada* (Davidson, NC: Lorimer Press, 2016); Gordon H. Chang, ed., *Morning Glory, Evening Shadow: Yamato Ichihashi and His Internment Writings, 1942–1945* (Stanford, CA: Stanford University Press, 1997); Muriel Kitagawa, *This Is My Own: Letters to Wes and Other Writings on Japanese Canadians, 1941–1948* (Vancouver, BC: Talonbooks, 1985); Arthur A. Hansen and Betty K. Mitson, eds., *Voices Long Silent: An Oral Inquiry into Japanese American Evacuation* (Fullerton: California State University, Fullerton, 1974); Charles Kikuchi,

The Kikuchi Diary: Chronicle from an American Concentration Camp, ed. John Modell (Urbana: University of Illinois Press, 1993); Naomi Hirahara and Gwenn Jensen, *Silent Scars of Healing Hands: Oral Histories of Japanese American Doctors in World War II Detention Camps* (Fullerton, CA: Center for Oral and Public History, 2004); Seiichi Higashida, *Adios to Tears: The Memoirs of a Japanese-Peruvian Internee in U.S. Concentration Camps* (Seattle: University of Washington Press, 2000); Richard Nishimoto, *Inside an American Concentration Camp: Japanese American Resistance at Poston, Arizona* (Tucson: University of Arizona Press, 1995); Mine Okubo, *Citizen 13660* (Seattle: University of Washington Press, 2014); May Matsuda Gruenewals, *Looking Like the Enemy: My Story of Imprisonment in Japanese-American Internment Camps* (Troutdale, OR: New Sage Press, 2005); Yuji Ichioka, ed., *Views from Within: The Japanese American Evacuation and Resettlement* (Los Angeles: UCLA Asian American Studies Center, 1989); and Arthur Kleinkopf, *Relocation Center Diary* (privately printed, 1945). Many more examples of personal accounts exist.

45. Quoted in Valerie Matsumoto, *City Girls: The Nisei Social World in Los Angeles, 1920–1950* (New York: Oxford University Press, 2014), 157. See also Chiang, *Nature Behind Barbed Wire*, 126–27; Valerie Matsumoto, "Japanese American Women During World War II," *Frontiers: A Journal of Women's Studies* 18, no. 1 (1984): 6–14; and Thomas Y. Fujita-Rony, "Remaking the 'Home Front' in World War II: Japanese American Women's Work and the Colorado River Relocation Center," *Southern California Quarterly* 88, no. 2 (2006): 161–204.

46. Chiang, *Nature Behind Barbed Wire*, xiv.

47. Chiang, *Nature Behind Barbed Wire*, xiv.

48. See Manu Karuka, *Empire's Tracks: Indigenous Nations, Chinese Workers, and the Transcontinental Railroad* (Berkeley: University of California Press, 2019).

49. See Andrew Urban, *Brokering Servitude: Migration and the Politics of Domestic Labor During the Long Nineteenth Century* (New York: New York University Press, 2017), for more on immigration policy and labor regulation and supply.

50. See Moon Ho Jung, *Coolies and Cane: Race, Labor, and Sugar in the Age of Emancipation* (Baltimore: Johns Hopkins University Press, 2006), for more on "coolie" Chinese labor, particularly in the South following the Civil War.

51. Myer, *Uprooted Americans*, 40–43.

52. John Dixon Ford, "Gov't Brief 'Race Doctrine' to Justify 'Jap-Crow' Evacuation," *New York New Lead*, June 12, 1943, 1, 4. See also Matthew Briones, *Jim and Jap Crow: A Cultural History of 1940s Interracial America* (Princeton, NJ: Princeton University Press, 2012), for more on the racial dynamics of Japanese American incarceration.

Chapter 1

1. Anders Tomlinson, "Born of Reclamation: Internment and World War II Veterans," https://anderstomlinson.com/tule-lake/towns/newell-california/ (accessed July 16, 2018). See Stan Turner, *Years of Harvest: A History of the Tule Lake Basin* (Port of Kalama, WA: Spencer Creek Press, 1987); Mark Fiege, *Irrigated Eden: The Making of an Agricultural Landscape in the American West* (Seattle: University of Washington Press, 2000); and Stephanie Pincetl, *Transforming California: A Political History of Land Use and Development* (Baltimore: Johns

Hopkins University Press, 1999), for more on the environmental history of Tule Lake and the Modoc region of northern California and Oregon. For more on the work of the Civilian Conservation Corps with the Reclamation Service, see Christine Pfaff, "The Bureau of Reclamation and the Civilian Conservation Corps: Legacy Revealed," Bureau of Reclamation Technical Services Center (undated).

2. See Brian Hayashi, *Democratizing the Enemy: The Japanese American Internment* (Princeton, NJ: Princeton University Press, 2004), 8–9.

3. Eric Walz, *Nikkei in the Interior West: Japanese Immigration and Community Building, 1882–1945* (Tucson: University of Arizona Press, 2012), 154–56; 172–75.

4. John L. DeWitt, *Final Report: Japanese Evacuation from the West Coast, 1942* (Washington, DC: Government Printing Office, 1943), 41.

5. DeWitt, *Final Report*, 43–45.

6. See Jason Scott Smith, *Building New Deal Liberalism: The Political Economy of Public Works, 1933–1956* (Cambridge: Cambridge University Press, 2006), 224–25.

7. Lieutenant General John L. DeWitt to Rex L. Nicholson, Regional WPA Supervisor, March 28, 1942, box 64, folder 333.1, Inspections—Vol. II, Records of the US Army Defense Commands (hereafter referred to as RG 499), National Archives and Records Administration II, College Park, Maryland.

8. DeWitt to Nicholson, March 28, 1942, reprinted in *Final Report*, 47.

9. DeWitt, *Final Report*, 151.

10. "Army to Use Longacres as Camp for Japs," *Seattle Post-Intelligencer*, April 2, 1942, 1.

11. Ted Nakashima, "Concentration Camp: US Style," *New Republic*, June 15, 1942, 828–35.

12. Bendetsen to Bruce Bliven, June 19, 1942, folder—Civil Affairs Division, box 611, Karl R. Bendetsen Papers—Record Group 75100 (hereafter referred to as Bendetsen Papers), Hoover Institution Archives, Stanford University, Stanford, California.

13. WCCA, "Joint Press Release, March 29, 1942," folder—Western Defense and Command and Fourth Army . . . , Vol. I, 3 of 4, box 621, Bendetsen Papers, 1.

14. Claude B. Washburne to Bendetsen, May 12, 1942, folder 230.145, box 25, RG 499.

15. Washburne to Bendetsen.

16. Washburne to Bendetsen.

17. WCCA, "Joint Press Release, March 29, 1942," 1.

18. Washburne to Bendetsen.

19. WRA, "A Statement of Guiding Principles of the War Relocation Authority," March 2, 1942, folder WRA—Committee on Fair Employment Practices, box 10, Office of Production Management (War Manpower Committee) Records, FDR Library, 2.

20. WRA, "Tentative Policy," May 29, 1942, folder—1942, box 1, OF 4849—War Relocation Authority Records, FDR Library, 1.

21. WRA, "Tentative Policy," 1.

22. Bendetsen, Memo: "Recommended procedure in establishing a proper public record in connection with the long staple cotton situation and in encouraging a maximum recruitment of evacuees,"May 12, 1942, folder 230.145, box 25, RG 499.

23. Hugh Fullerton to Minidoka County USDA Board, May 24, 1942, folder 230.145, box 25, RG 499.

24. War Relocation Authority, *Relocation Communities for Wartime Evacuees* (Washington, DC: Government Printing Office, September 1942), 2.

25. "History of WRA," undated, BANC MSS 67/14d, folder C1.00, 41–42, Japanese American Evacuation and Resettlement Records (hereafter referred to as JERS), Bancroft Library, University of California, Berkeley.

26. WRA, *Relocation Communities*, 2.

27. WRA, *Relocation Communities*, 2–3.

28. Peter R. Cooper to Harry Black, November 10, 1942, folder 319.1, box 47, RG 499, 6.

29. F. O. Hagie, "Report: Special to Our Members: RE: Establishment of Japanese Relocation Centers," May 20, 1942, folder 323.3—Relocation Centers—General, Vol. I, RG 499, 3.

30. Hagie, "Report," 3.

31. Office of Emergency Management-WRA, "War Relocation Authority Outlines Resettlement Plans for Evacuees," April 13, 1942, folder—Western Defense Command and Fourth Army . . . Vol. I, 3 of 4, box 621, Bendetsen Papers.

32. Hayashi, *Democratizing the Enemy*, 16–17.

33. "Let the Japs Build a Road," *New York Times*, March 8, 1942, 3.

34. Hayashi, *Democratizing the Enemy*, 16; Connie Y. Chiang, *Nature Behind Barbed Wire: An Environmental History of the Japanese American Incarceration* (New York: Oxford University Press, 2018), 13.

35. Eisenhower to Bendetsen, June 16, 1942, folder 323.2, box 54, RG 499.

36. WRA, *Relocation Communities*, 6.

37. WRA, *Relocation Communities*, 6.

38. WRA, *Relocation Communities*, 6–7.

39. WRA, *Relocation Communities*, 6–7.

40. WRA, *Relocation Communities*, 7.

41. WCCA, "Press Release No. 4-27," April 23, 1942, folder 4, box 720, Bendetsen Papers.

42. WCCA, "Press Release No. 4-27.".

43. See James Donald Holley, *Uncle Sam's Farmers: The New Deal Communities of the Lower Mississippi Valley* (Urbana: University of Illinois Press, 1973), for more on the FSA in Arkansas and other regions during the Depression.

44. "Proposed Relocation Center, Rohwer, Desha County, Arkansas," folder 601, box 92, RG 499, 1.

45. "Proposed Relocation Center," 1.

46. WRA, *Relocation Communities*, 12.

47. WRA, *Relocation Communities*, 8.

48. "Colorado's Part in the War Effort," *Colorado Springs News*, September 3, 1942, 1. See also Adam Schrager, *The Principled Politician: Governor Ralph Carr and the Fight Against Japanese American Internment* (Golden, CO: Fulcrum Publishing, 2009), for more on Carr's policies regarding Japanese Americans resettling in Colorado.

49. Herbert Maw to Bendetsen, March 13, 1942, folder 014.12—Governors, box 7, RG 499.

50. "Proposed Relocation Center."

51. Homer Adkins to DeWitt, June 12, 1942, folder 012.12, box 7, RG 499.

52. Adkins to DeWitt.

53. DeWitt to Adkins, June 17, 1942, folder 012.12, box 7, RG 499.

54. Consolidated Index Sheet, March 14, 1942, folder 113—Reimbursements, box 21, RG 499, 1.

55. William Durbin and Frank DuRette to Bendetsen, September 25, 1942, folder 123, box 21, RG 499.

56. Nicholson, Memo: Total Operating Budget Assembly Centers and Administrative Personnel, July 4, 1942, folder 110.01, box 21, RG 499.

57. DeWitt, *Final Report*, 350; Evans, Memo: Operating Agency Budget for Months of August and September," July 6, 1942, folder 110.01, box 21, RG 499.

58. Nicholson to Evans, March 31, 1942, folder 230.145, box 25, RG 499.

59. Hagie, "Report," 6.

60. "Final Report: WPA Occupational Titles by Wage Classification Approved for Use in Assigning Evacuees to Perform Work in the WCCA and Assembly Centers—Assistant Commissioner's Order No. 3–4," March 14, 1942, folder 319.1, box 47, RG 499, 1–2.

61. Hagie, "Report," 3.

62. Milton Eisenhower to Thomas Holland, May 4, 1942, folder C1.02, BANC MSS 67/14 c- (4 of 4), JERS.

63. Eisenhower to Holland, May 4, 1942.

64. United States Congress, House Select Committee Investigating National Defense Migration, 77th Congress, 2nd sess., *National Defense Migration* (hereafter Tolan Committee hearings), 11191. For more on the Tolan Committee hearings, see Robert Shaffer, "Cracks in the Consensus: Defending the Rights of Japanese Americans During World War II," *Radical History Review* 72 (Fall 1998): 84–120; and Matthew Saccento, "The Tolan Committee and the Internment of Japanese Americans" (BA thesis, Wilkes Honors College, Florida Atlantic University, 2008).

65. Tolan Committee hearings, 11189.

66. Tolan Committee hearings, 1191.

67. WRA, "Tentative Policy," 3.

68. WRA, "Tentative Policy," 2.

69. "WRA Policies," November 16, 1942, folder 5, box 1, JARC, Division of Rare and Manuscript Collections, Cornell University, Ithaca, New York, 5.

70. Hagie, "Report," 2.

71. See Rose Hayden-Smith, *Sowing the Seeds of Victory: American Gardening Programs of World War I* (Jefferson, NC: McFarland and Company, 2014); Lizzie Collingham, *The Taste of War: World War II and the Battle for Food* (New York: Penguin, 2013); and Tanfer Emin Tunc and Annessa Ann Babic, "Food on the Home Front, Food on the War Front: World War II and the American Diet," *Food and Foodways* 25 (2017): 101–6, for more on food, diet, and policy during both World Wars.

72. Chiang, *Nature Behind Barbed Wire*, 123–25, 146.

73. Hagie, "Report," 3.

74. Hagie, "Report," 4.

75. Eiichiro Azuma, *Between Two Empires: Race, History, and Transnationalism in Japanese America* (New York: Oxford University Press, 2005), 13–15.

76. WRA, "First Quarterly Report: March 18 to June 30, 1942," folder 6, box 1, JARC, 2.

77. For more on work and labor shortages during World War II, see Charles D. Chamberlain, *Victory at Home: Manpower and Race in the American South During World War II* (Athens: University of Georgia Press, 2003); Audra Jennings, *Out of the Horrors of War: Disability Politics in World War II America* (Philadelphia: University of Pennsylvania Press, 2016); Andrew E. Kersten, *Labor's Home Front: The American Federation of Labor During World War II* (New York: New York University Press, 2006); Stephanie A. Carpenter, *On the Farm Front: The Women's Land Army in World War II* (DeKalb: Northern Illinois University Press, 2003); Emily Yellin, *Our Mothers' War: American Women at Home and at the Front During World War II* (New York: Free Press, 2004); Cecilia Gowdy-Wygant, *Cultivating Victory: The Women's Land Army and the Victory Garden Movement* (Pittsburgh: University of Pittsburgh Press, 2013); and Matthew L. Basso, *Meet Joe Copper: Masculinity and Race on Montana's World War II Home Front* (Chicago: University of Chicago Press, 2013).

78. "Council Meeting Minutes, February 2, 1942," folder—Council Meetings, 1942–1945, box 1, Francis Biddle Papers, FDR Library.

79. Donald Nelson to Roosevelt, March 31, 1942, folder—Francis Biddle, box 38, James H. Rowe, Jr. Papers, FDR Library.

80. See Mary Ellen Curtin, *Black Prisoners and Their World, Alabama, 1865–1900* (Charlottesville: University of Virginia Press, 2000); Daniel Pete, *The Shadow of Slavery: Peonage in the South* (Urbana: University of Illinois Press, 1990); Ruth Gilmore, *Golden Gulag: Prisons, Surplus, Crisis, and Opposition in Globalizing California* (Berkeley: University of California Press, 2007); Alex Lichtenstein, *Twice the Work of Free Labor: The Political Economy of Convict Labor in the New South* (New York: Verso, 1996); Matthew Mancini, *One Dies, Get Another: Convict Leasing in the American South* (Chapel Hill: University of North Carolina Press, 1996); Martha Myers, *Race, Labor, and Punishment in the New South* (Columbus: Ohio State University Press,1998); David Oshinsky, *Worse Than Slavery: Parchman Farm and the Ordeal of Jim Crow Justice* (New York: Free Press, 1997); Douglas A. Blackmon, *Slavery by Another Name: The Re-enslavement of Black Americans from the Civil War to World War II* (New York: Anchor, 2009); Talitha L. LeFlouria, *Chained in Silence: Black Women and Convict Labor in the New South* (Chapel Hill: University of North Carolina Press, 2016); Clarence Jefferson Hall Jr., "Prisonland: Environment, Society, and Mass Incarceration on New York's Northern Frontier, 1845–1999" (PhD diss., State University of New York, Stony Brook, 2014); Volker Janssen, "When the 'Jungle' Met the Forest: Public Work, Civil Defense, and Prison Camps in Postwar California," *Journal of American History* 96, no. 3 (2009): 702–26; and Rebecca M. McLennan, *Crisis of Imprisonment: Protest, Politics, and the Making of the American Penal State, 1776–1941* (New York: Cambridge University Press, 2008).

81. "Abstract: March 30, 1942," folder—Department of Justice Abstracts, box 7, Department of Justice Records, FDR Library.

82. "Abstract: May, 10, 1942," folder—Department of Justice Abstracts, box 7, Department of Justice Records, FDR Library.

83. "Bulwinkle, Hon. A. L., U.S. House of Representatives, March 30, 1942," folder—Justice Department, 1942 Abstracts, Jan.-Apr., box 7, OF 10—Department of Justice, FDR Library.

84. "Press Release: Department of Justice, February 14, 1943," folder—Prisons, box 38, James H. Rowe, Jr. Papers, FDR Library.

85. Wartime Civilian Control Administration, "Instructions Governing Operation," March 5, 1942, folder 333.1, box 64, RG 499.

86. Hagie, "Report," 4.

87. Hagie, "Report," 4.

88. Commission on Wartime Relocation and Internment of Civilians, *Personal Justice Denied: Report of the Commission on Wartime Relocation and Internment of Civilians* (Seattle: University of Washington Press and Washington, DC: Civil Liberties Public Education Fund, 1997), 123.

89. "Japanese Till 226,094 Acres in California," *San Francisco Call-Bulletin*, March 5, 1942, 2.

90. Willard F. Williamson to Bendetsen, March 31, 1942, folder 230.145 (Employment of Japanese Vol. I), box 25, RG 499.

91. "Japanese Truck Gardens," *San Diego Tribune*, March 19, 1942, box 717, Bendetsen Papers.

92. "Evacuation May Hinge on Harvests," *Seattle Post-Intelligencer*, April 15, 1942, box 718, Bendetsen Papers.

93. E. R. Bitting to DeWitt, March 28, 1942, folder 230.145, box 25, RG 499.

94. "Elko County Ranchers Meet," May 6, 1942, box 718, Bendetsen Papers.

95. Dwight H. Green to Roosevelt, October 8, 1942, box 4, OF 227a Farm Matters, FDR Library.

96. "Conference Regarding Japanese Labor in Sacramento Delta and San Joaquin Valley, April 14, 1942, folder 230.145, box 25, RG 499.

97. Federal Reserve Bank of San Francisco, "Monthly Review," April 4, 1942, 1.

98. "Alien Farmers Are Advised to Continue Work," box 717, Bendetsen Papers, March 5, 1942. West Coast residents also feared the impact of a loss of Japanese fishermen on the seafood and specifically the oyster industry as shippers often depended on the haul of Japanese.

99. D. W. Rutherford, "Do We Need Japanese Farmers," *Pacific Rural Press*, February 21, 1942; "Japanese Garden Production Held Not Indispensable," March 8, 1942, box 717, Bendetsen Papers.

100. Charles Swain, "Make Them Work," *Grand Junction Sentinel*, February 20, 1942, 3.

Chapter 2

1. Bendetsen to Floyd Oles, April 28, 1942, folder 230.145, box 25, RG 499, 1.

2. Bendetsen to Oles, 2.

3. Lizzie Collingham, *The Taste of War: World War II and the Battle for Food* (New York: Penguin, 2013), 416–17.

4. "Food for Freedom: Information Handbook" (Washington, DC: Government Printing Office, 1943), 7.

5. "Food for Freedom," 9.

6. Connie Y. Chiang, *Nature Behind Barbed Wire: An Environmental History of the Japanese American Incarceration* (New York: Oxford University Press, 2018), vii, 121.

7. "Olson Again Asks Japs for Harvest," *San Francisco Examiner,* July 6, 1942, 1.

8. Simeon Man, *Soldiering Through Empire: Race and the Making of the Decolonizing Pacific* (Berkeley: University of California Press, 2018), 2.

9. Literature on the Bracero program and its effects is vast. For more on the Bracero program, see Deborah Cohen, *Braceros: Migrant Citizens and Transnational Subjects in the Postwar United States and Mexico* (Chapel Hill: University of North Carolina Press, 2013); Ronald Mize and Alicia Swords, *Consuming Mexican Labor: From the Bracero Program to NAFTA* (Toronto: University of Toronto Press, 2010); and Mireya Loza, *Defiant Braceros: How Migrant Workers Fought for Racial, Sexual, and Political Freedom* (Chapel Hill: University of North Carolina Press, 2016). Mae Ngai's *Impossible Subjects: Illegal Americans and the Making of Modern America* (Princeton, NJ: Princeton University Press, 2004) also includes information on the program, labor, and immigration policy.

10. *The Sugar Reference Book and Dictionary* (New York: Palmer Publishing Corporation, 1933), 84.

11. Raymond P. Barry, ed., *A Documentary History of Migratory Farm Labor in California* (Oakland, CA: Federal Writers Project, 1938), 1–4, 6–7.

12. Barry, *A Documentary History of Migratory Farm Labor,* 48–50.

13. Jim Norris, *North for the Harvest: Mexican Workers, Growers, and the Sugar Beet Industry* (Minneapolis: Minnesota Historical Society Press, 2009), 54–60.

14. Norris, *North for the Harvest,* 35.

15. Telephone conversation between Bendetsen and Colonel Tate, August 8, 1942, folder 230.145, box 25, RG 499.

16. Norris, *North for the Harvest,* 11–12.

17. Ford to DeWitt, April 11, 1942, folder 230.145, box 25, RG 499.

18. Qtd. in Richard Nishimoto, "Chapter V: Early Phase of Selective Migration: Student Relocation and Agricultural Furloughs" (1943), BANC MSS 67/14c, folder W.189, JERS, 44.

19. "Japanese Workers," *Sioux Falls Argus Leader,* June 21, 1942, 7.

20. Malta Commercial Club to Bendetsen, March 10, 1942, folder 230.145, box 25, RG 499.

21. Malta Commercial Club to Bendetsen.

22. Malta Commercial Club to Bendetsen. See also United States Department of Labor, "Wartime Wages, Income, and Wage Regulation in Agriculture," Bulletin Number 883 (Washington, DC: Government Printing Office, 1946), 11–12, and Nick Johnson, "Workers' Weed: Cannabis, Sugar Beets, and Landscapes of Labor in the American West, 1900–1946," *Agricultural History* 91, no. 3 (2017): 13.

23. Norris, *North for the Harvest,* 21.

24. Minutes from February meeting of SMECA, February 20, 1942, folder 014.12–Governors, Vol. I, box 27, RG 499.

25. Nishimoto, "Chapter V," 44.

26. Thomas Holland to Dillon Myer, September 10, 1943, folder C1.02, BANC MSS 67/14 (c), JERS.

27. H. E. Dodd to Eisenhower, May 1, 1942, qtd. in Nishimoto, "Chapter V," 43–44.

28. Dodd to Eisenhower.

29. Nishimoto, "Chapter V," 43–44.

30. Eisenhower to Claude Wickard, May 2, 1942, folder C1.02, BANC MSS 67/14 (c), JERS.

31. Eisenhower to Wickard.

32. Qtd. in Nishimoto, "Chapter V," 41.

33. "Meeting, Salt Lake City, Utah," April 7, 1942, folder 21, Box 1, WRA, JERS, 23–24.

34. Qtd. in Nishimoto, "Chapter V," 39; "Meeting, Salt Lake City, Utah," 24.

35. Herbert Maw to Bendetsen, April 13, 1942, folder 230.145, box 25, RG 499.

36. George Aiken to Bendetsen, April 11, 1942, folder 230.145, box 25, RG 499.

37. Eisenhower to G. H. Wells, May 5, 1942, folder C1.02, BANC MSS 67/14 (c), JERS.

38. Bendetsen to Albert H. Kruse, April 29, 1942, folder 230.145, box 25, RG 499, 1.

39. Eisenhower to Sprague, April 8, 1942, folder 2, box 12, Marvin Gavin Pursinger Collection, Mss 903, Oregon Historical Society, Portland, Oregon.

40. Charles Sprague to Karl Bendetsen, May 9, 1942, folder 2, box 12, Marvin Gavin Pursinger Collection.

41. "Governor Sprague Appeals to President for Action," *Eastern Oregon Observer* (Ontario, Oregon), May 14, 1942, 1.

42. See David Hamilton, *From New Day to New Deal: American Farm Policy from Hoover to Roosevelt* (Chapel Hill: University of North Carolina Press, 2011), for more on programs designed to assist agriculture during this period.

43. Press release from Governor Sprague, May 14, 1942, folder 16, box 4, Charles A. Sprague Papers (hereafter referred to as Sprague Papers), Oregon Historical Society, Portland, Oregon.

44. See Eric L. Muller, *The American Inquisition: The Hunt for Japanese American Disloyalty in World War II* (Chapel Hill: University of North Carolina Press, 2007), 24–25.

45. Maurice Walk, "The Status of Evacuees When Working in Private Employment Outside of the Military Zone," May 22, 1942, folder 230.145, box 25, RG 499, 1.

46. Walk, "Status of Evacuees," 1.

47. Walk, "Status of Evacuees," 1.

48. Walk, "Status of Evacuees," 1.

49. Walk, "Status of Evacuees," 2.

50. Walk, "Status of Evacuees," 2.

51. Fullerton to Bendetsen, September 15, 1942, folder 323.3—Assembly Centers, box 32, RG 499.

52. See Arnold Krammer, *Nazi Prisoners of War in America* (New York: Stein and Day, 1979); Robert D. Billinger, *Hitler's Soldiers in the Sunshine State: German POWs in Florida* (Lanham, MD: University Press of America, 2000); L. E. Keefer, *Italian Prisoners of War in America, 1942-1946* (New York: Praeger, 1992); and Derek R. Mallett, *Hitler's Generals in America: Nazi POWs and Allied Military Intelligence* (Lexington: University Press of Kentucky, 2013), for more on POWs and labor in the United States. See Arnold Krammer, "Japanese Prisoners of War in America," *Pacific Historical Review* 52, no. 1 (1983): 67–91, for more information on Japanese POWs held in the United States.

53. For more on economic and social mobilization in war, see Roger Chickering, Stig Forster, and Bernd Greiner, eds., *A World at Total War: Global Conflict and the Politics of Destruction, 1937-1945* (Cambridge: Cambridge University Press, 2010); Mark Harrison, *The Economics of World War II: Six Great Powers in International Comparison* (Cambridge: Cambridge University Press, 2000); Alan S. Milward, *War, Economy, and Society, 1939-1945* (Berkeley: University of California Press, 1980); Arthur Herman, *Freedom's Forge: How American Business Produced Victory in World War II* (New York: Random House, 2013); Harold G. Vatter, *The U.S. Economy in World War II* (New York: Columbia University Press, 1985); and Lance Janda, "Shutting the Gates of Mercy: The American Origins of Total War," *Journal of Military History* 59, no. 1 (Jan. 1995): 7-26.

54. Walk, "Status of Evacuees," 2.

55. Walk, "Status of Evacuees," 2.

56. Walk, "Status of Evacuees," 2.

57. Walk, "Status of Evacuees," 3.

58. Walk, "Status of Evacuees," 3.

59. Walk, "Status of Evacuees," 3.

60. William Boekel to Bendetsen and DeWitt, May 11, 1942, folder 230.145, box 25, RG 499.

61. Boekel to Bendetsen and DeWitt.

62. E. R. Fryer, "Memo to Persons of Japanese Ancestry who are released from Assembly or Relocation Centers . . . ," July 15, 1942, folder 230.145, box 25, RG 499.

63. United States Department of Agriculture, "Farmers' Attitude Toward the Use of Japanese Evacuees as Farm Labor: Part I—Sugar Beet and Long Staple Cotton Regions," January 30, 1943, folder 27, box 11, JARC, 24.

64. Bendetsen, "Memo: Transfer of Employees from one Employer to Another," July 15, 1942, folder 230.145, box 25, RG 499; Lewis A. Sigler to Dillon Myer, April 10, 1943, folder 4, box 1, JARC, 22.

65. H. A. Ketterman to Charles M. Paradis (Manager, U.S. Employment Service), May 22, 1942, folder 230.145, box 25, RG 499, 2.

66. Fryer, "Memo to Persons of Japanese Ancestry . . . ," 1.

67. United States Department of Agriculture, "Farmers' Attitudes," 26.

68. Lewis A. Sigler to Dillon Myer, April 10, 1943, folder 4, box 1, JARC, 27.

69. Sigler to Myer, 27-28.

70. Sigler to Myer, 27-28.

71. For more on New Deal labor policy, see Ira Katznelson, *Fear Itself: The New Deal and the Origins of Our Time* (New York: Liveright, 2014), 31-38; Lizabeth Cohen, *Making a New Deal: Industrial Workers in Chicago, 1919-1939*, 2nd ed. (New York: Cambridge University Press, 2008); and David M. Kennedy, *Freedom from Fear: The American People in Depression and War, 1929-1945* (New York: Oxford University Press, 2001).

72. E. R. Fryer to Bendetsen, May 19, 1942, folder 230.145, box 27, RG 499.

73. Governor Sprague to Bendetsen and Eisenhower, May 18, 1942, folder 230.145, box 27, RG 499.

74. DeWitt, "Civilian Restrictive Order No. 2," May 20, 1942, California State University American Digitization Project, sjs_fla_0887, https://cdm16855.contentdm.oclc.org/digital /collection/p16855coll4/id/12166 (accessed June, 20, 2017).

75. Boekel to Bendetsen, May 27, 1942, folder 230.145, box 25, RG 499.

76. "Japanese Evacuees Receive 'Clearance' for Work in Malheur Sugar Beet Fields," *Portland Oregonian*, May 20, 1942, 2.

77. "Only Twenty Japs to Aid in Oregon Beet Fields," May 22, 1942, *San Francisco Examiner*, 1.

78. "To Beet or Not to Beet; That Is Question Stumping Japs," *Portland Journal*, May 20, 1942, 1.

79. "Japanese on Way to Nyssa," *Idaho Daily Statesman* (Boise), May 20, 1942.

80. "Prisoners Favor Farm Labor Plan; Japanese Do Not," *Los Angeles Times*, June 19, 1942, 3.

81. Hito Okada to Sprague, May 25, 1942, folder 16, box 4, Sprague Papers, 1.

82. Okada to Sprague, 1.

83. Okada to Sprague, 2.

84. Okada to Sprague, 2.

85. "White Collar Japanese Men Saved Beets," *Idaho Daily Statesman*, June 17, 1942, 1.

86. "White Collar Japanese Men," 1.

87. Joe F. Dyer to George Aiken, November 6, 1942, folder 2, box 5, Sprague Papers.

88. Dyer to Aiken.

89. Okada to Sprague.

90. Hayashi, *Democratizing the Enemy*, 100–101, 155.

91. Frank Meek to Colonel Claude Washburne, May 30, 1942, folder 230.145, box 25, RG 499, 3.

92. Curfew Regulation Meeting Notes, September 4, 1942, folder 1, box 5, Sprague Papers.

93. Meek to Washburne, 3.

94. Meek to Washburne, 3.

95. Meek to Washburne, 3.

96. Meek to Washburne, 4.

97. Block E, Bar 13, Apartment 3-Santa Anita Assembly Center—Letter, August 1942, Folder 23, Box 11, JARC.

98. Telephone conversation between Bendetsen and DeWitt, July 4, 1942, folder 230.145, box 27, RG 499.

99. Telephone conversation between Bendetsen and DeWitt.

100. Omission in original.

101. Telephone conversation between Bendetsen and DeWitt.

102. Telephone conversation between Bendetsen and DeWitt.

103. Japanese American National Museum, *Uprooted: Japanese American Farm Labor Camps during World War II*, http://www.uprootedexhibit.com/farm-labor-camps/ (accessed December 12, 2019).

104. See Hayashi, *Democratizing the Enemy*, xv; and Greg Robinson, *A Tragedy of Democracy: Japanese Confinement in North America* (New York: Columbia University Press, 2009), 169–70. See also Takeya Mizuno, "The Creation of the 'Free' Press in Japanese-American Camps: The War Relocation Authority's Planning and Making of the Camp Newspaper Policy," *Journalism and Mass Communication Quarterly* 78, no. 3 (2001): 503–18; and Takeya Mizuno, "Journalism Under Military Guards and Searchlights: Newspaper Censorship at Japanese American Assembly Centers during WWII," *Journalism History* 29, no. 3 (2003): 98–106. In contrast, Jay Friedlander highlights the work of Japanese American editor Paul Yokata in achieving a relatively high level of authority over the *Denson Tribune* (the camp newspaper at Jerome) in his article "Journalism Behind Barbed Wire, 1942–44: An Arkansas Relocation Center Newspaper," *Journalism Quarterly* 62 (June, 1985): 243–71.

105. Mizuno, "Journalism Under Military Guards," 104.

106. H. A. Benning to Sprague, July 9, 1942, folder 12, box 4, Sprague Papers.

107. Ben Mitsuda, "First Impressions Described," *Santa Anita Pacemaker*, September 22, 1942, 3.

108. Mitsuda, "First Impressions," 3.

109. Mitsuda, "First Impressions," 3.

110. "250 Leaving Tonite," *Portland Evacuazette*, May 26, 1942, 1.

111. "Work Corps to Aid U.S.," *Manzanar Free Press*, May 21, 1942, 1.

112. "Victory Volunteers Are Loyal," *Santa Anita Pacemaker*, June 23, 1942, 4.

113. "Victory Volunteers," 3.

114. Jack Nakagawa to Hugh Evans, October 8, 1942, folder 28, box 11, JARC, 2.

115. Nakagawa to Evans, 1.

116. Nakagawa to Evans, 1.

117. Mitsukane Kaneko to Wade Head, undated latter, folder 28, box 11, JARC.

118. Kaneko to Head.

119. William Fujito to William Bonack, October 10, 1942, folder 28, box 11, JARC.

120. Yuji Funaki, Survey, November 13, 1942, folder 30, box 11, JARC, 3.

121. Jonathan Katano to Hugh Evans, October 15, 1942, folder 28, box 11, JARC, 1.

122. Katano to Evans, 1.

123. Katano to Evans, 1.

124. "Tak" to Spicer, October 15, 1942, 3.

125. Frank Meek to Colonel Washburne, July 22, 1942, folder 230.145, box 25, RG 499.

126. Letter from Shiro Yamami to "Kaz," September 23, 1942, folder 28, box 11, JARC, 1.

127. Yamami to Kaz.

128. Nakagawa to Evans, October 29, 1942, folder 28, box 11, JARC, 1.

129. "Outside Employment Observation: Poston Boys prepare to leave for Nevada," March 3, 1943, folder 28, box 11, JARC.

130. Nakagawa to Evans September 22, 1942, folder 28, box 11, JARC.

131. Mitsukane Kaneko to Vernon Kennedy, October 11, 1942, folder 28, box 11, JARC.

132. John Katano to Hugh Evans, October 12, 1942, Ag 1, 16.

133. Johnnie Fukushima, "Personal Journal: Re-location and Outside Employment," April 11, 1943, folder 30, box 11, JARC.

134. "Tak" to Spicer, October 19, 142, folder 28, box 11, JARC, 1.

135. Mitsukane Kaneko to Kennedy, October 12, 1942, folder 28, box 11, JARC.

136. Kaneko to Kennedy, October 12, 1942.

137. Kaneko to Kennedy, October 12, 1942.

138. "Olson Again Asks Japs for Harvest," *San Francisco Examiner*, June 6, 1942, 1.

139. "Olson Again Asks Japs for Harvest," 1.

140. Telephone conversation between DeWitt and John J. McCloy, September 9, 1942, folder 230.145, box 25, RG 499.

141. Telephone conversation between DeWitt and Bendetsen, July 8, 1942, 230.145, box 25, RG 499.

142. War Relocation Authority, "Daily Press Review," September 7, 1942, folder 20, box 1, JARC, 3.

143. Planning Branch Operations Report for the Secretary of War, June 2, 1942, folder 319.1, box 47, RG 499; telephone conversation between Bendetsen and Colonel Tate, August 8, 1942, folder 230.145, box 25, RG 499.

144. War Relocation Authority, "Daily Press Review," September 10, 1942, folder 20, box 1, JARC, 5.

145. Telephone conversation between DeWitt and McCloy, September 9, 1942, folder 230.145, box 25, RG 499.

146. Telephone conversation between DeWitt and McCloy, September 9, 1942.

147. Henry Stimson to DeWitt, September 12, 1942, folder 230.145, box 25, RG 499.

148. Telephone conversation between DeWitt and McCloy, September 9, 1942.

149. Alexander M. Leighton to Members of the Bureau of Sociological Research, October 22, 1942, folder 27, box 11, JARC; DeWitt to Chief of Staff, November 6, 1942, folder 230.145 Employment (Arizona Cotton), box 25, RG 499, 1.

150. Telephone conversation between DeWitt and McCloy, September 9, 1942.

151. "Farmers Attitudes Toward the Use of Japanese Evacuees as Farm Labor," folder 27, box 11, JARC, 15.

152. "Farmers Attitudes."

153. "Farmers Attitudes."

154. "Farmers Attitudes," 21.

155. John Howard, *Concentration Camps on the American Home Front* (Chicago: University of Chicago Press, 2008), 177–92.

Chapter 3

1. Telephone conversation between Colonel Moffitt and Colonel Austin, October 20, 1943, folder 323.3, box 60, RG 499, 1.

2. Telephone conversation between Moffitt and Austin.

3. John Howard, *Concentration Camps on the Home Front: Japanese Americans in the House of Jim Crow* (Chicago: University of Chicago Press, 2008), 178. See also Lane Ryo Hirabayashi, ed., *Inside an American Concentration Camp: Japanese American Resistance at Poston, Arizona* (Tucson: University of Arizona Press, 1995), xxvii.

4. "Fresno A.C.-May 18," folder—Internment of Japs on Indian Lands, 1942, Part I, box 21, RG 75—Records of the Bureau of Indian Affairs, Records of the Office of the Commissioner of Indian Affairs (hereafter referred to as RG 75), National Archives and Records Administration, Washington, DC.

5. Telephone conversation between Colonel Albert Moffitt and Colonel Meeks, May 23, 1943, folder 323.3, box 60, RG 499.

6. Howard, *Concentration Camps on the Home Front*, 177–80.

7. Robert H. Zieger, *American Workers, American Unions* (Baltimore: Johns Hopkins University Press, 1986), 139–42; Memo to H. L. Nicholson from Russell Amory, memo, June 23, 1942, roll 0484, RG 499.

8. For a discussion of viewing large infrastructure projects as labor history, see Julie Greene, *Canal Builders: Making America's Empire at the Panama Canal* (New York: Penguin Books, 2009), 38–42.

9. Ruth Y. Okimoto, interview by Tom Ikeda, April 8, 2011, in San Francisco, California, transcript, Densho Oral History Archives, https://encyclopedia.densho.org/media/encyc-psms/en-denshovh-oruth-01-0009-1.htm.

10. Greg Robinson, *A Tragedy of Democracy: Japanese Confinement in North America* (New York: Columbia University Press, 2009), 33. For more descriptions of life in the Tanforan detention center (also a former racetrack outside San Bruno, California), see Mine Okubo, *Citizen 13660* (Seattle: University of Washington Press, 2014); and Charles Kikuchi, *The Kikuchi Diary: Chronicle from an American Concentration Camp* (Urbana: University of Illinois Press, 1993).

11. Dillon S. Myer, *Uprooted Americans: The Japanese Americans and the War Relocation Authority During World War II* (Tucson: University of Arizona Press, 1971), 6.

12. Charles Iglehart, "Citizens Behind Barbed Wire," *Nation*, June 6, 1942, 3.

13. Iglehart, "Citizens," 3.

14. "Prison Rules for Evacuees," *American Civil Liberties Union-News*, August 2, 1942, 1.

15. "Prison Rules," 1.

16. "Prison Rules," 1.

17. Myer, *Uprooted Americans*, 40–42.

18. WCCA-Administration Notice 1, August 4, 1942, box 93, RG 499.

19. Yutaka Munakata to J. J. McGovern (manager of the WCCA), May 23, 1942, folder 333.1, box 64, RG 499.

20. Wartime Civilian Control Administration, "Instructions Governing Operation," March 5, 1942, folder 333.1, box 64, RG 499.

21. For example, nets decorated with Hollywood set trees were used by aircraft plants in the Los Angeles area to camouflage operations and lend the appearance of residential areas, while the military draped netting across entrances to harbors to prevent submarine attacks. Nikkei experience with fishing at Terminal Island also made netting a viable option for employment to take advantage of their skills.

22. Wartime Civil Control Administration, "Instructions Governing Operation."

23. "Prison War Work: Inmates Help the Fight," *LIFE*, December 7, 1942, 49–56.

24. For more on privatization of prison labor, see Laurin A. Wollan Jr., "Prisons: The Privatization Phenomenon," *Public Administration Review* 46, no. 6 (1986): 678–81.

25. Camouflage net work would later move to a piece-rate pay system (the same 0.48 per square 1,000 feet) again when another factory was established in Poston. Vernon R. Kennedy, Chief Employment Division, memo, December 29, 1942, folder 51, box 9, JARC.

26. Meeting Minutes of Labor Representatives of Poston Camp, December 19, 1942, folder 51, box 9, JARC, 3.

27. Colonel Archer Lerch, memo, April 27, 1942, folder 323.2, box 57, RG 499. Emphasis my own.

28. Report from Colonel Karl Bendetsen and Colonel I. K. Evans to Russell Amory, July 13, 1942, folder 323.3, box 58, RG 499; R. L. Nicholson, memo, July 28, 1942, folder 323.3, box 58, RG 499.

29. Nicholson, memo, May 26, 1942, folder 323.3, box 58, RG 499.

30. Ira K. Evans, "Report of Operations (Planning Branch), Office of the Commanding General-Project on Garnishing Camo Nets," May 5, 1942, folder 319.1, box 58, RG 499.

31. Evans, "Report of Operations."

32. Report to R. L. Nicholson, Chief, Reception and Induction Center Division of WCCA, roll 0485, RG 499.

33. F. H. Arrowood, "Report—Strike at Santa Anita," June 17, 1942, folder 370.61—Riots and Strikes, box 66, RG 499.

34. Fujii was from Los Angeles, where he was an editor of a communist newspaper (as reported by the administrators at Santa Anita). For more on the strike, see Brian Masaru Hayashi, *Democratizing the Enemy: The Japanese American Internment* (Princeton, NJ: Princeton University Press, 2004), 102–3.

35. Colonel Weckerling, "Sit-Down Strike at Santa Anita Assembly Center," June 17, 1942, folder 370.61, box 66, RG 499.

36. F. H. Arrowood to Major Ray Ashworth, June 17, 1942, roll 353, Records of the Assembly Center, RG 499.

37. "Five Japs to Face U.S. Jury," *Los Angeles Times*, June 26, 1942, 1; "Five Japs Face Trial in Santa Anita," *Los Angeles Times*, June 25, 1942; "U.S. Accuses Six Japs at Santa Anita," *Los Angeles Times*, June 25, 1942.

38. "Santa Anita," *Madera Times*, June 18, 1942, 6.

39. Arrowood to Ashworth, June 17, 1942.

40. "First Founder," folder 370.61, box 66, RG 499.

41. C. J. Beale to John Ingrams, April 28, 1943, folder 323.3, box 53, RG 499.

42. "First Founder."

43. Gordon H. Chang, ed., *Morning Glory, Evening Shadow: Yamato Ichihashi and His Internment Writings* (Stanford, CA: Stanford University Press, 1997), 119.

44. "Army Explains Camouflage Problems to Net Workers," *Santa Anita Pacemaker*, June 19, 1942, 1, 6.

45. Ashworth to Boekel, June 21, 1942 (original communication on meeting), folder 370.61, box 66, RG 499; "Five Japs to Face U.S. Jury," *Los Angeles Daily News*, June 26, 1942, 1.

46. William A. Boekel to Colonel Karl Bendetsen, June 29, 1942, folder 370.61, box 66, RG 499.

47. Boekel to Bendetsen, June 29, 1942.

48. Lieutenant General John L. DeWitt to Earl Warren, June 20, 1942, folder 370.61, box 66, RG 499,1.

49. DeWitt to Warren, 1.

50. Boekel to Bendetsen, June 29, 1942.

51. William Fleet Palmer, memo, June 29, 1942, folder 370.61, box 66, RG 499.

52. Palmer, memo, June 29, 1942.

53. Palmer, memo, June 29, 1942.

54. Boekel to Bendetsen, July 1, 1942, folder 370.61, box 66, RG 499.

55. Togo Tanaka, "A Report on the Manzanar Riot of Sunday, December 6, 1942," The Japanese American Evacuation and Resettlement: A Digital Archive, Bancroft Library, University of California, call number BANC MSS 67/14c, folder O.10.12 (2/2), 4, http://digitalassets.lib.berkeley.edu/jarda/ucb/text/cubanc6714_b211o10_0012_2.pdf (accessed March 25, 2019).

56. "Subject: Inspection of Santa Anita Assembly Center, to Assistant Chief of Staff, Civil Affairs Division, WDC 4th Army," October 16, 1942, folder 333.1, box 64, RG 499, 1.

57. "Inspection of Santa Anita Assembly Center," 1.

58. "Conference, Tule Lake Center," November 12, 1943, folder 337, box 65, RG 499, 2.

59. Hayashi, *Democratizing the Enemy*, 149.

60. Hayashi, *Democratizing the Enemy*, 148.

61. Alexander Leighton, *The Governing of Men: General Principles and Recommendations Based on Experience at a Japanese Relocation Camp* (Princeton, NJ: Princeton University Press, 1946), 110–11.

62. Leighton, *Governing of Men*, 112.

63. Ralph Merritt and Robert Brown, "Final Report: Manzanar Relocation Center," March 9, 1946, folder O1.05:2, MSS 67/14c, JERS.

64. Merritt and Brown, "Final Report."

65. Merritt and Brown, "Final Report." See Paul Spickard, "The Nisei Assume Power: The Japanese-American Citizens League, 1941–1932," *Pacific Historical Review* 52 (1983): 147–74; Donna K. Nagata, *Legacy of Injustice: Exploring the Cross-Generational Impact of the Japanese American Internment* (New York: Plenum Press, 1993); Frank S. Zelko, *Generation, Culture, and Prejudice: The Japanese American Decision to Cooperate with Evacuation and Internment During World War II* (Melbourne, Australia: Monash Publications, 1992); Jere Takahashi, *Nisei/Sansei: Shifting Japanese American Identities and Politics* (Philadelphia: Temple University Press, 1997); and Frank Chin, "Forgive and Forget?," *Amerasia Journal* 30, no. 3 (2004/2005): 61–93.

66. Merritt and Brown, "Final Report."

67. Hayashi, *Democratizing the Enemy*, 114.

68. Merritt and Brown, "Final Report."

69. Merritt and Brown, "Final Report."

70. Merritt and Brown, "Final Report."

71. Merritt and Brown, "Final Report." See also Eileen Tamura, *In Defense of Justice: Joseph Kurihara and the Japanese American Struggle for Equality* (Urbana: University of Illinois Press, 2013).

72. Merritt and Brown, "Final Report."

73. For more foundational works on Manzanar and the uprising, see Michi Weglyn, *Years of Infamy: Untold Story of America's Concentration Camps* (Seattle: University of Washington Press, 1996), 121–33; Roger Daniels, *Concentration Camps USA: Japanese Americans and World War II* (New York: Holt, Rinehart, and Winston, 1980), 107–8; Edward H. Spicer, Asael T. Hansen, Katherine Luomala, and Marvin K. Opler, *Impounded People: Japanese Americans in the Relocation Centers* (Tucson: University of Arizona Press, 1969), 135–37; Tetsuden Kashima and Commission on Wartime Relocation and Internment of Citizens, *Personal Justice Denied: Report of the Commission on Wartime Relocation and Internment of Citizens* (Seattle: University of Washington Press, 1997), 178–80; Audrie Girdner and Anne Loftis, *The Great Betrayal: The Evacuation of Japanese Americans During World War II* (New York: Macmillan, 1969), 263–66; Dorothy Swaine Thomas and Richard S. Nishimoto, *The Spoilage: Japanese American Evacuation and Resettlement During World War II* (Berkeley: University of California Press, 2010), 49–52; Myer, *Uprooted Americans*, 63–65; Daniel S. Davis, *Behind Barbed Wire: The Imprisonment of Japanese Americans During World War II* (New York: Dutton, 1982), 80–82; Lon Kurashige, "Resistance, Collaboration, and Manzanar Protest," *Pacific Historical Review* 70, no. 3 (2001): 387–417; and War Relocation Authority, US Department of the Interior, *WRA, A Story of Human Conservation* (Washington, DC: Government Printing Office, 1946), 49–50.

74. Bendetsen to DeWitt, December 7, 1942, folder 323.3, box 57, RG 499.

75. Bendetsen to Col. Wing, December 7, 1942, folder 323.3, box 57, RG 499, 5.

76. Merritt and Brown, "Final Report."

77. Arthur A. Hansen and David A. Hacker, "The Manzanar Riot: An Ethnic Perspective," *Amerasia Journal* 2, no. 2 (1974): 124.

78. Hayashi, *Democratizing the Enemy*, 114. See also Gary Y. Okihiro, "Religion and Resistance in America's Concentration Camps," *Phylon* 45, no. 3 (1984): 220–33.

79. Merritt and Brown, "Final Report."

80. Harland D. Unrau, *The Evacuation and Relocation of Persons of Japanese Ancestry During World War II: A Historical Study of the Manzanar War Relocation Center* (Washington, DC: United States Department of the Interior National Park Service, 1996), Chapter 12: Operation of Manzanar War Relocation Center, January 1943–November 1945—Administration Organization, https://www.nps.gov/parkhistory/online_books/manz/hrs12.htm (accessed May 12, 2019).

81. "An Interview with Harry Yoshio Ueno," by Sue Kunitoi, Arthur A. Hansen, and Betty Kulberg Mitson, October 30, 1976, San Jose, California, California State University, Fullerton, Oral History Program, Japanese American Project, 31.

82. Merritt and Brown, "Final Report."

83. Merritt and Brown, "Final Report."

84. Merritt and Brown, "Final Report."

85. Merritt and Brown, "Final Report."

86. Merritt and Brown, "Final Report."

87. "Evacuees Pay Indicated at $40 to $45," *San Francisco Call-Bulletin*, March 27, 1942, 1; Merritt and Brown, "Final Report."

88. Merritt and Brown, "Final Report."

89. Hayashi, *Democratizing the Enemy*, 153–54.

90. Merritt and Brown, "Final Report."

91. Merritt and Brown, "Final Report."

92. Alexander Leighton, "Labor Relations in Relocation Centers, Community Analysis Report No. 10," October 28, 1944, folder 28, box 1, JARC, 17–18.

93. Leighton, "Report No. 10," 18. For more on the Heart Mountain camp—particularly other strikes and protests—see Art Hansen, "The 1944 Nisei Draft at Heart Mountain, Wyoming: Its Relationship to Historical Representation of the World War II Japanese American Evacuation," *Magazine of History* 10, no. 4 (1996); Takashi Fujitani, "Cultures of Resistance: Japanese American Draft Resistance in Transnational Perspective," in *A Matter of Conscience: Essays on the World War II Heart Mountain Draft Resistance Movement*, ed. Mike Mackey (Powell, WY: Western History Publications, 2002), 21–38; Mike Mackey, *Heart Mountain: Life in Wyoming's Concentration Camp* (Powell, WY: Western History Publications, 2002); Louis Fiset, "The Hospital Strike of June 24, 1934," in *Remembering Heart Mountain: Essays on Japanese American Internment in Wyoming*, ed. Mike Mackey (Powell, WY: Western Historical Publications, 1998); Phil Roberts, "Temporarily Sidetracked by Emotionalism: Wyoming Residents Respond to Relocation," in Mackey, *Remembering Heart Mountain*, 38–39; Frank T. Inouye, "Immediate Origins of the Heart Mountain Draft Resistance Movement," in Mackey, *Remembering Heart Mountain*, 122–23; Frank Emi, "Draft Resistance at the Heart Mountain Concentration Camp and the Fair Play Committee," in *Frontiers of Asian American Studies: Writing, Research, Commentary*, ed. Gail M. Nomura, Russell Endo, Stephen H. Sumida, and Russell Leong (Pullman: Washington State University Press, 1989), 41–69; and Douglas Nelson, *Heart Mountain: The Story of an American Concentration Camp* (Madison: State Historical Society of Wisconsin, 1976).

94. Leighton, "Report No. 10," 16.

95. Leighton, "Report No. 10," 16.

96. Leighton, "Report No. 10," 17; Connie Y. Chiang, *Nature Behind Barbed Wire: An Environmental History of the Japanese American Incarceration* (New York: Oxford University Press, 2018), 82 (emphasis my own). For more on the Topaz camp, see Sandra Taylor, *Jewel of the Desert: Japanese American Internment at Topaz* (Berkeley: University of California Press, 1993); Leonard J. Arrington, *The Price of Prejudice: The Japanese-American Relocation Center in Utah During World War II*, 2nd ed. (Delta, UT: Topaz Museum, 1997); Eleanor Gerard, "A Teacher at Topaz," in *Japanese Americans: From Relocation to Redress*, ed. Roger Daniels, Sandra C. Taylor, and Harry H. L. Kitano (Salt Lake City: University of Utah Press, 1986), 38–43; Toyo Suyemoto and Susan B. Richardson, *I Call to Remembrance: Toyo Suyemoto's Years of Internment* (Brunswick, NJ: Rutgers University Press, 2007); Yoshiko Uchida, "Topaz, City of Dust," *Utah Historical Quarterly* 48, no. 3 (1980): 234–43; and Yoshiko Uchida, *Desert Exile: The Uprooting of a Japanese American Family* (Seattle: University of Washington Press, 1982).

97. Leighton, "Report No. 10," 18.

98. Leighton, "Report No. 10," 19.

99. Telephone conversation between Bendetsen and DeWitt, December 4, 1943, folder 323.3, box 59, RG 499. For more on Minidoka, see Eric Muller, "The Minidoka Draft Resisters in a Federal Kangaroo Court," in *Nikkei in the Pacific Northwest*, ed. by Louis Fiset and Gail M. Nomura (Seattle: University of Washington Press, 2005), 171–89; Jeffrey F. Burton and Mary M.

Farrell, *This Is Minidoka: An Archeological Survey of Minidoka Internment National Monument, Idaho* (Tucson, AZ: Western Archeological and Conservation Center, 2001); Laura Maeda, "Life at Minidoka: A Personal History of the Japanese-American Relocation," *Pacific Historian* 20, no. 4 (1976): 379–87; Amy Lowe Merger, *Minidoka Internment National Monument: Historic Resource Study* (Seattle: National Park Service, 2005); James M. Sakoda, "Minidoka: An Analysis of Changing Patterns of Social Interaction" (PhD diss., University of California, Berkeley, 1949); and Robert C. Sims, "The Japanese American Experience in Idaho," *Idaho Yesterdays* (1978): 2–10.

100. Chiyoko Yano, interview by Megan Asaka, Berkeley, California, August 1, 2008, transcript, Densho Digital Archive.

101. For more on the "civilian isolation centers," see Bruce D. Louthan and Lloyd M. Pierson, "Moab Japanese-American Isolation Center: The Dark Postlude in the History of the Dalton Wells CCC Camp," *Canyon Legacy: A Journal of the Dan O'Laurie Museum—Moab, Utah*, 19 (Fall/Winter 1993): 28–31; Lloyd Pierson, "The Moab Concentration Camp," *Zephyr*, July 1989, 20–21; Jeffery F. Burton, Mary M. Farrell, Florence B. Lord, and Richard W. Lord, "Citizen Isolation Centers," in *Confinement and Ethnicity: An Overview of World War II Japanese American Relocation Sites*, rev. ed. (Seattle: University of Washington Press, 2002), 325–30; Takako Day, *Show Me the Way to Go Home: The Moral Dilemma of Kibei No No Boys in World War II Incarceration Camps* (Middlebury, CT: Wren Song Press, 2014); Richard Drinnon, *Keeper of Concentration Camps: Dillon S. Myer and American Racism* (Berkeley: University of California Press, 1987); Tetsuden Kashima, *Judgment Without Trial: Japanese American Imprisonment During World War II* (Seattle: University of Washington Press, 2003); Eileen Tamura, *In Defense of Justice: Joseph Kurihara and the Japanese American Struggle for Equality* (Urbana: University of Illinois Press, 2013); Debra Bedsteer, "Leupp, Arizona: A Shared Historic Space for the Navajo Nation and Japanese Americans," *Discover Nikkei*, June 28, 2008, http://www.discovernikkei.org/en/journal/2008/6/28/enduring-communities/.

102. National Park Service, "Tule Lake Segregation Center," 3, https://www.nps.gov/tule/planyourvisit/upload/segregation_center_6-10.pdf (accessed August 21, 2018).

103. For more in-depth discussions of Tule Lake in the general literature, see Gary Okihiro, "Tule Lake Under Martial Law: A Study in Japanese Resistance," *Journal of Ethnic Studies* 5, no. 3 (1977): 71–85; Gary Okihiro, "Religion and Resistance in America's Concentration Camps"; William Minoru Hohri, *Resistance: Challenging America's Wartime Internment of Japanese-Americans* (Lomita, CA: Epistolarian, 2001); Cherstin M. Lyon, *Prisoners and Patriots: Japanese American Wartime Citizenship, Civil Disobedience, and Historical Memory* (Philadelphia: Temple University Press, 2012); Heather Fryer, "'The Song of the Stitches': Factionalism and Feminism at Tule Lake," *Signs* 35, no. 3 (2010): 673–98; Barney Shallit, *Song of Anger: Tales of Tule Lake* (Fullerton, CA: Oral History Program, 2001); Patrick O. Gudridge, "The Constitution Glimpsed from Tule Lake," *Law and Contemporary Problems* 68, no. 2 (2005): 88–118; Eric L. Mueller, *Free to Die for Their Country: The Story of the Japanese American Draft Resisters* (Chicago: University of Chicago Press, 2001); Teruko Kumei, "Skeleton in the Closet: The Japanese American Hokoku Seinen-dan and Their 'Disloyal' Activities at the Tule Lake Segregation Center During World War II," *Japanese Journal of American Studies* 7

(1996): 67–102; John Ross and Reiko Ross, *Second Kinenhi: Reflections on Tule Lake* (San Francisco: Tule Lake Committee, 2000); and Barbara Takei and Judy Tachibana, *Tule Lake Revisited* (San Francisco: Tule Lake Committee, 2012).

104. In 1944, President Roosevelt signed Public Law 405 (later codified with a denaturalization bill signed in July by Attorney General Francis Biddle), which allowed for US citizens to renounce their citizenship, but only during times of war. Only approximately 600 Nisei signed up for renunciation by December of the same year, yet as rumors grew that punishments would be swift and few would be accepted "on the outside" because of the negative affiliation with Tule Lake, more Nisei expressed their desire for renunciation. Ultimately 6,000 would apply for renunciation and repatriation to Japan, mainly out of frustration and fear. In October 1945, Tule Lake was transferred from the WRA to the Department of Justice, which agreed to hold hearings for anyone who wanted to change their minds of the renunciation after a hearing. More than 3,000 asked for a hearing, and only 406 remained on the list for deportation. For more on renunciation, repatriation, and resulting legal cases, see Mae Ngai, *Impossible Subjects: Illegal Americans and the Making of Modern America* (Princeton, NJ: Princeton University Press, 2004), 192; and Barbara Takei, "Legalizing Detention: Segregated Japanese Americans and the Justice Department's Renunciation Program," *Journal of the Shaw Historical Library* 19 (2005): 88–92.

105. National Park Service, "Tule Lake Segregation Center," 3.

106. "Translation: True Picture of This Camp," undated, folder 323.3—Tule Lake, box 59, RG 499.

107. "Meeting of the Spanish Consulate," November 3, 1943, folder 4, box 43, Verne Austin Papers, 20.

108. "Meeting of the Spanish Consulate," 20.

109. "Meeting of the Spanish Consulate," 20.

110. Telephone conversation between Colonel Meek and Colonel Moffitt, October 20, 1943, folder 323.3, box 60, RG 499, 2.

111. "Meeting in Mr. Best's Office at 8:45 A.M.," October 26, 1943, folder 4, box 43, Verne Austin Papers, 2.

112. "Meeting in Mr. Best's Office," 2.

113. "Meeting in Mr. Best's Office," 4.

114. "Meeting in Mr. Best's Office," 4.

115. Rosalie Wax, "Longitudinal Oral History of George and Joyce Kunitani, 1944–1945," BANCMSS 83/115c, Rosalie H. Wax Papers, Bancroft Library, 4. Wax originally did not list the true identity of Kuratomi in her oral history, using "Kunitani" instead.

116. Wax, "Longitudinal Oral History," 4.

117. Gary Okihiro, "Tule Lake Riot," https://reference.jrank.org/japanese/Tule_Lake_Riot .html (accessed May 17, 2019).

118. Telephone conversation between Colonel Washburne and Colonel Wilson, January 13, 1944 folder 323.3, box 60, RG 499.

119. Telephone conversation between Colonel Washburne and Colonel Wilson.

120. See Mark H. Leff, "The Politics of Sacrifice on the American Home Front in World War II," *Journal of American History* 77, no. 4 (1991): 1296–318.

121. For a more in-depth discussion, see Henry Yu's *Thinking Orientals: Migration, Contact, and Exoticism in Modern America* (New York: Oxford University Press, 2001).

122. "WRA Community Analysis Section, Community Analysis Report No. 10—Labor Relations in Relocation Centers," October 28, 1944, folder 1–28, box 1, JARC, 2, 9, 10.

123. "WRA Community Analysis Section, Community Analysis Report No. 10," 9.

Chapter 4

1. Speech by John Collier, June 17, 1942, folder—Internment of Japs on Indian Lands, 1942, Part I, box 21, RG 75, 1.

2. Speech by Collier, 2.

3. Kristen L. Michaud, "Japanese American Internment Centers on United States Indian Reservations: A Geographic Approach to the Relocation Centers in Arizona, 1942–1945" (master's thesis, University of Massachusetts Amherst, 2008), 35–36.

4. Collier to Harold Ickes, June 10, 1942, folder—Internment of Japs on Indian Lands, 1942, Part I, box 21, RG 75, 2.

5. See Orin Starn, "Engineering Internment: Anthropologists and the War Relocation Authority," *American Ethnologist* 13, no. 4 (1986): 700–720; Peter T. Suzuki, "Anthropologists in the Wartime Camps for Japanese Americans: A Documentary Study," *Dialectical Anthropology* 6, no. 1 (1981): 23–60; and Alice Yang Murray, *Historical Memories of the Japanese American Internment and the Struggle for Redress* (Stanford, CA: Stanford University Press, 2008), for more on the sociological and anthropological studies completed by Leighton and others at Poston. David Price's *Anthropological Intelligence: The Deployment and Neglect of American Anthropology in the Second World War* (Durham, NC: Duke University Press, 2008) also provides a thorough overview of the social sciences at work during the war.

6. See Wendi Yamashita, "The Colonial and the Carceral: Building Relationships Between Japanese and Indigenous Groups in the Owens Valley," *Amerasia Journal* 42, no. 1 (2016): 121–38; Cynthia Wu, "A Comparative Analysis of Indigenous Displacement and the World War II Japanese American Internment," *Amerasia Journal* 42, no. 1 (2016): 1–15; Karen J. Leong and Myla Vincenti Carpio, "Carceral States: Covering Indigenous and Asian American Experiences in the Americas," *Amerasia Journal* 42, no. 1 (2016): vii–xvii, and "Carceral Subjugations: Gila River Indian Community and Incarceration of Japanese Americans on Its Land," *Amerasia Journal* 42, no. 1 (2016): 103–20.

7. See Elmer R. Rusco, "John Collier: Architect of Sovereignty or Assimilation?," *American Indian Quarterly* 15, no. 1(1991): 49–54; John Laukaitis, "Indians at Work and John Collier's Campaign for Educational Reform, 1933–1945," *American Education History Journal* 32 (Fall 2007): 97–105; Karin Huebner, "An Unexpected Alliance: Stella Atwood, the California Clubwomen, John Collier, and the Indians of the Southwest, 1917–1934," *Pacific Historical Review* 78, no. 1(2009): 337–66; and Lawrence C. Kelly, *The Assault on Assimilation: John Collier and the Origins of Indian Policy Reform* (Albuquerque: University of New Mexico Press, 1983), for more on Collier's life and interest in Native Americans.

8. See Laurence Hauptman, "A Harbinger of the Indian New Deal," *American Indian Quarterly* 43, no. 1 (1991): 33–34; Jennifer McLerran, *A New Deal for Native American Art:*

Indian Arts and Federal Policy, 1933–1943 (Tucson: University of Arizona Press, 2009); and Graham D. Taylor, *The New Deal and American Indian Tribalism: The Administration of the Indian Reorganization, 1934–45* (Lincoln: University of Nebraska Press, 1980), for more on the Indian New Deal.

9. Taylor, *New Deal and American Indian Tribalism*, 120–22.

10. Felix S. Cohen, Office of the Solicitor, Department of the Interior, *Federal Indian Law* (Washington, DC: Government Printing Office, 1942), 296.

11. Memo to Collier, Subject: Pima W.R.A. Agreements, April 13, 1942, folder—Internment of Japs on Indian Lands, 1942, Part I, box 21, RG 75.

12. Memo of understanding between the Director of the WRA and the Secretary of the Interior, folder—Internment of Japs on Indian Lands, 1942, Part I, box 21, RG 75, 2.

13. Memo of understanding, 3–4.

14. Memo of understanding, 3–4.

15. Memo of understanding, 3–4.

16. Memo of understanding, 3–4.

17. Edward H. Spicer, "Attitude of Local Indians," October 18, 1942, folder J 10.10 (4 of 6), JERS.

18. Resolution of Tribal Council for Transfer of Land, April 13, 1942, folder—Internment of Japs on Indian Lands, 1942, Part I, box 21, RG 75; Brian Masaru Hayashi, *Democratizing the Enemy: The Japanese American Internment* (Princeton, NJ: Princeton University Press, 2004), 89.

19. Memo of understanding, 3–4.

20. Susan M. Rigdon, *The Culture Façade: Art, Science, and Politics in the Work of Oscar Lewis* (Urbana: University of Illinois Press, 1988), 27.

21. Rigdon, *The Culture Façade*, 27.

22. John Evans to Collier, June 7, 1942, folder—Internment of Japs on Indian Lands, 1942, Part I, box 21, RG 75, 2.

23. E. R. Fryer, "A Study of Administrative Experimentation in Relocating the Japanese," April 2, 1942, folder—Internment of Japs on Indian Lands, 1942, Part I, box 21, RG 75.

24. John Collier, "Annual Report," folder—Internment of Japs on Indian Lands, 1942, Part I, box 21, RG 75, 2.

25. Collier to Thompson, April 16, 1942, folder—Internment of Japs on Indian Lands, 1942, Part I, box 21, RG 75; Greg Robinson, *A Tragedy of Democracy: Japanese Confinement in North America* (New York: Columbia University Press, 2009), 154–55.

26. Alexander Leighton, *The Governing of Men: General Principles and Recommendations Based on Experience at a Japanese Relocation Camp* (Princeton, NJ: Princeton University Press, 1946), 49–51.

27. Woehlke to Collier, March 18, 1942, folder—Internment of Japs on Indian Lands, 1942, Part I, box 21, RG 75.

28. Woehlke to Collier.

29. Eisenhower to Collier, April 26, 1942, folder—Internment of Japs on Indian Lands, 1942, Part I, box 21, RG 75.

30. Eisenhower to Collier.

31. Leighton, *Governing of Men*, 55.

32. Leighton, *Governing of Men*, 55.

33. Leighton, *Governing of Men*, 61. For more on Poston, see Paul Bailey, *A City in the Sun: The Japanese Concentration Camp at Poston* (Los Angeles: Westmoreland Press, 1971); Matthew T. Estes and Donald H. Estes, "Hot Enough to Melt Iron: The San Diego Nikkei Experience, 1942–1946," *Journal of San Diego History* 42, no. 3 (1996): 126–73, and "Letters from Camp: Poston—the First Year," *Journal of the West* 38, no. 2 (1999): 22–33; Thomas Y. Fujita-Rony, "Arizona and Japanese American History: The World War II Colorado River Relocation Center," *Journal of the Southwest* 47, no. 2 (2005): 209–32; and Donald Teruo Hata Jr., "Inside an American Concentration Camp: Japanese American Resistance at Poston, Arizona," *Southern California Quarterly* 79, no. 1 (1997): 134–36, for more descriptions of Poston.

34. Leighton, *Governing of Men*, 68–70.

35. Leighton, *Governing of Men*, 64–65.

36. Edward H. Spicer, Asael T. Hansen, Katherine Luomala, and Marvin K. Opler, *Impounded People: Japanese Americans in the Relocation Centers* (Tucson: University of Arizona Press, 1969), 54.

37. Spicer et al., *Impounded People*, 55.

38. Spicer et al., *Impounded People*, 55.

39. Spicer et al., *Impounded People*, 57.

40. Spicer et al., *Impounded People*, 56.

41. Tamie Tsuchiyama, "Poston: The Characteristics of the Project Population: A Handbook of General Statistics," January 27, 1943, JERS, http://vm133.lib.berkeley.edu:8080/xtf3/search?rmode=jarda&docsPerPage=10&sort=title&keyword=Tamie (accessed February 13, 2020).

42. Speech by Ira K. Evans, July 16, 1942, folder 2, box 10, JARC, 1.

43. Speech by Evans, 2.

44. Speech by Evans, 2.

45. Leighton, *Governing of Men*, 96.

46. Leighton, *Governing of Men*, 92.

47. Leighton, *Governing of Men*, 92.

48. Leighton, *Governing of Men*, 92.

49. Leighton, *Governing of Men*, 96.

50. Leighton, *Governing of Men*, 96.

51. Leighton, *Governing of Men*, 81.

52. Leighton, *Governing of Men*, 107.

53. Leighton, *Governing of Men*, 104.

54. Leighton, *Governing of Men*, 104.

55. "Temporary Council Report," August, 19, 1942, folder 25, box 6, JARC, 3.

56. "Temporary Council Report," 4.

57. Leighton, *Governing of Men*, 104.

58. Leighton, *Governing of Men*, 104.

59. Leighton, *Governing of Men*, 104.

60. "Adobe Work Observation," June 14, 1942, folder 33, box 9, JARC, 1; "Structure of the Organization: An Interview with Bud Kinoshitani," July 1942, folder 33, box 9, JARC, 3.

61. "Adobe Project," 2, folder 33, box 9, JARC.

62. Iko Day, *Alien Capital: Asian Racialization and the Logic of Settler Colonial Capitalism* (Durham, NC: Duke University Press, 2016), 33–34.

63. Work Projects at Poston," January 31, 1943, folder 32, box 9, JARC, 2.

64. Leighton, *Governing of Men*, 105.

65. "Meeting of Temporary Council of Poston, "August 19, 1942, folder 25, box 6, JARC,15.

66. "Interview with Ben Sakamoto, Attitudes Toward Poston's Agricultural Project," June 16, 1943, folder 36, box 9, JARC, 1.

67. Karl Lillquist, "Imprisoned in the Desert: The Geography of World War II-Era Japanese American Relocation Centers in the Western United States," Washington State Office of Superintendent of Public Instruction through Interagency Agreement # 23-0782 Between OSPI and Central Washington University, September 2008, 410–12.

68. Lillquist, "Imprisoned in the Desert," 425.

69. Vernon Kennedy, "General Report of the Employment Situation," November 30, 1942, folder 3, box 10, JARC, 1; "Department of Agriculture Report," November 9, 1942, folder 3, box 10, JARC, 1.

70. Kennedy, "General Report of the Employment Situation," 4.

71. "Public Works, Engineering Department," June 1, 1943, folder 58, box 9, JARC, 4–5.

72. Michaud, "Japanese American Internment Centers on United States Indian Reservations," 50.

73. Leighton to Wade Head and John Collier, February 22, 1943, folder—Internment of Japs on Indian Lands, 1942, Part II, box 21, RG 75, 2.

74. Leighton to Head and Collier, 2.

75. Henry Suzuki to W. C. Sharp, August 22, 1942, Cornell, folder 39, box 9, JARC; "Over-All Committee Meeting (Agriculture Committee)," October 26, 1942, folder 36, box 9, JARC, 4.

76. Suzuki to Sharp.

77. Suzuki to Sharp.

78. "Meeting of the Temporary Council," August 19, 1942, folder 25, box 6, JARC, 3.

79. Suzuki to Sharp.

80. Richard Nishimoto, "The Firebreak Gang," folder 34, box 9, JARC, 4, 2.

81. For more information on the Japanese American Evacuation and Resettlement Study, Nishimoto, and Tsuchiyama, see Dorothy Swaine Thomas and Richard S. Nishimoto, *The Spoilage: Japanese-American Evacuation and Resettlement During World War II* (Berkeley: University of California Press, 2010); Richard S. Nishimoto, *Inside an American Concentration Camp: Japanese American Resistance at Poston*, ed. Lane Ryo Hirabayashi (Tucson: University of Arizona Press, 1995); and Lane Ryo Hirabayashi, *The Politics of Fieldwork: Research in an American Concentration Camp* (Tucson: University of Arizona Press, 1999). Nishimoto's employment by the administration at Poston and close dealings with the sociologists who stud-

ied the prison may have colored and shaped one of his other works, a history of the WRA and the Poston prison, but his descriptions of the firebreak gang as well as the challenges they faced are vibrant and dynamic and provide insight into the labor performed at Poston.

82. Nishimoto, "Firebreak Gang," 3.

83. Nishimoto, "Firebreak Gang," 3.

84. Nishimoto, "Firebreak Gang," 3.

85. Nishimoto, "Firebreak Gang," 7.

86. Nishimoto, "Firebreak Gang," 8.

87. Nishimoto, "Firebreak Gang," 9.

88. Nishimoto, "Firebreak Gang," 13.

89. Nishimoto, "Firebreak Gang," 15.

90. Nishimoto, "Firebreak Gang," 16.

91. Nishimoto, "Firebreak Gang," 16.

92. Nishimoto, "Firebreak Gang," 20.

93. Nishimoto, "Firebreak Gang," 20.

94. Yoshiki Yoshida to W. C. Sharp, August 22 and September 25, 1942, folder 48, box 9, JARC.

95. Yoshida to Sharp, 22.

96. Leighton, *Governing of Men*, 81–82.

97. Leighton, *Governing of Men*, 83.

98. Leighton, *Governing of Men*, 86.

99. Hayashi, *Democratizing the Enemy*, 28–29.

100. Nishimoto, "Firebreak Gang," 27.

101. Nishimoto, "Firebreak Gang," 28.

102. Nishimoto, *Inside an American Concentration Camp*, xxxvii.

103. United States Department of the Interior, "Community Government in War Relocation Centers" (Washington, DC: Government Printing Office, 1942), 25.

104. Hayashi, *Democratizing the Enemy*, 110–11.

105. Leighton, *Governing of Men*, 11.

106. "Community Government in War Relocation Centers," 22.

107. David McFadden, "Community Analysis—Strike at Poston," December 3, 1942, folder 3, box 10, JARC, 10.

108. McFadden, "Community Analysis," 10.

109. Leighton, *Governing of Men*, 164–65.

110. Leighton, *Governing of Men*, 165.

111. Leighton, *Governing of Men*, 166.

112. Leighton, *Governing of Men*, 167; "Monthly Report on the Colorado River War Relocation Project, No. 2, November 11–December 11, 1942, folder 28, box 2, JARC, 1; McFadden, "Community Analysis," 14.

113. Leighton, *Governing of Men*, 166.

114. Leighton, *Governing of Men*, 167.

115. McFadden, "Community Analysis," 16.

116. McFadden, "Community Analysis," 16.

117. Hayashi, *Democratizing the Enemy*, 131–33.

118. "The People of Poston II States Its Case," folder 4, box 10, JARC, 1.

119. "The People of Poston II States Its Case."

120. Leighton, *Governing of Men*, 167.

121. Leighton, *Governing of Men*, 170.

122. "Coddling Won't Work," *St. Louis Globe-Democrat*, November 10, 1943, 4; "Tule Hot Potato," *Indianapolis Star*, November 30, 1943, 2.

123. Leighton, *Governing of Men*, 190.

124. Leighton, *Governing of Men*, 186.

125. John Powell and Vernon Kennedy, memo, November 26, 1942, folder 4, box 10, JARC.

126. Kennedy, "General Report on Employment Situation," November 30, 1942, folder 3, box 10, JARC, 3.

127. Wade Head, "Cooperation of Loyal Citizens Lauded by Project Director in Public Statement Regarding Poston One Disturbance," *Press Bulletin*, November 24, 1942, 1.

128. Head, "Cooperation," 1.

129. "Staff Meeting," February 23, 1942, folder 19, box 2, JARC, 2.

130. Theodore Haas to Phillip Glick, January 1, 1943, folder 3, box 10, JARC, 1.

131. Haas to Glick, 3.

132. Bureau of Sociological Research, "We Came to the Beginning of the Year: A Brief History of Poston I, May to December," folder 11, box 2, JARC, 22–23.

133. Leighton, "Sociological Journal," November 12, 1942, folder 7, box 10, JARC, 2; Bureau of Sociological Research, "We Came to the Beginning," 16; Robinson, *Tragedy of Democracy*, 154–55.

134. Wade Head to Collier, February 6, 1943, folder—Correspondence regarding Evacuees, etc., box 22, RG 75.

135. McFadden, "Community Analysis," 3.

136. "Monthly Report on the Colorado River War Relocation Center," June 10, 1943, folder 28, box 2, JARC, 2.

137. Monthly Report on the Colorado River War Relocation Center," 5.

138. "Source of Information from an Issei," December 3, 1942, folder 3, box 10, JARC, 1.

139. Haas to Edwin Ferguson, October 13 1942, folder 3, box 10, JARC, 7.

140. Haas to Ferguson.

141. Mary Ellicott Arnold and Lionel Perkins, "Report of the Educational Work at the Japanese Relocation Center at Poston, Arizona," folder—Misc. WRA Publications I, box 22, RG 75, 9.

142. "Minutes of the Joint Meeting of the Block Managers and the Community Council," October 30, 1942, folder 9, box 4, JARC, 2; "Open Forum-Address by Mr. D. Myers," November 17, 1942, folder 9, box 4, JARC, 1.

143. Collier, Memo, "Unrealized Food Production Capacities at Japanese Centers," January 7, 1943, folder—Internment of Japs on Indian Lands, Part II, box 21, RG 75, 3.

144. Albert Wathan to Collier, April 16, 1932, folder—Correspondence Regarding Evacuees, box 21, RG 75.

145. Reflections on Administrative Problems, folder—Internment of Japs on Indian Lands, 1942, Part II, box 22, RG 75, 29.

146. "Official Statement Awaited on Strike at Japanese Center," *Los Angeles Times*, November 21, 1943, 3.

147. "Evacuee Camp Terrorized by Pro-Axis Japs," *San Francisco Examiner*, November 24, 1942, 1.

148. "Tenny Committee Will Probe Jap Camp Laxity," *San Francisco Examiner*, November 20, 1943, 6.

149. Dillon S. Myer, *Uprooted Americans: The Japanese Americans and the War Relocation Authority During World War II* (Tucson: University of Arizona Press, 1971), 44–45.

150. Myer, *Uprooted Americans*, 107; Hayashi, *Democratizing the Enemy*, 148–49.

151. Myer, *Uprooted Americans*, 93.

152. Myer, *Uprooted Americans*, 94; George Malone, "Record of the Hearing Held at Colorado River War Relocation Project," March 7, 1943, folder 26, box 11, JARC, 3.

153. "Local Administration-Report on Visit of the Dies committee," June 19, 1943, 1, folder 24, box 11, JARC, 1.

154. Local Administration-Report on Visit of the Dies committee," 4; Wade Head, "Report on the Visit of the Dies Sub-Committee to Poston," folder 25, box 11, JARC, 2.

155. R. N. Parnell to Wade Head, June 15, 1943, folder 24, box 11, JARC, 2.

156. Harold H. Townsend, "An American Battlefield: A Factual Report of Conditions at the Japanese Relocation Camps at Poston, Arizona," December 30, 1942, folder 25, box 11, JARC.

157. Statement from Father Clement, June, 23, 1942, folder 25, box 11, JARC.

158. Myer, *Uprooted Americans*, 100.

159. Myer, *Uprooted Americans*, 100; "Minority Report of the Honorable Herman P. Eberharter," August 25, 1943, folder 26, box 11, JARC, 1,3.

160. Robinson, *A Tragedy of Democracy*, 155.

161. "Monthly Report on the CRI," June 10, 1943, NARA; "Meeting Minutes—Block Managers," March 2, 1943, folder 11, box 4, JARC, 2; "Manpower Commission," August 23, 1943, folder 18, box 6, JARC, 2; "Manpower—Interview with Takahashi, Manpower Shortage," April 21, 1943, folder 13, box 19, JARC, 2.

162. Confidential Memo to the Secretary, July 6,1943, folder—Correspondence Regarding Evacuees, box 22, 4.

163. "Strike: Observation by EHS—Conversation with VK," November 25, 1942, folder 5, box 10, JARC, 1.

Chapter 5

1. See Robert Asahina, *Just Americans: How Japanese Americans Won a War at Home and Abroad* (New York: Gotham Books, 2006); Masayo Duus, *Unlikely Liberators: The Men of the 100th and 442nd* (Honolulu: University of Hawaii Press, 1987); and Linda Tamura, *Nisei Soldiers Break Their Silence: Returning Home to Hood River* (Seattle: University of Washington Press, 2012), for more on Nisei serving in the army during World War II.

2. Brenda L. Moore, *Serving Our Country: Japanese American Women in the Military During World War II* (Berkeley: University of California Press, 2003), 10–15.

3. Commission on Wartime Relocation and Internment of Civilians, *Personal Justice Denied: Report of the Commission on Wartime Relocation and Internment of Civilians* (Seattle: University of Washington Press, and Washington, DC: Civil Liberties Public Education Fund, 1997), 196. This document is also available as a PDF at https://www.archives.gov/files/research /japanese-americans/justice-denied/chapter-7.pdf. John Okada's classic novel *No-No Boy* (originally published in 1957) also provides an in-depth literary analysis of the questionnaire and its aftermath.

4. See Cherstin Lyon, *Prisons and Patriots: Japanese American Wartime Citizenship, Civil Disobedience, and Historical Memory* (Philadelphia: Temple University Press, 2011), for more on resistance to the questionnaire and the draft. Lucy Salyer's "Baptism by Fire: Race, Military Service, and U.S. Citizenship Policy, 1918–1935," *Journal of American History* 91, no. 3 (2004): 847–76, also provides an interesting discussion of military citizenship and masculinity more broadly.

5. US Congress, House, *Subcommittee on Japanese War Relocation Centers Report to the Committee on Military Affairs, United States Senate*, 78th Congress, 1st sess., 1943, S. Res. 101 and 111, 222–24, https://babel.hathitrust.org/cgi/pt?id=osu.32435007424989;view=1up;seq=3.

6. "'Parole' Plan Mapped for Interned Japanese," *Los Angeles Examiner*, August 1, 1942, 3.

7. See Ellen Wu, *The Color of Success: Asian Americans and the Origins of the Model Minority* (Princeton, NJ: Princeton University Press, 2013), 16–43, 150–52; and Madeline Y. Hsu, *The Good Immigrants: How the Yellow Peril Became the Model Minority* (Princeton, NJ: Princeton University Press, 2017), for more on the idea of the model minority in development in the post–World War II years. Although Hsu's work focuses more on Chinese Americans and foreign relations, her discussion adds important context.

8. "Interview with Takahashi, Phd. T. S.," April 21, 1943, folder 19, box 2, JARC, 1–3.

9. Dillon Myer, *Uprooted Americans: The Japanese Americans and the War Relocation Authority During World War II* (Tucson: University of Arizona Press, 1971), 132. Alice Yang Murray provides a brilliant discussion of using Myer's account of incarceration as a source in *Historical Memories of the Japanese American Internment and the Struggle for Redress* (Stanford, CA: Stanford University Press, 2008), 52–102. Myer's account is naturally celebratory and defensive of the WRA and his role in it yet also revealing for the views on labor and other facets of incarceration.

10. Myer, *Uprooted Americans*, 134.

11. Myer, *Uprooted Americans*, 133.

12. Myer, *Uprooted Americans*, 135. See also US Department of the Interior, War Agency Liquidation Unit, *People in Motion: The Postwar Adjustment of the Evacuated Japanese Americans* (Washington, DC: Government Printing Office, 1947).

13. Commission on Wartime Relocation and Internment of Civilians, *Personal Justice Denied*, 199–200.

14. Myer, *Uprooted Americans*, 139.

15. Myer, *Uprooted Americans*, 139; Commission on Wartime Relocation and Internment of Civilians, *Personal Justice Denied*, 202.

16. Commission on Wartime Relocation and Internment of Civilians, *Personal Justice Denied*, 202. For more on the Japanese American Joint Board, see Eric L. Muller, *The American Inquisition: The Hunt for Japanese American Disloyalty in World War II* (Chapel Hill: University of North Carolina Press, 2007), 39–67.

17. Myer, *Uprooted Americans*, 139; "WRA Institutes New Relocation Assistance Policy," *Minidoka Irrigator,* June 2, 1945, 1.

18. "Special Agricultural Meeting Held in Block 37 Office," July 8, 1943, folder 37, box 9, JARC, 1.

19. "Special Agricultural Meeting," 2–3; "Sentiments in Regard to Agriculture," folder 32, box 9, JARC, 2.

20. "Block Managers Meeting Minutes," June 25, 1943, 1, folder 16, box 4, JARC, 1.

21. "Monthly Report of the Colorado River War Relocation Center for Evacuated Japanese," July 10, 1943, folder 33, box 1, JARC, 4.

22. "Monthly Report of the Colorado River War Relocation Center," 4.

23. "Monthly Report of the Colorado River War Relocation Center," 5.

24. "Monthly Report of the Colorado River War Relocation Center," 5.

25. "Monthly Report of the Colorado River War Relocation Center," 5.

26. "Monthly Report of the Colorado River War Relocation Center," 5. See also "Report of the Co-ordinating Committee to the Spanish Consul," May 2, 1944, folder 1, box 44, Verne Austin Papers. Interestingly, this report from the Bureau of Sociological Research was one of the most direct admittances from any agency associated or affiliated with the incarceration project that Japanese Americans were, in fact, imprisoned in the "relocation centers."

27. "Monthly Report of the Colorado River War Relocation Center," 5.

28. "Monthly Report of the Colorado River War Relocation Center," 5.

29. "Monthly Report of the Colorado River War Relocation Center," 5.

30. "Monthly Report of the Colorado River War Relocation Center," 5.

31. Myer to Leighton, September 21, 1943, folder 33, box 1, JARC, 1.

32. Myer to Leighton

33. Myer to Leighton

34. Myer to Leighton, 2.

35. Myer to Leighton, 2.

36. Myer to Leighton, 2.

37. "Outgroup Relations: Personal Journal of T.S., Subjects: DeWitt's Statement in Poston Chronicle," April 14, 1943, JARC.

38. Bob Kazaki, "Re-evacuation," April 28, 1943, folder 22, box 10, JARC.

39. Kazaki, "Re-evacuation."

40. Kazaki, "Re-evacuation."

41. Kazaki, "Re-evacuation."

42. See Wu, *The Color of Success*, 157, and Patrick O. Gudridge, "Remember 'Endo'?," *Harvard Law Review* 116, no. 7 (2003): 1933–70, for more on the *Endo* case.

43. Elissa Kikuye Ouchida, "Nisei Employees vs. California State Personnel Board: A Journal of *Ex parte Mitsuye Endo, 1942–1947,*" *Pan Japan* 7 (Spring/Fall 2011): 2, 7–8. See also Brian Niiya, "Mitsuye Endo," http://encyclopedia.densho.org/Mitsuye_Endo/, and Peter H.

Irons, *Justice at War: The Story of the Japanese American Internment Cases* (Berkeley: University of California Press, 1993), 101–4.

44. "Washington Newsletter," *Heart Mountain Sentinel*, October 21, 1944, 1.

45. See Victoria W. Wolcott, *Remaking Respectability: African American Women in Interwar Detroit* (Chapel Hill: University of North Carolina Press, 2001); and Evelyn Brooks Higginbotham, *Righteous Discontent: The Women's Movement in the Black Baptist Church, 1880–1920* (Cambridge, MA: Harvard University Press, 1993), for more on respectability politics in the pursuit of civil rights for African Americans. An extensive body of literature also exists on the role of respectability politics in the fight against school segregation and other landmark cases for African Americans.

46. An active member of the Quaker community in Seattle, Hirabayashi consciously decided to violate the curfew in May by remaining in the university library in the evening. A little over a week later, Hirabayashi presented himself to the FBI office in Seattle and stated his intentions to continue to violate the curfew as well as other components of EO 9066, which resulted in his imprisonment. Hirabayashi received support from local Seattle-based activist organizations and later the ACLU to appeal his case after the King County court returned a guilty verdict on both counts in October 1942. Hirabayashi's case would eventually be heard by the Supreme Court in 1943 and become one of four lawsuits challenging the constitutionality of incarceration, including Endo's legal fight.

See Stephanie Bangarth, *Voices Raised in Protest: Defending Citizens of Japanese Ancestry in North America, 1942–1949* (Vancouver: University of British Columbia Press, 2008); Sidney Fine, "Mr. Justice Murphy and the Hirabayashi Case," *Pacific Historical Review* 33, no. 2 (1964): 195–209; Peter Irons, *The Courage of Their Convictions: Sixteen Americans Who Fought Their Way to the Supreme Court* (New York: Free Press, 1988); Jerry Kang, "Denying Prejudice: Internment, Redress, and Denial," *UCLA Law Review* 51, no. 4 (2004): 933–1013; Eric K. Yamamoto, Margaret Chon, Carol L. Izumi, Jerry Kang, and Frank H. Wu, *Race, Rights, and Repatriation: Law and the Japanese American Internment* (New York: Aspen Publishers, 2001); Greg Robinson and Toni Robinson, "Korematsu and Beyond: Japanese Americans and the Origins of Strict Scrutiny," *Law and Contemporary Problems* 68, no. 2 (2005): 29–55; and Roger Daniels, "The Japanese American Cases, 1942–2004: A Social History," *Law and Contemporary Problems* 68, no. 2 (2005): 159–71, for more on the extensively covered Hirabayashi case as well as its relations to *Korematsu v. United States* and *Yatsui v. United States*.

47. John Tateishi, *And Justice for All: An Oral History of the Japanese American Detention Camps* (New York: Random House, 1984), 60–61.

48. Earl Warren, "Martial Rule in Time of War," June 4, 1942, folder—KRB Japanese Loyalty Determination, box 610, Bendetsen Papers, 2.

49. See Patrick O. Gudridge, "The Constitution Glimpsed from Tule Lake," *Law and Contemporary Problems* 68 (2005): 81–118, for more on this case.

50. *Endo v. Eisenhower* (No. 70), "Outline," folder—Mitsui [*sic*] Endo v. Eisenhower (323 of U.S. 238), box 56, Charles Fahy Papers, FDR Library, 5.

51. *Endo v. Eisenhower* (No. 70), 6.

52. *Endo v. Eisenhower* (No. 70), 12.

53. *Endo v. Eisenhower* (No. 70), 6.

54. *Mitsuye Endo v. Milton Eisenhower, Director of the War Relocation Authority and Wartime Civilian Control Administration, et. al.*, Brief for Appellees, March 1, 1944, folder—Mitsui Endo v. Eisenhower, box 56, Fahy Papers, 1.

55. *Endo v. Eisenhower*, Brief for Appellees, 1.

56. *Endo v. Eisenhower* (No. 70), 6.

57. Charles Fahy to John McCloy, October 4, 1944, folder—Mitsui Endo v. Eisenhower, box 56, 1, Fahy Papers.

58. Fahy to John McCloy, 12.

59. *Endo v. Eisenhower*, Brief for Appellees, 2.

60. *Endo v. Eisenhower*, Brief for Appellees, 9.

61. *Ex parte Mitsuye Endo*, 323 U.S. 283, 284 (1944).

62. *Ex parte Mitsuye Endo*, 323 U.S. 283, 284 (1944).

63. *Ex parte Mitsuye Endo*, 323 U.S. 283, 284 (1944).

64. "Miss Mitsuye Endo Spurns Calif. Home," *Minidoka Irrigator*, June 2, 1945, 1.

65. "Supreme Court Case Winner Seeks Job in Windy City," *Colorado Times*, May 31, 1945, 1.

66. "Supreme Court Case Winner," 1.

67. "Burning Nisei Home Draws $1,000 Fine," *Colorado Times*, May 31, 1945, 1.

68. "Fresno Terrorism," *Colorado Times*, May 31, 1945, 1.

69. "Fresno Terrorism"; "Attacks Parley Held," *Colorado Times*, May 31, 1945, 1.

70. "'Parole' Plan Mapped for Interned Japanese," *Los Angeles Examiner*, August 1, 1942, 1.

71. See Stephanie Hinnershitz, "Demanding an 'Adequate Solution': The American Legion, the Immigration Act of 1924, and the Politics of Exclusion," *Immigrants and Minorities* 34 (2016): 1–21; Roger Daniels, *The Politics of Prejudice: The Anti-Japanese Movement in California and the Struggle for Japanese Exclusion* (Berkeley: University of California Press, 1999); Lon Kurashige, *Two Faces of Exclusion: The Untold History of Anti-Asian Racism in the United States* (Chapel Hill: University of North Carolina Press, 2016); and Erika Lee, *The Making of Asian America: A History* (New York: Simon and Schuster, 2016), for more on anti-Japanese discrimination in the early twentieth century.

72. Phillip M. Glick, "Summary of Anti-Japanese Legislation Proposed or Enacted in 1943," November 11, 1943, folder—Office of Production Management, Comm. on Fair Employ. Practice, War Relocation Authority, box 10, OF 4245g, Office of Production Management, War Manpower Commission, War Relocation Authority, FDR Library, 12.

73. Glick, Summary of Anti-Japanese Legislation," 3.

74. "Abstract of News Stories Appearing in *Pacific Citizen*," undated, folder—Office of Production Management, box 10, OF 4245g, 2.

75. List of West Coast Groups Which Have Passed Resolutions Unfavorable to Persons of Japanese Ancestry, folder—Office of Production Management, box 10, OF 4245g, 1.

76. "Former Residents Lost Land to California," *Poston Chronicle*, February 17, 1945, 1. See also Greg Robinson, *After Camp: Portraits in Midcentury Japanese American Life and Politics* (Berkeley: University of California Press, 2012), 181–90, for more on legal cases involving Japanese American land and escheat suits.

77. Calvert L. Dedrick to Colonel Miller, June 10, 1943, box 1733, RG 389, 1.

78. Dedrick to Miller, 2.

79. Dedrick to Miller, 3.

80. Commission on Wartime Relocation and Internment of Civilians, *Personal Justice Denied*, 196–98.

81. C. R. Young to Harry H. Schwartz, August 1, 1944, box 1723, RG 389, 1.

82. Young to Schwartz, 1.

83. Young to Schwartz, 2.

84. John O'Donnell and Harry Flanagan, Resolution of the Continental Motors Local No. 280 UAW-CIO, April 23, 1944, 1–2, folder—Communications on Fair Employment Practices, WRA, box 10—Office of Production MGT., War Manpower Comm., OF 4245g.

85. Minutes, Block manager, December 8, 1942, folder 19, box 2, JARC, 8.

86. Minutes, Block manager, December 8, 1942, 8.

87. Telegram, C. R. Young to Elmer Milliman, July 5, 1944, folder—Illinois Central Railroad, box 1723, RG 389.

88. Telegram, Young to Milliman.

89. Telegram, Young to Milliman. See also John W. Jeffries, *Wartime America: The World War II Home Front* (New York: Rowman and Littlefield, 2018), 97–98, for more on Executive Order 8802.

90. Telegram, Milliman to Young, July 6, 1944, folder—Illinois Central Railroad, box 1723, RG 389.

91. Telegram, Milliman to Young.

92. See Erasmo Gamboa, *Bracero Railroaders: The Forgotten World War II Story of Mexican Workers in the U.S. West* (Seattle: University of Washington Press, 2018), for more on the employment of Mexican migrants in the railroad industry during the war.

93. Telegram, Milliman to Young.

94. Young to George Harrison, July 22, 1944, folder—Illinois Central Railroad, box 1723, RG 389, 1.

95. Young to Harrison, 2.

96. C. R. Young to George Harrison, July 20, 1922, folder—Illinois Central, box 1723, RG 389, 2.

97. Young to Harrison, July 20, 1922, 2.

98. E. C. Millstead to Lieutenant General Ben Lear, July 25, 1944, folder—Illinois Central, box 1723, RG 389.

99. Millstead to Lear.

100. Myer to C. H. Mottier, August 4, 1944, folder—Illinois Central, box 1723, RG 389.

101. Robert Newton Reid, "Memo for Record: Threatened Illinois Central Railroad Strike, Chicago, of Maintenance Employees," July 28, 1944, folder—Illinois Central, box 1723, RG 389; Telephone Conversation between Miller and Gerhardt, July 29, 1944, folder—Illinois Central, box 1723, RG 389, 2.

102. Reid, "Memo for Record."

103. "Jap-American Fired, Rail Strike Averted," July 28, 1944, *Chicago Sun*; "Railroad Relieves Jap Workers from Duty," *Chicago Sun*, July 28, 1944; "Jap-Americans Laid Off to Avert Strike," *Chicago Sun*, July 29, 1944.

104. For conflicts and interactions between Japanese Americans and other racial and ethnic minorities, see Scott Kurashige, *The Shifting Grounds of Race: Black and Japanese Americans in the Making of Multiethnic Los Angeles* (Princeton, NJ: University of Princeton Press, 2010); Shana Bernstein, *Bridges of Reform: Interracial Civil Rights Activism in Twentieth-Century Los Angeles* (New York: Oxford University Press, 2011); and Mark Brilliant, *The Color of America Has Changed: How Racial Diversity Shaped Civil Rights Reform in California, 1941–1978* (New York: Oxford University Press, 2012).

105. See Stephanie Hinnershitz, *Race, Religion, and Civil Rights: Asian Students on the West Coast, 1900–1968* (New Brunswick, NJ: Rutgers University Press, 2015), 185–86. For conflicts and interactions between Japanese Americans and other racial and ethnic minorities, see Kurashige, *Shifting Grounds of Race.*

106. See Charlotte Brooks, "In the Twilight Zone Between Black and White: Japanese American Resettlement and Community in Chicago, 1942–1945," *Journal of American History* 86, no. 4 (2000): 1655–87.

107. "Where Do We Go from Here?" *Poston Chronicle*, March 7, 1945, 1.

108. "Offers of Outside Employment," June 30, 1943, folder 1, box 14, JARC, 1.

109. "Offers of Outside Employment," June 30, 1943, folder 1, box 14, JARC, 1–2.

110. Robinson, *After Camp*, 48.

111. "Chicago: Japanese Home Buying Protested," *Topaz Times*, May 31, 1944; "Walkout Ends as FEPC and CIO Support Nisei," *Topaz Times*, May 13, 1944, 5.

112. "Editorial: Evanston's Still Safe," *Topaz Times*, May 2, 1944, 2.

113. Thomas M. Linehan, "Japanese American Resettlement in Cleveland During and After World War II," *Journal of Urban History* 20, no. 1 (1993): 56–59.

114. Linehan, "Japanese American Resettlement in Cleveland," 57; Erna Risch, *The Quartermaster Corps: Organization, Supply, and Services*, vol. 1 (Washington, DC: Center of Military History, United States Army, 2014), 310–11.

115. Linehan, "Japanese American Resettlement in Cleveland," 57.

116. "Weekly Intelligence Summary," January 15–January 22, 1944, folder—Publicity, box 1733, RG 389, 2.

117. Brian Albrecht and James Banks, *Cleveland in World War II* (Charleston, SC: History Press, 2015), 122.

118. Albrecht and Banks, *Cleveland in World War II*, 122.

119. Linehan, "Japanese American Resettlement in Cleveland," 62–63, 65–66.

120. "Japanese Resettle in Cleveland," *Cleveland Plain Dealer*, March 1, 1944, 4.

121. Joseph D. Hughes to Captain Harbert, March 13, 1944, folder—Publicity, box 1733, RG 389.

122. "Relocation Analysis: Occupational Study of Relocation Given," *Topaz Times*, May 13, 1944, 5.

123. Relocation Analysis," 5.

124. "Two Hundred Girls Sought for Utah Canneries," *Poston Chronicle*, July 14, 1945, 1.

125. "Arne Discusses Bamboo Industry in Louisiana," *Topaz Times*, April 20, 1945, 2.

126. "Final Details from Georgia Farm on the Way," *Rohwer Outpost*, February 2, 1944, 2.

127. "Warren Farmers Demand Exclusion of Jap Labor," *Easton Express* (Pennsylvania), April 12, 1944, 1.

128. Charles H. Harrison, *Growing a Global Village: Making History at Seabrook Farms* (New York: Holmes and Meier, 2003), 4–6. See also Koji Shimada, "Education, Assimilation, and Acculturation: A Case Study of a Japanese American Community in New Jersey" (PhD diss., Temple University, 1975).

129. Harrison, *Growing a Global Village*, 7.

130. "Seabrook Farm Described by Visiting Recruiters," *Topaz Times*, October 28, 1944, 3.

131. "Seabrook Farm Described," 3.

132. "Seabrook Offers Transportation," *Topaz Times*, October 28, 1944, 1.

133. See Karleen Chinen, "Japanese Peruvians," *Hawaii Herald*, October 7, 1988, 22–24; Harvey C. Gardiner, *Pawns in a Triangle of Hate: The Peruvian Japanese and the United States* (Seattle: University of Washington Press, 1981); Lee, *Making of Asian America*, 214, 223–24; and Seiichi Higashide, *Adios to Tears: the Memoirs of a Japanese-Peruvian Internee in U.S. Concentration Camps* (Seattle: University of Washington Press, 2000), for more on Japanese Latin Americans in the United States.

134. Shigeo Kihara, interview by Richard Potashin, April 1, 2011, transcript, Densho Digital Archive, https://densho.org/category/oral-history/.

135. Shigeo Kihara, interview by Richard Potashin,

136. Shigeo Kihara, interview by Richard Potashin.

137. Sumiko Yamauchi, interview by Whitney Peterson, July 23, 2013, in Chula Vista, California, transcript, Densho Digital Archive, https://densho.org/category/oral-history.

138. Sumiko Yamauchi, interview by Whitney Peterson.

139. Lee, *Making of Asian America*, 224–27.

140. Elsa Kudo, interview by Kelli Nakamura, February 2, 2012, in Honolulu, Hawaii, transcript, Densho Digital Archive, https://densho.org/category/oral-history.

141. Elsa Kudo, interview by Kelli Nakamura.

142. Grace K. Seto, interview by Erin Brasfield, March 16, 2006, in Los Angeles, California, transcript, Densho Digital Archive, https://ddr.densho.org/media/ddr-manz-1/ddr-manz-1-140-transcript-771ff0bf56.htm.

143. Myer, *Uprooted Americans*, 185.

144. Myer, *Uprooted Americans*, 186.

145. Myer, *Uprooted Americans*, 192.

146. Leonard Broom and John I. Kitsuse, *The Managed Casualty: The Japanese-American Family in World War II* (Berkeley: University of California Press, 1973), 34.

147. "Center Closes as 345 Japs Leave for West," *McGehee Times*, December 6, 1945, 1.

148. "Truck Farming in Desha County," *McGehee Times*, January 3, 1946, 2.

149. "13,300 Acres of Topaz Farm Land on Sale," *Topaz Times*, February 21, 1945, 1.

150. "Indian Families Slated to Enter 208 September 1," *Poston Chronicle*, August 8, 1945, 1.

Conclusion

1. For more on the fight for redress, see Roger Daniels, Sandra C. Taylor, and Harry H. L. Kitano, eds., *Japanese Americans: From Relocation to Redress* (Salt Lake City: University of Utah Press, 1986); Mitchell T. Maki, Harry Kitano, S. Megan Berthold, *Achieving the Impossible Dream: How Japanese Americans Obtained Redress* (Urbana: University of Illinois Press, 1999); and Eric K. Yamamoto, Margaret Chon, Carol L. Izumi, Jerry Kang, and Frank H. Wu, *Race, Rights, and Reparation: Law and the Japanese American Internment* (New York: Aspen Publishers, 2001). Public Law 100-383, http://www.wwnorton.com/college/history/archive/resources/documents/ch30_06.htm.

2. "Redress to Japanese Americans," April 28, 1986, C-SPAN Video Library, https://www.c-span.org/video/?126246-1/redress-japanese-americans.

3. "Redress to Japanese Americans."

4. Leslie Hatamiya, *Righting a Wrong: Japanese Americans and the Passage of the Civil Liberties Act* (Stanford, CA: Stanford University Press), 95.

5. Hatamiya, *Righting a Wrong*, 95.

6. Greg Robinson, "Japanese American Evacuation Claims Act," Densho Encyclopedia, http://encyclopedia.densho.org/Japanese_American_Evacuation_Claims_Act/.

7. Robinson, "Japanese American Evacuation Claims Act." See also Aimee Chin, "The Long-Run Market Effects of Japanese American Internment During World War II on Working-Age Male Internees" (PhD diss., University of Houston, 2004); and Molly Malloy Cooper, "Japanese American Wages, 1940–1990" (PhD diss., Ohio State University, 2003), for more on wages and work.

8. For more on Mike Masaoka, see Mike Masaoka, *They Call Me Moses Masaoka: An American Saga* (New York: William Morrow, 1987); Bill Hosokawa, *Nisei: The Quiet Americans* (Boulder: University of Colorado Press, 2002); and Paul Spickard, "The Nisei Assume Power: The Japanese American Citizen's League, 1941–1942," *Pacific Historical Review* 52, no. 2 (1983): 147–74. Attorney and Asian American studies scholar Deborah Lim was hired in 1989 by the JACL to conduct an in-depth investigation into incarceration and the JACL's role in the process, resulting in the "Research Report prepared for Presidential Select Committee on JACL Resolution #7," or the Lim Report. It is a detailed and complex document that sheds light on various aspects of the JACL during the war as well as memory and perception of incarceration.

9. Robinson, "Japanese American Evacuation Claims Act."

10. "Redress to Japanese Americans," April 12, 1986, C-SPAN, https://www.c-span.org/video/?126246-1/redress-japanese-americans.

11. Inflation calculator, https://www.officialdata.org/1800-dollars-in-2016.

12. Nicole Goodkind, "Prisoners Are Fighting California's Wildfires on the Frontlines, but Getting Little in Return," *Fortune*, November 1, 2019, https://fortune.com/2019/11/01/california-prisoners-fighting-wildfires/.

SELECTED BIBLIOGRAPHY

Manuscript Collections

Verne Austin Papers. Special Collections, Charles E. Young Research Library, University of California, Los Angeles.

Karl R. Bendetsen Papers. Hoover Institution Archives, Stanford University.

Francis Biddle Papers. Franklin D. Roosevelt Presidential Library and Museum (FDR Library).

California State University Digitization Project.

Densho Digital Repository. http://ddr.densho.org.

Charles Fahy Papers. FDR Library.

Farm Matters (OF 227). FDR Library.

Japanese American Evacuation and Resettlement Study (JERS). Bancroft Library, University of California, Berkeley, Microfilm.

Japanese American Internment Collection. FDR Library.

Japanese-American Relocation Center Records, 1935–1953 (JARC). Division of Rare and Manuscript Collections, Cornell University Library.

Manzanar War Relocation Records. Special Collections, Charles E. Young Research Library, University of California, Los Angeles.

National Archives and Records Administration, College Park, Maryland. Records of the Office of the Provost Marshal General (Record Group/RG 389); Records of the US Army Defense Commands (RG 499).

National Archives and Records Administration, Washington, DC. Records of the Bureau of Indian Affairs (RG 75); Records of the War Relocation Authority (RG 210).

Oregon Historical Society. Marvin Gavin Pursinger Collection; Charles A. Sprague Papers.

Records of the Bureau of the Budget. FDR Library.

Records of the Department of Justice (OF 10). FDR Library.

Records of the Department of the Interior (OF 6). FDR Library.

Records of the Office of Production Management (OF 4245). FDR Library.

Records of the War Department (OF 25). FDR Library.

Records of the War Relocation Authority (OF 4849). FDR Library.

Rohwer Relocation Center Closing Roster, Arkansas State Archives, Little Rock, Arkansas.

Published Primary Sources

Barry, Raymond P., ed. *A Documentary History of Migratory Farm Labor in California*. Oakland, CA: Federal Writers Project, 1938.

Chang, Gordon H., ed. *Morning Glory, Evening Shadow: Yamato Ichihashi and His Internment Writings*. Stanford, CA: Stanford University Press, 1997.

DeWitt, John L. *Final Report: Japanese Evacuation from the West Coast, 1942*. Washington, DC: Government Printing Office, 1943.

"Food for Freedom: Information Handbook." Washington, DC: Government Printing Office, 1943.

Hansen, Arthur A., and Betty K. Mitson, eds. *Voices Long Silent: An Oral Inquiry into Japanese American Evacuation*. Fullerton: California State University, Fullerton, 1974.

Ichioka, Yuji, ed. *Views from Within: The Japanese American Evacuation and Resettlement*. Los Angeles: UCLA Asian American Studies Center, 1989.

Kashima, Tetsuden, and Commission on Wartime Relocation and Internment of Citizens. *Personal Justice Denied: Report of the Commission on Wartime Relocation and Internment of Citizens*. Seattle: University of Washington Press, 1997.

Kikuchi, Charles. *The Kikuchi Diary: Chronicle from an American Concentration Camp*. Edited by John Modell. Urbana: University of Illinois Press, 1993.

Leighton, Alexander. *The Governing of Men: General Principles and Recommendations Based on Experience at a Japanese Relocation Camp*. Princeton, NJ: Princeton University Press, 1946.

Masaoka, Mike. *They Call Me Moses Masaoka: An American Saga*. New York: William Morrow, 1987.

Myer, Dillon S. *Uprooted Americans: The Japanese Americans and the War Relocation Authority During World War II*. Tucson: University of Arizona Press, 1971.

Nakashima, Ted. "Concentration Camp: US Style." *New Republic*, June 15, 1942, 828–35.

Okubo, Mine. *Citizen 13660*. Seattle: University of Washington Press, 2014.

Spicer, Edward H., Asael T. Hansen, Katherine Luomala, and Marvin K. Opler. *Impounded People: Japanese Americans in the Relocation Centers*. Tucson: University of Arizona Press, 1969.

Thomas, Dorothy Swaine, and Richard S. Nishimoto. *The Spoilage: Japanese American Evacuation and Resettlement During World War II*. Berkeley: University of California Press, 2010.

United States. Congress. House. Select Committee Investigating National Defense Migration. 77th Congress, 2nd sess. *National Defense Migration*.

US Department of Labor. *Wartime Wages, Income, and Wage Regulation in Agriculture*. Bulletin Number 883. Washington, DC: Government Printing Office, 1946.

US Department of the Interior, War Agency Liquidation Unit. *People in Motion: The Postwar Adjustment of the Evacuated Japanese Americans*. Washington, DC: Government Printing Office, 1947.

War Relocation Authority, US Department of the Interior. *Relocation Communities for Wartime Evacuees*. Washington, DC: Government Printing Office, 1942.

———. *WRA: A Story of Human Conservation*. Washington, DC: Government Printing Office, 1946.

Periodicals

American Civil Liberties Union-News
Boise Daily Statesman
Chicago Sun
Cleveland Plain Dealer
Eastern Oregon Observer
Fresno Vignette
Gila Courier-News
Granada Pioneer
Grand Junction Sentinel (Colorado)
Heart Mountain Sentinel
Indianapolis Star
LIFE
Los Angeles Times
Madeira Times
Manzanar Free Press
McGehee Times
Minidoka Irrigator
The Nation
Pacific Rural Press
Portland Oregonian
Poston Chronicle
San Diego Tribune
San Francisco Examiner
Santa Anita Pacemaker
Seattle Post-Intelligencer
Sioux Falls Argus Leader
Tucson Daily Citizen
WRA Daily Press Review

INDEX

Adkins, Homer, 39, 40, 66

African Americans: convict lease labor and, 12; farm labor and, 60; relations with Japanese Americans, 230, 232–33

Agricultural Adjustment Administration, 44, 65

'Aha Makhav, 146

Aiken, George, Oregon Plan, 66–68

Alabama, 12

all-out relocation, 21, 217, 229–30, 232, 234, 236–37, 239, 244, 247

Amalgamated Sugar Company: history of, 61; requesting Japanese Americans for labor, 74, 76, 78–80

American Beet Sugar Company, 61

American Civil Liberties Union (ACLU), 107

American Federation of Labor (AFL): Japanese American laborers in Chicago and, 226; no-strike pact during WWII and, 142

Amory, Russell, 104–5; replacement of, 122; Santa Anita detention center strike and, 114–15, 117–18, 144; use of Japanese American labor and, 111

Angel Island, 8

anti-Japanese discrimination: Japanese American laborers and, 18–19, 89; land laws and, 51, 223–24; in the prison camps, 177, 186; removal and, 7, 35, 38–39; resettlement and, 202, 222–24, 245–46; wartime hysteria and, 6, 138

Ariyoshi, Koji, 114

Arizona: consideration for prison camp, 33, 38; cotton and, 97–100; Japanese American laborers in, 59; Leupp isolation center, 137. *See also* Poston prison camp

Arkansas: Desha County, 246; discrimination against Japanese Americans in, 66; improvements to land in, 101, 246–47; Jerome prison camp and, 36, 149; McGehee, 246; Rohwer prison camp and, 36; selection as a prison camp site, 36–37, 39–40. *See also* Adkins, Homer

Arrowood, F. H., 114–15

Ashworth, Ray, 114

Austin, Verne, 140–41

Ban, Jotaro, 114

Barge, Jennings B., 34

beet farming: army clearance and, 79–80, 99; *betabaleros* and, 62; Bracero program and, 62, 14; Colorado and, 101; corporations, 60–61; Idaho and, 82, 85, 88, 197, 243; Japanese Americans' experiences with, 86–87, 89–90; labor disputes and, 91, 93–94, 96, 101, 142; Montana and, 85; Nebraska and, 89; Oregon and, 78–79, 85; Oregon Plan and, 68–69; politicians and, 38, 59, 66, 68; in prewar period, 60–61; recruiting Japanese Americans for, 80–83, 85, 87–88, 197, 243; regulations for Japanese Americans working in, 75–76; requests for Japanese American laborers for, 55, 62, 64, 67, 74, 84; Utah and, 86; WRA and, 74, 78–79, 83–84, 205

ACKNOWLEDGMENTS

I would like to thank the editorial and production team at Penn Press for all of their assistance in creating this book. Bob Lockhart saw this project through from the beginning and dedicated time to reading the manuscript multiple times and getting it into shape. John Howard and other reviewers provided insightful comments that shaped the final product and made it a more comprehensive and nuanced addition to the literature on Japanese American incarceration.

Many archivists including those at the National Archives and Records Administration in College Park and Washington, DC, the FDR Library, the Charles E. Young Research Library at the University of California at Los Angeles, the Rare and Manuscript Collections at Cornell University, the Hoover Institution Archives, and the Bancroft Library at the University of California at Berkeley assisted with locating key documents for this project. Scott Daniels at the Oregon Historical Society deserves special recognition for tracking down documents for Chapter 2.

Cleveland State University as well as the United States Military Academy at West Point provided much-needed resources and support for research and writing.

Finally, Robert Hutchinson once again served as my unofficial editor while working on his own scholarship.